Vegan
PLanet

Vegan Planet

400 Irresistible Recipes
with Fantastic Flavors from Home
and Around the World

Robin Robertson

The Harvard Common Press
Boston, Massachusetts

The Harvard Common Press
535 Albany Street
Boston, Massachusetts 02118
www.harvardcommonpress.com

Printed in the United States of America

Printed on acid-free paper

Library of Congress Cataloging-in-Publication Data

Robertson, Robin (Robin G.).
   Vegan planet : 400 irresistible recipes with fantastic flavors from home and around the world / Robin Robertson.
      p. cm.
Includes index.
   ISBN 1-55832-210-8 ((cl) : alk. paper) — ISBN 1-55832-211-6 ((pbk) : alk. paper)
   1. Vegan cookery. 2. Cookery, International. I. Title.
   TX837.R6253 2003
   641.5'636—dc21

                                                     2002007435

ISBN-13: 978-1-55832-211-0
ISBN-10: 1-55832-211-6

DESIGN BY RENATO STANISIC
ILLUSTRATIONS BY SUSY PILGRIM WATERS

Special bulk-order discounts are available on this and other Harvard Common Press books. Companies and organizations may purchase books for premiums or resale, or may arrange a custom edition, by contacting the Marketing Director at the address above.

21

For the animals

Contents

Acknowledgments

This book is the culmination of many years of study, experience, inspiration, and dedication. I am indebted to many people who have helped to shape my career and philosophy over the years, including the individuals and organizations who work to refine the art of vegan cooking and promote compassion for all life.

Special appreciation goes to Neal Barnard, M.D., of the Physicians Committee for Responsible Medicine (PCRM), for his generous spirit and vital work and for writing the foreword to this book. Thanks also to Jen Keller, R.D., also of PCRM, for her assistance with nutritional information. I extend my heartfelt gratitude to Gloria Siegel for her diligent testing of many of these recipes, and to several other dear friends who tasted, tested, and helped in many ways during the creation of this book: Samantha Ragan, Lochlain Lewis, Lisa Lange, B. J. Atkinson, Kay and Larry Sturgis, Kerri Kyle, Pat Davis, Darlene Ellenburg, and my sister, Carole Lazur.

I especially thank my husband, Jon Robertson, for his ongoing support, assistance, and encouragement. My deep appreciation extends to my agent, Stacey Glick of Jane Dystel Literary Management, and the expert team at The Harvard Common Press for their fine work and enthusiasm, in particular, publisher Bruce Shaw, executive editor Pam Hoenig, managing editor Valerie Cimino, copyeditor Barbara Jatkola, publicity manager Skye Stewart, and marketing director Christine Alaimo.

Foreword

As you page through the recipes in this book—from appetizers to desserts—you'll find that not only are they mouthwateringly delicious, but these great tasting foods can change your life.

In research studies at the Physicians Committee for Responsible Medicine, conducted in partnership with Georgetown University Medical Center in Washington, D.C., we have put various diets to the test. Whether our goal is cutting cholesterol levels, taming diabetes or high blood pressure, or trimming waistlines, the clear winner is a lowfat, vegan diet. As savory as spaghetti marinara, split pea soup, or rice pilaf may be, they are also incredibly powerful for health. They contain no animal fat and no cholesterol—if they are properly made. And that means they, along with other vegan foods, can tackle cholesterol problems like no other diet can, and weight loss kicks in effortlessly without our having to impose any artificial calorie limit—even when people do not change their exercise routines.

Young people who eat this way can stay trim and healthy and keep their arteries open throughout life. Older people whose unhealthy diets may have already brought health problems—heart disease, for example—can use these foods to get a new lease on life. The research studies of Dr. Dean Ornish and his colleagues at the Preventive Medicine Research Institute showed that diets based on plant foods rather than animal products actually reversed existing heart disease in more than 80 percent of participants without medications or surgery. We have shown that two-thirds of people with adult-onset diabetes can either reduce their medications or stop them completely within 12 weeks of the diet change. Other researchers have found much the same benefit for people with high blood pressure.

A vegan diet is as close to a perfect menu as you can have. Unfortunately, many people have made wrong turns. A switch from red meat to white meat, for example, really does not do the job. If a person scrupulously limits meat intake to no more than six ounces per day, choosing only chicken and fish while trimming away visible fat, and chooses skim over whole milk and egg whites over whole eggs, the results are embarrassingly modest. Cholesterol levels fall by only about 5 percent. Body weight and blood pressure improve only modestly. Inside the arteries, blockages continue to worsen. All in all, there is little reward for all this effort. Americans now eat, believe it or not, 1 million chickens per hour, and collectively we are more out of shape than at any time in our nation's history.

A vegan diet puts health into high gear, cutting cholesterol by 20 to 25 percent, trimming body weight by about a pound or more per week, and helping most people with diabetes or high blood pressure free themselves from their medications.

If you are tempted to put it to the test, I suggest that you take a week or two and try out as many of these delicious recipes as you can. Then, when you've found your favorites, block out a three-week period to eat lowfat, vegan foods exclusively. Don't dabble with it—do it all the way. As you get started, your body will begin to transform itself. In all likelihood, you'll start to lose weight, your cholesterol level will fall, your energy will improve, and you'll feel better than you've felt since you were a kid. After three weeks, see how you feel. If you like the feeling of a trimmer, healthier body, you can stick with it, and you now have the tools you need to do it.

These foods give you a chance to be on as perfect a diet as humanly possible, and your body will be delighted that you made this choice. Robin has done a magnificent job in bringing this volume together, and I hope you enjoy *Vegan Planet* as much as I have.

— Neal D. Barnard, M.D.
President, Physicians Committee for Responsible Medicine

Introduction

Over the years, our society has grown more comfortable with vegetarianism. Polls show that the majority of Americans eat one or more meatless meals per week and many people have vegetarian friends or family members. In 1992, when the USDA released its new Food Guide Pyramid, the U.S. government officially recognized the vegetarian option as a healthy way to eat.

Although vegetarians choose not to eat meat, many of them do include eggs, dairy, and other animal products in their diets. These products can be high in cholesterol and saturated fat. A vegan diet, on the other hand, includes no animal products of any kind and may well be the logical dietary choice for optimum health.

People choose veganism chiefly for reasons of health, environment, ethics, or religion. If vegetarianism appeals to you for health reasons, the health benefits of a vegan diet should appeal to you even more. By eliminating eggs and dairy, you can have a diet that is cholesterol-free and lower in saturated fat, while at the same time reducing your intake of antibiotics, hormones, and other man-made additives that are found in many of these foods.

From an environmental standpoint, the vegetarian and vegan views are much the same: the production of animal products is notoriously wasteful of resources such as water and land (both for grazing and for raising feed crops) and is one of the chief sources of land and water pollution.

People who go vegan for ethical reasons believe that animals should not be killed or exploited for food. Although it is true that animals aren't killed for their eggs or dairy products, these animals undergo horrendous treatment in factory farms and are eventually slaughtered when they are no longer productive. Vegans choose not to support such industries and therefore omit eggs and dairy from their diets.

It is easier to enjoy a vegan diet now than ever before. Vegan-friendly ingredients are becoming more visible in natural food stores and many supermarkets, and creative vegan cookbooks are showing up on bookshelves everywhere. Although the vegetarian menu choices of many restaurants remain dairy-laden, vegan selections are becoming more widely available. At the same time, upscale vegan restaurants in metropolitan areas are thriving.

Those of us who enjoy a plant-based diet are often quizzed with questions such as these: "Do you live on salad?" "No meat or dairy? What *do* you eat?" And, of course, "Where do you get your protein?"

The 400 recipes in *Vegan Planet* are my answer to those questions. Quite simply, a well-balanced vegan diet can provide all the nutrition we need with astonishingly varied recipes. The fact is, there is a world of choice in the vegan diet. In fact, I hesitate to use the word *diet* because it may imply austerity or deprivation, and a vegan diet is anything but that. In this book, fresh vegetables and fruits, whole grains, beans, and nuts are used to make infinitely varied, full-flavored dishes for breakfast, lunch, dinner, and everything in between.

Chapter 1 introduces the basics of a vegan diet, from its history and health benefits to an overview of ingredients, cooking tips, and basic recipes. From there, you will discover that by creatively using a variety of vegetables, beans, grains, and other healthful ingredients, you can make soups, stews, entrées, breads, and even desserts that are satisfying and delicious—good food that just happens to be meatless and dairy-free. From *Chilled Ginger-Peach Soup with Cashew Cream* and hearty *White Bean Cassoulet* to *Five-Spice Chocolate Layer Cake* and *Maple-Pecan French Toast*, the dishes you prepare will be noticed for their great taste rather than for "what's missing."

When you first begin to cook without animal products, it can be a liberating experience. No longer bound by the former habits of pork chops on Tuesdays and chicken breasts on Thursdays, you are free to explore the cuisines of other lands, using ingredients you never knew existed. Fragrant spices, colorful vegetables, and numerous beans, grains, and other ingredients await your pleasure. What will it be tonight? A Moroccan stew or a Thai stir-fry? How about a Tuscan soup or a French gratin? It can be an exciting experience to try a new cuisine each week, pick up new vegetables at the market that you've never cooked before, and learn how to prepare them. Soon you will find creative ways to incorporate more fresh vegetables into your meals, perhaps by making a lovely composed salad or whipping up a relish or chutney.

For those times when only good old-fashioned comfort food will do, you can explore new ways to make old favorites with healthier vegetable-based ingredients. Use tofu to make creamy sauces, lasagna, and even cheesecake. Sauté some seitan when you crave a "meaty" entrée. When you cook vegan, you can have it all—the flavors you crave, the nutrients you need, and, best of all, the freedom to step beyond the confines of the same old meat- and dairy-based meals.

The twenty chapters in this book range from appetizers, soups, and sauces to breads, beverages, and desserts. In between, there are a number of main-course chapters that are organized by ingredients such as grains, beans, and pasta, and others that are grouped by cooking method, such as sautés and stir-fries, stews, and oven-baked dishes. Also included are chapters on sandwiches, pizza, and even one devoted to breakfast.

Within these chapters, you will find a wide range of recipes. First are the naturally vegan recipes that celebrate the natural goodness of vegetables, grains, beans, and other plant-based ingredients. Recipes such as *Ancient Grains on Wild Greens*, *Brandy-Glazed Winter Squash with Apple-Pecan Topping*, and *Marjoram-Scented Artichoke and Chickpea Stew* fall under that heading.

Other recipes drawn from the cuisines of the world include exciting, robust dishes such as *African Sweet Potato and Peanut Stew*, Thai *"Drunken" Noodles*, and *Cuban Black Bean Soup*, as well as recipes that feature some of the world's best vegetable-based protein sources, such as tofu, tempeh, and seitan.

Many of the recipes are what I call transformation recipes. They include dishes that traditionally contain meat or dairy but that have been transformed into vegan versions by changing some of the ingredients. Examples include *Eggless Hollandaise*, *Seitan Reuben*, and *Key Lime "Cheesecake."*

In developing the recipes, it was important to me that they be accessible to everyone. The great majority of the ingredients in my recipes are available in most supermarkets and natural food stores, and the remainder can be found in ethnic markets. I have made a point not to use heirloom produce or other esoteric ingredients that are available only to a small portion of the population. For those who do not live near a natural food store or ethnic grocer, mail-order and online sources for ingredients are provided in the resource list at the back of the book.

In *Vegan Planet*, you will traverse the globe with internationally inspired, straightforward recipes that show how varied, flavorful, and exciting vegan food can be. It is my hope that, with this book, you will discover new ways to enjoy the many natural ingredients available to us, and a whole new world of delicious vegan cuisine.

1

Vegan Basics

By the close of the 20th century, the steady increase of diet-related maladies such as high cholesterol, heart disease, and diabetes had prompted many Americans to look at switching to a diet that emphasizes whole grains, vegetables, and fruits. In this way, the vegetarian diet established itself as an important fixture in mainstream America. Among the types of vegetarian diets now shared by millions are lacto-vegetarian, which includes dairy; lacto-ovo-vegetarian, which includes dairy and eggs; and vegan, which contains no eggs, dairy, or other animal products, including honey.

If the vegetarian option was the healthier choice of the previous century, the vegan diet is destined to become the diet of the new millennium. It is the logical next step as people become more aware that animal products not only are unnecessary for a healthy diet but also are associated with many health risks.

In some editions of the *Oxford English Dictionary*, a vegan is defined as a "strict vegetarian." Other sources refer to a vegan diet as "pure vegetarian," since it consists solely of plant-based ingredients. The reasons for going vegan are usually based on health, ethics, environment, or religion.

In terms of health, people give up meat because they need to avoid cholesterol and saturated fat. If they still rely on eggs and dairy products, however, they have not solved their cholesterol problem. A vegan diet is cholesterol-free and naturally low in saturated fat. Other health concerns include food allergies, such as lactose (milk sugar) intolerance or other dairy allergies; the hormones and antibiotics that are given to livestock; and the pesticides from animal feed that find their way into many meat and dairy products.

People who initially go vegan for their health are often compelled to remain vegan for ethical reasons. Some vegetarians give up meat because they do not believe in killing animals for food and prefer to rely on eggs and dairy for their protein because "it doesn't kill the animal." What they often do not realize is that the factory-farming practices of the egg and dairy industries can be just as brutal as the meat industry. For that reason, ethically based vegans eliminate all animal-derived products—and their commitment doesn't end with diet. Many ethical vegans wear no leather, silk, fur, or wool and avoid products such as soaps and cosmetics that contain animal byproducts or are tested on animals. Vegans espouse compassion for all life, holding that animals should not be exploited for food, clothing, or any other reason.

PROTEINS COMPLETE AND INCOMPLETE

Protein is made up of amino acids. There are 9 essential amino acids that we need to obtain from the foods we eat. Animal products such as meat, dairy, and eggs contain large amounts of all 9 essential amino acids and are called *complete proteins*. However, animal foods also contain high amounts of cholesterol and saturated fat, which put you at a higher risk for developing heart disease, cancer, hypertension, and diabetes. In fact, too much protein can damage your heart, kidneys, and bones. When you eat a diet that includes meat, dairy, and eggs, it is easy to get too much protein, which is another reason to get your protein from plant foods.

With the exception of soybeans, which are a complete protein, individual plant foods are *incomplete proteins*, because they do not contain a perfect balance of all the essential amino acids. When you eat a variety of plant foods throughout the day, however, by day's end the various amounts of amino acids in the foods have combined to make complete proteins. Plant foods have the added benefit of being naturally cholesterol-free, high in fiber and complex carbohydrates, and low in fat.

Although there have long been vegetarians who do not eat or use any animal products, the term *vegan* (pronounced VEE-gun) came into being in 1944 in London. The first official Vegan Society in America was established in 1948, and today the American Vegan Society is a thriving entity that publishes a quarterly magazine, *American Vegan* (formerly *Ahimsa*, a Sanskrit word meaning "harmlessness to all life").

Veganism is actually as old as recorded history if you consider Genesis 1:29, where God says, "Behold, I have given you every herb-bearing seed, which is upon the face of all the earth, and every tree, in which is the fruit of a tree-yielding seed; to you it shall be for meat." In the archaic English usage, *meat* merely meant "meal."

ENJOYING A HEALTHY VEGAN DIET

To successfully adopt a vegan diet, common sense and an understanding of basic nutritional needs are important. For example, choosing a diet of French fries and diet colas may qualify as vegan, but that doesn't make it healthy. The key to a healthful vegan diet is eating a variety of fresh fruits and vegetables, whole grains, legumes, nuts, and seeds every day, in order to acquire adequate amounts of protein, calcium, fat, and iron.

Protein is made up of amino acids, and there are nine essential amino acids that we need to obtain from the foods we eat. All nine of these essential amino acids are found in animal products such as meat, milk, and eggs. However, it is quite easy to get too much protein by eating a diet that includes these products. Too much protein can damage your bones and organs. Animal products also contain high amounts of cholesterol and saturated fat, which put us at a higher risk for developing heart disease, cancer, hypertension (high blood pressure), and diabetes, among other ailments. For this reason, it is best to get protein from plant foods, since they are naturally cholesterol-free, low in fat, and high in fiber and complex carbohydrates.

Since most individual plant foods, such as whole grains, legumes, and vegetables, contain varying amounts of the essential amino acids, they are said to be *incomplete proteins*. An exception is the soybean, which contains an abundance of all nine essential amino acids and is, therefore, a *complete protein*. It was once thought that certain foods, such as beans and grains, needed to be carefully combined at the same meal to make a complete protein. In recent years, we have learned that these and other wholesome plant-based ingredients can be eaten at any time during the day to have the same benefits. Of course, since grains and beans are frequently paired in scores of tasty dishes, it's often a simple matter to enjoy them at the same meal.

The dairy industry tells us that if we don't drink milk, we won't get enough calcium. But calcium is found in abundance in tofu, nuts, vegetables such as broccoli and dark leafy greens, and sea vegetables. In addition to providing enough protein and calcium, a well-balanced vegan diet has ample sources of vitamins, minerals, and other nutrients.

Since iron is abundant in many plant foods, vegans are not at any particular risk for iron deficiency, as long as they include daily servings of iron-rich foods. Beans, dark green vegetables, dried fruits, nuts, and seeds, as well as blackstrap molasses and whole-grain or fortified breads and cereals, all contain high amounts of iron.

Did You Know...

Drinking coffee and tea with meals can significantly decrease the absorption of iron? It is believed that this happens because of tannins and other substances in the beverages that bind with the iron, thus making it less absorbable.

If you're wondering how you'll get your vitamin D if you stop drinking milk, you should know that cow's milk does not naturally contain vitamin D; it's added later, just as it is in soy milk. Vitamin D, in fact, is not really a "vitamin" but a hormone that our bodies manufacture when our skin is exposed to as little as 15 minutes of sunlight.

Vitamin A is readily stored in the liver, and thus daily sources are not critical. In fact, since it is not excreted, overdoses can be toxic. Good sources of vitamin A are yellow and dark green vegetables and orange fruits, as well as fortified soy milk and margarine.

NUTRITIONAL YEAST

Nutritional yeast is an inactive yeast that is used as a food supplement and seasoning. It is yellow in color, with a distinctive, some say "cheesy," flavor. Because it has no leavening power, it cannot be used in baking. Nutritional yeast is extremely high in protein, B complex vitamins, and folic acid and very low in fat and sodium. Perhaps its greatest merit is that it provides vegans with a reliable, nonanimal source of vitamin B_{12}. Nutritional yeast will keep indefinitely if stored in a tightly closed container. It is widely available at natural food stores under the Red Star label.

Vitamin B_{12} is found mostly in animal products, but it is also found in some fortified foods, as well as in our own mouths and intestines. Since we require only 2 micrograms per day and our bodies store vitamin B_{12} and recycle it, a B_{12} deficiency is not a problem for most vegans. Still, if you are concerned about getting enough, you can take a vitamin B_{12} supplement.

Some dietitians maintain that omega-3 fatty acids are best when derived from fish and fish oils. Other researchers, however, have found that the omega-3 molecules from fish sources can be unstable and release free radicals as they decompose. The more stable form of omega-3s is found in vegetables, fruits, beans, and, most notably, flaxseeds. Additionally, the antioxidants present in certain vegetables and fruits help neutralize the free radicals.

Many respected medical doctors and other health professionals conclude that a vegan diet not only is safe but also can produce many significant health benefits. (For more information on the health benefits of a vegan diet, read the foreword by Dr. Neal Barnard on page xi.)

By learning to think of plant-based ingredients in new ways, you can help make your vegan meals more interesting and delicious. For example, whereas you may have once thought of nuts as simply an occasional snack food, you are now encouraged to consider them as a good protein source and versatile ingredient for sauces, spreads, salads, and entrées. In addition, many Asian, Indian, Italian, Mexican, and Middle Eastern dishes are inherently vegan or easily adaptable and use wonderful combinations of grains, beans, and vegetables. The vast diversity of ethnic cuisines and ingredi-

THE FACTS ABOUT VITAMIN B_{12}

- All vitamin B_{12} comes from bacteria that live in the soil or in animal intestines.
- Animal products are a primary source of B_{12} for humans.
- Vitamin B_{12} is produced by bacteria in the human mouth and intestines.
- Humans store vitamin B_{12} in their bodies for years.
- The human body requires only 2 micrograms of vitamin B_{12} per day.
- Vitamin B_{12} deficiency is not common among vegans.
- The best way for vegans to get vitamin B_{12} is through fortified foods (such as breakfast cereals and soy milk) and supplements.

ents offers opportunities for tremendous variety in your meals. Cooking vegan has given me a broader appreciation for the natural flavors of foods and at the same time has inspired me to develop ways to use these ingredients to their full potential.

Whatever your reason for cooking vegan, it is almost certain to have far-reaching benefits for you, your fellow beings, and the entire planet. If you wish to learn more about a vegan lifestyle, see the resource list at the back of the book.

THE VEGAN KITCHEN

A vast array of culinary resources can add flavor, texture, and nutrition to your meals. From fresh organic produce to protein-rich beans, nuts, and soy foods to exotic global seasonings, quality ingredients are the key to enjoying satisfying vegan meals.

A Firm Foundation

Cooking with a variety of whole grains, beans or legumes, and fresh vegetables and fruits can provide the firm foundation of a healthful vegan diet.

Considered staple foods throughout the world, grains can be an economical source of high quality nutrition. Among the many grains to choose from are rice, millet, quinoa, barley, wheat, kamut, and many others. Grains can be used in soups, stuffings, pilafs, puddings, and desserts, as well as to make breads and pasta. Each type of grain has its own nutritional value, unique flavor, and cooking characteristics. When combined with beans, vegetables, and seasonings, grains provide great taste and texture, in addition to good nutrition. Grains are discussed in more detail in chapter 8.

Dried beans, also known as legumes, are widely used throughout the world as a major protein source. Beans are inexpensive, easy to prepare, low in fat, and an important part of a well-balanced vegan diet. Popular bean varieties include chickpeas, black-eyed peas, lentils, split peas, black beans, pinto beans, kidney beans, lima beans, fava beans, and white beans (Great Northern, navy, and cannellini). Once called "poor man's meat," beans are high in protein, fiber, carbohydrates, and B vitamins. They are becoming more popular on dinner tables throughout the United States, where they are used to make soups, stews, burgers, breads, spreads, and more. More information about beans can be found in chapter 10.

Whereas some vegetables are especially high in vitamin C, others are loaded with iron. For that reason, eating a wide variety of vegetables helps ensure optimum nutritional benefits. It also can add interest and variety to your meals. Many vegetables are delicious raw as well as steamed, stir-fried, baked, or boiled. In a plant-based diet, you are more apt to find vegetables featured as an integral part of a meal rather than as a side dish. However you prepare them, vegetables are best when grown without pesticides and eaten while at their peak of freshness.

Naturally sweet fruit is a refreshing, ready-to-eat snack or dessert that can be eaten raw with little or no preparation. In addition, many fruits, from the tiniest berry to the largest melon, can be found in appetizers, soups, entrées, salads, and sauces.

Always wash fruits and vegetables well before using to rinse off pesticides and bacteria. Potatoes and root vegetables should be well scrubbed, and any wilted or damaged areas should be removed from produce before using.

Organically Yours

Coming up with an enforceable standard for what can be called "organic produce" has been debated for a long time. In 2001, the USDA passed strict guidelines for labeling organic foods. Taking effect in late 2002, these guidelines will make it easier for consumers to understand what they are buying. Previously, organic labeling was mostly unregulated and varied largely based on geographic region.

When buying organic foods, check that they are labeled "organic." The new USDA organic seal for foods that are at least 95 percent organic will make it easier for you to make your selections. This label means that synthetic pesticides or fertilizers were not used in the growing of the produce and that the ingredients were not exposed to irradiation or biotechnology. Until such guidelines go into effect, calling something "organic" doesn't necessarily mean that the food is completely pesticide-free. Try to buy locally grown organic produce, not only for maximum nutrition and

What Does *Organic* Mean?

Organic refers to farming practices that sustain soil health and fertility in a natural way without relying on synthetic fertilizers and that use natural methods to control pests, diseases, and weeds. Instead of chemicals, for example, weeds, insects, and other pests are managed with earth-friendly methods such as beneficial insects.

Produce labeled "100 percent organic" was grown by a farm certified organic by the USDA. Only certified operations may apply the USDA seal to their products.

that "just picked" flavor but also for the peace of mind you get by buying from some-one you trust.

Egg and Dairy Alternatives

In childhood we learned to associate milk and other dairy products with nurturing and comfort, as well as good health. Much of this association is due to the advertising campaigns that taught us from an early age that dairy is good for us and that we need to drink milk to "build strong bones." But recent medical studies show that dairy products contribute to heart disease, many forms of cancer, psoriasis, respiratory ailments, allergies, sinus trouble, migraines, and other problems. Once thought to aid in the prevention of osteoporosis, meat and dairy products in excessive amounts can actually contribute to osteoporosis. Medical researchers now report that excessive consumption of protein raises the acid level in the blood, which causes calcium to be lost. In fact, the protein in milk can actually inhibit the body's ability to absorb calcium from dairy products. Fortunately, calcium is found in abundance in some nondairy foods, such as tofu, nuts, and many vegetables.

Humans are the only animals that drink the milk of another species and the only animals that drink milk after childhood. One might conclude that people who use dairy products often do so out of deeply ingrained habit and because they taste good. Indeed, many American "comfort foods" are made with dairy products. For this reason, vegetarians who find it easy to give up meat may find it difficult to renounce dairy products, especially if they have come to rely on these products for protein. Luckily, there are plant-based alternatives to dairy products that allow us to re-create many of our favorite "creamy" dishes.

Did You Know...

Osteoporosis is less a disease of calcium deficiency than one of protein excess? Studies show that osteoporosis tends to occur in countries where calcium intake via dairy products is highest. Instead, it's better to get your calcium from plant sources such as figs, rice, fortified cereals, nuts, sesame seeds, molasses, dark greens, sea vegetables, and soy foods.

Eggs served sunny-side up and milk in a carton are easy ingredients to recognize. The trick is learning to detect them when they are hidden in baked goods and prepared foods. In addition to reading labels closely, the best defense against hidden dairy products may be to "bake your own," using some of the many available egg and dairy alternatives. Soy, rice, oat, and even nut or coconut milk can be used to replace cow's milk in cooking. Soy milk and oat milk are best for savory dishes, although oat milk can be difficult to find. Rice milk and almond milk have a sweeter taste and should be used for desserts or over cereal. Coconut milk is best where its distinctive flavor will be appreciated, such as in Thai or Indian recipes or in certain desserts. These milks are available in most supermarkets and natural food stores. A few brands of soy milk are found in the refrigerator case and must stay refrigerated even if unopened, but many brands of soy milk, as well as milk made with rice or almonds, are sold in one-quart aseptic containers that may be stored unrefrigerated until opened. You may find vanilla or chocolate soy milk in addition to the regular flavor, which can pass for cow's milk in recipes.

Eggless mayonnaise and dairy-free sour cream, cream cheese, and several other cheeses are made from soy. When buying soy cheeses, read the label to be sure the product does not contain casein or other dairy byproducts that are sometimes added to make the cheese melt better. Vegan cheese is usually labeled as such or has the words "contains no animal products" on the label.

Instead of butter, you can opt for high-quality expeller-pressed or cold-pressed oils, which are made without the use of harsh solvents and heat. I prefer corn oil for baking and extra virgin olive oil for most savory dishes. When only a solid butter alternative will do, check out the refrigerator case of your natural food store for a nonhydrogenated spread made from soy. Consider switching to nut butters for toast. They contain about the same amount of calories as butter but with no cholesterol and lots of protein and essential fatty acids.

To replace eggs in recipes, use Ener-G Egg Replacer, an egg replacement powder made from vegetable starch and leaveners. I like this brand because it can be readily found in natural food stores and is easy to use in recipes. Other egg alternatives include ground flaxseeds (page 22) and silken tofu (page 12).

Meat Alternatives

Although it is possible to fulfill all our nutritional needs with a plant-based diet, many people hold firm to the habit of eating meat. Since most people do not eat their meat raw but prefer it cooked and sauced in a variety of ways, it seems apparent that the surrounding flavors play a role in their choices. Taste and tradition, it would seem, are an important part of why we eat what we do.

But the change to a vegan diet doesn't mean you must give up familiar flavors, textures, and traditions. You can often enjoy many of the same dishes by simply swapping some ingredients. Soy foods such as tofu, tempeh, and textured vegetable protein (TVP), along with seitan (also called wheat-meat) and the many varieties of beans, are excellent protein choices that can be used to make soups, stews, and other dishes with many of the same flavors and chewy textures you enjoy.

Although a vegan menu doesn't have to include tofu, soy foods can add variety and nutritional benefits to a vegan diet and are worth considering. Evidence indicates that eating more soy protein can produce a number of health benefits, whether you're trying to lower your cholesterol, relieve the symptoms of menopause, or reduce the risks of heart disease, osteoporosis, and certain cancers. A recent medical study on soy protein's effect on menopause showed such remarkable results that tofu is now being referred to as "natural estrogen." Indeed, in Japan, where soy is a dietary staple, there is no word for "hot flash." In 1999, the FDA permitted soy food manufacturers to label their products as being associated with a reduced risk of coronary disease.

TOFU TALK

If you're among those who avoid tofu because you don't know what to do with it, I encourage you to give it a try. Think of it as an ingredient, like flour, rather than a ready-to-eat food, like bread. This will make it easier to understand that tofu needs to be combined with other ingredients to be at its best. You wouldn't eat raw chicken without first cooking and seasoning it, and the same is true for tofu. It's like an empty canvas waiting for the creative cook to transform it into a masterpiece.

Regular tofu is also known as Chinese bean curd, and silken tofu is also called Japanese-style tofu. Both are available in soft, firm, and extra-firm varieties. Firm and extra-firm regular tofu are generally used in stir-fries and other dishes that require a sturdy texture that retains its shape during cooking. Soft regular tofu can be used in recipes where a softer texture is desired. Silken tofu is more or less the same whether soft or firm; the softer kind just contains more water. Silken tofu is primarily used in recipes requiring a smooth, creamy texture, such as smoothies, sauces, and puddings. Both regular and silken tofu are available in lowfat versions. Regular tofu is also sold baked and marinated in a number of flavors, which you can use without further seasoning. For best results, regular and silken tofu should be treated as different products and not used interchangeably in most recipes.

Storing Tofu

Regular tofu may be stored unopened in the refrigerator up to the expiration date on the package. Once tofu is opened, it is best to use it right away, although it can be submerged in fresh water in a covered container (to prevent it from absorbing surrounding flavors) and kept in the refrigerator for several days. Silken tofu is usually sold in aseptic containers that can be kept unrefrigerated until opened. Once opened, however, it should be used within two to three days.

Draining, Blotting, and Pressing Tofu

Since tofu is generally packaged in water, it is essential to drain it before using it in recipes. To remove even more moisture, cut the tofu into slabs and place them on a cutting board or baking sheet lined with two or three layers of paper towels. Cover the tofu with paper towels and blot to help enable the tofu better absorb flavors. To remove most of the moisture from regular tofu (you can't do this with silken tofu) and thereby achieve a firmer texture, place a baking sheet on top of the tofu after blotting. Weight down the sheet with canned goods or a heavy skillet and allow to sit for one hour, then use as desired.

Freezing and Thawing Tofu

Another way to change the texture of regular tofu is to freeze it. (Do not freeze silken tofu.) Once thawed, the tofu will be chewier and more porous, making it ideal for marinating and sautéing. It is also easily crumbled for use in chili and other recipes.

To freeze tofu, cut drained and pressed tofu into thin slices and wrap in plastic or place in an airtight container. When you're ready to use the tofu, defrost it, then squeeze it to remove any excess moisture. Once thawed, it should be used within two to three days. Since frozen tofu will keep for several months, this is a good way to store tofu that is near its expiration date.

Baked Tofu

Baked tofu is widely available in natural food stores and supermarkets in a variety of flavors, including teriyaki, Italian, and Thai. It is ready to eat and can be served hot or cold, but it is also expensive. A more economical choice is to bake your own, using whatever seasonings you like—such as this simple soy-sesame marinade. To give it a teriyaki taste, add a teaspoon or two of pure maple syrup or brown rice syrup and a little grated fresh ginger to the marinade. For a Thai flavor, add a little peanut butter and Asian chili paste. If you want an Italian flavor, simply marinate the tofu in your favorite Italian salad dressing. Baked tofu is extremely versatile and can be sliced, cubed, or cut into strips. It's great cold when added to salads, made into sandwiches, or eaten as a snack. Served hot it can be added to pasta and grain dishes or served as an entrée.

One 16-ounce package firm tofu, drained	1/4 cup water
1/3 cup tamari or other soy sauce	2 tablespoons toasted sesame oil
	2 tablespoons fresh lemon juice

1. Blot the tofu to remove excess liquid, then cut it into 1/2-inch-thick slices. Place the tofu slices on a baking sheet lined with paper towels. Cover with more paper towels and place another baking sheet on top. Weight it down with some canned goods and let sit for 20 minutes.
2. In a small bowl, combine the tamari, water, oil, and lemon juice. Blend well.
3. Place the tofu slices in a glass baking dish and pour the marinade on top. Cover and refrigerate for 3 hours or overnight, turning the tofu once.
4. Preheat the oven to 375 degrees F. Remove the tofu from the marinade and place on a lightly oiled baking sheet. Bake until the tofu is well browned and very firm, turning once about halfway through, about 1 hour total. Serve hot or allow to cool. Store in a tightly covered container in the refrigerator for up to a few days.

SERVES 4

TEMPEH: THE OTHER SOY MEAT

Tempeh is a versatile meat alternative made from fermented soybeans that are compressed into a cake. Like tofu, tempeh readily absorbs flavors and is especially suited to hearty stews, stir-fries, and sautés. It marinates well and turns a crisp, golden brown when fried. Indonesian in origin, tempeh is a good source of high-quality soy protein with a chewy, meat-like texture. Some varieties of tempeh contain only soy; others are blended with one or more grains, giving them a mellower flavor. I prefer the tempeh-grain blends because they lend themselves to a wider variety of preparations.

Purchasing and Storing Tempeh

Tempeh is available in the refrigerator or freezer case of natural food stores and some supermarkets. Sold in slabs, it can be found in 8- or 12-ounce packages, depending on the brand. The slabs can be sliced lengthwise, cut into strips, cubed, or grated. Tempeh must be stored in the refrigerator, where it will keep unopened for several weeks (check the expiration date). Once opened, however, it should be tightly wrapped and used within three to four days. Tempeh also may be stored in the freezer for a month or so.

Poaching Tempeh

As a general rule, I recommend poaching tempeh before using in it recipes to mellow the flavor and increase digestibility. To poach tempeh, place it in a saucepan with water to cover and bring to a simmer. Continue to simmer gently for 10 minutes, then remove from the water and pat dry. Use as desired.

TEXTURED VEGETABLE PROTEIN

With the huge influx of vegetarian products that include everything from meatless Buffalo wings to bratwurst, textured vegetable protein (TVP) is found more often as an ingredient in other products than on its own.

Back in the early 1970s, when I first attempted vegetarianism, TVP was one of the few meat substitutes I could find. Sold as dehydrated granules or chunks that doubled in size when reconstituted with a hot liquid, TVP was one of the most economical meat alternatives you could buy. Made from compressed soy flour, it often tasted "grainy" and flavorless, but its ability to take on the flavor of surrounding ingredients made it popular for use in vegetarian chili, spaghetti sauce, and other "ground beef" recipes. TVP is a registered trademark of the Archer Daniels Midland Company, but it has come to be used generically to describe all dehydrated textured soy or vegetable protein products.

Although you can still find grainy and flavorless textured soy protein on the market, some new and improved varieties have a better texture and taste. Because of their convenience and superior flavor, I prefer the new generation of textured vegetable protein—frozen vegetarian burger crumbles—but I still keep some dehydrated TVP on hand for emergencies. Look for TVP in natural food stores and well-stocked supermarkets, where it is often sold in bulk. To rehydrate, place the desired amount in a heatproof bowl and cover with boiling water.

THE MEAT OF WHEAT

Seitan is one of the few meat alternatives not made from soy. Also known as wheatmeat, seitan is made from the protein part of wheat, which is known as gluten when mixed with liquid and agitated. Seitan is perhaps the most versatile meat alternative, owing to its meaty texture and chameleon-like qualities. It can be sliced thinly and sautéed; diced or cut into strips for stir-fries, stews, and soups; shredded or ground to use as you would ground beef; or even turned into a roast. If you're looking for an ingredient to win over a meat eater, this is the one that could do the trick.

Although it's fairly simple to make seitan from scratch, it can be time-consuming, since it must be kneaded and rinsed several times. For that reason, it's best to make a large amount at once and freeze the rest. The process of making seitan is intriguing: at certain points, you could swear the messy glob is going to go down the drain, then suddenly you have a firm ball of high-protein wheat gluten just waiting to be used in recipes. If you don't have the time or patience to make your own, look for Seitan Quick Mix, a packaged mix that produces fresh seitan in minutes without all the bother. Precooked seitan is available in natural food stores and Asian markets, but it is often sold in a marinade that may not be compatible with your recipe. To remedy this, drain and rinse the seitan before using.

Seitan (Wheat-Meat)

Some cooks make seitan with a combination of wheat and white flours, while others add a small amount of wheat gluten flour to the mix, all resulting in slight variations in texture. I prefer to keep it simple: my version uses only whole wheat flour, which produces a medium-texture seitan. Be sure to save the stock the seitan is cooked in and strain it for use in sauces, soups, and other recipes.

1 large yellow onion, quartered

1 large carrot, coarsely chopped

1 celery rib, coarsely chopped

2 garlic cloves, crushed

3/4 cup tamari or other soy sauce

2 bay leaves

16 cups water, or more as needed

4 pounds whole wheat flour (about 9 cups)

1. In a large pot, combine the onion, carrot, celery, garlic, tamari, and bay leaves with 12 cups of the water. Place over high heat and bring to a boil. Reduce the heat to low and simmer while you prepare the seitan.

2. Place the flour in a large bowl, add the remaining 4 cups water, and stir to form a firm dough, adding a little more water if the dough is too dry. Knead the dough on a flat work surface until it is smooth and elastic, about 10 minutes. Place the dough in the bowl and add warm water to cover completely. Let rest for 20 minutes.

3. Place the bowl in the sink and knead until the water turns white (that is the starch coming out). Drain the milky water, then cover with fresh water and knead again until the water turns white. Repeat the process until the kneading water is almost clear. The contents of the bowl will be quite loose and messy, but you will soon have a smooth ball of wheat gluten, or raw seitan.

4. Divide the seitan into smaller pieces and add to the simmering stock. Simmer, uncovered, for 1 hour, keeping the seitan submerged. Do not boil. When the seitan is cooked, remove from the pot and place on a baking sheet to cool. To store in the refrigerator, place the seitan and its stock in a tightly covered bowl and keep for 4 to 5 days. You also may freeze the seitan, either in its stock or not, for several weeks.

MAKES ABOUT 2½ POUNDS

BEYOND THE BASICS

As mentioned in the section on TVP, a number of products are made from tofu, seitan, and TVP. Manufacturers have discovered ways to add spices and seasonings to one or more of these basic ingredients to create products that resemble foods normally made with meat, such as burgers, hot dogs, bacon, pepperoni, Buffalo wings, and pastrami. The number of products and companies making them has skyrocketed in recent years. Many of the products are vegan, but some are not. It is important to read the labels, looking for ingredients such as egg whites, cheese, casein, and milk solids. (See page 32 for a list of hidden animal ingredients in foods.)

There are two main schools of thought on these products. One is that they are processed foods and not natural; therefore, no self-respecting vegan would want to eat them. The other is that they are a godsend to families with limited time to cook, finicky children, or reluctantly vegan spouses. They also are great transitional foods to have on hand when you're new to veganism and trying new recipes. A veggie burger slathered with barbecue sauce goes a long way when you're too tired to cook and want something quick and easy.

On the one hand, I agree that fresh, unadulterated foods are best. Vegetables, fruits, grains, beans, and the basic meat alternatives (tofu, tempeh, and seitan) offer as much variety and nutrition as I need. On the other hand, it sure is fun to grill a tofu hot dog on the Fourth of July or to enjoy the crisp, smoky flavor of tempeh bacon in a BLT. Does this mean I miss eating animal flesh? Not at all. It's not the flavor of animal flesh that I love but the seasonings, textures, cooking methods, and even condiments. Processed meats and processed vegetarian meats have much in common. They both start with a protein source (a pig or a soybean, for example), which is then turned into a usable mass that can be seasoned, colored, flavored, and shaped to fit in that hot dog bun. In my estimation, anyone who chooses vegetable-based processed

Stocking the Pantry

A well-stocked pantry is the first step toward making meatless and dairy-free cooking convenient, fun, and delicious. With a variety of ingredients at your fingertips, you can prepare interesting, healthful meals in a snap.

The following list of pantry items is especially important in a vegan kitchen. It includes staples such as canned and dried beans, grains, pasta, and tomato products. Also included are meal enhancers such as peanut butter, tahini, tamari, salsa, and chutney—indispensable ingredients for the creative cook.

Many of the ingredients integral to a vegan pantry are highly perishable. This applies not only to fresh fruits and vegetables but also to nuts, seeds, certain oils, and whole-grain flours, which can go rancid quickly. As an extra precaution against spoilage, I suggest storing such items in the refrigerator. For that reason, my list is broken down into perishable and nonperishable items. Once packages are opened, many of the items on the nonperishable list also will require refrigeration. In addition to the items listed here, you should, of course, keep on hand a supply of dried herbs, spices, sea salt, and other basic seasonings, as well as various flours, baking soda, baking powder, and extracts. Your vegan larder should include a number of perishable staples, such as onions, carrots, and celery, so that you always have the makings for a soup or stew; fresh lettuce and other salad ingredients; fresh vegetables and fruits; and fresh herbs.

Vegan Pantry: Nonperishables

- Dried and canned beans: kidney beans, chickpeas, lentils, pintos, etc.
- Dairy-free milk: soy, rice, oat, or almond (aseptic package)
- Unsweetened coconut milk (canned)
- Silken tofu (aseptic package)
- Pasta and noodles: Italian pasta, rice sticks, soba, etc.
- Whole-grain cereals
- Canned tomato products (diced, whole, puree, paste)
- Canned vegetables: artichokes, hearts of palm, roasted red peppers, etc.

- Condiments: soy sauce (tamari and shoyu are best), salsa, chutney, mustard, soy mayonnaise, etc.
- Dried fruits
- Thickeners: cornstarch, arrowroot, kudzu
- Egg replacement powder (Ener-G Egg Replacer is the brand most widely available)
- Sweeteners: pure maple syrup, raw sugar (sold under the brand names Rapadura, Sucanat, or Florida Crystals), brown rice syrup, barley malt
- Vegetable broth (aseptic containers, canned, powdered—preferably low sodium)
- Dried mushrooms (porcinis, shiitakes, etc.)
- Dried chiles
- Sun-dried tomatoes (dehydrated or oil-packed)
- Dried sea vegetables, including nori and agar
- Miscellaneous: vinegars, pickles, jellies, capers, Asian chili paste, hoisin sauce, wasabi powder, etc.

Vegan Pantry: Perishables

- Grains: rice, millet, barley, bulgur, couscous, rolled oats, popcorn
- Soy foods: tofu, tempeh, miso paste, veggie burgers, soy hot dogs, etc.
- Whole-grain flours, cornmeal, etc.
- Bread products: whole-grain breads, tortillas, pita breads, bagels, etc.
- Oils: olive, flaxseed, sesame, peanut, corn
- Peanut butter, tahini, almond butter
- Dairy-free ice cream
- Nuts and seeds
- Lemons and limes (for cooking)
- Fresh ginger
- Garlic
- Olives (bulk)

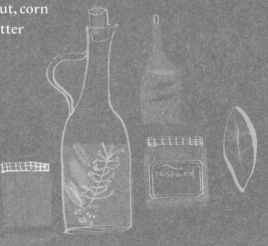

meat alternatives has taken a giant step in the right direction ethically, as well as for his or her health and the environment.

To me, the main caveat about vegetarian meat alternative products is that some taste wonderful and others taste awful. You'll have to determine which is which by trial and error. The main thing is, don't give up. If you find one brand of tofu dogs that tastes like an inner tube, it doesn't mean the next one will. The same goes for veggie burgers and cold cuts. So don't stock up on a brand until you know you like it, and keep track of which ones you like and which ones you don't. My favorite veggie burger, hands down, is the Original Vegan Boca Burger.

Another product I am especially partial to is frozen vegetarian burger crumbles. With the flavor and appearance of cooked ground beef, these crumbles can be used to replace the meat in most recipes. If you can't find a brand you like, finely chopped or crumbled veggie burgers make a reasonable substitute.

For the most part, I steer clear of any product that is marinated or flavored. I'd rather be the one to do the flavoring. But for a quick fix, for the kids, or just for fun, tofu dogs, veggie burgers, and other meat alternative products can fit the bill.

Oils

Since vegan meals are naturally low in fat, a moderate use of cooking and salad oils can add some "good" fat to your diet. The best-quality oils are cold-pressed, or un-refined. I like to use extra virgin olive oil for salads and most cooking, except for high-heat stir-fries, where you want an oil that has a higher smoking point and won't start breaking down before you get it to the right temperature. In addition to great flavor, olive oil provides many health benefits.

For high-heat cooking, peanut oil is a good choice because it is stable at high temperatures. Corn oil has a slightly "buttery" flavor, so I often use it for baking. Toasted sesame oil adds an Asian flavor to salads and other recipes, but think of it as a season-ing rather than a cooking oil, because it is unstable at high temperatures. Add it at the last minute for flavor. Flaxseed oil is an excellent source of omega-3 fatty acids, which are so important for good health. Like toasted sesame oil, flaxseed oil is unstable at high temperatures and should not be used for cooking. Unlike toasted sesame oil, it is virtually flavorless, but you can use it on salads to boost your intake of omega-3s. All of these oils are highly perishable, so be sure to store them in the refrigerator.

Coconut oil is another choice you may want to consider. It can withstand high temperatures and is especially useful for frying. Studies show a very low incidence of heart disease among people who consume coconut oil on a regular basis. In addition, coconut oil aids calcium absorption and is rich in antimicrobial properties. Organic, unrefined coconut oil is available at natural food stores. Be sure you buy food-grade oil, not the cosmetic grade meant for external use.

Nuts and Seeds

Nuts and seeds are staple foods in many cultures and important protein sources for vegans. Many nuts and seeds are available both in and out of the shell, whole, halved, sliced, chopped, raw, roasted, or made into nut butter. Nuts are popular in both sweet and savory dishes and are often enjoyed as a snack food. Due to their high oil content, nuts and seeds go rancid quickly once shelled and should be stored in an airtight container in the refrigerator, where they will keep for several months. Some nuts are sold shelled in cans, jars, and bags. Many are available in bulk at natural food stores and many supermarkets.

Studies have shown that eating just two ounces of almonds, pecans, or other nuts each day as part of a high-fiber vegan diet can dramatically lower "bad" low-density lipoprotein (LDL) cholesterol.

NUT AND SEED BUTTERS

When nuts or seeds are ground into a paste, they are referred to as butters. Not long ago, the only nut butter found in most pantries was peanut butter, and a highly processed version at that. Over the past several years, however, a wide variety of natural nut butters have come on the scene, including almond butter, cashew butter, hazelnut butter, macadamia butter, pistachio butter, tahini (sesame paste), and even soy nut butter (page 549).

Nut and seed butters are rich in protein, fiber, and essential fatty acids and can be used to replace butter or margarine on bread or toast. At least half of the fat in nuts is monounsaturated, which can actually be good for blood cholesterol. Nut butters are a boon to vegans as a versatile source of protein and can be used to make sauces, to enrich soups and stews, and as a healthy fat replacement in baking. They are easier to digest than whole nuts and are easy to make at home using a blender. They should

FABULOUS FLAXSEEDS

The tiny flaxseed is a nutritional powerhouse that is especially prized for its high amounts of omega-3 and omega-6 essential fatty acids. High in protein, flaxseeds also contain good amounts of calcium, phosphorus, potassium, magnesium, and boron. Flaxseeds provide abundant soluble fiber, which is helpful in controlling blood-sugar levels and reducing cholesterol. Flaxseeds are also the richest known source of the anticarcinogens known as lignans and phytoestrogens.

Flaxseeds can be purchased in bulk at natural food stores and well-stocked supermarkets. They should be ground in a blender or coffee grinder before using to provide maximum nutrient absorption and increase digestibility. Since they go rancid quickly, they should be stored in the refrigerator or freezer. They can be sprinkled on breakfast cereals, salads, or grain dishes or added to smoothies for an energy boost. Blended with water, ground flaxseeds can be used to replace eggs in baking (page 509).

be stored in tightly covered jars in the refrigerator, where they will keep for about a month. Since nut butters become stiff when chilled, it is best to bring them to room temperature before using. In addition, the oil in nut butters will rise to the top of the jar, so you will need to stir the butter before using.

Natural nut butters do not contain the stabilizers and additives found in most national brands. They are made, quite simply, with nuts and perhaps a little salt. Nothing more.

Dried Fruits

Dried fruits have become increasingly popular in recent years, showing up in sweet and savory dishes from breads, muffins, and compotes to sauces, chutneys, stuffings, and stews. Choices range from dried cranberries and papaya spears to banana chips and apple rings. Raisins, dried dates, dried figs, and even dried apricots are important ingredients in many cuisines, and prunes are now called dried plums in an effort to update their image.

Because most of the water content has been removed from dried fruits, they have a higher concentration of sugar than fresh fruits, which results in more calories on a weight-for-weight basis. Still, dried fruits are a chewy, sweet snack with good nutritional content, despite the fact that some of the nutrients are lost during the drying process. To keep the nutritional losses to a minimum, store your dried fruits in airtight containers in a cool, dark place. Dried fruits can be reconstituted by soaking them in hot water for 30 minutes.

Although their vitamin C content is diminished, virtually all dried fruits are high in potassium, calcium, and fiber, and many actually have an increased mineral content when dried. In particular, raisins, dried pears, and dried figs are abundant in iron, phosphorus, and magnesium, while dried apples and dates contain a good amount of magnesium. Dried apricots, peaches, and plums (prunes) are high in vitamin A, iron, and magnesium, and dried papayas are abundant in vitamin A.

Miso

Miso is a salty fermented paste made from soybeans, often in combination with a grain such as rice or barley. It is versatile and can be used in soups and stews casseroles, marinades, sauces, dressings, and dips. Available in different colors and degrees of saltiness, miso is high in protein and rich in enzymes.

Know Your Nuts and Seeds

Most of us know that nuts and seeds are important sources of protein, but did you also know that they are rich in a number of vitamins, minerals, and other nutrients as well? In addition, although most nuts and seeds are high in fat, most of that is unsaturated fat—the "good" fat we all need. Here's a look at the nutrient content of some nuts and seeds.

- *Almonds:* High in calcium, potassium, magnesium, and zinc, almonds also contain folic acid, phosphorus, and iron and are about 18 percent protein.
- *Brazil nuts:* Rich in calcium, magnesium, thiamine, and potassium, Brazil nuts contain significant amounts of vitamin B_6, zinc, and iron.
- *Cashews:* They contain high amounts of calcium, magnesium, iron, and zinc, as well as phosphorus and potassium.
- *Chestnuts:* High in carbohydrates, chestnuts are a source of calcium, potassium, B complex vitamins, magnesium, and iron.
- *Coconuts:* High in fiber, coconuts contain a good amount of calcium, potassium, iron, phosphorus, zinc, and magnesium.
- *Flaxseeds:* Especially high in protein and rich in essential fatty acids, flaxseeds also contain good amounts of calcium and phosphorus.
- *Hazelnuts:* Also known as filberts, they are high in fiber and a good source of calcium, iron, potassium, magnesium, and vitamins A, B complex, and E.
- *Macadamia nuts:* They are rich in magnesium, calcium, potassium, iron, thiamine, and niacin.
- *Peanuts:* Rich in protein (about 26 percent) peanuts are an excellent source of niacin and contain other B complex vitamins—thiamine and riboflavin—as well as potassium, magnesium, calcium, and iron.
- *Pecans:* High in fiber, pecans are a good source of calcium, iron, magnesium, and potassium. They also contain small amounts of vitamins A, B complex, C, and E.

- *Pine nuts:* A rich source of fiber, pine nuts contain iron, magnesium, potassium, and folic acid.
- *Pistachios:* Pistachios are a good source of calcium, magnesium, potassium, iron, folic acid, and vitamins B$_6$ and C.
- *Pumpkin seeds:* Extremely high in protein (29 percent), pumpkin seeds are rich in iron, calcium, phosphorus, and vitamins A and B complex.
- *Sesame seeds:* They are rich in iron, calcium, and vitamins A, B, and E.
- *Sunflower seeds:* Rich in omega-6 fatty acids, sunflower seeds are a good source of calcium, iron, and other nutrients.
- *Walnuts:* An excellent source of vitamin E, copper, and magnesium, walnuts also contain potassium, vitamin B$_6$, thiamine, and essential fatty acids.

Miso paste is generally aged from one month to three years and can be made using either traditional or commercial methods. The traditional method relies on natural ingredients and sea salt and allows the miso to age in large, wooden fermentation casks. The commercial method accelerates the fermentation process in plastic or stainless steel holding tanks.

The longer the soybeans are fermented, the darker and stronger in flavor the miso is. Miso paste can range in color and pungency from white to dark brown, with white being the weakest in flavor and dark brown the most pungent. White and yellow miso are well suited for soups, salad dressings, and sauces. Red and brown miso are strong and salty and are generally used for stews, soups, and braised foods. Often two or more kinds of miso are combined in a recipe. Some of the more common varieties are *hatcho miso*, made with soybeans and sea salt; *genmai miso*, made with soybeans and brown rice; and *mugi miso*, made with soybeans and barley.

Several varieties of miso paste are available in natural food stores and Asian markets under different brand names. Miso paste may be stored for up to a year in a tightly sealed container in the refrigerator.

Salt

From the delicate, pricey *fleur de sel* to the coarse, economical kosher variety, salt is an important element in cooking. Just a pinch can sometimes make the difference between a well-seasoned dish and one that lacks flavor. The best salt for general use is sea salt, because it is naturally derived, has a good flavor, and contains minerals that are nutritionally beneficial. Steer clear of refined table salt. It is bitter, devoid of nutrition, and loaded with chemicals that are added to make it flow freely.

If you do not need to avoid salt for medical reasons, I encourage a judicious use of sea salt in your cooking to bring out and balance the natural flavors of foods. If you must eliminate salt from your diet, consider using an herbal salt substitute. You also may want to experiment with spices, herbs, and ingredients such as garlic, onions, lemon juice, and wine to add flavor to your dishes.

The more processed a food is, the higher its sodium content. Therefore, the more naturally you eat, with lots of fresh vegetables, fruits, and grains, the less sodium you will consume. For that reason, most people can use sea salt when they cook and not worry about getting too much sodium. It is important to add salt to your food *while it is cooking*, not afterward, so that the salt has a chance to dissolve into the dish, thus allowing your body to absorb the minerals in the salt. If you add salt at the table, the absorption process is bypassed, and the salt is simply flushed out of your system, which can overtax your kidneys.

Soy sauce is often used to replace salt, although many brands of soy sauce are full of sodium and additives and the flavor can be bitter and harsh. Read the label when buying soy sauce to avoid any undesirable ingredients. For the best flavor and nutritional value, use a traditionally brewed shoyu or tamari. Although these products do contain salt, they are naturally fermented and have a mellow flavor. A low-sodium tamari also is available. The downside of these soy sauces is the cost: the best-quality, cold-pressed organic tamari and shoyu can be very expensive.

Sea Vegetables

Not long ago, the only sea vegetable on the American horizon was nori, famed for its use in sushi. These days, however, you can find several varieties of sea vegetables on supermarket shelves and seaweed salads on some restaurant menus.

Sea vegetables are sold in dehydrated form and will keep indefinitely when stored in airtight containers in a cool, dark place. With flavors ranging from delicate and mild to salty and spicy, sea vegetables contain high concentrations of protein, iron, calcium, and other nutrients. Because most sea vegetables are dried, they require soaking in water prior to use. Two exceptions are nori sheets and dulse, which can be eaten right from the package. The soaking time for sea vegetables varies, and some expand more than others when soaked. For correct preparation, follow the instructions on the package or in a particular recipe.

Many sea vegetables are best enjoyed in soups or salads or cooked with vegetables or grains. A few have other uses. For example, agar has natural jelling properties, making it useful as a vegan alternative to gelatin. Kombu or kelp can be added to the cooking water of dried beans to help them cook faster and to make them easier to digest.

It is best to buy only certified organic sea vegetables. Although Asian markets carry less expensive products, they are not of the same high quality as certified organic brands. If you're worried about the extra expense, remember that sea vegetables expand dramatically when soaked and only a small amount is needed.

Flours

When considering what kind of flour to use in baking, you have a "field of flours" from which to choose, each with its own flavor and textural characteristics. Here is a bouquet of the more common (and some uncommon) flours.

- *Amaranth flour:* Though difficult to find, it can be made at home by grinding the tiny amaranth grains. Because of its strong, distinctive flavor, it is best used in small quantities to add nutrients and flavor to your favorite bread recipes.
- *Brown rice flour:* This is especially useful for people allergic to wheat. However, because rice contains no gluten, it is best to use rice flour in quick-bread recipes.
- *Buckwheat flour:* Just a small amount of this flour added to a bread recipe creates a hearty, dense loaf with a strong, distinctive flavor.
- *Cornmeal:* Available in both white and yellow varieties, cornmeal is used to make breads, muffins, and other baked goods. Because many of the nutrients are removed during processing, cornmeal is often sold enriched with vitamins and minerals.
- *Wheat gluten flour:* This high-protein flour is refined from wheat flour and rises better because it is low in starch.
- *Oat flour:* Oat flour has a delicate, sweet flavor and can be used in cookies, quick breads, and muffins. Because it contains no gluten, it is often used by people with wheat allergies. You can make your own oat flour by grinding rolled oats to a powder in a blender.

Know Your Sea Vegetables

Here is a list of the most common sea vegetables.

- *Agar:* Also called kanten, this is a tasteless natural gelatin alternative used to make gelatin-type desserts. Available in bars or flakes, it is extremely high in iodine.
- *Alaria:* Resembling wakame in appearance, taste, and nutrition, alaria is high in calcium, vitamin A, and B vitamins. Blackish green in color, it is good in stews, grain dishes, and miso soup.
- *Arame:* Similar to hijiki in appearance, arame is rich in calcium and iodine. It has a delicate flavor and can be used in soups or combined with tofu or land vegetables.
- *Carrageen:* Also called Irish moss, it is rich in vitamin A, iodine, and other minerals. It is used to thicken commercial products such as soups, stews, and sauces.
- *Dulse:* Reddish in color with a soft, chewy texture and a salty, spicy flavor, this is an appealing choice for those new to sea vegetables. Native to the North Atlantic coast, dulse is high in protein, iron, potassium, and vitamins B_6 and B_{12}. It cooks quickly when added to recipes but also is a nice snack right from the package or when lightly fried.
- *Hijiki:* The strongest-tasting sea vegetable, hijiki is often paired with onions and root vegetables or added to soups. Dehydrated, hijiki looks like black strings. When cooked, it expands to up to five times its dry volume. Hijiki is high in calcium and iron.
- *Kelp:* Light brown to dark green in color, kelp is similar to Japanese kombu and is used in much the same ways—in stews and soups or cooked with grains or beans. It contains a natural tenderizer that helps beans cook quickly and aids in digestion. Kelp is high in calcium, iron, potassium, magnesium, chromium, and iodine.
- *Kombu:* Sometimes called "natural MSG," kombu is used to brighten the flavors of soups and stews and to tenderize beans. It is usually sold as dried strips that are blackish green in color.

- *Nori:* Though deep purple in color, nori turns dark green when toasted, which is how it is commonly sold. Known for its role in sushi making, nori is available in pretoasted, ready-to-use sheets and can be chopped or crumbled to use in soups and salads.
- *Wakame:* The traditional leafy addition to miso soup, wakame has a mild flavor that works well in salads or stir-fries with other vegetables or grains. It is high in calcium, B vitamins, and vitamin C.

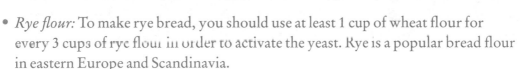

- *Rye flour:* To make rye bread, you should use at least 1 cup of wheat flour for every 3 cups of rye flour in order to activate the yeast. Rye is a popular bread flour in eastern Europe and Scandinavia.
- *Soy flour:* Extremely rich in high-quality protein, soy flour also is an excellent source of iron, calcium, and B vitamins. Made from finely ground roasted soybeans, soy flour added protein to baked goods, as well as a dense texture and nutty flavor. Because it has no gluten, you should use only a small amount of soy flour in combination with wheat flour for baking. Toasting soy flour lightly will give it a nuttier flavor.
- *Triticale flour:* This hybrid of rye and wheat has a hearty flavor and extra protein. Boost the protein in your bread recipe by replacing half of the whole wheat flour with triticale flour.
- *Unbleached all-purpose flour:* Refined wheat flour is less nutritious than whole wheat flour. Combine unbleached all-purpose flour and whole wheat flour in bread recipes to provide the nutrients of whole wheat and the lighter texture and mellower flavor of all-purpose.
- *Whole wheat flour:* For bread recipes, use whole wheat bread flour, which is made from hard red spring wheat or red winter wheat and is high in gluten or protein, which helps produce light, airy loaves. For pastries, muffins, and cookies, use whole wheat pastry flour, which has less protein than regular whole wheat.

The Buzz About Honey

Although honey may be considered a "natural" sweetener by many, it is not considered a vegan ingredient. This is because many bees are killed, harmed, or otherwise exploited to procure honey from their hives.

During the harvesting of honey and other bee byproducts, bees are removed from their hives by harsh methods, such as shaking or smoking the hives or dousing them with gases or blasts of air. A number of bees are invariably killed in the process.

Although the exploitation of bees may be inconsequential to many vegetarians, especially when compared to the cruel and inhumane treatment of other animals raised for food, to many vegans not using honey is a matter of principle. Ethical vegans strive to eliminate from their lives any product that involves the exploitation or suffering of any creature.

A vast number of alternative sweeteners, candles, and personal care products that do not contain bee products are available.

Sweeteners

Although honey, an animal product, is not considered vegan, the use of white sugar in a vegan diet is a matter of personal preference. Many people need to avoid sugar for health reasons. Others don't use it because it is devoid of nutritional value. If you need another reason to avoid sugar, consider the fact that about one-quarter of the white table sugar in the United States is processed using charred animal bones. To many vegans, this is considered a minuscule point in the grand scheme of things, and they continue to use sugar.

Among the alternatives to sugar and honey are natural sweeteners such as maple syrup, barley malt, rice syrup, pureed fruit (such as raisins or dates), and natural fruit sweeteners available under a variety of brand names. In addition to providing nutritional benefits, natural sweeteners do not cause a sugar "rush," because they metabolize more slowly in the system.

The sweetness level of sugar alternatives can vary greatly, so it is best to experiment to find the ones you like best. Several alternatives can be substituted in equal measure for white table sugar. Among the most reliable brands are granulated FruitSource, made from fruit juice concentrate and brown rice syrup, and naturally processed granulated sugar cane, sold as Rapadura, Sucanat, or Florida Crystals.

Among the natural liquid sweeteners that can be substituted in equal measure for honey are pure maple syrup and liquid FruitSource. These work best when the liquid-to-solid ratio is important to the outcome of a recipe. Sweeteners such as barley malt and brown rice syrup are about half as sweet as honey, so you may need to experiment to achieve the desired results. Soaked and pureed dates and raisins, as well as molasses, are good natural sweeteners, but their dark color and distinctive flavors make them appropriate for only certain recipes. Another option is date or palm sugar, which can be found in ethnic markets. Its deep, almost caramelized flavor is ideally suited to Southeast Asian recipes and can be fun to experiment with, although it doesn't dissolve as well as other sugars.

When substituting a natural liquid sweetener for granulated sugar in recipes, you will need to reduce the amount of the other liquids in the recipe so that the finished product retains the intended texture. For each cup of liquid sweetener added, figure on reducing the other liquids by a total of 1/4 cup.

Stevia is another sweetener worth considering. Available in liquid or powder form, stevia is derived from dried stevia leaves, an herb native to Paraguay. It differs from other sweeteners in that it is highly concentrated. Just a drop or pinch of this natural sugar alternative can sweeten a cup of liquid. Stevia can be used for baking, as it is stable to 390 degrees F, although determining the proper ratio can be hit or miss. If you use too much, it can leave a strong, overly sweet aftertaste.

Hidden Animal Ingredients

Many animal-based ingredients lurk in seemingly vegetarian and vegan foods. Beyond the obvious anchovy-laced Worcestershire sauce and the "milk" contained in milk chocolate, animal products such as gelatin and lard can be found in foods such as marshmallows, cookies, crackers, chips, candies, pastries, and refried beans.

Vegetarians who eat cheese should know that most dairy cheese is made with pepsin, rennet, or lipase, coagulated enzymes from the stomach linings of slaughtered cows and pigs. An alternative to dairy cheese is soy cheese, which contains no slaughtered animal byproducts. However, this is of little help to the vegan, since most soy cheeses are made with casein, which is

Avoiding Hidden Animal Ingredients

Here are some common hidden animal-based ingredients and the types of foods in which they are often found.

- *Albumin:* Used to thicken or bind in baked goods, soups, cereals, puddings, and other products, albumin is a protein found in eggs, milk, and blood.
- *Carmine, cochineal, or carminic acid:* A common red food dye made from ground beetles, it is used to color juices, baked goods, candies, and other processed foods.
- *Casein:* A protein derived from animal milk that is used in dairy products such as sour cream and cream cheese. It is also added to nondairy cheese to improve the texture.
- *Gelatin:* This thickener is made by boiling the bones, skin, and other parts of cows and other animals. It is found in gelatin desserts, marshmallows, candies, puddings, and other products.
- *Lactose:* Also called milk sugar, it is derived from cow's milk and is found in baked goods and processed foods.
- *Lard:* This fat taken from hogs is an ingredient in crackers, pie crusts, and baked goods, as well as refried beans and other fried or processed foods.
- *Suet:* This hard, white fat from cattle and sheep is sometimes found in margarine and baked goods.
- *Whey:* Derived from milk as it is processed into cheese, whey is found in commercial food products such as crackers and breads.

obtained from cow's milk. A few brands of soy cheese are casein-free, but they do not melt well. They are usually labeled as "vegan."

Vegans also should be aware that many products labeled as "vegetarian" may contain egg and dairy byproducts. In addition to avoiding products that contain butter, milk, eggs, and honey, vegans should be on the lookout for products with ingredients such as casein, albumin, whey, and lactose.

Fortunately, virtually every animal-based ingredient has a plant-based alternative. For example, there are vegan versions of Worcestershire sauce and chocolate chips, and gelatin-like desserts and puddings can be made with vegetable-based jelling ingredients such as the sea vegetables agar and carrageen.

The best defense against unwittingly buying foods with animal-derived ingredients is quite simple: read the labels. As a rule, the more processed a food item is, the more likely it is to contain animal products—often not listed in easily recognizable terms. To cut down on the chances of ingesting hidden animal ingredients, try to eat more fresh whole foods, such as vegetables, fruits, grains, and beans, and to make more foods, such as salad dressings, from scratch. Not only will this help you avoid hidden animal ingredients, but homemade dressings and other foods generally taste better and are more economical.

2

Love at First Bite

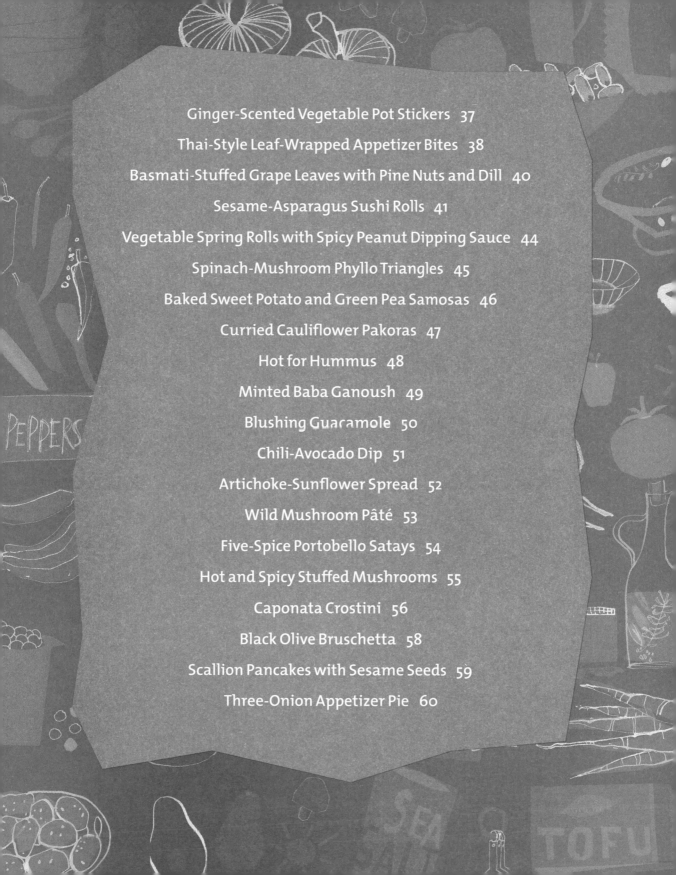

Appetizers usually herald a special event, be it an intimate dinner for two, a family celebration, or a party. Whether you call them hors d'oeuvres, finger foods, or even *amuse-bouches*, these tasty bites don't have to be reserved for special occasions. Serving a first course prior to Tuesday night's casserole or setting out a plate of crostini before your usual Thursday night pasta dinner can have an amazing effect on the rest of the meal. On nights when you're serving leftovers or a light supper, an appetizer can elevate the meal from dull to dramatic and add substance and nutrition at the same time. Your family will feel special for the extra effort, and that will make you feel good, too.

Appetizers are a great way to introduce new tastes and recipes to your family—in little bites. Plus, they're a good way to be sure your family is getting enough veggies. A finicky child (or spouse) who avoids certain vegetables on the dinner plate is almost certain to enjoy them served up as "fun food" in a fritter, alongside (or in) a dip, or wrapped in a savory pastry.

Planning an appetizer party without meat and dairy removes the guesswork from entertaining friends, since most people can enjoy the food whether they are vegetarians or meat eaters. This chapter contains a planet full of naturally vegan appetizers, including a spicy rendition of Middle Eastern hummus, *Basmati-Stuffed*

Grape Leaves with Pine Nuts and Dill, and *Minted Baba Ganoush*, as well as Italian *Caponata Crostini*, *Black Olive Bruschetta*, and *Hot and Spicy Stuffed Mushrooms*. Asian bites include tempting *Vegetable Spring Rolls with Spicy Peanut Dipping Sauce*, *Scallion Pancakes with Sesame Seeds*, and *Five-Spice Portobello Satays*, as well as elegant *Sesame-Asparagus Sushi Rolls*. Other worldly wonders include Indian *Baked Sweet Potato and Green Pea Samosas*, a French-inspired *Wild Mushroom Pâté*, and an all-American *Artichoke-Sunflower Spread*.

Ginger-Scented Vegetable Pot Stickers

These vegetable dumplings are called pot stickers because—you guessed it—they tend to stick to the bottom of the pot. Look for wonton or dumpling wrappers in the produce section of well-stocked supermarkets and Asian grocery stores. They can be served with a small bowl of plain soy sauce or your favorite dipping sauce.

1 cup minced napa cabbage
1 cup drained and crumbled
　extra-firm tofu
1/4 cup finely shredded carrots
1 garlic clove, minced
1 tablespoon peeled and minced fresh
　ginger
1 teaspoon toasted sesame oil

1/2 teaspoon cornstarch
Salt and freshly ground black pepper
24 dumpling or wonton wrappers,
　thawed if frozen
2 tablespoons peanut oil
1 tablespoon tamari or other soy sauce
1 cup water

1. In a food processor, combine the cabbage, tofu, carrots, garlic, ginger, sesame oil, cornstarch, and salt and pepper to taste. Process until well combined.
2. Place 1 wonton wrapper on a work surface and spoon 1 tablespoon of the filling mixture on the lower third of the wrapper. Fold the wrapper over the filling to form a triangle (if using square wrappers) or a semicircle (if using round wrappers). Moisten the edges of the wrapper with water to seal. Repeat with the remaining wrappers and filling.
3. Heat 1 tablespoon of the peanut oil in a large nonstick skillet over medium-high heat. Place half the dumplings in the pan and cook until golden, about 3 minutes. Do not crowd.

4. Stir in half the tamari, then half the water. Cover, reduce the heat to medium, and cook for 5 minutes. Uncover and cook until the water evaporates, 2 to 3 minutes.

5. Repeat with the remaining dumplings, tamari, and water. Keep the first batch covered with a lid or aluminum foil so they stay warm. Serve hot.

MAKES 24 DUMPLINGS

Thai-Style Leaf-Wrapped Appetizer Bites

This unusual appetizer is a popular snack food in Thailand, where it is called *miang kam* and is often sold by street vendors. I've enjoyed it served elegantly at Arun's, an extraordinary Thai restaurant in Chicago, and have since begun making it at home. The key to the amazing flavor is a small amount of several ingredients—sweet, sour, hot, and salty—which, when wrapped in a leaf and popped in the mouth, provide an experience not unlike a burst of fireworks. Since the wild leaves (often *shaploo*, wild pepper, or wild betel leaves) used to make *miang kam* can be difficult to find, I use leaf lettuce, torn into small pieces, but spinach or tender young kale leaves may be used instead.

5 or 6 large leaf lettuce leaves

Sauce:
1/2 cup unsweetened shredded coconut, toasted (page 491)
1/4 cup unsalted dry-roasted peanuts
1/4 cup palm sugar or other natural sweetener
3 tablespoons tamari or other soy sauce
1/3 cup water

Filling:
2 or 3 Thai chiles, to your taste, seeded and cut into very thin rounds
1 lime, sliced and finely chopped, including peel
1/2 cup coarsely chopped unsalted dry-roasted peanuts
1/2 cup unsweetened shredded coconut, toasted (page 491)
1/4 cup minced shallots
1/4 cup peeled and minced fresh ginger
1/4 cup chopped fresh cilantro leaves

1. Carefully wash and dry the lettuce leaves and tear into 20 pieces total, about 4 inches square. Arrange on a serving platter and set aside.

2. To make the sauce, combine the ingredients in a small saucepan over medium heat and bring to a boil. Reduce the heat to low and simmer until thickened, about 5 minutes. Remove from the heat and allow to cool slightly. Transfer to a blender or food processor and process until smooth. Place in a small serving bowl and set the bowl on the platter with the leaves. Set aside.

3. For the filling, place each of the ingredients in a small bowl and arrange on a large platter or tray.

4. To eat, cup one of the lettuce leaves in your hand and place a small amount of each filling in the center of the leaf. Top with a bit of sauce, close up the leaf, and pop it in your mouth.

SERVES 4

ALTERNATE SERVING IDEAS: Having your guests assemble their own *miang kam* can be fun, but you may prefer a more elegant presentation. Arrange 5 lettuce leaves on each of 4 plates (square plates are perfect for this) and place a small amount of each filling and a small amount of sauce in the center of each leaf. Then the diners simply have to close up their leaf packets, place in their mouths, and enjoy.

When serving a crowd, you can go one step further and turn the appetizer into easy "pickup" food by closing up the leaf bundles and skewering them shut with a toothpick.

"I have no doubt that it is part of the destiny of the human race, in its gradual improvement to leave off eating animals, as surely as the savage tribes have left off eating each other when they came into contact with the more civilized."

—HENRY DAVID THOREAU

Basmati-Stuffed Grape Leaves with Pine Nuts and Dill

Piquant grape leaves wrap tightly around a tasty filling of basmati rice and pine nuts to make the classic Middle Eastern appetizer called *dolmas* or *dolmades*. Jars of grape leaves packed in brine are available in well-stocked supermarkets and specialty food stores.

One 16-ounce jar grape leaves
3 tablespoons olive oil
1 medium-size yellow onion, minced
3/4 cup basmati rice
1/4 cup pine nuts, toasted (page 110)
3 tablespoons minced fresh dill

1/2 teaspoon ground cinnamon
Salt and freshly ground black pepper
1 1/4 cups Basic Vegetable Stock
   (page 68)
1 tablespoon fresh lemon juice

1. Remove the grape leaves from the jar and rinse under running water to remove the brine. Pat dry and trim off the stems. Set aside.

2. Heat 1 tablespoon of the olive oil in a large skillet over medium heat. Add the onion, cover, and cook until softened, about 5 minutes. Stir in the rice, pine nuts, dill, cinnamon, salt and pepper to taste, and 1 cup of the stock. Cover and simmer, stirring occasionally, until all of the liquid has evaporated, about 20 minutes. The rice should be *al dente*. Transfer the filling to a bowl and allow to cool completely.

3. On a work surface, place one of the grape leaves shiny side down, with the stem end toward you. Place a tablespoon of the cooled filling near the stem end and fold in the sides of the leaf over the filling. Roll up the leaf away from you, firmly but not too tightly, because the rice will expand more as it continues to cook. Repeat the process with the remaining leaves and filling. Transfer the *dolmas* to a large skillet.

4. Pour the remaining 1/4 cup stock, the remaining 2 tablespoons olive oil, and the lemon juice over the *dolmas*, adding water to just barely cover them with liquid. Bring to a simmer over medium heat and cook, covered, until the grape leaves are tender, about 30 minutes. Remove from the heat, uncover, and allow to cool.

5. Using a slotted spoon, transfer the *dolmas* to a serving plate and serve. They will keep for 3 to 5 days in a tightly sealed container in the refrigerator but are best served at room temperature.

MAKES 20 TO 24 *DOLMAS*

Sesame-Asparagus Sushi Rolls

Asushi roll, called *nori maki*, can be filled with vegetables instead of fish. Tender, thin asparagus is used here, but other choices include strips of avocado, cucumber, carrot, and bell pepper. Nori seaweed sheets, as well as wasabi powder, pickled ginger, and short-grain rice (sometimes called sushi rice), are now available in well-stocked supermarkets, natural food stores, and Asian markets.

2 cups short-grain white rice
2³/₄ cups water
¹/₄ cup rice vinegar
2 tablespoons sugar or natural
    sweetener
1 teaspoon salt
6 nori sheets
2 tablespoons sesame seeds, toasted
    (page 192)

6 thin asparagus spears, bottoms
    trimmed and lightly steamed
    until crisp-tender
1 tablespoon wasabi powder
1 tablespoon warm water
2 tablespoons pickled ginger
    for garnish
Tamari or other soy sauce

1. Rinse the rice under cold running water until the water runs clear, then drain in a colander for 1 hour.
2. Place the drained rice in a medium-size saucepan with a tight-fitting lid. Add the water, cover, and bring to a boil over medium-high heat. Boil for about 2 minutes, then reduce the heat to medium and simmer for 5 minutes. Reduce the heat to low and cook until all the water has been absorbed, about 12 minutes. Remove from the heat, remove the lid, and place a clean kitchen towel over the pot. Replace the lid and let stand for 10 minutes.

3. While the rice is cooking, heat the vinegar, sugar, and salt in a small saucepan over low heat, stirring until the sugar is dissolved. Remove from the heat and let cool to room temperature.

4. While the rice is still warm, place in a wide nonreactive container and spread out evenly using a rice paddle or large wooden spoon. Bring the paddle through the rice in slicing motions to separate the grains. While doing this, slowly pour the vinegar mixture over the rice, fanning the rice as you add the mixture. Continue to fan until the rice is cool. Set aside and cover with a damp cloth while you prepare the sushi. Do not refrigerate.

5. Place one nori sheet on a bamboo sushi mat or cloth napkin. Spread $1/2$ cup of the rice evenly over the nori, spreading it right to the side edges and to within $1/2$ inch of the top and bottom edges. Sprinkle the rice evenly with the sesame seeds. Along the edge nearest you, place one asparagus spear on top of the rice. Beginning at that edge, roll up the mat or napkin, pressing firmly against the nori. Use your fingers to keep the edge of the sushi mat from rolling into the sushi. Continue rolling slowly up to the top edge. Wet the exposed edge of the nori with a little water to seal the roll. Gently squeeze the mat around the sushi roll and remove the mat.

6. Using a sharp knife, cut the sushi roll into 6 pieces. Stand the pieces on end and place on a large platter. Repeat with the remaining nori sheets, rice, sesame seeds, and asparagus.

7. In a small bowl, combine the wasabi powder and warm water to form a paste. Shape the wasabi paste into a small mound and place it on the sushi platter. Also place the pickled ginger in a mound on the platter. Serve with small dipping bowls of tamari. Sushi is best eaten shortly after it is made, since refrigeration can toughen the rice and cause the nori to go limp. If you must make it ahead, it should be no longer than an hour or two.

MAKES 6 ROLLS OR 36 PIECES

HOT LIKE WASABI

Wasabi is best known as a sushi sidekick, although it isn't just for sushi anymore. Thanks to the popularity of fusion food, wasabi, among many other Asian ingredients, is being used in a number of Western dishes, with tasty results. The fiery green paste has found its way into marinades, salad dressings, sauces, spreads, and even mashed potatoes.

The wasabi plant is a semiaquatic member of the cabbage family. Its stem is ground into a powder that is in turn blended into a paste. A 10th-century Japanese medical encyclopedia documents wasabi as an antidote for food poisoning. In fact, it is traditionally served as a sushi condiment because of its ability to kill bacteria in food.

Prepared wasabi paste and powdered wasabi can be bought at Asian markets and well-stocked supermarkets. Powdered wasabi is prepared in much the same way as dry mustard. Simply add water to form a paste, and this bright green condiment with the pungent, fiery flavor is ready to use. Just remember—a little goes a long way.

Vegetable Spring Rolls with Spicy Peanut Dipping Sauce

Unlike deep-fried egg rolls, these fresh-tasting spring rolls are uncooked. Spring roll wrappers made of delicate rice paper are available in Asian markets. Vietnamese and Thai brands are common, and the shape can be round or square. The wrappers are brittle and quite fragile when you buy them, but they soften quickly in water just prior to use. Vary the filling ingredients according to personal preference.

8 spring roll wrappers

Filling:
1 cup shredded napa cabbage
3/4 cup shredded carrots
1 small red bell pepper, seeded and cut
    into thin strips

1/2 cup fresh bean sprouts
1/2 cup chopped fresh cilantro or Thai
    basil leaves

Spicy Peanut Dipping Sauce (page 160)

1. Dip a wrapper into a shallow bowl of warm water to soften. Remove from the water and place on a piece of plastic wrap that has been placed on a flat work surface.
2. To make the filling, arrange a small amount of each ingredient on the bottom third of the wrapper. Bring the bottom edge over the filling and fold in the sides tightly. Dab the top edge with water and roll up tightly, using the plastic wrap to help you roll. Place the roll seam side down on a serving platter. Repeat with the remaining wrappers and filling ingredients.
3. Serve the rolls with small bowls of the sauce. These spring rolls are best eaten shortly after they are assembled, but they will keep for a few hours in the refrigerator if wrapped tightly in plastic wrap.

SERVES 4

Spinach-Mushroom Phyllo Triangles

These bite-size versions of spanakopita are the hit of any party. The great taste of the spinach filling enveloped by the flaky phyllo pastry is a testimony to the vegan ingredients: olive oil and tofu stand in for the traditional butter and feta cheese. For a variation, use cooked kale or other greens instead of the spinach.

Two 10-ounce packages frozen
    chopped spinach
1 tablespoon olive oil, plus more
    for brushing
1 medium-size yellow onion, minced
2 garlic cloves, minced
2 cups chopped white mushrooms
One 12-ounce package soft silken tofu,
    drained

1 tablespoon fresh lemon juice
1 teaspoon salt
1/4 teaspoon freshly ground black
    pepper
Pinch of freshly grated nutmeg
One 16-ounce package phyllo pastry,
    thawed overnight in the
    refrigerator

1. Cook the spinach according to the package directions. Drain well, then squeeze it inside a clean tea towel to remove any remaining moisture. Set aside.

2. Heat the olive oil in a large skillet over medium heat. Add the onion, cover, and cook until softened, about 5 minutes. Add the garlic and mushrooms and cook, uncovered, for 3 minutes. Add the spinach and cook until all the liquid is absorbed, about 3 minutes.

3. Transfer the spinach mixture to a food processor. Add the tofu, lemon juice, salt, pepper, and nutmeg and process until smooth.

4. Preheat the oven to 375 degrees F. Unwrap the phyllo pastry and remove about half of the sheets. Rewrap the remaining phyllo and set it aside. Cut the phyllo sheets lengthwise into thirds. Take 1 strip and place it on a flat surface. Cover the remaining pastry with a damp towel. Lightly brush the phyllo strip with olive oil. Top with another strip and brush with a little more oil. Spoon a small spoonful of the filling in one corner of the pastry and fold over into a triangular shape. Continue folding the triangle as if you were folding a flag, until you end up with a small triangular packet. Place on a lightly oiled baking sheet and brush with oil. Repeat with the remaining ingredients until all the filling is used.

5. Bake until golden brown, about 15 minutes. Serve warm or at room temperature.

MAKES ABOUT 18 TRIANGLES

Baked Sweet Potato and Green Pea Samosas

These are actually twice-baked—if you count the fact that the sweet potato is baked before being turned into the fragrant samosa filling. This is a good way to use leftover sweet potatoes. Since these samosas are baked instead of fried, there's no need to feel guilty about filling your plate.

1 cup unbleached all-purpose flour

1/4 cup water

1 tablespoon plus 2 teaspoons peanut oil, plus more for brushing

1 small yellow onion, minced

1 large sweet potato, baked until tender, peeled, and diced

1/2 cup frozen green peas, thawed

1 garlic clove, minced

2 teaspoons curry powder

1/8 teaspoon cayenne, or to taste

Salt

1. In a medium-size bowl, combine the flour, water, and the 2 teaspoons peanut oil until well blended. Cover and let stand for 30 minutes.

2. Heat the 1 tablespoon peanut oil in a large skillet over medium heat. Add the onion, cover, and cook until softened, about 5 minutes. Add the remaining ingredients and cook until the vegetables are soft, about 10 minutes. Set aside to cool.

3. Preheat the oven to 375 degrees F. On a floured work surface, roll out the dough into an approximately 16-inch square that is about 1/8 inch thick. Cut into sixteen 4-inch squares. Place a small amount of the filling in the center of each square and fold one corner over the filling to the opposite corner to make a triangular shape. Seal the edges with water. Place the samosas on a lightly oiled baking sheet and brush lightly with peanut oil. Bake until golden brown, about 20 minutes. Serve hot.

SERVES 4

Curried Cauliflower Pakoras

Much like the *tempura* of Japan or *fritto misto* of Italy, these classic batter-dipped fritters of India lend themselves to almost any vegetable. Try the cauliflower as suggested here, or use sliced zucchini, bell pepper, broccoli, or onion—or any combination. Serve with chutney.

1 head cauliflower	3/4 teaspoon baking powder
1 cup unbleached all-purpose flour	1 tablespoon corn oil
2 teaspoons curry powder	3/4 cup water, or as needed
1 teaspoon salt	Peanut oil for frying

1. Preheat the oven to 275 degrees F. Place the cauliflower on a cutting board and cut into slices no more than 1/2 inch thick. You will end up with cross sections of the florets. Set aside.

2. In a large bowl, combine the flour, curry powder, salt, baking powder, corn oil, and enough water to make a smooth batter. Mix well.

3. Heat about 1 inch of peanut oil in a large, deep skillet over medium-high heat. It's hot enough when a small piece of bread dropped in the oil turns golden brown in about 1 minute. Place the cauliflower slices in the batter to coat, letting any excess drip off, then place them in the hot oil. Do not crowd. Cook until golden brown on both sides, turning once, about 2 minutes per side. Transfer to paper towels to drain, then place in a baking pan and keep warm in the oven until all the slices are fried. Serve hot.

SERVES 4

Did You Know...

Cauliflower is rich in vitamin C and potassium? Believed to be more than 2,500 years old, this member of the cabbage family also contains a fair amount of vitamin B6 and copper.

Hot For Hummus

Hummus is an ideal vegan food, at once creamy and flavorful, while also being loaded with calcium and protein. No wonder everyone loves it, whether served as a dip or used as a spread for sandwiches. To keep your hummus from becoming ho-hum, try this spiced-up variation made with fiery harissa, a North African chili sauce that contains garlic, cumin, and coriander. Canned harissa is available at ethnic markets for those who don't want to make it from scratch. For a more traditional hummus, omit the harissa.

1 1/2 cups cooked or one 15-ounce can chickpeas, drained and rinsed
1/4 cup tahini (sesame paste)
2 teaspoons harissa, homemade (page 159) or store-bought, or to taste

3 tablespoons fresh lemon juice
2 garlic cloves, chopped
1 tablespoon minced fresh parsley leaves
1/2 teaspoon salt

1. Place the chickpeas in a food processor and process until smooth. Add the remaining ingredients and process until smooth and well blended.
2. Transfer to a tightly covered container and refrigerate for at least 1 hour before serving to allow the flavors to develop. Stored tightly covered in the refrigerator, hummus will keep for up to 3 days. Serve chilled or at room temperature.

MAKES ABOUT 2 CUPS

Minted Baba Ganoush

Baba ganoush is a delicious eggplant puree that can be used in much the same way as hummus. It is a must-have on any Middle Eastern *meze* platter (small dishes similar to Spanish *tapas*), where it is delicious accompanied by brine-cured black olives and warm pita wedges. Roasting the eggplant brings out its natural sweetness, which the mint complements nicely. Traditional baba ganoush usually contains a small amount of yogurt to enhance the creamy texture, but that is omitted here with good results.

1 large or 2 medium-size eggplants	1 tablespoon extra virgin olive oil
2 large garlic cloves, slivered	Salt
1/3 cup tahini (sesame paste)	2 tablespoons minced fresh mint leaves
Juice of 1 lemon	

1. Preheat the oven to 375 degrees F. Using a sharp knife, make several deep cuts in the eggplant and place the garlic pieces inside. Place on a baking sheet and bake until soft, about 40 minutes. Allow to cool. Remove the eggplant skin and discard.
2. Transfer the eggplant flesh and garlic to a food processor or blender. Add the tahini, lemon juice, olive oil, and salt to taste and process until smooth.
3. Transfer to a serving bowl and sprinkle with the mint. Serve at room temperature.

SERVES 4 TO 6

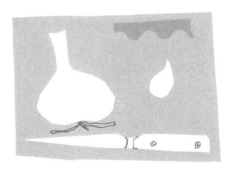

Blushing Guacamole

Fresh tomato and a touch of chili powder add a rosy blush to this popular avocado dip. Serve with tortilla chips or raw vegetables. Guacamole is best made just before serving. If you must make it a few hours ahead, place the avocado pit in the center of the guacamole, cover tightly with plastic wrap, and refrigerate. This will help prevent the guacamole from turning brown.

2 medium-size, ripe avocados, peeled
   and pitted
1 medium-size, ripe tomato, peeled,
   seeded, and minced
1 tablespoon grated onion

2 teaspoons fresh lemon juice,
   or to taste
3/4 teaspoon chili powder
Salt and freshly ground black pepper

1. Place all the ingredients in a medium-size bowl. Mash with a potato masher until well blended. Taste and adjust the seasonings.
2. Transfer to a serving bowl and serve at once, or make a few hours ahead and refrigerate as described in the headnote.

SERVES 4

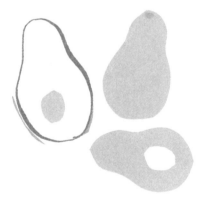

Chili-Avocado Dip

A fun way to serve this dip is in what I call "chili parfaits." Instead of a large serving bowl, use individual dessert glasses and proceed with the recipe, dividing the ingredients evenly among the glasses. Each guest will have his or her own personal dip goblet.

2 medium-size, ripe avocados
1 tablespoon fresh lime juice
1/4 teaspoon salt
1/8 teaspoon cayenne
2 cups vegetarian chili, homemade
    (pages 314–326) or store-bought,
    heated

1 cup Fresh Tomato Salsa (page 174) or
    your favorite salsa
One 4-ounce can diced hot green chiles,
    drained
1/2 cup pitted and sliced black olives
1/2 cup shredded vegan cheddar cheese
Tortilla chips for serving

1. Halve, peel, and pit the avocados and mash well. Add the lime juice, salt, and cayenne and blend until well combined.

2. In a serving bowl (preferably clear glass), spread half of the chili in a layer, followed by the salsa. Spread the avocado mixture over the salsa and top with the remaining chili. Sprinkle the chiles, olives, and vegan cheese evenly over the top and serve with the tortilla chips.

SERVES 6

Artichoke-Sunflower Spread

This flavorful spread can be used on crackers, with warm pita bread, or to top crostini. Thin with a little soy milk to use as a dip for vegetables or crackers.

1/2 cup hulled raw sunflower seeds
One 9-ounce package frozen artichoke
    hearts, cooked according to
    package directions and drained
2 garlic cloves, peeled

2 tablespoons extra virgin olive oil
1 teaspoon minced fresh oregano
    leaves or 1/4 teaspoon dried
Tabasco sauce
Salt

1. Soak the sunflower seeds in warm water to cover for several hours or overnight.
2. Drain the sunflower seeds, then process in a food processor until smooth. Add the artichoke hearts and garlic and process until minced. Add the olive oil, oregano, and Tabasco and salt to taste and process until well blended. Serve at once or transfer to a tightly covered bowl and refrigerate until ready to serve. This spread is best eaten the day it is made.

MAKES ABOUT 1 1/2 CUPS

Knife Knowledge

No matter how many fancy kitchen gadgets you may have, a good set of knives is among the most important. A well-equipped cook can get by with only a few carefully chosen knives for most jobs: a small paring knife, a medium-size paring knife, a 10-inch chef's knife, and a serrated knife will do the trick. Many home cooks prefer stainless steel knives because they don't rust or react chemically with food, but many professional chefs prefer high-carbon steel knives because they are easy to keep well sharpened. It is important, however, to wash and dry them immediately after each use. Another option is a set of Japanese ceramic knives, which stay sharp and are good for delicate work. A sharp knife can actually be safer than a dull one, as it keeps you from forcing the knife and possibly losing your grip. In addition, a well-sharpened knife can make short work of almost any cutting job.

Wild Mushroom Pâté

Garnish this pâté with ground nuts and fresh herbs, and serve whole or sliced on a buffet table with an assortment of crackers and breads. If displaying whole, consider sautéing a few more mushrooms to garnish the top.

1/2 cup dried porcini mushrooms, soaked in very hot water to cover for 20 minutes
2 tablespoons olive oil
1 medium-size yellow onion, minced
1 garlic clove, minced
2 cups chopped white mushrooms
1 cup fresh shiitake mushroom caps, chopped
1 cup cremini mushrooms, chopped

2 tablespoons white wine
1 teaspoon dried thyme
1/2 teaspoon salt
1/8 teaspoon cayenne
1/2 cup pecan pieces (or other nuts)
2 tablespoons chopped fresh parsley leaves
2 tablespoons unbleached all-purpose flour

1. Drain the porcinis and chop. Set aside.

2. Lightly oil a 6-cup loaf pan or pâté mold. Preheat the oven to 350 degrees F.

3. Heat the olive oil in a large skillet over medium heat. Add the onion and garlic, cover, and cook until softened, about 5 minutes. Add all the mushrooms, the wine, thyme, salt, and cayenne. Cook until all the liquid evaporates, about 5 minutes. Remove from the heat and set aside.

4. Coarsely grind the pecans in a food processor. Add the parsley and flour and pulse to combine. Add the mushroom mixture and process until combined but not pureed, leaving some texture. Taste and adjust the seasonings, then spoon into the prepared pan. Bake until firm, about 45 minutes.

5. Let the pâté cool in the pan, then refrigerate until well chilled for easier slicing.

6. When ready to serve, remove the pâté from the pan and transfer to a plate. If necessary, run a knife along the edge of the pan to loosen the pâté. Serve at room temperature.

SERVES 6

Five-Spice Portobello Satays

Traditional Indonesian satays are made with marinated meat or seafood threaded onto skewers and are usually served with a spicy peanut sauce. Here the flavor of the peanut sauce is built right into the marinade. The five spices used in this dish are not those that go into Chinese five-spice powder (Szechuan peppercorns, star anise, cloves, cinnamon, and fennel). Rather, the spices were chosen to complement the other marinade ingredients. If you like, you may grill or broil these satays until lightly browned. If grilling or broiling, soak the bamboo skewers in water for 30 minutes before using to prevent them from burning.

1 tablespoon olive oil
4 large portobello mushrooms, stems removed
1/4 cup tamari or other soy sauce
2 garlic cloves, chopped
2 tablespoons fresh lime juice
2 tablespoons firmly packed light brown sugar
1 tablespoon smooth natural peanut butter
1/2 teaspoon ground cumin
1/2 teaspoon ground allspice
1/2 teaspoon ground coriander
1/2 teaspoon ground ginger
1/8 teaspoon cayenne

1. Heat the olive oil in a large skillet over medium heat. Add the portobello caps and cook until softened, turning once, about 5 minutes total. Set aside to cool.

2. In a food processor, combine the remaining ingredients and process until smooth. Transfer to a shallow bowl.

3. Cut the mushrooms into 1/4-inch-thick slices and add to the marinade. Cover and marinate at room temperature for 30 minutes.

4. Preheat the oven to 425 degrees F. Remove the mushrooms from the marinade, reserving the marinade. Thread the mushrooms onto bamboo skewers. Place on a lightly oiled baking sheet and bake until lightly browned, 6 to 8 minutes, turning once and brushing with the marinade. Serve hot.

SERVES 4

Hot and Spicy Stuffed Mushrooms

The spicy hotness of the cherry peppers combines with the sweetness of the raisins for a balance of flavors that makes these mushrooms a favorite at our house. Jars of hot cherry peppers are available in well-stocked supermarkets and Italian specialty stores.

8 ounces white mushrooms
2 tablespoons olive oil
1 garlic clove, minced
4 hot cherry peppers, seeded and
    minced
2 cups fresh bread crumbs

1/2 teaspoon sugar or natural sweetener
1/2 cup raisins
1 tablespoon minced fresh parsley
    leaves
Salt and freshly ground black pepper

1. Remove the stems from the mushroom caps and set the caps aside. Chop the mushroom stems and set aside.

2. Preheat the oven to 400 degrees F. Heat 1 tablespoon of the olive oil in a large skillet over medium heat. Add the mushroom caps and cook for 2 minutes to soften slightly. Remove from the pan with a slotted spoon and set aside.

3. Return the skillet to the heat. Add the garlic and cook until fragrant, about 1 minute. Add the reserved mushroom stems, cherry peppers, bread crumbs, sugar, raisins, parsley, and salt and pepper to taste. Cook for 2 minutes, mixing well. Add a little of the remaining 1 tablespoon olive oil, if necessary, to get the stuffing to stick together.

4. Fill the mushroom caps evenly with the stuffing mixture and arrange on a lightly oiled baking sheet. Drizzle with any remaining olive oil, if desired, and bake until the mushrooms are soft and the tops are lightly browned, about 10 minutes. Serve hot.

SERVES 4 TO 6

Caponata Crostini

Caponata is a piquant eggplant salad that hails from southern Italy. I think it makes an ideal topping for crostini. Make the caponata ahead of time so the flavors can mingle. Caponata is best served at room temperature.

Caponata:

3 tablespoons olive oil

1 small yellow onion, finely chopped

1 medium-size eggplant, peeled and chopped

1 small red bell pepper, seeded and finely chopped

2 garlic cloves, minced

One 14.5-ounce can plum tomatoes, drained and chopped

Salt and freshly ground black pepper

2 tablespoons capers, drained and chopped

1 tablespoon red wine vinegar

2 teaspoons sugar or natural sweetener

1 tablespoon minced fresh parsley leaves

Crostini:

Eight to twelve 1/2-inch-thick slices French bread

1/4 cup olive oil, or as needed

1. To make the caponata, heat 1 tablespoon of the olive oil in a large skillet over medium heat. Add the onion, cover, and cook until softened, about 5 minutes. Remove the lid. Add 1 tablespoon of the remaining oil and stir in the eggplant. Cook, stirring occasionally, until the eggplant begins to soften, about 5 minutes. Add the bell pepper, garlic, tomatoes, and salt and pepper to taste. Cook until the vegetables soften but still hold some shape, about 15 minutes. Stir in the capers, vinegar, sugar, and parsley. Taste and adjust the seasonings.

2. Transfer to a bowl and allow to cool to room temperature. (You can make the caponata ahead up to this point, refrigerate, and bring back to room temperature before serving. It will keep, tightly covered, in the refrigerator for 3 to 4 days.)

3. To make the crostini, preheat the oven to 400 degrees F. Lightly brush both sides of the bread slices with the olive oil and place on a baking sheet. Bake until lightly browned, 1 to 2 minutes. Remove from the oven, spread the caponata on the bread, and serve at once.

SERVES 4

PARTY PLANNING

When I think of parties, I think of appetizers. Whether you're hosting an intimate dinner party or a lavish gathering of scores of your closest friends, appetizers can help make the party special. When planning your menu, strive for variety in shape, color, and texture, but with a theme of some kind to tie it together.

My personal favorite is an international appetizer buffet—a festive mix of hot and cold, savory and sweet, and mostly fun finger foods. Include items that are special but not fussy—easy to make ahead with a quick reheat or other final touch. To reduce stress, plan no more than 2 hot appetizers that require last-minute attention, concentrating on dishes that do well cold or at room temperature. If a meal is to follow the appetizers, plan on 3 to 5 small hors d'oeuvres per person. If the appetizers are the main event, allow 10 to 12 per person.

Black Olive Bruschetta

Use any crusty Italian or French bread to make the bruschetta. In this recipe, the bread is run under the broiler, but it can be grilled or toasted instead. The topping for this bruschetta is a black olive tapenade. Although the name *tapenade* refers to the requisite capers (*tapeno* means capers in the Provençal dialect) it is made with, the olives are really the star of the show. Oil-cured black olives have a deeper flavor than those cured in brine. If you prefer a lighter taste, go with the brine-cured. In any event, avoid using regular canned supermarket olives, because they lack the true olive flavor you want in a tapenade.

1/3 cup extra virgin olive oil, plus more for brushing

2 garlic cloves, chopped

1 1/2 cups pitted oil-cured black olives

2 tablespoons capers, drained

3 tablespoons chopped fresh Italian parsley leaves

1/2 teaspoon salt

Eight 1/2-inch-thick slices Italian or French bread

1. Preheat the broiler. Heat 1 tablespoon of the olive oil in a small skillet over medium heat. Add the garlic and cook until soft and fragrant, about 1 minute. Transfer to a food processor. Add the remaining olive oil, the olives, capers, parsley, and salt and pulse to blend, retaining some texture. Set aside. (The tapenade may be prepared ahead of time and refrigerated in a tightly sealed container. It will keep for 3 to 4 days. Bring it back to room temperature before using.)

2. Lightly brush both sides of the bread with olive oil and place on a baking sheet. Broil until golden brown on both sides.

3. Spread the tapenade on the prepared bread and serve at once.

SERVES 8

Scallion Pancakes with Sesame Seeds

These golden brown pancakes make a delicious first course for an Asian meal or a wonderful addition to a *dim sum* buffet.

2 cups unbleached all-purpose flour

3/4 teaspoon salt

1 cup boiling water, or more as needed

1 tablespoon toasted sesame oil

3/4 cup minced scallions

2 tablespoons sesame seeds

1 tablespoon peanut oil

Ginger-Lime Dipping Sauce (page 160)

1. Place the flour and salt in a food processor. With the machine running, slowly add the water through the feed tube, adding a little more water, if necessary, until a dough ball forms. Remove from the food processor, cover with plastic wrap or a damp cloth, and let rest for 30 minutes.

2. Divide the dough into 2 pieces. Set one aside and cover. On a floured work surface, roll out the other piece of dough into a circle about 1/4 inch thick. Brush on half the sesame oil and press half the scallions and half the sesame seeds into the dough. Set aside and repeat with the remaining dough ball, sesame oil, scallions, and sesame seeds.

3. Heat half of the peanut oil in a large nonstick skillet over medium heat. Place one of the pancakes in the pan and cook until golden brown on both sides, turning once, 5 to 7 minutes total. Repeat with the remaining peanut oil and pancake.

4. Cut the pancakes into wedges and serve hot with the dipping sauce on the side.

MAKES 2 LARGE PANCAKES

Three-Onion Appetizer Pie

Onion lovers will enjoy this fresh take on the ever-popular onion dip, turned into an appetizer pie with a potato or corn chip crust. Although it looks like a pie, it is essentially still a dip and should be served with raw vegetables or more chips. Soy-based vegan cream cheese is available at natural food stores.

6 ounces potato or corn chips

1/4 cup coarsely chopped red onion

1 large shallot, quartered

2 scallions, coarsely chopped

One 8-ounce package vegan cream cheese, softened

3/4 cup drained and crumbled soft silken tofu

2 tablespoons soy mayonnaise, home-made (page 140) or store-bought

1 teaspoon Dijon mustard

1/4 cup minced fresh parsley leaves

1/2 teaspoon Tabasco sauce

1/2 teaspoon salt

Cherry tomatoes, cut in half, for garnish

Black olives, pitted and halved, for garnish

1. Grind the chips in a food processor until they are fine crumbs. Reserve 2 tablespoons of the crumbs and press the remaining crumbs in the bottom of a lightly oiled 9-inch pie plate or tart pan or 8-inch springform pan. Set aside.

2. Place the onion, shallot, and scallions in a food processor and process until minced. Add the vegan cream cheese, tofu, soy mayonnaise, mustard, parsley, Tabasco, and salt and process until well combined. Spread the onion mixture evenly over the crumb crust and smooth the top.

3. Cover and refrigerate for at least 2 hours or overnight.

4. Just before serving, arrange a border of cherry tomato halves along the edge of the pie. Then arrange a ring of olive halves inside the tomatoes. Repeat with additional concentric rings of tomatoes and olives, if desired, leaving the center of the pie uncovered. Sprinkle the reserved chip crumbs in the center and serve.

SERVES 8

Kitchen Timesavers

Too busy to cook? Here are some great ways to save time in the kitchen.

1. Plan ahead. It can be easier than it sounds. List your family's favorite dishes and rotate them regularly—use a calendar, if it's easier. When you plan your meals in advance, you can schedule easy dishes such as veggie burgers, stir-fries, or make-ahead one-dish meals for busy nights.

2. Keep your pantry, refrigerator, and freezer organized and well stocked with a variety of healthy "convenience" foods, such as canned beans, couscous, quick-cooking pasta, frozen vegetarian burger crumbles, and an arsenal of condiments for last-minute inspirations.

3. Give leftovers a makeover. Make a double recipe, serving it one way the first time, then transforming it into something else for a future meal. For instance, you can turn leftover roasted vegetables into a soup, stew, or potpie or combine them with beans and pasta or rice.

4. Once a week, have a cooking marathon, where you prepare several dishes for the week. Once you put on a pot of chili and a hearty soup, they cook themselves. While they simmer, put together a casserole, stuffed peppers, or maybe a rice dish.

5. Cook double recipes of beans, grains, and other dishes and freeze half for later use.

6. Double up on your oven time. If you're baking a casserole, also bake a few potatoes or some long-cooking vegetables such as winter squash, carrots, and onions to use the next day.

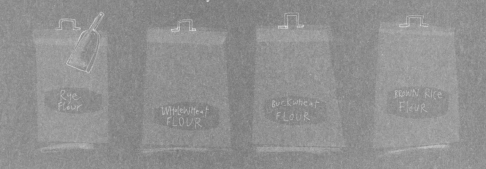

3

Soups that Satisfy

oup is the common denominator of the world's cuisines. Since ancient times, when
humankind first made fire and learned to boil water, pots of soup have been simmering everywhere on the planet. Throughout history, the wealthy and impoverished
alike have shared in the pleasure of soup, where countless combinations of both
humble and opulent ingredients have been ladled for sustenance.

Many warming soups are naturally vegan, such as those that feature beans and
vegetables. Others can be made vegetarian by simply using a vegetable stock to
replace a meat-based one. Where the real vegan magic comes into play is in transforming "cream" soups into dairy-free marvels. Creaminess is accomplished in
several ways, through the use of either a dairy-free milk or pureed vegetables, beans,
or nuts.

This chapter includes brothy vegetable soups, such as *Italian Wedding Soup*,
Sassy Vegetable Gumbo, *Szechuan Hot and Sour Soup*, and *Miso Soup with Tofu and
Baby Spinach*; hearty bean soups, such as *Tuscan White Bean Soup*, *Cuban Black
Bean Soup*, and *Yellow Split Pea Soup with Green Pea Garnish*; and creamy soups, in-
cluding velvety *Winter Vegetable Bisque*, *Potato-Watercress Soup with Sesame*, and
Orange and Chipotle–Kissed Butternut Squash Bisque. For those hot summer nights,

you can enjoy a selection of cold soups, including *Chilled Ginger-Peach Soup with Cashew Cream* and *Cool Cucumber Soup with Cilantro and Lime*.

STOCK OPTIONS

The use of vegetable stocks can add flavor and nutrition to many recipes. Making vegetable stock is not difficult, nor does it need to be time-consuming. It can be as easy as boiling water—all you have to do is add some vegetables and walk away. After about an hour of simmering, you can strain out the vegetables, and the resulting liquid is your stock.

Making an all-purpose vegetable stock with little more than onions, carrots, celery, and water is a modest investment that will provide dividends to your meals. When I make vegetable stock, I like to begin by sweating the vegetables in a little oil to deepen the flavors. I usually roughly chop the vegetables, often keeping the skins, peels, stems, and leaves on for added taste. Just be sure that all the ingredients are well washed before adding them to the pot. Many of the recipes in this book call for stock or water. In these cases, water will work just fine in the recipe, but using stock will enrich the flavor. If you're trying to get as much flavor (and nutrition) as possible out of a recipe, use the stock option.

When there's no time to make homemade stock but you want a more complex flavor than you would achieve with water, you can buy commercial vegetable broth available in cans or aseptic cartons or use vegetable bouillon cubes or powdered vegetable soup base as a quick and easy substitute. These products vary in saltiness, so experiment to find ones you like, and remember to adjust the seasonings in your recipes accordingly. Sometimes when I don't have stock, I add a splash of tamari soy sauce or a little dissolved miso paste to enrich the flavor of a recipe.

These three stock recipes are examples of the subtle differences the ingredients can make. *Basic Vegetable Stock* is an all-purpose stock that can be used as a soup base or to make sauces, risottos, pilafs, or any recipe requiring stock. *Mushroom Stock* and

12 Really Great Health Reasons to Go Vegan

As most vegans will tell you, a diet without animal products can be good for your health. Of the more than 12 million vegetarians in the United States, it is estimated that nearly 50 percent made the choice for health reasons. Consider these facts:

1. A vegan diet has been shown to reduce your risk of heart disease, stroke, cancer, adult-onset diabetes, and osteoporosis.

2. The *Journal of the American Medical Association* has reported that a vegetarian diet can prevent 97 percent of coronary obstructions.

3. Osteoporosis is a disease of protein excess. The protein in milk actually inhibits the body's ability to absorb the calcium from milk. Many plant-based sources of calcium are easily assimilated into the body.

4. Dairy consumption has been linked to heart disease, cancer (especially breast cancer), allergies, sinus trouble, migraines, and psoriasis.

5. Dairy foods can create excess mucus in the body, which can host cold and virus germs in the respiratory tract.

6. Vegans and vegetarians tend to be slimmer than meat eaters.

7. Studies show that a plant-based diet can increase your life expectancy by 7 to 15 years.

8. The feed given to livestock is sprayed with pesticides. More than 90 percent of the toxic chemical residues found in foods consumed by Americans come from animal products.

9. More than 60 million pounds of antibiotics per year are fed to livestock. These are passed on to people in meat and dairy products. This results in a diminished effectiveness of antibiotics used to treat human illnesses.

10. Meat also contains bovine growth hormone, which can cause early sexual maturity in children. Statistics show that 100 years ago,

American girls reached puberty at the average age of 17; today girls as young as 8 are beginning puberty.

11. A vegan diet can reduce the risk of food poisoning. According to the Centers for Disease Control, campylobacter infects up to 90 percent of all chickens. In addition, each year up to 20,000 Americans become ill from E. coli found in meat.

12. Cornell University's long-term study of diet and health, called the China Project, showed that 80 to 90 percent of all cancer, cardiovascular disease, and other forms of degenerative illness can be prevented by adopting a plant-based diet.

Super-Rich Vegetable Stock can be used in the same ways as the basic recipe, but they impart more complex flavor notes.

Another variation is to roast the vegetables before adding them to the water. To do this, toss the vegetables with olive oil and spread in a baking pan. Roast in a preheated 425 degree F oven for about 45 minutes, turning frequently to brown. Transfer the vegetables to the stockpot, add the remaining ingredients, and proceed with the recipe. Roasting the vegetables intensifies the flavors and deepens the color of the final stock.

Regarding salting the stocks, in addition to a little salt, I like to use a splash of tamari because it also adds its own flavor and a little color. The amount of salt you add is up to you, but less is better than more. Although salt does help bring out the flavors of the vegetables, adding too much salt will impair the flavors, especially if the stock is reduced further, which will intensify the saltiness. I usually begin with 1 teaspoon of salt, then adjust the seasoning toward the end, after the flavors have had a chance to develop. At that time, I decide whether the stock will benefit from a bit more salt or perhaps another dash of tamari. More often than not, I leave it alone.

Basic Vegetable Stock

Use this basic stock as a guideline, adding other vegetables or seasonings according to personal preference. It is best to stay away from boldly colored or strongly flavored vegetables, which will overpower the stock. Feel free to add vegetable trimmings, such as carrot peelings, parsley stems, and other discards.

1 tablespoon olive oil
1 large yellow onion, coarsely chopped
2 celery ribs, chopped
2 medium-size carrots, coarsely
    chopped
8 cups water
2 garlic cloves, crushed

1/2 cup coarsely chopped fresh parsley
    leaves
1 large bay leaf
1/2 teaspoon black peppercorns
1 tablespoon tamari or other soy sauce
Salt

1. Heat the olive oil in a large stockpot over medium heat. Add the onion, celery, and carrots. Cover, and cook until slightly softened, about 5 minutes. Add the water, garlic, parsley, bay leaf, peppercorns, tamari, and salt to taste. Bring to a boil, then reduce the heat to medium-low and simmer, uncovered, for 1 hour to reduce the liquid and bring out the flavors of the vegetables.

2. Strain through a fine-mesh sieve into another pot, pressing the juices out of the vegetables with the back of a large spoon. The stock is now ready to use. If a stronger stock is desired, return the stock to a boil and reduce the volume by one-quarter. If stored tightly covered in the refrigerator, the stock will keep for up to 3 days. Alternatively, it can be portioned and frozen for 3 to 4 months.

MAKES ABOUT 6 CUPS

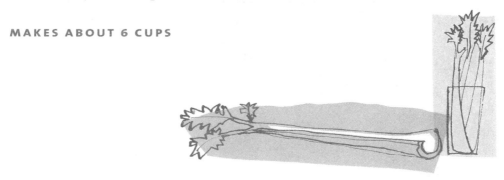

Mushroom Stock

Mushroom stock adds a depth of flavor to recipes. It is especially good used in soups, sauces, risottos, and pilafs. I like to make this stock with mushrooms that are a bit past their prime for a richer taste. The addition of a few dried mushrooms lends a deep, woodsy flavor to the stock.

4 dried shiitake or porcini mushrooms, soaked in 1 cup very hot water for 20 minutes
1 tablespoon olive oil
1 large yellow onion, quartered
1 celery rib, coarsely chopped
8 cups water
8 ounces white mushrooms, coarsely chopped

3 garlic cloves, crushed
1/2 cup coarsely chopped fresh parsley leaves
2 bay leaves
1/2 teaspoon black peppercorns
1 tablespoon tamari or other soy sauce
Salt

1. Drain the shiitakes, reserving the soaking liquid. Strain the liquid and set aside.
2. Heat the olive oil in a stockpot over medium heat. Add the onion and celery, cover, and cook until softened, about 5 minutes. Add the water, all the mushrooms, the mushroom soaking liquid, garlic, parsley, bay leaves, peppercorns, tamari, and salt to taste. Bring to a boil, then reduce the heat to low and simmer for 1 hour.
3. Strain through a fine-mesh sieve into a large bowl or pot, pressing against the solids with the back of a large spoon. The stock can now be used. If not using immediately, cool the stock and refrigerate it for up to 3 days, or portion and freeze for up to 3 months.

MAKES ABOUT 6 CUPS

ASIAN-STYLE MUSHROOM STOCK: Omit the bay leaves and add a few slices of peeled fresh ginger, a piece of kombu sea vegetable, and a splash of sake, mirin, or dry sherry.

Super-Rich Vegetable Stock

This full-bodied stock tastes similar to chicken stock and can be used in any recipe to enrich the flavor. The use of potatoes and root vegetables gives the stock more body and a deeper character than Basic Vegetable Stock (page 68). You may add other vegetables, such as leeks or mushrooms, but stay away from anything too assertive in color or flavor, such as beets or broccoli. Note: If celery root is unavailable, use regular celery instead.

1 tablespoon olive oil

1 large yellow onion, unpeeled and quartered

2 large Yukon Gold potatoes, unpeeled and quartered

2 medium-size carrots, coarsely chopped

1 medium-size parsnip, peeled and coarsely chopped

1 cup peeled and chopped celery root (celeriac)

8 cups water

3 garlic cloves, unpeeled and crushed

1/2 cup coarsely chopped fresh parsley leaves

2 bay leaves

1/2 teaspoon black peppercorns

1 tablespoon tamari or other soy sauce

Salt

1. Heat the olive oil in a stockpot over medium heat. Add the onion, potatoes, carrots, parsnip, and celery root. Cover and cook until the vegetables are slightly softened, about 5 minutes. Add the water, garlic, parsley, bay leaves, peppercorns, tamari, and salt to taste. Bring to a boil, then reduce the heat to low and simmer, uncovered, for 1 hour.

2. Strain the stock through a fine-mesh sieve into a large bowl or pot, pressing against the solids with the back of a large spoon to release the liquid. Use at once or let cool and refrigerate, covered, for up to 3 days. Alternatively, you may portion the stock and freeze it for 3 to 4 months.

MAKES ABOUT 6 CUPS

Cool Cucumber Soup with Cilantro and Lime

"**C**ool as a cucumber" takes on new meaning with this light and luscious soup, made smooth and creamy with unsweetened coconut milk, which, along with the cilantro and lime juice, adds a hint of Southeast Asian flavor.

1 garlic clove, peeled
1 teaspoon salt
2 large cucumbers, peeled, seeded, and chopped
2 cups Basic Vegetable Stock (page 68)
One 14-ounce can unsweetened coconut milk

2 tablespoons fresh lime juice
1 tablespoon minced fresh cilantro leaves
8 thin cucumber slices for garnish
Whole fresh cilantro leaves for garnish

1. Place the garlic and salt in a food processor and process to form a paste. Add the chopped cucumbers and process until smooth. Add the stock, coconut milk, lime juice, and minced cilantro and process until smooth. Taste and adjust the seasonings.
2. Transfer the soup to a container and refrigerate, covered, for a few hours to blend the flavors.
3. To serve, ladle the soup into bowls and garnish with the cucumber slices and whole cilantro leaves.

SERVES 4

Cooling the Heat with Chilled Soups

Combining the comforting goodness of hot soup with the invigorating coolness we crave in the summer, a chilled soup can be a welcome addition to a hot-weather meal. Since most chilled soups need to be refrigerated before eating, they are best made ahead, so plan to prepare them the night before or early in the day. Additionally, many chilled soups require no cooking, so you can be in and out of the kitchen quickly without heating it up.

Two of the best-known chilled soups, vichyssoise and gazpacho, couldn't be more different from each other. Vichyssoise, the cold leek and potato soup from France, with its delicate flavor and silky texture, is on the opposite end of the spectrum from the zesty Spanish gazpacho, a spicy tomato-based elixir brimming with refreshing chopped vegetables.

In addition to vegetables, fruits are often used to make chilled soups, with some so decadent they beg to be served as dessert and others sublime enough to be enjoyed as a dazzling first course. Making chilled soups can be as simple as pureeing your favorite fruits or vegetables in a blender or food processor with some fruit juice or vegetable stock, depending on the type of soup you are making. To add creaminess, finish the soup with a swirl of soy yogurt or whisk in a small amount of dairy-free milk, such as soy, oat, or rice milk. Garnish with a sliver of an appropriate fruit or vegetable, chopped nuts, or a fresh herb sprig.

Chilled Ginger-Peach Soup with Cashew Cream

A fresh fruit soup is a refreshing way to begin or end a meal during the summer. This is best made when peaches are ripe and plentiful. For a decadent flourish, make some extra cashew cream and swirl a spoonful into each portion of soup.

1/2 cup raw cashews

1 cup water, or more as needed

1 1/2 pounds ripe peaches, peeled, pitted, and sliced

2 teaspoons peeled and grated fresh ginger

1/4 cup frozen orange juice concentrate

1 tablespoon fresh lemon juice

Sugar or natural sweetener, if needed

Fresh mint sprigs for garnish

Chopped raw cashews for garnish

1. Place the 1/2 cup cashews in a dry blender and grind into a paste. Add the water and blend until smooth. Set aside.

2. Place the peach slices and ginger in a food processor and process until smooth. Add the cashew cream, orange juice concentrate, and lemon juice and blend well. Add a little more water if the soup is too thick. Taste and adjust the seasonings, adding a little sugar, if needed, for sweetness.

3. Pour into a container with a tight-fitting lid and refrigerate for several hours.

4. Serve chilled, garnished with the mint sprigs and chopped cashews.

SERVES 4

Gazpacho Verde

This refreshing gazpacho is nontraditional in that it features mostly green vegetables, including green tomatoes, although it is garnished with chopped red tomatoes. If green tomatoes are unavailable, you can substitute tomatillos or an additional cucumber. Omit the jalapeño if you don't like the heat.

2 large green tomatoes, peeled, seeded, and chopped

2 medium-size cucumbers, peeled, seeded, and chopped

1 small green bell pepper, seeded and chopped

1/4 cup chopped sweet yellow onion

2 tablespoons minced celery

1 jalapeño, seeded and minced

2 garlic cloves, minced

3 tablespoons minced scallions

2 tablespoons capers (optional), drained and chopped

3 tablespoons rice vinegar

2 tablespoons olive oil

1 teaspoon salt

1 teaspoon green Tabasco sauce (optional)

3 cups Basic Vegetable Stock (page 68)

1/4 cup minced fresh parsley leaves

1 large, ripe red tomato, seeded and chopped, for garnish

1. In a food processor, combine the green tomatoes, half of the cucumbers, half of the bell pepper, and the onion and process until smooth.

2. Transfer the vegetable puree to a large bowl and add the remaining cucumbers and remaining bell pepper. Stir in the celery, jalapeño, garlic, scallions, capers (if using), vinegar, olive oil, salt, and Tabasco (if using). Stir in the stock and 2 tablespoons of the parsley.

3. Cover and refrigerate for at least 2 hours. Taste and adjust the seasonings.

4. Serve chilled, garnished with the remaining 2 tablespoons parsley and the red tomato.

SERVES 4 TO 6

Szechuan Hot and Sour Soup

This version is as spicy and flavorful as the original but is made lighter with vegetable stock and slivers of tofu instead of the traditional pork.

1/2 cup dried cloud ear or shiitake mushrooms, soaked in very hot water to cover for 20 minutes
1 cup canned or fresh sliced bamboo shoots
4 teaspoons peanut oil
8 ounces extra-firm tofu, drained and cut into thin strips
1 garlic clove, minced
1 tablespoon peeled and minced fresh ginger
4 cups Basic Vegetable Stock (page 68)

2 tablespoons tamari or other soy sauce
2 tablespoons rice vinegar
1/2 teaspoon sugar or natural sweetener
1 teaspoon Asian chili paste
1 teaspoon cornstarch dissolved in 2 teaspoons water
1 tablespoon toasted sesame oil
2 tablespoons chopped scallions
1 tablespoon chopped fresh cilantro leaves
Salt and freshly ground black pepper

1. Drain the mushrooms and discard the stems. Cut the caps into thin strips and set aside.

2. If using canned bamboo shoots, drain and rinse, then cut into thin strips and set aside. If using fresh, soak in water to cover for 30 minutes. Cut into thin strips, cook in boiling water until tender, and set aside.

3. Heat 2 teaspoons of the peanut oil in a medium skillet over medium-high heat. Add the tofu and cook, stirring, until golden brown, about 5 minutes. Set aside.

4. Heat the remaining 2 teaspoons peanut oil in a large pot. Add the garlic and ginger and cook until fragrant, about 30 seconds. Add the stock, tamari, vinegar, sugar, chili paste, and mushroom strips. Bring to a boil over high heat, then reduce the heat to medium and simmer until the mushrooms are tender, about 5 minutes.

5. Add the tofu and bamboo shoots and bring the liquid back to a simmer. Stir in the cornstarch mixture and cook until heated through, about 5 minutes. Stir in the sesame oil, scallions, cilantro, and salt and pepper to taste. Serve hot.

SERVES 4

Miso Soup with Tofu and Baby Spinach

Because of its many health benefits, miso soup is considered the "chicken soup" of a macrobiotic diet. Unlike chicken soup, however, which people often eat after they catch a cold, miso soup can help strengthen the immune system, thus warding off illness in the first place. Miso paste is made from aged soybeans that are often combined with other ingredients to make several varieties, from the salty, assertive barley miso to the slightly sweet, mellow white miso.

6 cups water
1 1/2 cups baby spinach leaves, cut into
    thin strips
1/2 cup thinly sliced white mushrooms
3 tablespoons minced scallions

1 tablespoon tamari or other soy sauce
1/3 cup mellow white miso paste
4 ounces extra-firm silken tofu,
    drained and cut into 1/4-inch dice

1. Place the water in a large pot and bring to a boil over high heat. Add the spinach, mushrooms, scallions, and tamari. Reduce the heat to medium and simmer until the vegetables soften, 3 to 6 minutes. Reduce the heat to low.
2. Place about 1/4 cup of the hot soup mixture in a small bowl and add the miso, blending well. Stir the mixture back into the soup, add the tofu, and simmer for 2 minutes, being careful not to boil. Taste, adjust the seasonings, and serve hot.

SERVES 4

Thai-Style Coconut Soup

I love the creamy elegance of Thai coconut soup. A favorite in many Thai restaurants, this soup is often made with chicken as well as exotic Thai ingredients such as kaffir lime leaves, lemongrass, and galangal, which can be difficult for many people to find. I've devised a recipe that comes close to the original. Made substantial with tofu and mushrooms, it is seasoned with ingredients that are available in most supermarkets.

1 tablespoon peanut oil or other
   neutral-tasting oil

3 shallots, minced

2 cups thinly sliced white mushrooms

3 cups Basic Vegetable Stock (page 68)

1¹/₂ tablespoons peeled and grated
   fresh ginger

2 tablespoons tamari or other soy sauce

1 tablespoon firmly packed light brown
   sugar or natural sweetener

1 teaspoon Asian chili paste, or
   to taste

One 14-ounce can unsweetened
   coconut milk

6 ounces extra-firm tofu, drained and
   cut into ¹/₄-inch dice

Juice and grated zest of 1 lime

2 tablespoons fresh lemon juice

1 tablespoon chopped fresh cilantro
   leaves for garnish

1. Heat the peanut oil in a large pot over medium heat. Add the shallots and cook, stirring, until tender, about 5 minutes. Add the mushrooms and cook, stirring, for 3 minutes. Stir in the stock, ginger, tamari, brown sugar, and chili paste and bring to a boil. Reduce the heat to low and simmer for 2 to 3 minutes, stirring to dissolve the sugar.

2. Stir in the coconut milk, tofu, lime juice and zest, and lemon juice and simmer until the flavors have blended and the soup is hot, about 5 minutes. Taste and adjust the seasonings. Serve hot, garnished with the cilantro.

SERVES 4

Indian-Spiced Lentil Soup

Although lentils are enjoyed in various parts of the world, I think they are most flavorful prepared with Indian spices. Instead of the traditional dal, or lentil puree, the flavors here are combined in an aromatic soup, made colorful with the addition of diced sweet potato.

2 tablespoons corn oil

1 small yellow onion, chopped

1 celery rib, chopped

1 small sweet potato, peeled and diced

1 garlic clove, minced

One 14.5-ounce can diced tomatoes, undrained

1 teaspoon peeled and minced fresh ginger

1/2 teaspoon ground cumin

1/2 teaspoon ground coriander

1/4 teaspoon cayenne

1 1/2 cups dried brown lentils, picked over and rinsed

6 cups Basic Vegetable Stock (page 68) or water

1/4 cup minced fresh cilantro leaves

Salt and freshly ground black pepper

1. Heat the corn oil in a large pot over medium heat. Add the onion, celery, sweet potato, and garlic. Cover and cook until softened, about 10 minutes. Add the juice from the tomatoes, then finely chop the tomatoes and add them to the pan. Stir in the ginger, cumin, coriander, and cayenne. Add the lentils and stock and bring to boil. Reduce the heat to low, cover, and simmer, stirring occasionally, until the lentils are tender, about 30 minutes.

2. Add the cilantro, season with salt and pepper to taste, and cook for 10 minutes to blend the flavors. Serve hot.

SERVES 4 TO 6

Vegan Road Food

The thought of a vacation may conjure up images of four-star hotels, family visits, or fun day trips, but for a vegan, it often also includes the question "What am I going to eat?"

Although many urban restaurants now offer more choices in vegan and vegetarian fare, roadside restaurants generally do not. To get through any road trip, whether it be for a few hours or several days, it's best to plan ahead and pack the cooler.

One of my favorite road foods is hummus, a protein- and calcium-rich spread made with chickpeas and tahini that can be enjoyed with raw veggies, crackers, or as a pita sandwich filling. Other options include pasta or grain salads, marinated baked tofu, or even vegetable sushi. Kids always enjoy peanut butter and jelly sandwiches. Bring along a good supply of cut vegetables, fresh and dried fruits, trail mix, nuts, raisins, or granola bars. Eat the most perishable foods first, saving the nonperishables for later in the journey. On the return trip, look for a natural food store or a well-stocked supermarket to replenish your supplies. For a quick lunch, there's usually a supermarket salad bar or a Taco Bell, where you can get a bean burrito (no cheese).

When seeking out a restaurant in an unfamiliar town, ethnic restaurants generally offer the best choices. Chinese, Thai, Indian, Italian, and Mexican menus usually include vegan alternatives. Many restaurants are willing to accommodate a vegan and will prepare a special meal upon request. If you don't see it, ask for it. If you're staying in a hotel, the concierge can help.

When traveling by air, I've been served everything from a lovely vegetable curry over rice pilaf to a wilted and gummy (canned) fruit plate. Since airlines vary greatly (some have no meal service at all), call ahead and ask the airline representative for menu details. It takes a little time, but it's well worth the effort. It pays to confirm your meal the day before and again just prior to boarding. Still, it's a good idea to bring along a backup food stash, just in case: a PBJ sandwich can seem like a banquet on a long flight with little or no meal service.

Lentil Soup with Chard and Orzo

Although chard is often called "Swiss" chard after a Swiss botanist, it is actually a Mediterranean vegetable. Nutrient-rich chard and lentils combine for a healthful wintertime soup with a rich, complex flavor. A loaf of crusty bread is all that you need for a complete and satisfying meal.

2 tablespoons olive oil

1 small yellow onion, minced

1 medium-size carrot, grated

1/3 cup minced celery

2 garlic cloves, minced

7 cups Basic Vegetable Stock (page 68) or water

1 cup dried brown lentils, picked over and rinsed

2 tablespoons tomato paste

1/2 cup dry red wine

1/3 cup minced fresh parsley leaves

1/2 teaspoon minced fresh thyme leaves or 1/4 teaspoon dried

1 bay leaf

Salt and freshly ground black pepper

2 cups coarsely chopped Swiss chard (tough stems removed)

1/2 cup orzo

1. Heat the olive oil in a large pot over medium heat. Add the onion, carrot, celery, and garlic. Cover and cook until softened, about 5 minutes. Add the stock, lentils, tomato paste, wine, parsley, thyme, bay leaf, and salt and pepper to taste. Bring to a boil, then reduce the heat to medium-low and simmer, stirring occasionally, until the lentils are tender, about 30 minutes.

2. About 10 minutes before the end of the cooking time, remove the bay leaf and stir in the chard.

3. Meanwhile, cook the orzo in a pot of boiling salted water, stirring occasionally, until *al dente*, about 5 minutes. When ready to serve, stir the cooked orzo into the hot soup, then ladle immediately into bowls.

SERVES 4 TO 6

Yellow Split Pea Soup with Green Pea Garnish

You can make this soup using green split peas, but the yellow ones have a milder flavor, and I like the color contrast when garnished with the vivid green peas.

1 tablespoon olive oil

1 small yellow onion, chopped

1 medium-size carrot, minced

1 medium-size Yukon Gold potato, peeled and diced

6 cups Basic Vegetable Stock (page 68) or water

1 3/4 cups dried yellow split peas, picked over and rinsed

1 teaspoon minced fresh summer savory leaves or 1/2 teaspoon dried

1/4 teaspoon ground allspice

1 bay leaf

1 teaspoon salt

Cayenne

1/2 cup frozen baby green peas, thawed

1. Heat the olive oil in a large saucepan over medium heat. Add the onion, carrot, and potato. Cover and cook, stirring occasionally, until the vegetables are soft, about 10 minutes. Stir in the stock, split peas, savory, allspice, bay leaf, salt, and cayenne to taste. Bring to a boil, then reduce the heat to low, cover, and cook, stirring occasionally, until the vegetables are soft and the soup thickens, about 40 minutes. If the soup becomes too thick, add a little water. Remove and discard the bay leaf.

2. Just before serving, heat the green peas in a small saucepan of boiling water. Drain and set aside. To serve, ladle the soup into bowls and garnish with the green peas.

SERVES 4 TO 6

Cuban Black Bean Soup

Black beans are popular in Cuban cooking, and this spicy soup is a terrific way to enjoy them. The cayenne is optional, since it adds another layer of heat beyond the chile. If you prefer a milder taste, you may omit the chile and cayenne with good results. This recipe calls for dried black beans. If you're short on time, substitute two 15-ounce cans of black beans, drained and rinsed.

$1\frac{1}{2}$ cups dried black beans, picked over and rinsed

8 cups water

2 bay leaves

1 tablespoon olive oil

1 large red onion, chopped

1 medium-size carrot, chopped

1 small red bell pepper, seeded and minced

3 garlic cloves, minced

1 small, fresh hot chile, seeded and minced

One 14.5-ounce can diced tomatoes, undrained

6 cups Basic Vegetable Stock (page 68) or water

1 teaspoon dried oregano

1 teaspoon ground cumin

1 teaspoon salt

$\frac{1}{4}$ teaspoon cayenne (optional)

$\frac{1}{4}$ cup dark rum (optional)

2 tablespoons minced fresh cilantro leaves for garnish

1. Soak the beans in water to cover for several hours or overnight (or use the quick-soak method on page 275).

2. Drain the beans and transfer to a large pot. Add the water and bay leaves and bring to a boil over medium heat. Reduce the heat to medium-low, cover, and simmer until the beans are soft, about $1\frac{1}{2}$ hours. Stir occasionally, skimming off any foam that rises to the top. Drain the beans, discard the bay leaves, and set the beans aside.

3. Heat the olive oil in a large pot over medium heat. Add the onion, carrot, bell pepper, garlic, and chile. Cover and cook until softened, about 5 minutes. Add the juice from the tomatoes, then mince the tomatoes and add to the pan. Stir in the beans, stock, oregano, cumin, salt, and cayenne (if using). Simmer for 30 minutes.

4. Carefully transfer 2 cups of the soup to a blender or food processor. Process until smooth and return to the pot. Add a little water if the soup is too thick. Simmer for 15 minutes to blend the flavors. Taste and adjust the seasonings.

5. About 5 minutes before serving, stir in the rum (if using). Serve hot, garnished with the cilantro.

SERVES 4 TO 6

Tuscan White Bean Soup

Also known as *pasta e fagioli*, this classic bean soup has many variations. This version, made with cannellini beans and a touch of red pepper flakes, is thick with chewy pasta and makes a hearty and economical meal when served with a green salad.

8 ounces elbow macaroni or other
    small pasta
1 tablespoon olive oil
1 small yellow onion, minced
1 large garlic clove, minced
One 6-ounce can tomato paste
    blended with 1 cup warm water
1 1/2 cups cooked or one 15-ounce can
    cannellini or other white beans,
    drained and rinsed

6 cups Basic Vegetable Stock
    (page 68)
1/4 teaspoon red pepper flakes,
    or to taste
2 bay leaves
1/4 teaspoon dried oregano
Salt and freshly ground black pepper

1. Cook the pasta in a pot of boiling water, stirring occasionally, until just *al dente*, 6 to 8 minutes. Drain and set aside.
2. Heat the olive oil in a large pot over medium heat. Add the onion, cover, and cook until softened, about 5 minutes. Add the garlic and cook for 1 minute. Reduce the heat to low and stir in the diluted tomato paste. Add the beans, stock, red pepper flakes, bay leaves, oregano, and salt and pepper to taste. Bring to a boil, reduce the heat to low, and simmer for 30 minutes.
3. Add the reserved pasta and cook for 10 minutes to blend the flavors. Serve hot.

SERVES 4 TO 6

Thyme-Scented Wild Mushroom Bisque

This creamy, elegant soup is a far cry from the canned mushroom soup we grew up with. Use white button mushrooms for all or part of the fresh mushrooms to cut down on the cost. The dried porcinis will impart a sufficient "wild" mushroom flavor.

2 tablespoons olive oil

2 leeks (white parts only), washed well and thinly sliced

4 shallots, chopped

1 celery rib, thinly sliced

2 garlic cloves, chopped

1 teaspoon salt

1 teaspoon minced fresh thyme leaves or 1/2 teaspoon dried

1/4 cup dry vermouth or white wine

8 ounces cremini mushrooms, thinly sliced

4 ounces oyster mushrooms, thinly sliced

4 ounces large portobello mushrooms, stems removed and caps thinly sliced

1 cup dried porcini mushrooms, soaked in very hot water to cover for 20 minutes and drained

6 cups Mushroom Stock (page 69)

4 ounces soft silken tofu, drained and chopped

Fresh thyme sprigs for garnish (optional)

1. Heat the olive oil in a large pot over medium heat. Add the leeks, shallots, and celery. Cover and cook until softened, about 10 minutes. Add the garlic, salt, and thyme and cook for 2 minutes. Stir in the vermouth, increase the heat, and cook for about 2 minutes to reduce the liquid slightly. Add all the fresh mushrooms, reduce the heat to medium, and cook for 5 minutes, stirring occasionally.

2. Slice the porcinis and add to the pot along with the stock. Reduce the heat to medium-low and simmer for 20 to 30 minutes. Taste and add more salt, if necessary.

3. Carefully transfer the soup to a blender or food processor, add the tofu, and process until

Did You Know...

Mushrooms are a good source of potassium and riboflavin? These flavorful fungi are also extremely low in calories and are credited with having several medicinal qualities, from antibiotic to aphrodisiac.

smooth. Return to the saucepan and place over low heat to keep warm until ready to serve, being careful not to boil.

4. Serve hot, garnished with the thyme sprigs, if desired.

SERVES 6

Winter Vegetable Bisque

Made with those dependable vegetables that are often overlooked during summer's bounty, this velvety soup soothes on a cold winter night. A garnish of fresh chives adds a fresh taste and a bit of contrast.

1 tablespoon olive oil

1 medium-size yellow onion, chopped

3 large parsnips, peeled and thinly sliced

2 large carrots, thinly sliced

1 medium-size all-purpose potato, peeled and diced

1 celery rib, thinly sliced

1 garlic clove, minced

1/4 cup white wine

5 cups Super-Rich Vegetable Stock (page 70) or Basic Vegetable Stock (page 68)

1 1/2 teaspoons minced fresh thyme leaves or 1 teaspoon dried

Salt and freshly ground black pepper

2 tablespoons snipped fresh chives for garnish

1. Heat the olive oil in a large pot over medium heat. Add the onion, cover, and cook until softened, about 5 minutes. Add the parsnips, carrots, potato, and celery. Cover and cook until the vegetables are soft, about 10 minutes. Stir in the garlic, wine, and stock. Increase the heat to medium-high and bring to a boil, then reduce the heat to low. Add the thyme, season with salt and pepper to taste, and simmer for 20 to 30 minutes.

2. Working in batches, carefully transfer the mixture to a blender or food processor and process until smooth. Return to the pot and heat through. Taste and adjust the seasonings.

3. To serve, ladle into bowls and garnish with the chives.

SERVES 4 TO 6

Orange and Chipotle-Kissed Butternut Squash Bisque

The smoky chipotle chile and sweet hint of orange add layers of flavor to this creamy bisque. Chipotle chiles are smoke-dried jalapeños, also available canned in adobo sauce, and can be found in ethnic markets and well-stocked supermarkets.

1 canned or dried chipotle chile

1 tablespoon olive oil

1 medium-size yellow onion, chopped

1 medium-size butternut squash, peeled, seeded, and thinly sliced

1 celery rib, chopped

Salt to taste

5 cups Basic Vegetable Stock (page 68)

2 tablespoons frozen orange juice concentrate

2 tablespoons roasted pumpkin seeds or pepitas for garnish (optional)

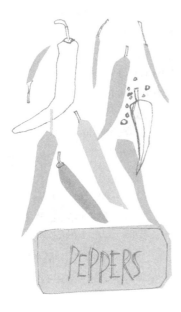

PEPPERS

1. If using a dried chipotle, soak it in very hot water to cover for 30 minutes. Drain and set aside.

2. Heat the olive oil in a large pot over medium heat. Add the onion, cover, and cook until softened, about 5 minutes. Add the squash, celery, and salt to taste. Cook, stirring, until softened slightly, about 5 minutes. Add the stock, cover, and cook until the vegetables are soft, about 15 minutes.

3. In a blender or food processor, puree the chipotle. Working in batches, add the orange juice concentrate and squash mixture and process until smooth. Return the soup to the pot and heat through. Taste, adjust the seasonings, and serve hot, garnished with the pumpkin seeds, if desired.

SERVES 4 TO 6

Roasted Corn Chowder

Roasting (or grilling) intensifies the naturally sweet flavor of the corn in this wholesome chowder. A garnish of fresh tomato and basil completes my favorite summer produce trilogy. Although you can make this chowder using frozen corn kernels, it will not be as flavorful as when using roasted fresh corn.

4 ears corn

1 tablespoon olive oil

1 small yellow onion, chopped

1 celery rib, chopped

1 large Yukon Gold potato, peeled
    and diced

4 cups Basic Vegetable Stock (page 68)

1 cup soy milk or other dairy-free milk

Salt and freshly ground black pepper

1 large, ripe tomato, peeled, seeded,
    and finely chopped, for garnish

2 tablespoons minced fresh basil leaves
    for garnish

1. Preheat the oven to 450 degrees F. Pull back the green husks to expose the corn. Remove the corn silk and bring the husks back up to cover the kernels. Place the corn on a baking sheet and roast for 25 to 30 minutes. Remove from the oven and set aside until the corn is cool enough to handle. Remove and discard the husks. Use a sharp knife to cut the kernels from the cobs. Discard the cobs and set the kernels aside in a bowl.

2. Heat the olive oil in a large pot over medium heat. Add the onion and celery, cover, and cook until softened, about 5 minutes. Add the potato and stock and bring to a boil. Reduce the heat to low, cover, and cook until the vegetables are tender, about 25 minutes. Uncover, add the corn, and cook for 15 minutes.

3. Remove from the heat, ladle 2 cups of the soup into a food processor or blender, and process until smooth. Stir the puree back into the chowder, add the soy milk, and season with salt and pepper to taste. Ladle the soup into bowls and garnish with the tomato and basil.

SERVES 4 TO 6

New England-Style Chowder

This chowder gets its ocean-fresh taste from the vitamin-rich kombu sea vegetable and its creamy texture from pureeing part of the soup. Coarsely chopped oyster mushrooms make this soup reminiscent of a traditional New England clam chowder. Look for certified organic kombu and other sea vegetables at natural food stores.

2 tablespoons corn oil

1 leek (white part only) washed well
   and chopped

1 inner celery rib, chopped

1 large Yukon Gold potato, peeled and
   diced

4 cups Basic Vegetable Stock
   (page 68)

One 2-inch-square piece kombu
   sea vegetable

1 bay leaf

Salt

1 cup soy milk or other dairy-free milk

1 tablespoon mellow white miso paste
   dissolved in 2 tablespoons hot
   (not boiling) water

8 ounces oyster mushrooms, coarsely
   chopped

1/2 teaspoon Old Bay seasoning

1. Heat 1 tablespoon of the corn oil in a large pot over medium heat. Add the leek and celery, cover, and cook until softened, about 5 minutes. Add the potato, stock, kombu, bay leaf, and salt to taste. Bring to a boil, then reduce the heat to medium-low and simmer until the vegetables are soft, 20 to 30 minutes. Remove the kombu and bay leaf.

2. Carefully transfer 2 cups of the soup solids plus 1/4 cup of the broth to a food processor or blender and process until smooth. Return the mixture to the pot and stir in the soy milk and dissolved miso. Keep the soup warm over low heat, being careful not to boil.

3. Heat the remaining 1 tablespoon corn oil in a large skillet over medium heat. Add the mushrooms and cook, stirring constantly, until softened, 3 to 5 minutes. Sprinkle with the Old Bay seasoning, stirring to coat. Stir the cooked mushrooms into the chowder and serve hot.

SERVES 4 TO 6

Farmhouse Vegetable Soup

This is a good old-fashioned vegetable soup that can be made with just about any vegetables you have on hand. Kidney beans boost the protein, making this a great one-dish meal when served with a loaf of warm crusty bread.

1 tablespoon olive oil

1 medium-size yellow onion, chopped

1 large carrot, halved lengthwise and cut into 1/4-inch-thick half-moons

1 celery rib, chopped

2 or 3 small red potatoes, unpeeled and diced

1/2 small red bell pepper, seeded and diced

3 ounces green beans, ends trimmed and cut into 1-inch pieces

1 medium-size zucchini or yellow squash, halved lengthwise and cut into 1/4-inch-thick half-moons

1 large garlic clove, minced

6 cups Super-Rich Vegetable Stock (page 70) or Basic Vegetable Stock (page 68)

1 1/2 cups cooked or one 15-ounce can dark red kidney beans, drained and rinsed

Salt and freshly ground black pepper

2 tablespoons chopped fresh parsley leaves

1. Heat the olive oil in a large pot over medium heat. Add the onion, carrot, and celery. Cover and cook until softened, about 5 minutes. Add the potatoes, bell pepper, green beans, zucchini, and garlic. Cover and cook for 5 minutes. Add the stock, increase the heat to high, and bring to a boil. Reduce the heat to low, add the kidney beans, season with salt and pepper to taste, and simmer until the vegetables are tender and the flavors have developed, about 40 minutes.

2. Stir in the parsley, then taste and adjust the seasonings. Serve hot.

SERVES 4 TO 6

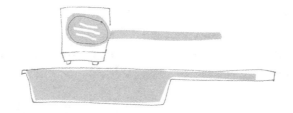

Sassy Vegetable Gumbo

Gumbo is a thick soup served over rice that is synonymous with spicy Cajun cooking. Since the word *gumbo* means "okra," it is included among the ingredients. But if you don't like it, don't use it—there'll be plenty of other vegetables in the pot, including the New Orleans vegetable "trinity" of onions, celery, and green bell pepper, as well as tomatoes and corn. This soup is made "sassy" with the addition of a smoky chipotle chile and a generous sprinkling of ground sassafras leaves, called filé powder. The filé, along with the okra, helps thicken the soup and adds traditional flavor. The optional barley miso, though nontraditional, enriches the broth and deepens its color.

1 dried chipotle chile, soaked in very
    hot water to cover for 30 minutes
1 tablespoon olive oil
1 large onion, diced
1 medium-size green bell pepper,
    seeded and diced
1/2 cup chopped celery
2 garlic cloves, minced
6 cups Basic Vegetable Stock (page 68)
    or water
One 14.5-ounce can diced tomatoes,
    undrained

11/2 cups fresh or frozen sliced okra
11/2 teaspoons filé powder
1 teaspoon dried thyme
Salt and freshly ground black pepper
1 tablespoon barley miso paste
    (optional)
1 cup fresh or frozen corn kernels
1 teaspoon Tabasco sauce, or to taste
2 to 3 cups freshly cooked long-grain
    white or brown rice

1. Drain the chipotle, mince, and set aside.
2. Heat the olive oil in a large pot over medium heat. Add the onion, bell pepper, celery, and garlic. Cover and cook until softened, about 5 minutes. Add the stock, tomatoes and juice, okra, filé, thyme, and salt and pepper to taste. Reduce the heat to low and simmer for 30 minutes, stirring occasionally.
3. Place the miso, if using, in a small bowl. Add 2 tablespoons of the hot broth and stir to thin the miso, then add it to the gumbo along with the corn, Tabasco, and minced chipotle. Taste and adjust the seasonings, then cook for 10 minutes.

4. To serve, spoon about $^1/_2$ cup of the cooked rice into each soup bowl and top with the gumbo. Serve hot.

SERVES 4 TO 6

A SOUP BY ANY OTHER NAME

- *Stock:* A clear, flavorful liquid made by simmering ingredients (such as vegetables for vegetable stock) with water to release the flavor of the ingredients. The strained liquid is used to make soups, stews, and sauces.
- *Broth:* Stock that is served on its own as a soup.
- *Consommé:* Stock that has been reduced to intensify the flavor and then filtered for clarity.
- *Bisque:* Traditionally made with shellfish, but the term also can refer to any smooth, creamy soup. To make a vegan bisque, vegetables are cooked in liquid and then pureed. For added creaminess, dairy-free milk may be added near the end of the cooking time.
- *Chowder:* A hearty, chunky soup usually associated with seafood and dairy. A vegan chowder can be made with vegetables such as corn or potatoes.
- *Gumbo:* A traditional Cajun dish, gumbo is a spicy, thick, stew-like soup that is served over rice. Usually thickened with okra (the word *gumbo* means "okra") and filé powder (ground sassafras leaves), gumbo may be made with a variety of vegetables instead of the traditional meat and seafood. (Hint: Chunks of browned soy sausage added at the end of the cooking time are delicious.)

Ribollita

This flavorful cabbage and bean soup from Tuscany is made thick by spooning it over a slice of toasted Italian bread. To me, it's the ultimate in simple, economical comfort food that nourishes both body and soul. Canned borlotti beans can be found in Italian markets and some supermarkets. If unavailable, use cannellini beans. If you prefer to use dried beans, soak, cook, and drain them, then proceed with the recipe.

1 small head green cabbage, quartered
   and cored
2 tablespoons olive oil
1 medium-size yellow onion, chopped
1 medium-size carrot, halved
   lengthwise and cut into
   $1/4$-inch-thick half-moons
2 garlic cloves, minced
2 small white potatoes, peeled
   and diced

$1/3$ cup tomato paste blended with
   1 cup warm water
5 cups Basic Vegetable Stock (page 68)
   or water
2 bay leaves
Salt and freshly ground black pepper
$1 1/2$ cups cooked or one 15-ounce can
   borlotti or cannellini beans,
   drained and rinsed
4 to 6 slices Italian bread, toasted

1. Cut the cabbage into $1/2$-inch-wide strips and set aside.

2. Heat the olive oil in a large pot over medium heat. Add the onion, carrot, and garlic. Cover and cook until softened, about 5 minutes. Add the cabbage, potatoes, diluted tomato paste, stock, bay leaves, and salt and pepper to taste. Bring to a boil, then reduce the heat to low and simmer until the vegetables are soft, about 45 minutes. Add the beans and cook for 20 minutes. Remove the bay leaves, then taste and adjust the seasonings.

3. To serve, place a slice of toasted bread in the bottom of each bowl and ladle the soup over the bread. Serve hot.

SERVES 4 TO 6

Italian Wedding Soup

In the ever-evocative Italian language, minestrone is often called wedding soup. There are infinite variations of this classic vegetable soup—the only requirement is a variety of vegetables. My mother often added tiny meatballs (which you can do by thawing frozen veggie burgers, breaking off small pieces, rolling them into balls, and browning in a skillet) just before serving. In this version, I use the traditional borlotti beans, available at Italian markets, but you may use chickpeas or cannellini beans instead. For additional substance, add some cooked small pasta a few minutes before serving—just long enough to warm the pasta.

2 tablespoons olive oil

1 medium-size yellow onion, minced

1 large carrot, chopped

1 celery rib, chopped

1 cup trimmed green beans cut into
    1-inch pieces

One 14.5-ounce can diced tomatoes,
    undrained

6 cups Basic Vegetable Stock
    (page 68) or water

Salt and freshly ground black pepper

1 medium-size zucchini, diced

1 1/2 cups cooked or one 15-ounce can
    borlotti or other beans (see
    headnote), drained and rinsed

1 tablespoon minced fresh parsley
    leaves

1/4 cup vegan pesto, homemade
    (page 157) or store-bought,
    for garnish (optional)

1. Heat 1 tablespoon of the olive oil in a large pot over medium heat. Add the onion, carrot, and celery. Cover and cook until softened, about 5 minutes. Add the green beans, tomatoes and juice, stock, and salt and pepper to taste. Bring to a boil, reduce the heat to low, and simmer for 30 minutes.

2. Add the zucchini, borlotti beans, and parsley and cook for 15 minutes. Serve hot, garnished with a small spoonful of the vegan pesto, if desired.

SERVES 4 TO 6

Potato-Watercress Soup with Sesame

Buttery Yukon Gold potatoes combine with the peppery flavor of watercress to make a luxurious soup accented by a touch of toasted sesame oil.

1½ tablespoons peanut oil

4 or 5 shallots, to your taste, chopped

4 cups Basic Vegetable Stock (page 68)

1½ pounds Yukon Gold potatoes, peeled and diced

Salt

½ cup soy milk or other dairy-free milk

Cayenne

2 bunches watercress, tough stems removed and finely chopped

1 tablespoon toasted sesame oil

1 tablespoon sesame seeds, toasted (page 192), for garnish

1. Heat 1 tablespoon of the peanut oil in large pot over medium heat. Add the shallots, cover, and cook until softened, about 5 minutes. Add the stock and potatoes and bring to a boil. Reduce the heat to low, season with salt to taste, and simmer until the potatoes are soft, about 30 minutes.

2. Pass the potato mixture through a food mill into a large bowl. Stir in the soy milk and season with cayenne to taste. Return to the pot and keep warm over low heat.

3. Heat the remaining ½ tablespoon peanut oil in a medium-size skillet over high heat. Add the watercress and stir-fry until just wilted, about 2 minutes. Remove from the heat, toss with the sesame oil, and add to the soup, stirring to combine. Serve hot, garnished with the sesame seeds.

SERVES 4 TO 6

Udon Noodles in Shiitake-Ginger Broth

Udon noodles and shiitake mushrooms swim in a broth flavored with ginger and a hint of toasted sesame oil. Once the miso has been added to the broth, be sure the broth does not return to a boil, as boiling will destroy the beneficial enzymes in the miso.

8 ounces udon noodles
1 teaspoon toasted sesame oil
6 cups Basic Vegetable Stock
   (page 68)
4 ounces fresh shiitake mushrooms,
   stems removed and caps thinly
   sliced

1 tablespoon peeled and minced
   fresh ginger
4 scallions, minced
2 tablespoons tamari or other soy sauce
1 tablespoon mellow white miso paste
1 tablespoon minced fresh parsley
   leaves for garnish

1. Cook the udon in a pot of boiling water until just tender, 6 to 8 minutes. Drain and transfer to a large bowl. Add the sesame oil and toss to coat. Set aside.

2. Place the stock, shiitakes, ginger, scallions, and tamari in a large pot over medium heat. Bring to a boil, reduce the heat to low, and simmer until the shiitakes soften, about 5 minutes.

3. In a small bowl, blend the miso with 1/4 cup of the hot broth. Stir into the soup and add the noodles. Serve immediately, garnished with the parsley.

SERVES 4 TO 6

Sherry-Laced Garlic Soup with Pasta Stars

Both garlic and soup have long been used as home remedies for colds, so combining them would seem to be a sure-fire cure. Long, slow simmering helps mellow the flavor of the garlic. Tiny pasta stars, called stellini, add substance to this restorative soup.

10 garlic cloves, peeled

2 tablespoons extra virgin olive oil

5 cups Basic Vegetable Stock
    (page 68)

Salt

Cayenne

1/2 cup stellini or other tiny pasta

2 tablespoons dry sherry

1. Place the garlic and olive oil in a blender or food processor and process until smooth. Transfer to a large pot over medium heat and cook until very fragrant, about 3 minutes, being careful not to let the garlic brown. Stir in the stock and season with salt and cayenne to taste. Bring to boil, reduce the heat to medium-low, and simmer for 20 to 30 minutes.

2. Meanwhile, cook the pasta in a pot of boiling salted water, stirring occasionally, until *al dente*, about 5 minutes. Drain and divide among 4 soup bowls.

3. When ready to serve, add the sherry to the soup, ladle into the bowls, and serve at once.

SERVES 4 TO 6

"Custom will reconcile people to any atrocity; and fashion will drive them to acquire any custom."
—GEORGE BERNARD SHAW

Barley Soup with Porcinis and Dill

Barley soups are especially popular in eastern European cultures, where they often contain mushrooms. Here dried porcinis add a rich, woodsy element, while minced dill heightens the flavor. Using water as the liquid will yield a fine soup, but mushroom stock may be used for a more pronounced mushroom flavor.

1/2 cup dried porcini mushrooms, soaked in 1 cup very hot water for 20 minutes
1 tablespoon olive oil
6 shallots, chopped
1 small carrot, grated

1 cup pearl barley
5 cups water or Mushroom Stock (page 69)
Salt and freshly ground black pepper
1 tablespoon minced fresh dill or 1 teaspoon dillweed

1. Remove the porcinis from the soaking liquid and strain the liquid. Thinly slice the porcinis and return to the strained liquid. Set aside.

2. Heat the olive oil in a large pot over medium heat. Add the shallots and carrot, cover, and cook, stirring a few times, until softened and lightly caramelized, about 10 minutes. Add the barley and water and bring to a boil. Season with salt and pepper to taste, reduce the heat to medium-low, and simmer for 20 minutes. Add the porcinis and their soaking liquid and half the dill. Cook until the barley is tender, about 10 minutes.

3. Serve hot, garnished with the remaining dill.

SERVES 4 TO 6

10 Environmental Reasons to Go Vegan

Animal agriculture takes a heavy toll on the environment. Here are some of the consequences.

1. Since 1967, forests have been destroyed at a rate of 1 acre every 5 seconds to create grazing land for beef cattle to ensure a continuous supply of inexpensive meat for our fast-food restaurants.

2. Economists estimate that for every person who switches to a vegan diet, 1 acre of trees is spared each year.

3. Runoff from animal waste is linked to a 7,000-square-mile "dead zone" in the Gulf of Mexico that no longer supports aquatic life.

4. At the present rate, many rain forests—a natural resource on which we rely for everything from lifesaving medicines to the very air we breathe —will be gone in 30 years.

5. Livestock produces 7 trillion tons of manure every year, and it all finds its way into our water systems.

6. Sixty percent of all water used in America is used for meat production.

7. It takes 16 pounds of grain and 2,500 gallons of water to produce 1 pound of meat. Yet 16 people can be fed on the grain it takes to produce that pound of meat. Growing that amount of grain requires only 250 gallons of water.

8. Countries such as Ethiopia and some Central American countries use their farmland to supply the United States with cheap burgers instead of growing healthful grain foods for their own starving people. Every 2 seconds, a child starves to death somewhere in the world.

9. The livestock population of the United States consumes enough grain and soybeans to feed more than 5 five times its human population. Ninety percent of all corn grown in the United States goes to livestock. Eighty percent of all grains and beans go to feed these animals.

10. Food grown directly for human consumption occupies 60 million acres. Food grown to feed livestock occupies 1.2 billion acres.

Tuscan Spelt Soup

Also known as farro, emmer, or German wheat, this ancient grain was mentioned in the Bible (Ezekiel 4:9 and Exodus 9:32). A type of wheat with large grains that resemble brown rice, it has a chewy texture and hearty flavor and is popular in soups, especially in Tuscany and the Provence region of France. It is also used to make a dark German bread. Like its cousin kamut, spelt can often be tolerated by those with wheat allergies. Spelt breads and pasta are available in natural food stores. This recipe was inspired by one contained among the writings of Apicius, a first-century food writer credited with writing the first cookbook.

3/4 cup spelt
2 tablespoons olive oil, plus more for drizzling, if desired
1 small yellow onion, chopped
1 medium-size carrot, chopped
1 celery rib, chopped
2 garlic cloves, minced

5 cups Basic Vegetable Stock (page 68) or water
1 1/2 cups or one 15-ounce can cannellini or other white beans, drained and rinsed
Salt and freshly ground black pepper

1. In a medium-size bowl, soak the spelt in cold water to cover for 12 hours to soften. Drain and set aside.

2. Heat the olive oil in a large pot over medium heat. Add the onion, carrot, celery, and garlic. Cover and cook until the vegetables soften, about 5 minutes. Add the stock and bring to a boil. Add the spelt and reduce the heat to low. Cover and simmer until the spelt is tender, 1 1/2 to 2 hours. Add more water if soup becomes too thick.

3. Add the beans and season with salt and pepper to taste. Simmer for 30 minutes to allow the flavors to blend.

4. Serve hot, drizzled with a little olive oil, if desired.

SERVES 4

4

Salads & Slaws

Salads have come a long way since that crunchy wedge of iceberg lettuce drowning in bottled dressing that many of us grew up with. These days salad greens abound, with choices ranging from the usual romaine, butter, and leaf lettuces to arugula, chicory, and baby spinach. And the greens are just the beginning. Look for them topped with anything from grilled vegetables to marinated bean and grain medleys. Intricate main-dish salads are now featured entrées on many restaurant menus, and a salad course has become an important part of many dinner parties. Marinated salads are great choices for picnics and potlucks, and some of the more substantial salads can stand in for an entire meal.

Vegetarians and vegans alike are sometimes jokingly referred to as "salad eaters," but with salads such as the ones in this chapter, that's not necessarily a bad label. Consider the elegance of *Eggplant Salad Towers* or *Artichoke Salad Parfaits*, or the rustic goodness of two different bread salads, *Panzanella* from Tuscany and Lebanese *Fattoush*. A selection of slaws and potato salads, a variety of grain salads such as *Five-Spice Moroccan Couscous Salad* and *Quinoa Tabbouleh*, and some global salads from Asia such as *Thai-Style Papaya Salad* and *Asian Noodle Salad with Spicy Peanut Sauce* help round things out.

Asian Pear and Baby Spinach Salad with Warm Walnut Dressing

Asian pears are increasingly available in supermarkets and can be found in Asian markets as well. If they're unavailable, you may substitute another variety of pear. A final drizzle of walnut oil adds a luxurious touch, but the salad is quite delicious without it, too.

3/4 cup walnut pieces

1/3 cup peanut oil or other neutral-tasting oil

3 tablespoons fresh lemon juice

1/2 teaspoon sugar or natural sweetener

Salt and freshly ground black pepper

6 cups baby spinach leaves

2 Asian pears, peeled, cored, and thinly sliced

1 tablespoon walnut oil (optional)

1. Place the walnuts in a dry skillet over medium heat and toast, stirring or shaking a few times, until fragrant and lightly browned, about 3 minutes. Be careful not to let burn.

2. Remove about 1/2 cup of the walnuts from the skillet and set aside to cool. Add the peanut oil to the remaining walnuts in the skillet and warm over low heat for 5 minutes. Add the lemon juice, sugar, and salt and pepper to taste. Transfer to a blender and process until smooth. Return to the saucepan and keep warm over very low heat.

3. Place the spinach and all but 12 of the pear slices in a large bowl. Add the dressing and toss to coat. Divide the salad among 4 plates. Arrange the remaining pear slices on top of the spinach and drizzle with the walnut oil, if using. Scatter the reserved walnuts on top and serve immediately.

SERVES 4

Thai-Style Papaya Salad

This recipe was inspired by the classic green papaya salads often served in Thai restaurants. This refreshing salad is sweet, hot, tangy, and crunchy all at the same time—typical of the amazingly complex flavors of Thai cuisine. I created this version out of desperation because most restaurants make theirs with fish sauce and shrimp. Now I can enjoy a vegan version at home. Look for green papayas in Asian markets. The best way to shred them is with a mandoline or other slicer, such as the Benriner brand, a less expensive Japanese version that makes similar cuts.

4 garlic cloves, minced
1 teaspoon peeled and minced
    fresh ginger
1 teaspoon Asian chili paste, or to taste
2 tablespoons palm sugar, firmly
    packed light brown sugar, or
    raw sugar
1/3 cup fresh lime juice
2 tablespoons tamari or other soy sauce

2 medium-size green papayas
    (about 1 1/2 pounds)
1 small carrot, peeled
1/2 cup chopped unsalted dry-roasted
    peanuts
4 large Boston lettuce leaves
12 very thin cucumber slices for
    garnish
4 cherry tomatoes for garnish

1. In a small bowl, combine the garlic, ginger, chili paste, and palm sugar. Slowly stir in the lime juice and tamari, blending well. Set aside.

2. Peel the papayas, halve lengthwise, and seed. Use a mandoline or similar slicer to cut the papayas into long, thin shreds. Alternatively, use a box grater, food processor with a shredding disk, or sharp knife to achieve the same kind of shreds. Place in a large bowl. Shred the carrot the same way and add to the papayas.

3. Pour the dressing over the papayas and carrot, add the peanuts, and toss to combine well.

4. To serve, place a lettuce leaf on each of 4 salad plates, top with a mound of papaya salad, and garnish each plate with 3 cucumber slices and a cherry tomato.

SERVES 4

Cooking in the Raw

As people become more aware that fresh fruits and vegetables are essential for good health, the raw, or "living," foods diet is gaining increased attention, especially from vegetarians and many nutrition professionals. The raw foods diet consists mainly of fresh fruits, leafy greens and other vegetables, soaked nuts and seeds, and occasionally soaked or sprouted beans and grains.

The main reason advocates of living foods eat foods raw is that they believe that cooking foods destroys the enzymes and most of the vitamins. They also believe that the human body is better suited to eating and assimilating plant foods rather than animal foods.

Although the stove may fall into disuse when you begin to "cook raw," your blender, food processor, or juicer will be humming as you prepare raw appetizers, entrées, and desserts. If you have a food dehydrator, you can make yummy pizzas, breads, cookies, and crackers with soaked grains, seeds, and nuts. It's easy to include more raw foods at meals and as between-meal snacks by eating more fresh fruits, raw vegetables, and salads.

Walnut-Crusted Apple-Cranberry Salad Pie

Here elements of the classic Waldorf salad—tasty bits of apples, celery, and walnuts—are transformed into a salad "pie" with dried cranberries and soy mayonnaise. Who says we can't begin our meal with dessert? The choice of apple is up to you—if you like a sweeter apple, use Delicious or perhaps Fuji or Gala. If you like a slightly tart, crisp taste, go for Granny Smith.

1/2 cup dates, pitted and soaked in
    hot water to cover until soft
2 cups walnut pieces
4 apples (see headnote)
1 tablespoon fresh lemon juice
1/2 cup sweetened dried cranberries

1 cup minced celery
2 scallions, minced
1/2 cup soy mayonnaise, homemade
    (page 140) or store-bought
1/2 teaspoon sugar or natural sweetener
1/4 teaspoon salt

1. Drain the dates and set aside.

2. In a food processor, combine 1 1/2 cups of the walnuts with the drained dates and process into a sticky paste. Press the mixture evenly into the bottom and sides of a lightly oiled 9-inch pie plate and set aside.

3. Peel, core, and shred the apples or cut into very thin slices and place in a large bowl. Add the lemon juice and toss to coat to prevent discoloration. Drain any liquid from the apples, then add the cranberries, celery, scallions, soy mayonnaise, sugar, and salt. Stir gently to combine. Taste and adjust the seasonings, then transfer to the prepared pie plate and spread over the crust. Press the apple mixture into the crust and smooth the top. Sprinkle the remaining 1/2 cup walnuts on top.

4. Cover and refrigerate for at least 30 minutes or up to 2 hours before serving. Cut into wedges and serve.

SERVES 6

Indonesian-Style Vegetable Salad

The pleasing crunch of cabbage, carrots, and jicama against the backdrop of a creamy, peanutty dressing makes for a tasty salad combination and a nice change from the usual raw vegetable salads. Toss this with cold rice or noodles for a substantial one-dish meal. The coconut milk adds a rich finish to the sauce, but water will work if you want to reduce the fat.

1 tablespoon peanut oil

1/2 cup chopped shallots

2 garlic cloves, minced

2 teaspoons peeled and grated
   fresh ginger

1/2 cup smooth natural peanut butter

2 teaspoons light brown sugar or
   natural sweetener

1/4 teaspoon cayenne

3 tablespoons fresh lemon juice

2 tablespoons tamari or other soy sauce

1 cup unsweetened coconut milk or
   water, or as needed

1 small head green cabbage, cored and
   finely shredded

1 small carrot, shredded

1 cup peeled and shredded jicama

1/3 cup chopped unsalted dry-roasted
   peanuts

1/4 cup raisins

1/2 cup fresh bean sprouts

1. Heat the peanut oil in a medium-size skillet over medium heat. Add the shallots, garlic, and ginger. Cover and cook until softened, about 5 minutes. Stir in the peanut butter, brown sugar, cayenne, lemon juice, tamari, and as much coconut milk as

SPROUTING UP ALL OVER

Loaded with concentrated flavor and nutrition, a wide variety of fresh sprouts are available in supermarkets and natural food stores. In addition to the familiar mung bean sprouts common in Asian cooking and the popular fluffy salad garnish sprouted from alfalfa seeds, we now have radish sprouts, broccoli sprouts, lentil sprouts, soybean sprouts, and numerous other types grown from various vegetable and herb seeds, beans, and grains. When buying sprouts, be sure they are very firm and fresh. Most sprouts will keep well in the refrigerator for several days.

necessary to make a thick sauce. Reduce the heat to low and simmer for 5 minutes, stirring a few times.

2. Transfer to a blender or food processor and process until smooth.

3. Place the cabbage, carrot, jicama, peanuts, and raisins in a large serving bowl. Pour in the sauce and toss to combine. Sprinkle the bean sprouts on top and serve immediately.

SERVES 4

Here's My Heart Salad with Raspberry Vinaigrette

Valentine's Day was my inspiration for this heartwarming salad made with four kinds of vegetable "hearts." A blushing raspberry vinaigrette adds a touch of pink, which is picked up by the sliced beets and radishes. If you want to go all out, cut beet slices into heart shapes for garnish. The white wine vinegar combines with the raspberry spread to create an economical alternative to the pricey raspberry vinegars available in specialty food shops.

2 hearts of romaine lettuce

One 9-ounce package frozen artichoke
    hearts, cooked according to
    package directions, drained,
    and thinly sliced

One 14-ounce can hearts of palm,
    drained and thinly sliced

1/2 cup minced celery hearts

2 red radishes, thinly sliced

3 tablespoons white wine vinegar

1 shallot, minced

1 or 2 teaspoons fruit-sweetened
    raspberry spread, to your taste

Salt and freshly ground black pepper

1/3 cup extra virgin olive oil

1/2 cup sliced cooked or canned beets

1. Tear the romaine into bite-size pieces and place in a large bowl. Add the artichoke hearts, hearts of palm, celery, and radishes. Set aside.

2. In a small bowl, combine the vinegar, shallot, raspberry spread, and salt and pepper to taste. Whisk in the olive oil until blended. Pour the dressing over the salad.

3. If using plain sliced beets, add them now and toss the salad to combine. If using heart-shaped beets, toss the salad first, then divide among 4 plates, garnishing each salad with the beet slices.

SERVES 4

Artichoke Salad Parfaits

The ingredients in these salad "parfaits" can be varied according to personal preference. Presentation is the key—ice-cream sundae glasses are best, but large wineglasses or even martini glasses can be used instead.

1/4 cup extra virgin olive oil

2 tablespoons balsamic vinegar

1/2 teaspoon minced garlic

1 teaspoon minced fresh basil leaves or
    1/2 teaspoon dried

1/2 teaspoon salt

1/8 teaspoon freshly ground black
    pepper

1 small cucumber, peeled, seeded,
    and chopped

1 small carrot, grated

1 small red bell pepper, seeded and
    chopped

Romaine lettuce, cut into thin strips

One 9-ounce jar marinated artichoke
    hearts, drained and chopped

2 tablespoons pine nuts, lightly toasted
    (page 110)

4 pitted Kalamata olives

1. In a small bowl, combine the olive oil, vinegar, garlic, basil, salt, and pepper, whisking until blended. Set aside.

2. Place the cucumber, carrot, and bell pepper in separate small bowls and drizzle a little dressing on each. Toss to coat.

3. Arrange the salad ingredients in layers in 4 glasses (see headnote), beginning with a layer of romaine lettuce, followed by bell pepper, cucumber, carrot, and artichoke hearts, adding more lettuce if there is room in the glass.

4. Drizzle with a little of the remaining dressing, top each salad with pine nuts and an olive, and serve.

SERVES 4

Pseudo Caesar Salad

This salad is great for those who enjoy the crunchy goodness of romaine lettuce tossed with fresh croutons and a garlicky dressing but want to avoid the raw eggs and anchovies found in a classic Caesar salad.

4 thick slices Italian bread, crusts removed

2 garlic cloves, minced

1 tablespoon tahini (sesame paste)

1 tablespoon mellow white miso paste

2 tablespoons fresh lemon juice

1 teaspoon tamari or other soy sauce

1/4 teaspoon vegetarian Worcestershire sauce (optional)

1/3 cup olive oil

Salt and freshly ground black pepper

1 head romaine lettuce

1. Preheat the oven to 325 degrees F. Cut the bread into 1-inch cubes and spread on a baking sheet. Bake, turning occasionally, until lightly toasted on all sides, about 20 minutes. Set aside to cool.

Toasting Nuts

Toasting brings out the flavor in nuts. For small quantities of nuts (less than a cup), it is easy to toast them in a dry skillet over medium heat, shaking or stirring constantly until toasted. When toasting larger amounts, however, the oven works better.

Preheat the oven to 350 degrees F. Spread the nuts on a baking sheet and bake until lightly browned and dry. Walnuts can take up to 25 minutes, pecans and hazelnuts, about 15 minutes, and almonds and pine nuts, about 10 minutes. Be sure to remove the toasted nuts from the hot baking sheet or skillet, or they will continue to cook.

Allow the nuts to cool completely and store in an airtight container until ready to use. They are best eaten within a few days.

2. In a small bowl or food processor, combine the garlic, tahini, miso, lemon juice, tamari, vegetarian Worcestershire (if using), and olive oil until blended. Taste and adjust the seasonings, adding salt and pepper to taste. Set aside.

3. Tear the romaine leaves into bite-size pieces and place in a large serving bowl. Pour the dressing over the salad and toss until evenly coated. Add the croutons, toss again, and serve immediately.

SERVES 4

Fennel, Pecan, and Watercress Salad with Orange Vinaigrette

The vibrant colors, complementary flavors, and contrasting textures in this salad create a sparkling combination that will make it a favorite.

1 navel orange, peeled

2 large fennel bulbs, trimmed

2 bunches watercress, tough stems
   removed and coarsely chopped

1/2 cup pecan halves, toasted (see left)

1/4 cup white wine vinegar

2 tablespoons frozen orange juice
   concentrate, thawed

2 tablespoons water

1 teaspoon Dijon mustard

1/2 teaspoon salt

1/4 teaspoon freshly ground black
   pepper

1/4 cup olive oil

1. Remove the white pith from the orange. Cut sections of orange from between the membranes and set aside.

2. Halve each fennel bulb lengthwise, then cut crosswise into paper-thin slices. Place in a large serving bowl. Add the watercress, orange sections, and pecans.

3. In a small bowl, combine the vinegar, orange juice concentrate, water, mustard, salt, and pepper. Whisk in the olive oil until blended and pour the dressing over the salad. Toss gently to coat evenly and serve immediately.

SERVES 4

Eggplant Salad Towers

A stacked salad makes a striking first course. Instead of the eggplant slices, you can substitute slices of grilled portobello mushroom caps, if you prefer.

1 large roasted red bell pepper
  (page 143), minced
1/2 cup frozen green peas, thawed
1/3 cup minced red onion
1 garlic clove, minced
1/4 cup extra virgin olive oil
1 tablespoon balsamic vinegar
1 tablespoon fresh lemon juice

Salt and freshly ground black pepper
1 medium-size eggplant
4 slices Italian bread, crusts removed
1 large, ripe tomato
4 Boston lettuce leaves
1 tablespoon minced fresh parsley
  leaves

1. In a medium-size bowl, combine the bell pepper, peas, onion, and garlic. Add the olive oil, vinegar, lemon juice, and salt and pepper to taste. Toss to combine and set aside.

2. Preheat the oven to 400 degrees F. Cut the middle section of the eggplant into twelve 1/4-inch-thick slices and place on a lightly oiled baking sheet. Season with salt and pepper to taste and bake until soft, turning once, 12 to 15 minutes total.

3. Toast the bread in the oven or under the broiler to make 4 large croutons. Set aside.

4. Cut four 1/4-inch-thick slices from the tomato and set aside.

5. Set out 4 salad plates and place 1 lettuce leaf on each. Top each leaf with a large crouton. Using a slotted spoon, place an eggplant slice on top of the crouton. Top with a spoonful of the marinated salad, followed by another eggplant slice and then a tomato slice. Repeat with the remaining marinated salad and top with the remaining eggplant slice. Sprinkle with the parsley and drizzle with any extra dressing from the marinated vegetables. Serve at once.

SERVES 4

Chili Taco Salad

This recipe is a refreshing way to stretch a small amount of chili into a satisfying lunch for six and is great served in bowls made from tortillas.

6 cups shredded lettuce

3 cups vegetarian chili, homemade (pages 314–326) or store-bought, heated

1 cup Fresh Tomato Salsa (page 174) or your favorite salsa

1 cup vegan sour cream

1 cup shredded vegan cheddar cheese

1 small red bell pepper, seeded and chopped

1 large, ripe avocado, peeled, pitted, and diced

1/4 cup pitted and sliced brine-cured black olives

Tortilla chips for serving

1. Place a bed of lettuce on each of 6 salad plates. Top with the chili, dividing it evenly among the plates.

2. In a small bowl, combine the salsa and vegan sour cream until well mixed, then spoon over the chili. Top each serving with the vegan cheese and scatter the bell pepper, avocado, and olives evenly over the top. Serve with the tortilla chips.

SERVES 6

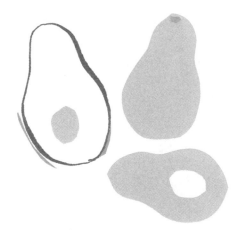

"People often say that humans have always eaten animals, as if this is a justification for continuing the practice. According to this logic, we should not try to prevent people from murdering other people, since this has also been done since the earliest of times."
—ISAAC BASHEVIS SINGER

Carrot-Mung Bean Salad

In addition to being rich in protein and complex carbohydrates, this flavorful salad is also very low in fat. Yellow split mung beans can be found in natural food stores and Indian markets. For variation, chopped fresh mango may be substituted for the apple.

1/4 cup yellow split mung beans, picked over and rinsed

2 cups water

1 large carrot, grated

1/2 Granny Smith apple, cored and chopped

1/2 red bell pepper, seeded and chopped

1 teaspoon peeled and grated fresh ginger

2 tablespoons fresh lemon juice

1 tablespoon peanut oil

1/2 teaspoon black mustard seeds

1 small, fresh hot green chile, seeded and minced

1 tablespoon chopped fresh cilantro leaves

Salt

1. Soak the mung beans in the water for at least 2 hours or up to 8 hours.

2. Drain the beans and place them in a large serving bowl. Add the carrot, apple, bell pepper, ginger, and lemon juice. Set aside.

3. Heat the peanut oil in a small saucepan over medium heat. Add the mustard seeds, cover, and cook until the seeds start popping. When the popping stops, add the chile and stir for 30 seconds to bring out the flavor. Add the mustard seeds and chile to the salad mixture.

4. Just before serving, add the cilantro and salt to taste, tossing gently to combine.

SERVES 4

Gold and Black Bean Salad

Black beans, corn, and yellow bell peppers make for a striking contrast in this salad with a southwestern accent. Serve as is, or toss with a cup or so of cold rice or other grain and spoon over torn salad greens for a more substantial dish.

3 cups cooked or two 15-ounce cans
    black beans, drained and rinsed
2 cups fresh or frozen corn kernels,
    cooked and cooled
1 small yellow bell pepper, seeded
    and chopped
2 shallots, minced

2 tablespoons fresh lime juice
1/4 teaspoon ground cumin
1/2 teaspoon salt
1/8 teaspoon cayenne
1/4 cup olive oil
2 tablespoons minced fresh cilantro
    leaves

1. In a large serving bowl, combine the beans, corn, and bell pepper. Set aside.
2. In a small bowl, combine the shallots, lime juice, cumin, salt, and cayenne. Whisk in the olive oil until blended.
3. Pour the dressing over the salad and toss lightly to coat. Taste and adjust the seasonings. Sprinkle with the cilantro and serve at room temperature.

SERVES 4 TO 6

Fresh Herbs

Fresh herbs can work like magic to elevate an ordinary dish to the extraordinary. A sprinkling of minced fresh parsley, basil, tarragon, or chives can brighten almost any salad, grain, or vegetable dish in the same way a little thyme, oregano, or sage can do wonders for soups, stews, and stuffings. Because most fresh herbs are expensive and highly perishable, it is a wise and rewarding investment to plant your own. Whether a few small pots on the windowsill or a garden full of lush plants, a variety of fragrant herbs can be an indispensable tool for the creative cook.

Mediterranean Lima Bean Salad with Grape Tomatoes, Kalamata Olives, and Marinated Tofu

Frozen lima beans are readily available, economical, and simple to prepare. They also happen to look and taste great in this main-dish salad. Grape tomatoes tend to be much sweeter than cherry tomatoes, but if you can't find them, feel free to use cherry tomatoes instead.

2 tablespoons mellow white miso paste

1/4 cup water

2 tablespoons fresh lemon juice

Salt and freshly ground black pepper

4 ounces extra-firm tofu, drained and pressed (page 12)

3 cups frozen lima beans, cooked according to package directions and drained

1 cup grape tomatoes, cut in half

1/2 cup minced scallions

1/2 cup minced fresh parsley leaves

1/4 cup Kalamata olives, pitted and thinly sliced

3 tablespoons extra virgin olive oil

1. In a small bowl, combine the miso and water, stirring to blend. Stir in 1 tablespoon of the lemon juice and a pinch of salt and pepper and set aside.

2. Cut the pressed tofu into 1/2-inch cubes and place in a shallow bowl. Pour the marinade over the top and stir gently to coat. Cover and refrigerate for at least 2 hours or overnight.

3. In a large serving bowl, combine the lima beans, tomatoes, scallions, parsley, olives, and tofu and its marinade. Add the olive oil and remaining 1 tablespoon lemon juice and season with salt and pepper to taste. Toss gently to combine, then cover and let stand at room temperature for about 20 minutes to allow the flavors to blend before serving.

SERVES 4

Tomato and White Bean Salad with Watercress

Sweet ripe tomatoes combine with creamy white beans and refreshing crisp watercress for a lovely salad combination that tastes as good as it looks. Add a loaf of warm crusty bread, and you have a delicious light meal.

2 shallots, peeled
1 garlic clove, peeled
2 tablespoons fresh lemon juice
1 teaspoon Dijon mustard
1/4 cup extra virgin olive oil
Salt and freshly ground black pepper
1 1/2 cups cooked or one 15-ounce can
   cannellini or other white beans,
   drained and rinsed

2 bunches watercress, tough stems
   removed and coarsely chopped
12 grape or cherry tomatoes,
   cut in half
8 brine-cured black olives, pitted
2 tablespoons chopped fresh
   basil leaves

1. Place the shallots and garlic in a food processor and process until smooth. Add the lemon juice, mustard, olive oil, and salt and pepper to taste. Process until well blended and set aside.

2. In a large serving bowl, combine the beans, watercress, tomatoes, olives, and basil. Pour the dressing over the salad and toss gently to combine. Serve immediately.

SERVES 4

Panzanella (Tuscan Bread Salad)

I know firsthand how thrifty Italians can be—my grandmother once saved three peas left over from dinner to be used the next day. So this luscious salad, traditionally made with stale bread, came as no surprise to me. The bread absorbs the surrounding flavors and becomes the focal point of the dish. I don't know about your house, but around my kitchen, good Italian bread doesn't last long enough to go stale, so I begin with a fresh loaf. Panzanella is especially good served over salad greens.

1 loaf Italian bread, crust removed and cut into 3/4-inch cubes (about 5 cups)

1 shallot, peeled

1 garlic clove, peeled

3 tablespoons red wine vinegar

1/2 teaspoon sugar or natural sweetener

1 teaspoon chopped fresh oregano leaves

1/2 teaspoon salt

1/3 cup extra virgin olive oil

Freshly ground black pepper

1 pound ripe grape or cherry tomatoes, cut in half

1/2 large yellow bell pepper, seeded and chopped

1/2 cup brine-cured black olives, pitted and halved

1/4 cup minced fresh Italian parsley leaves

1. Preheat the oven to 325 degrees F. Spread the bread cubes on a baking sheet and bake until lightly toasted, 15 to 20 minutes.

2. In a blender or food processor, combine the shallot, garlic, vinegar, sugar, oregano, and salt and process until smooth. With the machine running, slowly add the olive oil in a steady stream through the feed tube, processing until blended. Season with pepper to taste.

3. In a large serving bowl, combine the bread cubes, tomatoes, bell pepper, olives, and parsley. Pour the vinaigrette over the salad and toss to combine. Let stand at room temperature for 15 to 20 minutes to let the flavors develop before serving.

SERVES 6

Fattoush (Lebanese Bread Salad)

Not to be outdone by the Italians, the Lebanese have their own delicious bread salad, which they make with stale pita bread. I use whole wheat pita for added flavor and nutrition. The addition of chickpeas and tahini is a departure from the traditional, but they add lots of protein and turn this refreshing salad into a one-dish meal.

2 garlic cloves, mashed into a paste

2 teaspoons tahini (sesame paste)

1/3 cup fresh lemon juice

1/3 cup extra virgin olive oil

1/2 teaspoon salt

Pinch of cayenne

2 large or 4 small white or whole wheat pita breads

1 large cucumber, peeled, seeded, and chopped

1 large, ripe tomato, seeded and chopped

1/2 small green bell pepper, seeded and chopped

1/2 cup minced red onion

1 cup cooked or canned chickpeas, drained and rinsed

1/3 cup chopped fresh parsley leaves

1/3 cup chopped fresh mint leaves

2 cups shredded romaine lettuce

1. Preheat the oven to 350 degrees F. In a small bowl, whisk together the garlic, tahini, lemon juice, olive oil, salt, and cayenne until blended. Set aside.

2. Place the pitas on a baking sheet and bake until lightly toasted, turning once, 10 to 12 minutes. Remove from the oven, cut or tear into bite-size pieces, and place in a large bowl. Add the cucumber, tomato, bell pepper, onion, chickpeas, parsley, mint, and as much of the dressing as needed to coat. Toss well to combine, then let sit for 10 to 15 minutes to let the flavors develop.

3. Divide the lettuce among 4 salad plates, top with the salad, and serve.

SERVES 4

Did You Know...

The greener the lettuce the more nutritious it is? Dark green lettuce varieties such as romaine contain more vitamins and minerals than pale varieties such as iceberg.

Close to Mom's Potato Salad

This is very close to my mom's recipe, except she used to add diced hard-cooked eggs and sliced pimiento-stuffed green olives. I keep the olives in as a nod to nostalgia, but I'll pass on the eggs. It has all the great taste of a classic potato salad, but it's better for you because it's made with soy mayonnaise. Look for soy mayonnaise at natural food stores or well-stocked supermarkets, or make it yourself.

1 1/2 pounds red or white waxy potatoes

1 inner celery rib, minced

2 tablespoons grated onion

1/4 cup sliced pimiento-stuffed green olives

3/4 cup soy mayonnaise, homemade (page 140) or store-bought

1 tablespoon white wine vinegar

1 teaspoon Dijon mustard

Salt and freshly ground black pepper

Paprika

1. Place the potatoes in a large saucepan with salted water to cover. Bring to a boil over medium-high heat and continue to boil until tender, about 30 minutes. Drain and allow to cool.

2. Peel the potatoes, cut into bite-size chunks, and place in a large serving bowl. Add the celery, onion, and olives and set aside.

3. In a small bowl, combine the soy mayonnaise, vinegar, mustard, and salt and pepper to taste. Mix well and add to the potato mixture, stirring gently to combine. Sprinkle the top with paprika. Serve right away or cover and refrigerate until ready to serve. This is best eaten within a day or two of being made.

SERVES 4 TO 6

Less-Dressed Potato Salad with Fennel and Chives

Sometimes less is more. This sophisticated salad is lightly dressed in a simple lemony vinaigrette to let the flavors of the potatoes and fennel come through. As a variation, add some cooked green beans cut into 1-inch pieces.

1¹/₂ pounds small red potatoes
¹/₂ cup minced fennel bulb
¹/₄ cup niçoise olives, pitted
¹/₄ cup chopped fresh chives
¹/₃ cup extra virgin olive oil

2 tablespoons fresh lemon juice
1 teaspoon Dijon mustard
1 shallot, minced
Salt and freshly ground black pepper

1. Place the potatoes in a large saucepan with salted water to cover. Bring to a boil over medium-high heat and continue to boil until tender, about 30 minutes. Drain and cut into halves or quarters, depending on the size. Transfer to a large serving bowl and add the fennel, olives, and chives. Set aside.

2. In a small bowl, whisk together the olive oil, lemon juice, mustard, shallot, and salt and pepper to taste until blended. Pour the dressing over the potato mixture and toss gently to combine. Taste and adjust the seasonings. Serve right away or cover tightly and refrigerate until ready to serve. This will keep for 2 to 3 days.

SERVES 4 TO 6

Red Flannel Cole Slaw

The term *cole slaw* comes from the Dutch, *koolsla*, for "cabbage salad." The vibrant red colors from the cabbage, bell pepper, radishes, and beets make this a pretty "cool" slaw in more ways than one.

2 medium-size beets

1 small head red cabbage, cored and shredded

1/2 small red bell pepper, seeded and minced

3 red radishes, shredded

1/4 cup extra virgin olive oil

2 tablespoons orange juice

1 tablespoon fresh lemon juice

1 teaspoon sugar or natural sweetener

1/4 teaspoon celery salt

1/8 teaspoon Tabasco sauce

Salt and freshly ground black pepper

1. Place the beets in a medium-size saucepan, cover with water, and bring to a boil. Reduce the heat to low, cover, and simmer until just tender, about 30 minutes. Drain and rinse under cold running water, then peel and cut into matchsticks. Place in a large serving bowl along with the cabbage, bell pepper, and radishes. Set aside.

2. In a small bowl, whisk together the olive oil, orange juice, lemon juice, sugar, celery salt, Tabasco, and salt and pepper to taste until blended. Pour the dressing over the vegetables and stir to coat. Taste and adjust the seasonings.

3. Cover and refrigerate for several hours or 2 to 3 days. Serve chilled.

SERVES 6 TO 8

THE BEET GOES ON

My mother rarely had to coax me to eat my vegetables. Even as a child, I enjoyed the flavors and textures of everything from asparagus to zucchini. One notable exception was beets. Mom always lost the battle when trying to force me to "eat my beets."

My beet aversion continued into adulthood, as I snubbed borscht and avoided the pickled beets on salad bars and buffets. I was perfectly content to live an off-beet lifestyle—until I discovered the joy of fresh beets. After my first taste, it became clear that I had disliked the beets of my youth for the simple reason that my mom had always served the tasteless canned variety. Tinned beets bear little resemblance to fresh ones, which are amazingly sweet and full of flavor. Had I been served fresh beets as a child, I'm sure they would have ranked among my top ten favorite vegetables.

One of the best things about fresh beets is that you get two vegetables for the price of one since both the round red beetroots and bushy green tops are edible and nutritious. Beetroots and greens are both high in iron, calcium, potassium, and magnesium, as well as in vitamins A, C, and B complex. The vibrancy of the dramatic magenta and green hues is surpassed only by the delicious taste of the lightly steamed tops combined with the sweet and tender roots.

The most flavorful beets are tender baby beets. Look for small, round beetroots with crisp green leaves. Beetroots will keep well in the refrigerator for a week or two, but the greens will last for only a few days. Try to cook them both within a day or two of purchase to minimize the loss of nutrients that occurs with any fresh vegetable after it is picked.

To retain the nutrients, flavor, and appearance of beetroots, cook them whole with the skins on, as cutting them prior to cooking disperses the color and nutrients into the cooking water. You can add a splash of lemon juice or vinegar to the water to minimize color loss. Small beetroots cook in 15 to 30 minutes, depending on size. Larger beets may take up to 1 hour. Check for doneness by piercing the beet with a knife. Once the beets are cooked, the skins will slip off easily when pressed with your fingers.

Beets can also be baked and are especially good cut in half, brushed with olive oil, and sprinkled with salt and pepper before baking. Place them on a baking sheet or in a casserole dish and bake at 375 degrees F until tender, 20 to 30 minutes, depending on size. You can also wrap them in aluminum foil and bake them like potatoes at 400 degrees F until tender, about 1 hour, depending on their size. The greens can be eaten raw in salads or cooked like spinach: steamed, sautéed, or boiled. Grated raw beetroots also make a colorful addition to salads.

Asian Cole Slaw

Fragrant ginger and cilantro are just two of the great flavor elements in this Asian-style slaw. You could use napa cabbage, if you like, but I prefer regular green cabbage because it has a crunchier texture. Daikon is a large, white radish available in many supermarkets and Asian grocery stores.

2¹/₂ cups cored and shredded green cabbage

1 cup peeled and grated daikon radish

¹/₂ cup grated carrots

1 large scallion, minced

2 tablespoons chopped fresh cilantro leaves

1 tablespoon peeled and minced fresh ginger

2 tablespoons fresh lime juice

1 tablespoon rice vinegar

1 tablespoon toasted sesame oil

1 teaspoon tamari or other soy sauce

1 teaspoon sugar or natural sweetener

Salt and freshly ground black pepper

1. In a large serving bowl, combine the cabbage, daikon, carrots, scallion, and cilantro. Set aside.

2. In a small bowl, whisk together the ginger, lime juice, vinegar, sesame oil, tamari, sugar, and salt and pepper to taste until well blended. Pour the dressing over the vegetables and toss gently to coat well. Taste and adjust the seasonings.

3. Refrigerate, covered, until ready to serve. This slaw will keep for up to 3 days, although the flavors will get stronger the longer it sits. Serve chilled.

SERVES 4 TO 6

"Cool" Slaw

Cole slaw has a long history in America, having arrived in the 1620s with Dutch immigrants, who called it *koolsla*, which means "cabbage salad." Originally made with shredded cabbage and a boiled dressing, it now exists in many variations, including those made with vegetables other than cabbage.

Quinoa Tabbouleh

This classic Middle Eastern salad is normally made with bulgur, tomato, and loads of chopped parsley and mint. Here it is given a new twist with quinoa, the protein-rich "super grain" of the Incas, and yellow tomatoes, although red tomatoes may be substituted if yellow are unavailable. Be sure to rinse the quinoa well before using to remove the bitter white coating called saponin. Fresh cilantro replaces the mint, and the optional tiny red adzuki beans can be added for substance. These mild-tasting, highly digestible beans are available dried or canned at natural food stores.

1 cup quinoa
2 cups water
Salt
2 medium-size, ripe yellow tomatoes,
    seeded and chopped
1/4 cup minced red onion
1/2 cup cooked or canned adzuki beans
    (optional), drained and rinsed

Leaves from 1 bunch fresh parsley,
    minced
3 tablespoons chopped fresh cilantro
    leaves
1/3 cup olive oil
2 tablespoons fresh lemon juice
Freshly ground black pepper

1. Wash the quinoa thoroughly to remove any trace of the bitter white coating, then rinse and drain.
2. Bring the water to a boil in a medium-size saucepan. Add salt to taste and the quinoa. Reduce the heat to low, cover, and simmer until all the water is absorbed, about 15 minutes. Blot the quinoa with paper towels to remove excess moisture.
3. Place the quinoa in a large serving bowl and set aside to cool. Add the tomatoes, onion, adzuki beans (if using), parsley, and cilantro.
4. In a small bowl, whisk together the olive oil, lemon juice, and salt and pepper to taste until blended. Pour the dressing over the salad and toss well to combine.
5. Cover and refrigerate for at least 1 hour before serving. For the best flavor, this salad should be served the day it is made. Serve chilled.

SERVES 4 TO 6

Ancient Grains on Wild Greens

Kamut, a large-grain member of the wheat family, is said to have its origins in ancient Egypt, while quinoa, a small protein-rich grain with a faintly popcorn-like aroma, is called "the mother grain" by the Incas. Together, they are tossed in a light vinaigrette and served on a bed of mesclun for a hearty salad that is visually appealing and full of great taste and nutrition.

1/3 cup olive oil

2 tablespoons balsamic vinegar

1 garlic clove, minced

1 tablespoon Dijon mustard

Salt and freshly ground black pepper

6 cups mesclun salad mix

2 cups cooked kamut (page 220)

2 cups cooked quinoa (page 220)

1 cup cherry tomatoes, cut in half

1 large cucumber, peeled, seeded, and
   thinly sliced

1 small carrot, shredded

1/3 cup chopped pecans

3 scallions, minced

1. In a small bowl, whisk together the olive oil, vinegar, garlic, mustard, and salt and pepper to taste until blended. Set aside.

2. Place the salad greens in a large bowl. Add about half the dressing and toss gently to coat lightly. Divide the dressed greens among 4 salad plates.

3. Place the kamut and quinoa in the same bowl and add the remaining dressing. Stir to combine. Mound 1/2 cup of each of the grains in the center of each salad plate on top of the greens. Arrange the tomatoes and cucumber slices decoratively alongside the grains. Scatter the carrot, pecans, and scallions over the salads and top with several grindings of black pepper. Serve immediately.

SERVES 4

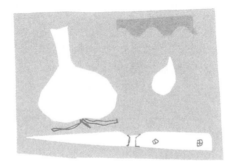

Asian Noodle Salad with Spicy Peanut Sauce

Crisp vegetables play nicely against the chewy noodles and creamy sauce. The ingredients are available at Asian markets and many supermarkets. The salad components may be made ahead, covered, and refrigerated. When ready to serve, bring the sauce to room temperature, thinning with additional water, if necessary. Udon noodles are thick Japanese wheat noodles. If they're unavailable, linguine may be substituted.

3/4 cup smooth natural peanut butter

1/4 cup tamari or other soy sauce

2 tablespoons rice vinegar

1 tablespoon Asian chili paste

3 garlic cloves, minced

1/2 cup water

12 ounces udon noodles

1 tablespoon toasted sesame oil

1 large carrot, shredded

2 cups cored and finely shredded napa cabbage

1/2 small red bell pepper, seeded and cut into matchsticks

1 bunch scallions, minced

1. In a medium-size bowl, combine the peanut butter, tamari, vinegar, chili paste, and garlic, stirring to blend well. Add the water, whisking to make a thick sauce. Set aside.

2. Cook the noodles in large pot of boiling water until just tender, 6 to 8 minutes. Drain and rinse the noodles under cold running water, then transfer to a large serving bowl. Toss with the sesame oil to coat.

3. Add the carrot, cabbage, bell pepper, and scallions to the noodles. Add just enough of the peanut sauce to coat, tossing gently to combine. Serve at room temperature.

SERVES 4

Five-Spice Moroccan Couscous Salad

Heady Moroccan spices add an exotic touch to this colorful salad bursting with flavor. Although couscous is often thought of as a grain, it is actually bits of dried semolina.

¼ cup peanut oil

¼ teaspoon turmeric

¼ teaspoon ground cinnamon

¼ teaspoon ground ginger

¼ teaspoon ground cumin

¼ teaspoon cayenne

1½ cups instant couscous

2½ cups Basic Vegetable Stock
    (page 68) or water

3 tablespoons orange juice

1 teaspoon light brown sugar or
    natural sweetener

Salt

1½ cups cooked or one 15-ounce can
    chickpeas, drained and rinsed

1 small red onion, finely chopped

½ large red bell pepper, seeded and
    cut into ¼-inch pieces

⅓ cup dates, pitted and chopped

¼ cup golden raisins

2 tablespoons minced fresh cilantro
    leaves for garnish

2 tablespoons chopped unsalted
    dry-roasted peanuts for garnish

1. Heat 1 tablespoon of the peanut oil in a medium-size saucepan over medium heat. Add the turmeric, cinnamon, ginger, cumin, cayenne, and couscous. Cook, stirring, until fragrant, about 2 minutes, being careful not to burn. Stir in the stock and bring to a boil. Reduce the heat to very low, cover, and cook until all the liquid is absorbed, about 5 minutes. Remove from the heat and let stand for 5 minutes.

2. Transfer the couscous to a large serving bowl, using a fork to fluff it up. Set aside.

3. In a small bowl, combine the remaining 3 tablespoons peanut oil, orange juice, brown sugar, and salt to taste. Stir to blend well and set aside.

4. To the couscous, add the chickpeas, onion, bell pepper, dates, and raisins. Add the dressing and toss gently to combine well. Garnish with the cilantro and peanuts and serve.

SERVES 4

Springy Tarragon Pasta Salad with Roasted Asparagus and Baked Tofu

"Springy" because of the pencil-thin asparagus plentiful at that time of year, but also for the rotini pasta "springs" that are used in the salad. Fresh tarragon adds a sweetly aromatic accent. Baked tofu is available in natural food stores, or you can make your own.

8 ounces rotini

1/4 cup plus 1 tablespoon extra virgin olive oil

1 pound thin asparagus, bottoms trimmed

Salt and freshly ground black pepper

2 tablespoons fresh lemon juice

Cayenne

1/2 medium-size yellow bell pepper, seeded and chopped

2 shallots, minced

1 large, ripe yellow tomato, seeded and diced

8 ounces baked tofu, homemade (page 13) or store-bought, cut into small cubes

2 tablespoons minced fresh tarragon leaves

1. Cook the pasta in a pot of boiling salted water, stirring occasionally, until *al dente*, 8 to 10 minutes. Drain and rinse under cold running water. Place in a large bowl, toss with 1 teaspoon of the olive oil, and set aside.

2. Preheat the oven to 425 degrees F. Place the asparagus on a lightly oiled baking sheet, season with salt and pepper to taste, and drizzle with 1 teaspoon of the olive oil. Roast until soft and lightly browned, about 10 minutes. Set aside to cool.

3. In a small bowl, combine the lemon juice and salt and cayenne to taste. Whisk in the remaining olive oil until blended and pour over the pasta. Add the bell pepper, shallots, tomato, tofu, and tarragon and toss to combine well.

4. Divide among 4 individual plates and top with the asparagus. Serve immediately.

SERVES 4

Pasta Salad Niçoise

Classic *salade niçoise* ingredients team up with penne pasta for a great-tasting Mediterranean fusion salad perfect for *al fresco* dining. Accompany with grilled portobello mushrooms and crusty bread for a terrific meal.

1 pound penne
1/2 cup extra virgin olive oil
1 1/2 cups trimmed green beans,
 blanched in salted boiling water
 until crisp tender, for 3 to 5 minutes, and drained
1 1/2 cups cooked or one 15-ounce can
 cannellini or other white beans,
 drained and rinsed
1 cup cherry or grape tomatoes,
 cut in half

1/3 cup niçoise olives, pitted
1/4 cup minced fresh parsley leaves
1/4 cup white wine vinegar
1 garlic clove, pressed
2 teaspoons Dijon mustard
1/2 teaspoon salt
Freshly ground black pepper
Salad greens

1. Cook the penne in a pot of boiling salted water, stirring occasionally, until *al dente*, 8 to 10 minutes. Drain, rinse under cold running water, and place in a large bowl.

2. To the pasta add 1 tablespoon of the olive oil, the green beans, cannellini beans, tomatoes, olives, and parsley. Toss gently to combine.

3. In a small bowl, combine the vinegar, garlic, mustard, salt, and pepper to taste. Whisk in the remaining olive oil and add to the pasta and vegetables. Toss gently to coat evenly. Taste and adjust the seasonings.

4. Divide the salad greens among 4 individual plates, top with the pasta salad, and serve.

SERVES 4

Lighten Up Macaroni Salad

When I crave the old-fashioned macaroni salad I grew up with, I "lighten up" and make it with heart-healthy soy. Serve it alongside grilled tofu hot dogs and veggie burgers for a healthful cookout with all the trimmings.

8 ounces elbow macaroni

1/2 cup minced celery

1/2 cup drained soft silken tofu

1/3 cup soy milk or other dairy-free milk

1/4 cup grated onion

1/4 cup sweet pickle relish

1 tablespoon fresh lemon juice

1 teaspoon Dijon mustard

1/2 teaspoon salt

Cayenne

1. Cook the elbows in a pot of boiling salted water, stirring occasionally, until *al dente*, about 8 minutes. Drain, rinse under cold running water, and transfer to a large serving bowl. Add the celery and set aside.

2. In a blender or food processor, combine the tofu and soy milk and process until smooth. Add the onion, relish, lemon juice, mustard, salt, and cayenne to taste and blend well. Add the tofu mixture to the pasta and mix well to coat evenly. Taste and adjust the seasonings.

3. Cover with plastic wrap and refrigerate for at least 1 hour before serving. Serve chilled.

SERVES 4

Pasta Salad: The Rinse Cycle

When cooking pasta for salad, be sure to rinse it after it's cooked. This will stop the cooking process and wash away the outer coating of starch, which would otherwise make your pasta gummy, sticking to itself and the other ingredients.

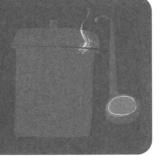

Summer Sunshine Pasta Salad

Evocative of a summer day, seashell and butterfly pasta combine with broccoli florets and sunflower seeds for a whimsical ray of sunshine any time of year. If serving as an entrée, add cooked chickpeas or kidney beans to the salad.

8 ounces farfalle

1/4 teaspoon turmeric

8 ounces small pasta shells

1/3 cup plus 1 tablespoon extra virgin olive oil

2 cups broccoli florets

Juice and grated zest of 1 orange

2 tablespoons fresh lemon juice

Salt

Cayenne

1 small yellow bell pepper, seeded and cut into thin strips

1 small red onion, chopped

1 cup cherry or grape tomatoes, cut in half

1/4 cup hulled raw sunflower seeds

1. Cook the farfalle in a pot of boiling salted water, stirring occasionally, until *al dente*, 8 to 10 minutes. While the farfalle is cooking, add the turmeric to the water to turn the pasta a bright yellow color.

2. Cook the pasta shells in a separate pot of boiling salted water, stirring occasionally, until *al dente*, about 8 minutes. Drain the farfalle and shells and rinse under cold running water. Place in a large serving bowl, toss with the 1 tablespoon olive oil, and set aside.

3. In a medium-size saucepan of boiling salted water, blanch the broccoli until bright green, about 30 seconds. Drain, rinse under cold running water, and add to the pasta.

4. In a small bowl, combine the orange juice and zest, lemon juice, and salt and cayenne to taste. Whisk in the remaining 1/3 cup olive oil until blended, then pour the dressing over the pasta. Add the bell pepper, onion, and tomatoes and toss to coat evenly with the dressing. Sprinkle on the sunflower seeds right before serving.

SERVES 4 TO 6

Cumin-Spiced Wagon Wheels with Jalapeño Pesto

Ruote, sometimes called rotelle, are shaped like the small wagon wheels of the Old West—a fitting choice for this taste of the Southwest. Cumin, jalapeños, and lime juice add a nice piquant touch to this substantial salad.

2 tablespoons extra virgin olive oil

1 teaspoon ground cumin

12 ounces ruote or rotelle

1 small red onion, chopped

Jalapeño pesto:

2 jalapeños, seeded

1 large garlic clove, peeled

1/2 cup cooked or canned pinto beans, drained and rinsed

1/4 cup coarsely chopped fresh parsley leaves

2 tablespoons fresh lime juice

1 teaspoon light brown sugar or natural sweetener

1/2 teaspoon chili powder

Salt

1/3 cup extra virgin olive oil

Salad greens

1. Heat the olive oil in a small skillet over medium heat. Add the cumin and stir until fragrant, about 30 seconds. Remove from the heat and set aside.

2. Cook the pasta in a pot of boiling salted water, stirring occasionally, until *al dente*, 8 to 10 minutes. Drain, rinse under cold running water, and place in a large bowl. Add the cumin-scented oil and onion and toss to combine. Set aside.

3. To make the pesto, process the jalapeños and garlic in a food processor until minced. Add the pinto beans, parsley, lime juice, brown sugar, chili powder, and salt to taste. With the machine running, add the olive oil and process to form a smooth paste. Add the pesto to the pasta and toss to coat.

4. Line 4 to 6 individual plates with the salad greens. Divide the pasta salad among the plates and serve at room temperature.

SERVES 4 TO 6

ORANGES AT CHRISTMAS

Each Christmas, a favorite relative sends us a case of sweet Florida oranges as a gift. I'm always thrilled when they arrive because, to me, it's not the holiday season without oranges. This association comes from my childhood, when I'd always find an orange in my stocking on Christmas morning. Whatever gifts waited under the tree, I'd make a beeline for my stocking, which held small treasures such as tiny puzzles and games, gold foil–wrapped chocolate coins, candy canes, and—at the very bottom—one perfect orange.

Placing an orange in each Christmas stocking has long been a family tradition. This practice is believed to have begun a few generations back when the now familiar fruit was a rare and precious treat. Even though oranges originated in China more than 4,000 years ago, it is only during the past century that they have become common in the United States. Oranges are now widely available year round, with most varieties designated for either juicing or eating. They keep well in the refrigerator but taste best when brought to room temperature before eating. In addition to the sheer pleasure of eating oranges out of hand, they add a refreshing sparkle to salads, dressings, sauces, and desserts.

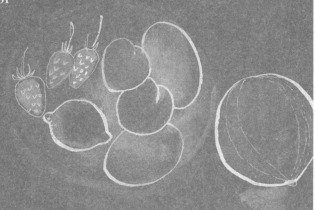

Tropical Pasta Salad with Fresh Fruit and Coconut

Juicy fresh fruit and creamy coconut milk add a taste of the tropics to this colorful salad. Try it on a warm summer night served with jerk-spiced tempeh cooked on the grill. For a spectacular presentation, serve in hollowed-out pineapple shells (cut in half lengthwise).

12 ounces small pasta shells

2 cups fresh pineapple chunks

1 medium-size, ripe mango, peeled, pitted, and cut into 1/2-inch pieces

1 navel orange, peeled, white pith removed, and cut into 1-inch chunks

1 small red bell pepper, seeded and cut into thin strips

1/3 cup minced celery

2 tablespoons minced scallions

2 tablespoons chopped fresh mint leaves

1 cup unsweetened coconut milk

1/2 cup orange juice

Juice and grated zest of 1 lime

1 teaspoon light brown sugar or natural sweetener, or to taste

1/8 teaspoon ground allspice

1/8 teaspoon cayenne

Salt

Salad greens

1/4 cup unsweetened shredded coconut, toasted (page 491)

1. Cook the pasta in a pot of boiling salted water, stirring occasionally, until *al dente*, about 8 minutes. Drain, rinse under cold running water, and place in a large bowl. Add the pineapple, mango, orange, bell pepper, celery, scallions, and mint and set aside.

2. In a small bowl, combine the coconut milk, orange juice, lime juice and zest, brown sugar, allspice, cayenne, and salt to taste. Mix well. Pour the dressing over the pasta salad and toss gently to coat evenly.

3. Arrange the salad greens on 4 individual plates. Divide the pasta salad among the plates, sprinkle with the toasted coconut, and serve.

SERVE 4 TO 6

5

Sauces & Dressings

From the simple vinaigrette to the temperamental hollandaise, the world of dressings and sauces is vast. Used to enhance and even define many salads, vegetables, pastas, and desserts, sauces can be the most important flavor elements of numerous dishes.

Included in the sweeping category of dressings and sauces are the roux-thickened brown and béchamel sauces, as well as egg-based hollandaise and mayonnaise, characteristic of the classic European kitchen. Thanks to the innovations of nouvelle cuisine in the 1970s, however, lighter sauces also have become popular. Although many traditional sauces are made with butter, cream, and eggs, as you will see in this chapter, even these can be made without dairy products, using soy products, nut butters, and bean purees instead. As an added benefit, sauces made with these protein-rich ingredients are low in fat and cholesterol-free.

Also included in this chapter are Asian soy-based sauces, oil-based dressings, tomato sauces, and many tempting toppings made with vegetable and fruit purees, ground herbs, beans, and seeds.

Many of the sauces presented here require no cooking, making them simple to whip up in a blender or food processor.

Tofu Sour Cream

This sour cream alternative couldn't be easier. Blend in some minced chives and try it on baked potatoes, or use it in recipes calling for sour cream.

6 ounces soft silken tofu, drained

1 1/2 tablespoons fresh lemon juice

1 tablespoon sunflower oil or other
    neutral-tasting oil

1/2 teaspoon salt

1/4 teaspoon sugar or natural sweetener
    (optional)

1. Place all the ingredients in a food processor or blender and process until smooth and creamy.

2. Transfer to a container with a tight-fitting lid. Cover and refrigerate until ready to use, up to 3 to 4 days.

MAKES ABOUT 1 CUP

Soy Mayonnaise

This is a lowfat, cholesterol-free version of the versatile condiment. Use it in any way you'd use the original—from sandwich spread to salad dressing. If you prefer the convenience of store-bought, vegan mayonnaise is available commercially in natural food stores and some supermarkets.

6 ounces firm silken tofu, drained
1 1/2 tablespoons white wine vinegar
1/4 teaspoon dry mustard
1/2 teaspoon salt

Pinch of sugar or natural sweetener (optional)
3 tablespoons corn oil or other neutral-tasting oil

1. Place the tofu, vinegar, mustard, salt, and sugar (if using) in a food processor or blender and process until smooth. With the machine running, slowly add the corn oil in a thin stream through the feed tube until it is incorporated. Taste and adjust the seasonings.

2. Transfer to a glass jar or other container with a tight-fitting lid. Cover and refrigerate until ready to use, up to 4 to 5 days.

MAKES ABOUT 1 CUP

Did You Know...

Soy products are high in protein and a good source of calcium, B vitamins, phosphorus, and potassium? In addition, soy has been shown to help lower blood cholesterol in some people.

7 Great Reasons to Eat Soy Every Day

The versatile soybean comes in many guises, from tofu and tempeh to soy nuts and edamame. By eating soy foods every day, you can do the following:

1. Boost your immune system. Studies show that soybean peptides can boost the immune system, helping the body fight disease.

2. Live longer. Soy foods contain isoflavones—phytonutrients that are believed to increase longevity. Studies done with Seventh-Day Adventists show that they live on average between 4.5 and 7 years longer than the rest of the population; the major lifestyle difference is that they are vegetarians who eat soy regularly. The country with the longest average life span is Japan, where people eat soy in abundance.

3. Reduce hot flashes. Half of all menopausal women in the United States complain of hot flashes, a problem that is so rare in Japan (where they eat lots of soy) that there's not even a word for it. Some researchers believe that this is due to the phytoestrogens found in soy foods.

4. Enjoy easy, delicious meals. You can enjoy almost all of your favorite meals by simply replacing high-fat, artery-clogging meat, eggs, and dairy with versatile soy foods, which can be used to mimic the flavors and textures of your old-style dishes—all with no cholesterol, fewer calories, lots of fiber, and plenty of great taste.

5. Help prevent cancer. Soy foods contain antioxidants—compounds that protect cells from damage caused by free radicals, which are believed to cause many forms of cancer. Numerous studies link regular consumption of soy foods to significantly lower rates of breast cancer, colon cancer, and prostate cancer, among others.

6. Reduce the risks of osteoporosis and kidney disease. Studies suggest that soy may help retain bone mass. Soy protein is easier for the kidneys to process than animal protein.

7. Lower your cholesterol. Scores of studies from around the world attest to soy's cholesterol-lowering properties, especially for people with high cholesterol levels. One study showed that consumption of 25 to 47 grams of soy protein per day can reduce cholesterol levels by an average of 9.3 percent in a month in people with high cholesterol.

Red Bell Pepper and Caper Mayonnaise

There are a number of mayonnaise-based sauces in French cooking that can be used in a variety of ways. Among the most versatile (and flavorful) are rémoulade, made with fresh herbs and capers, and andalouse, made with tomato and red bell pepper. I've combined elements of the two using soy mayonnaise, resulting in a flavorful sauce that can be used on veggie burgers, on grilled or steamed vegetables, or as a binder for chopped vegetable salads.

1 cup soy mayonnaise, homemade
  (page 140) or store-bought
1 tablespoon tomato paste
1/4 teaspoon Tabasco sauce
1/3 cup chopped roasted red bell pepper
  (page 143)

1 tablespoon capers, drained and
  minced
1 tablespoon minced fresh parsley
  leaves
Salt

In a small bowl, combine the mayonnaise, tomato paste, and Tabasco. Stir in the roasted pepper, capers, parsley, and salt to taste. Blend thoroughly, then cover and refrigerate until ready to use, up to 3 to 5 days. Serve chilled.

MAKES ABOUT 1 1/4 CUPS

"While we ourselves are the living graves of murdered beasts, how can we expect any ideal conditions on this earth?"
—GEORGE BERNARD SHAW

Roasted Red Bell Peppers

Roasting bell peppers gives them a deep, rich flavor, which may account for their amazing popularity on everything from salads and sandwiches to entrées and pizza. Although you can buy roasted red peppers in the supermarket, try making them yourself with fresh peppers. They are much more flavorful.

2 large red bell peppers

1. Hold the peppers over an open flame with a pair of tongs or place on a baking sheet under a preheated broiler until the skin is blackened on all sides.

2. Place the charred peppers in a paper bag and let stand for 5 minutes to steam. Remove from the bag and scrape off the charred skin. Cut open and remove the stem, seeds, and white ribs. The peppers are now ready to use in recipes.

Roasted peppers will keep for up to 1 week in the refrigerator if properly stored. For best results, place them in a tightly sealed container (a glass jar is ideal) and cover with olive oil.

MAKES ABOUT 1¹/₂ CUPS

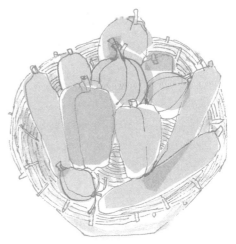

Rouille Redux

Try this egg-free version of the garlicky red mayonnaise from France on grilled or steamed vegetables or as a dipping sauce for crudités. It's also delicious as a spread on sandwiches or veggie wraps.

2 or 3 garlic cloves, to your taste, peeled
1/3 cup canned pimientos, drained
1 cup soy mayonnaise, homemade
   (page 140) or store-bought

Pinch of cayenne
Salt

1. Place the garlic and pimientos in a blender or food processor and process until smooth. Add the soy mayonnaise, cayenne, and salt to taste and process again until smooth.
2. Transfer to a tightly covered container and store in the refrigerator for up to 3 to 5 days.

MAKES ABOUT 1¼ CUPS

Eggless Hollandaise

Healthful hollandaise may sound like an oxymoron, but with this eggless, butter-free version, you can literally dip your asparagus to your heart's content. Add the turmeric if you want a brighter yellow color.

2/3 cup soy mayonnaise, homemade
   (page 140) or store-bought
1 tablespoon fresh lemon juice
1 teaspoon Dijon mustard

Pinch of cayenne
Pinch of turmeric (optional)
Salt

Place all the ingredients in a food processor or blender and process until smooth. This will keep, tightly covered, in the refrigerator for up to 3 days.

MAKES ABOUT 1 CUP

Faux Choron Sauce

Many years ago, I worked in a restaurant that served choron sauce, an opulent variation of hollandaise sauce that combined chopped tomato in a tangy béarnaise (a hollandaise flavored with a white wine, shallot, and tarragon reduction). Here's my vegan version, which tastes amazingly like the original. It's delicious served with grilled or steamed vegetables or sautéed seitan. I especially like it with the roasted cauliflower on page 199.

$^1/_3$ cup dry white wine

2 shallots, minced

$1^1/_2$ teaspoons minced fresh tarragon leaves or $^1/_2$ teaspoon dried

$^2/_3$ cup soy mayonnaise, homemade (page 140) or store-bought

Pinch of cayenne

Pinch of turmeric (optional)

Salt

1 large, ripe tomato, peeled, seeded, and finely chopped

1. Place the wine, shallots, and tarragon in a small saucepan over medium-high heat and boil until the liquid is reduced by one half.

2. Place the reduced wine mixture in a food processor or blender along with the soy mayonnaise, cayenne, turmeric (if using), and salt to taste and process until smooth. Stir in the tomato, then taste and adjust the seasonings. This will keep, tightly covered, in the refrigerator for 2 to 3 days.

MAKES ABOUT 1 CUP

Vegan Béchamel Sauce

This rich, creamy white sauce is wonderful because it is protein-rich, dairy-free, and delicious. Use it anytime you want a creamy white sauce without the cream.

1 tablespoon corn oil or other
   neutral-tasting oil
1/4 cup grated yellow onion
1 tablespoon dry white wine
1/4 cup raw cashews

1 1/2 cups soy milk or other dairy-free
   milk
1/2 cup drained soft silken tofu
Pinch of freshly grated nutmeg
Salt and freshly ground black pepper

1. Heat the corn oil in a small skillet over medium-low heat. Add the onion, cover, and cook until softened, about 5 minutes. Do not brown. Stir in the wine and set aside.

2. Place the cashews in a blender or food processor and grind into a powder. Add 3/4 cup of the soy milk and process until smooth. Add the remaining 3/4 cup soy milk and the tofu and process until blended. Add the onion mixture and process until thoroughly smooth.

3. Transfer to a medium-size saucepan over low heat. Season with the nutmeg and salt and pepper to taste. Serve hot.

MAKES ABOUT 2 1/2 CUPS

New Millennium Mornay

Classic Mornay sauce is made by adding grated Gruyère or a similar cheese to a basic béchamel or white sauce. Thanks to the popularity of lighter sauces, you don't see this heavy, high-fat sauce all that much anymore. Still, for macaroni and cheese and similar casseroles, a creamy, cheesy sauce is essential—or is it? Instead, try this vegan "cheese" sauce for the 21st century to bind your next casserole or as a creamy adornment for steamed broccoli. Nutritional yeast flakes are available at natural food stores. They add a "cheesy" flavor to recipes.

1 cup cooked or canned cannellini or other white beans, drained and rinsed

1 tablespoon chopped onion

2 tablespoons tahini (sesame paste)

1 tablespoon mellow white miso paste

1 tablespoon nutritional yeast flakes

1/2 cup soy milk or other dairy-free milk

1 1/2 tablespoons fresh lemon juice

Salt

Cayenne

1. Place the beans, onion, tahini, miso, and nutritional yeast in a blender or food processor and process until smooth. Add the soy milk and lemon juice, season with salt and cayenne to taste, and process until creamy.

2. Use as is in casserole recipes. To use as a sauce for vegetables, warm in a saucepan over low heat, stirring constantly, being careful not to boil.

MAKES ABOUT 1 1/2 CUPS

Basic Brown Sauce

As the name implies, this is the most basic of brown sauces. Instead of the traditional roux thickener (butter or oil and flour), it is thickened with cornstarch. Additions to this infinitely versatile sauce include minced herbs, sautéed shallots, or a splash of wine. It also can be transformed into a creamy gravy with the addition of 1/4 cup of soy milk. Use it like a gravy over mashed potatoes or rice, veggie meat loaf, stuffed portobellos, sautéed seitan, or veggie burgers.

2 cups Basic Vegetable Stock
   (page 68)
2 tablespoons tamari or other soy sauce

1 tablespoon cornstarch dissolved in
   2 tablespoons water
Salt and freshly ground black pepper

Combine the stock and tamari in a small saucepan over high heat and bring to a boil. Reduce the heat to low, whisk in the cornstarch mixture, and stir until the sauce thickens, 2 to 3 minutes. Season with salt and pepper to taste and serve hot.

MAKES ABOUT 2 CUPS

Double Mushroom Sauce

Fresh and dried mushrooms deepen the flavor of this sauce, which can be used in the same ways as Basic Brown Sauce (page 148) but provides more texture and flavor. Die-hard mushroom lovers might want to use Mushroom Stock instead of Basic Vegetable Stock for a triple layering of mushroom flavor.

1/2 cup dried porcini or other mushrooms, soaked in 1 cup very hot water for 20 minutes
1 tablespoon olive oil
3 shallots, minced
1 cup sliced white mushrooms

1 1/2 cups Basic Vegetable Stock (page 68) or Mushroom Stock (page 69)
1 tablespoon tamari or other soy sauce
Salt and freshly ground black pepper
1 tablespoon cornstarch dissolved in 2 tablespoons water

1. Drain the mushrooms, reserving the soaking liquid. Strain the liquid and set aside. Chop the mushrooms.

2. Heat the olive oil in a medium-size saucepan over medium heat. Add the shallots, cover, and cook until softened, about 5 minutes. Add all the mushrooms and cook for 2 minutes. Stir in the stock, tamari, and reserved mushroom soaking liquid and season with salt and pepper to taste. Bring to a boil, then reduce the heat to low. Whisk in the cornstarch mixture and cook, stirring, until thickened, 2 to 3 minutes. Serve hot.

MAKES ABOUT 2 CUPS

Summertime Tomato Sauce

The window of opportunity for making sauce with fresh, ripe tomatoes is woefully brief, but if you have a bumper crop and want to dress your pasta with the fresh taste of summer, this is the way to go. You can also make a raw version of this sauce—just combine the ingredients, leaving the garlic whole but crushed. Let the sauce stand in a covered bowl at room temperature for one hour, then remove the garlic before tossing with hot pasta. In addition to pasta, I like to use this simple, fresh-tasting sauce with steamed green beans or as a dipping sauce for fried potato sticks.

3 pounds ripe tomatoes
2 tablespoons olive oil
1 large garlic clove, minced

Salt and freshly ground black pepper
1 tablespoon chopped fresh parsley or
   basil leaves

1. Core the tomatoes by cutting out the stem end. Score a small X in the bottom of each tomato and plunge them into boiling water for 30 seconds. Remove from the water and plunge into ice water to stop the cooking process. Peel off the skins—they will come off easily. Cut each tomato in half crosswise and remove the seeds. Coarsely chop the tomatoes and set aside.

2. Heat the olive oil in a large saucepan over medium heat. Add the garlic and cook until fragrant, about 30 seconds. Add the tomatoes, season with salt and pepper to taste, and simmer for 20 minutes to reduce the liquid and thicken the sauce. Add the parsley, then taste and adjust the seasonings. This sauce can be frozen, but to fully appreciate the flavor of the fresh tomatoes, it's best to enjoy it within a day or two of making it.

MAKES ABOUT 3 CUPS

9 COMPELLING ETHICAL REASONS TO GO VEGAN

A vegan lifestyle is one of compassion, nonviolence, and respect for all sentient life. The slaughter of animals for food is a violent act, but modern agriculture inflicts other extraordinary cruelties that add incentive for going vegan.

1. More than 7 billion animals die each year for human consumption. That's more than 600,000 animals killed every hour in the United States alone. The average American eats 2,600 animals in his or her lifetime. Going vegan can help end the needless suffering and deaths of thousands of animals.

2. Food animals are not protected by the Animal Welfare Act. With virtually no laws to protect them, cruelty and abuse on farms go unchecked.

3. Lack of enforcement of the Humane Slaughter Act allows cattle, pigs, horses, and sheep to be shackled and throat-slit without first being stunned. Animals often are skinned, boiled, and butchered alive.

4. Factory-farm hens are forced to live in "battery" cages—stacked in rows 4 high—by the thousands. Each hen is confined to a tiny space, where it ends up suffering from blisters, bare wings, torn feet, and bloody combs. "Spent" birds are sometimes ground up while alive to be used as feed for the next flock.

5. A factory-farm dairy cow must endure a painfully swollen udder and spend her entire life in a stall, being milked up to 3 times a day. She is kept pregnant most of her life, and her young are usually taken from her at birth.

6. Egg producers can force spent hens to lay again by starving them for up to 14 days. No U.S. law prevents this practice.

7. Sick or crippled animals, called downers, are not protected from cruelty by federal law. These animals are bulldozed or dragged by chains and may be left to starve or freeze to death.

8. Mutilation occurs throughout animal agriculture. Animals are branded, ear-notched, and tail-docked. Birds are debeaked to reduce stress-related violence. Bulls, calves, and piglets are routinely castrated.

9. Veal calves—byproducts of the dairy industry—are locked up in stalls and chained by the neck so they cannot turn around their entire lives. They are kept in darkness and fed a diet without iron or roughage in order to produce tender, milky white meat.

Tomato Sauce in Winter

Actually, this is a good tomato sauce to serve in the spring, fall, and most of the summer, too—virtually anytime you don't have fresh, ripe tomatoes. Be sure you buy San Marzano tomatoes (available under various brand names at Italian markets and gourmet shops) for the best-tasting canned tomatoes. Omit the red pepper flakes if you prefer to delete the heat.

1 tablespoon olive oil
1 small yellow onion, minced
1 large garlic clove, minced
1/4 teaspoon red pepper flakes
    (optional)
2 tablespoons tomato paste

1/4 cup dry red wine
One 28-ounce can crushed tomatoes
Salt and freshly ground black pepper
1 tablespoon chopped fresh parsley
    leaves

1. Heat the olive oil in a large saucepan over medium heat. Add the onion and garlic and cook, stirring, until fragrant, about 1 minute, being careful not to burn the garlic. Stir in the red pepper flakes, if using, and tomato paste and cook, stirring, for 1 minute to heat through. Add the wine, blending until smooth. Stir in the crushed tomatoes and bring to a simmer. Reduce the heat to low, season with salt and pepper to taste, and cook for about 15 minutes to thicken the sauce, stirring occasionally.

2. Stir in the parsley, taste and adjust the seasonings, and serve hot. This sauce freezes well.

MAKES ABOUT 3 1/2 CUPS

Bourbon-Spiked Barbecue Sauce

If you prefer a nonalcoholic version, substitute apple juice for the bourbon. Use this sauce to make the tempeh recipe on page 344 or combine it with shredded seitan or vegetarian burger crumbles for a delicious meatless barbecue. Omit the chile for a mild version.

1 dried chipotle chile, soaked in very
    hot water to cover for 30 minutes
1 small yellow onion, cut into pieces
1 garlic clove, peeled
1 tablespoon olive oil
One 6-ounce can tomato paste
1/4 cup bourbon

1/4 cup molasses
2 tablespoons pure maple syrup
1 teaspoon dry mustard
1/4 cup tamari or other soy sauce
2 tablespoons cider vinegar
3/4 cup water
Salt and freshly ground black pepper

1. Drain the chile, cut into small pieces, and set aside.

2. Place the onion and garlic in a blender and process until smooth. Heat the olive oil in a large skillet over medium heat. Add the onion and garlic puree and cook, stirring a few times, to mellow the flavor, about 5 minutes.

3. Place the chipotle chile pieces in the blender and process until smooth. Add to the puree along with the tomato paste, bourbon, molasses, maple syrup, mustard, tamari, vinegar, and water. Bring to a boil, then reduce the heat to low. Season with salt and pepper to taste and simmer, stirring occasionally, until the sauce thickens slightly and the flavor develops, about 15 minutes. This sauce will keep for several days, tightly covered, in the refrigerator. It also freezes well.

MAKES ABOUT 2 CUPS

Gloria's Glorious Garlic Sauce

Necessity is often the mother of invention, and it was certainly true with this sauce. When her favorite brand of garlic sauce was no longer available, my friend and recipe tester Gloria Siegel wanted to develop a sauce to replace it. After much tinkering, we've come up with a versatile sauce that can be used on steamed or grilled vegetables or to perk up sauces and stews. I've even thinned it a little and used it as a salad dressing.

1 head garlic, broken into cloves
3 tablespoons extra virgin olive oil,
    plus more for drizzling
2 tablespoons blanched almonds

1 tablespoon balsamic vinegar
1/2 teaspoon salt
1 tablespoon water, or more as needed

1. Preheat the oven to 350 degrees F. Place the garlic cloves, with the skins still on, in a small baking dish. Drizzle with a bit of olive oil, cover tightly with aluminum foil, and bake until soft, about 45 minutes.

2. Remove the garlic from the skins and place in a blender or food processor. Add the almonds and process until smooth. Add the olive oil, vinegar, salt, and water and process until well blended. Add a little more water if a thinner consistency is desired.

3. Transfer to a container with a tight-fitting lid and refrigerate until ready to use, up to several days.

MAKES ABOUT 2/3 CUP

Did You Know...

Garlic has been widely touted for its medicinal properties? In addition to perking up bland-tasting food, garlic has been credited with relieving ailments such as the common cold, bronchitis, hypertension, and high cholesterol. Garlic was even used for its antibiotic properties during World War I.

Avocado-Wasabi Sauce

My favorite sushi roll is made with creamy avocado strips and fiery wasabi paste. Although these two ingredients are the same color, their flavors couldn't be more different. Here this odd couple joins forces to make a lovely green sauce with an Asian accent. Use it to dress salads, to spread on sandwiches, or as a dipping sauce for fried tofu.

1 large, ripe avocado, peeled and pitted
2 tablespoons fresh lemon juice
1 tablespoon chopped fresh cilantro or
    parsley leaves
1 scallion, minced

1 tablespoon toasted sesame oil
1 teaspoon tamari or other soy sauce
2 teaspoons wasabi powder
2/3 cup soy mayonnaise, homemade
    (page 140) or store-bought

1. Combine all the ingredients in a food processor or blender and process until smooth.

2. Transfer to a tightly covered container and refrigerate. This sauce is best used within an hour or so after it is made.

MAKES ABOUT 1¹/₂ CUPS

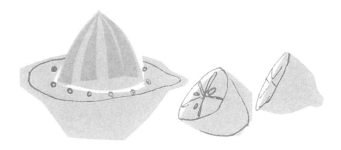

Mango Sunburst Sauce

This sauce is great for a number of reasons. Most obvious, of course, are its gorgeous golden orange color and fresh mango flavor. Also, it couldn't be easier to make. Use it as a dipping sauce for spring rolls, samosas, or fried tofu. If you omit the chili paste, you can transform it into a dessert sauce and serve it with cut fruit or sliced teacakes.

1 large, ripe mango

Juice of 1 orange

1/2 teaspoon Asian chili paste

1/2 teaspoon sugar or natural sweetener

1. Peel the mango and cut the flesh from the pit. Place the mango flesh in a blender or food processor with the remaining ingredients and process until smooth.
2. Transfer to a container, cover tightly, and refrigerate until ready to use. I like to use this sauce within 24 hours of making it for the best flavor.

MAKES ABOUT 1 CUP

Yellow Pepper Coulis

This smooth puree of sweet yellow bell peppers is especially good with grilled or steamed vegetables, but it can also be used to add flavor and color to soups, salad dressings, or other sauces.

1 tablespoon olive oil

1 small yellow onion, chopped

3 medium-size yellow bell peppers,
    seeded and chopped

1/4 cup water

Salt and freshly ground black pepper

1. Heat the olive oil in a large skillet over medium heat. Add the onion and bell peppers, cover, and cook, stirring a few times, until softened, about 5 minutes. Add the water, season with salt and pepper to taste, and cook until the vegetables are very soft, about 15 minutes.

2. Transfer the cooked vegetables to a food processor or blender and process until smooth.

3. Push the mixture through a fine-mesh strainer into a small saucepan and heat over low heat. Use immediately or allow to cool and store in a tightly sealed container until ready to use. Reheat over low heat.

MAKES ABOUT 2 CUPS

Basil Pesto with Variations

Pesto isn't just for pasta. You can use it to flavor salad dressings, swirl it into soups at serving time, or serve it with grilled vegetables or sliced ripe tomatoes. But the variations don't end there. Experiment with the ingredients themselves for different taste sensations. Try parsley and walnuts, or mint and almonds, instead of the usual basil and pine nuts. Pesto will keep in the refrigerator for several weeks. Before refrigerating it in a tightly sealed container, spread a thin layer of olive oil on top to prevent it from discoloring.

2 garlic cloves, peeled

$1/3$ cup pine nuts or other nuts (see headnote), toasted (page 110)

$1/2$ teaspoon salt

2 cups loosely packed fresh basil or other herb leaves (see headnote)

$1/4$ cup extra virgin olive oil

1. Finely grind the garlic, pine nuts, and salt together in a food processor or blender. Add the basil and process until minced. With the machine running, slowly add the olive oil in a steady stream through the feed tube until the pesto is blended into a paste.

2. Transfer to a bowl, cover tightly, and refrigerate until ready to use.

MAKES ABOUT 1$1/2$ CUPS

Black Bean Sauce with Jalapeños and Cilantro

If you can't take the heat, eliminate the jalapeños, and the sauce will still be delicious. Use it over grain dishes, polenta, veggie burgers, or sautéed tofu slices.

1 tablespoon olive oil

1 garlic clove, chopped

1 or 2 jalapeños, to your taste, seeded and minced

1/4 teaspoon ground cumin

1 1/2 cups or one 15-ounce can black beans, drained and rinsed

1 tablespoon tamari or other soy sauce

1 teaspoon fresh lime juice

1/3 cup water, or more as needed

2 tablespoons minced fresh cilantro leaves

1. Heat the olive oil in a large skillet over medium heat. Add the garlic and jalapeños and cook for 1 minute. Stir in the cumin, beans, and tamari and simmer for 5 minutes to blend the flavors.

2. Transfer the mixture to a blender or food processor, add the lime juice and water, and process until smooth.

3. Transfer to a medium-size saucepan and add the cilantro and more water, if necessary, to get the consistency you prefer. Taste and adjust the seasonings. Heat over low heat, stirring, until hot.

MAKES ABOUT 1 1/2 CUPS

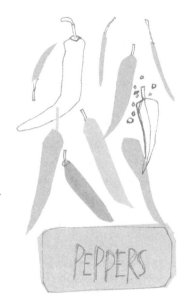

PEPPERS

Harissa

Use this Tunisian hot sauce in the traditional manner—to enliven vegetable tagines and similar stews from that part of the world—or use your imagination and let it spice up your life in unexpected ways: as a condiment for sautéed tofu or veggie burgers or as an addition to soy mayonnaise or any sauce where you want a bit of flavorful heat.

1/2 cup dried chiles, seeded, cut into small pieces, and soaked in very hot water to cover for 30 minutes
1 tablespoon caraway seeds
2 teaspoons coriander seeds
3 small, fresh hot chiles, seeded

5 garlic cloves, peeled
1/2 teaspoon salt
2 tablespoons extra virgin olive oil
1 tablespoon white wine vinegar
1/4 cup water

1. Drain the dried chiles and set aside.
2. Place the caraway and coriander seeds in a small skillet over low heat and toast them until fragrant, 1 to 2 minutes, stirring frequently so they don't burn. Remove from the heat and grind finely in a spice grinder.
3. In a food processor, grind the fresh chiles, garlic, ground spices, and salt. Add the dried chiles to the processor along with the olive oil, vinegar, and water. Process into a smooth paste. This will keep, tightly covered, in the refrigerator for several weeks.

MAKES ABOUT 1 CUP

Spicy Peanut Dipping Sauce

Serve this delicious and extremely versatile sauce with steamed vegetables or spring rolls (page 44), or toss with hot or cold cooked noodles.

1/2 cup smooth natural peanut butter
1 tablespoon minced garlic
1/4 cup tamari or other soy sauce
1/4 cup water, or more as needed
1 tablespoon rice vinegar

1 teaspoon Asian chili paste
1 teaspoon sugar or natural sweetener
2 tablespoons finely chopped fresh
    cilantro leaves

1. In a small bowl or food processor, combine the peanut butter, garlic, tamari, water, vinegar, chili paste, and sugar until well blended. Taste and adjust the seasonings. Add more water if the sauce is too thick.
2. Use at once, or cover and refrigerate until ready to use. Stir in the cilantro just before using. Stored properly, this sauce will keep for 4 to 5 days.

MAKES ABOUT 1 CUP

Ginger-Lime Dipping Sauce

This light and refreshing sauce is ideal with the scallion pancakes on page 59. It can also be used to dress a salad.

1 scallion, finely chopped
1 tablespoon peeled and minced
    fresh ginger
1 teaspoon minced garlic
1/2 cup tamari or other soy sauce

1/4 cup fresh lime juice
1 tablespoon rice vinegar
2 tablespoons toasted sesame oil
1/2 teaspoon red pepper flakes
1 teaspoon sugar or natural sweetener

1. In a small bowl, combine the scallion, ginger, and garlic. Stir in the tamari, lime juice, vinegar, sesame oil, red pepper flakes, and sugar. Blend well.

2. Cover tightly and refrigerate until ready to use. This sauce will keep for several days, but the flavors will intensify the longer it is kept.

MAKES ABOUT 1 CUP

Garlicky Herb Marinade

I especially like to use this marinade for tofu or portobello mushrooms. Sometimes I'll feature one herb prominently, and other times I'll include a pinch of virtually every herb in my garden. Feel free to vary the type and amount of herbs according to personal preference and availability.

3 large garlic cloves, chopped

1/2 cup tamari or other soy sauce

1/4 cup extra virgin olive oil

1/4 cup white wine vinegar

1/4 teaspoon salt

2 tablespoons minced fresh tarragon leaves

1 tablespoon minced fresh basil leaves

1 tablespoon minced fresh chervil leaves

In a small bowl, combine the garlic, tamari, olive oil, vinegar, and salt. Whisk until well blended. Stir in the tarragon, basil, and chervil. Cover and refrigerate until ready to use. Be sure to use this marinade the same day you make it to ensure the fresh taste of the herbs.

MAKES ABOUT 1 CUP

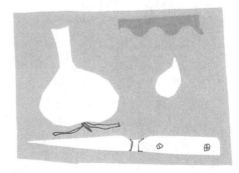

Fresh Herb and Scallion Dressing

This creamy dressing is bursting with the flavors of fresh herbs, which can be varied according to personal taste and availability. Use it to dress romaine lettuce, sliced ripe tomatoes, or a cucumber salad. It also makes a flavorful topping for baked potatoes.

3 scallions, minced

1/2 cup drained soft silken tofu

3 tablespoons extra virgin olive oil

2 tablespoons fresh lemon juice

1 tablespoon cider vinegar

1/2 teaspoon Dijon mustard

1/8 teaspoon Tabasco sauce

Salt and freshly ground black pepper

1/4 cup chopped fresh parsley leaves

2 tablespoons minced fresh basil, tarragon, dill, or other herb

1. In a food processor, combine the scallions, tofu, olive oil, lemon juice, vinegar, mustard, Tabasco, and salt and pepper to taste and process until smooth.

2. Transfer to small bowl and stir in the fresh herbs. Refrigerate, covered, until ready to use, up to 3 to 5 days.

MAKES ABOUT 1 CUP

Dressed for Success

The dressing can make or break a salad. No matter how crisp your lettuce, if the dressing you use is bitter, bland, or just plain blah, the entire salad will suffer. A good dressing doesn't have to be complicated—it just needs to enhance the flavors of the salad ingredients. It can be a simple vinaigrette consisting of nothing more than a good oil and vinegar blended in just the right amounts. Add a touch of salt and a grinding of pepper, and you can approach salad perfection. Extra virgin olive oil is standard, but other flavored oils, such as hazelnut, walnut, or sesame oil, may be used. The choice of vinegar can range from the deeply flavored balsamic, to lighter-tasting vinegars such as sherry, wine, or champagne, to those infused with fresh herbs or fruits. Remember to toss your salads with the dressing just before serving to keep the greens from wilting.

Balsamic Vinaigrette with Garlic and Sun-Dried Tomatoes

The addition of heady garlic and smoky sun-dried tomatoes adds an assertive note to the traditional oil and vinegar pairing. This dressing can also be made in a bowl or a jar with a tight-fitting lid. Simply chop the tomatoes and garlic before combining them with the rest of the ingredients. Then whisk or shake well. It can be used on almost any salad, and it stands up well to strong-flavored greens.

3 oil-packed or rehydrated sun-dried
  tomatoes
2 garlic cloves, crushed
1 shallot, chopped
1/2 teaspoon sugar or natural sweetener

1/4 teaspoon salt
3 tablespoons balsamic vinegar
1/2 cup extra virgin olive oil
Freshly ground black pepper

Place the tomatoes, garlic, shallot, sugar, and salt in a blender or food processor and process until smooth. Add the vinegar, olive oil, and pepper to taste and blend well. This will keep, tightly covered, in the refrigerator for up to 1 week.

MAKES ABOUT 3/4 CUP

6

Chutneys, Salsas, & Other Condiments

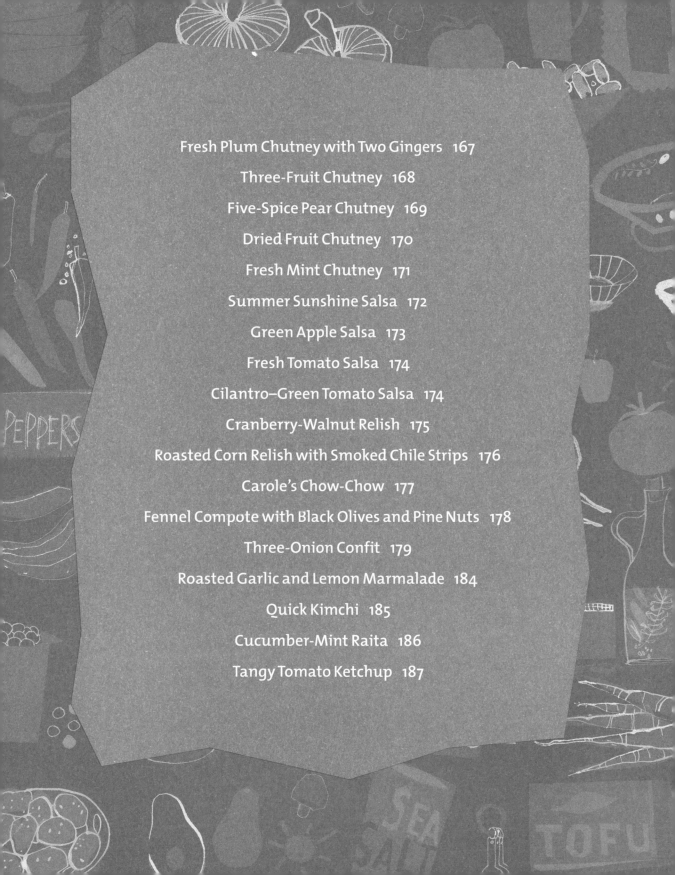

Like sauces, chutneys, salsas, and other condiments can be the crowning glory of a meal, often providing the flavor that defines the dish with which it is served.

Condiments not only add their special flavors to vegan foods, but they also can provide the link to make foods taste like familiar family favorites. Slather ketchup on a veggie burger, and you've got a great-tasting burger. Serve cranberry sauce or relish with a seitan roast and mashed potatoes, and it's suddenly Thanksgiving.

This chapter traverses the globe to deliver a selection of delectable condiments to enliven your next meal. Choose from a number of fresh salsas, from refreshing *Cilantro–Green Tomato Salsa* to vibrant *Summer Sunshine Salsa*, made with a variety of yellow vegetables. Tangy chutneys include *Fresh Plum Chutney with Two Gingers*, *Five-Spice Pear Chutney*, and tasty *Fresh Mint Chutney*, which looks more like pesto than a typical chutney. All-American favorites with a twist include *Roasted Corn Relish with Smoked Chile Strips*, *Tangy Tomato Ketchup*, and dazzling *Cranberry-Walnut Relish*. Sophisticated condiments such as *Three-Onion Confit* and *Fennel Compote with Black Olives and Pine Nuts* can elevate even the simplest fare.

Fresh Plum Chutney with Two Gingers

Fresh plums team up with two kinds of ginger in this fruity chutney, best made when plums are plentiful. Use underripe or barely ripe fruit for best results. You may use peaches instead of plums, if you prefer.

1½ pounds ripe plums
4 dates, pitted and chopped
3 shallots, finely chopped
½ small red bell pepper, seeded and minced
1 small, fresh hot chile, seeded and finely chopped
1 tablespoon peeled and minced fresh ginger

1 tablespoon chopped crystallized ginger
½ cup water
2 tablespoons balsamic vinegar
3 tablespoons sugar or natural sweetener
⅛ teaspoon salt

1. Cut a small X in the bottom of each plum and place in a large saucepan of boiling water for about 30 seconds. Drain and transfer to a bowl of cold water. Peel the skins from the plums, then pit and coarsely chop.

2. Place in a medium-size saucepan over medium heat. Add the remaining ingredients and bring to a boil. Reduce the heat to low and simmer, stirring occasionally, until the fruit and vegetables have softened and most of the liquid has evaporated, about 30 minutes. Taste and adjust the seasonings. Let cool to room temperature before serving.

3. If not serving right away, cover and refrigerate until ready to serve. Bring back to room temperature for the best flavor. This chutney is best used within 2 to 3 days.

MAKES ABOUT 2 CUPS

Three-Fruit Chutney

I like the balance of flavors with the tart apples, sweet pears, and dried apricots, but other fruits may be used, such as pineapple or peaches.

1 pound Granny Smith apples, peeled, cored, and chopped

1 pound ripe pears, peeled, cored, and chopped

³/4 cup firmly packed light brown sugar or natural sweetener

³/4 cup cider vinegar

1 small onion, minced

1 small, fresh hot red chile, seeded and minced

1 cup dried apricots, chopped

2 tablespoons peeled and minced fresh ginger

1 tablespoon grated lemon zest

1 teaspoon ground cinnamon

¹/2 teaspoon ground allspice

¹/2 teaspoon salt

1. Place all the ingredients in a large saucepan over medium heat and bring to a boil, stirring occasionally. Reduce the heat to low and simmer until the mixture is very thick, stirring frequently toward end of the cooking time, about 45 minutes.

2. Let cool to room temperature, then refrigerate in tightly sealed containers (small glass jars are best) until ready to serve. This chutney will keep for several weeks in the refrigerator. Bring to room temperature before serving for the best flavor.

MAKES ABOUT 3 CUPS

Five-Spice Pear Chutney

This chutney highlights the sweet taste of ripe pears complemented by the fragrant blend of five flavorful spices. I like to use a firmer pear, such as Anjou, for this recipe.

3 large, ripe pears, peeled, cored, and
    coarsely chopped
1/2 cup minced onion
1 small, fresh hot red chile, seeded and
    minced
1/4 cup golden raisins
1/2 cup firmly packed light brown sugar
    or natural sweetener

1/2 cup rice vinegar
1/4 teaspoon ground allspice
1/4 teaspoon ground ginger
1/4 teaspoon ground coriander
1/4 teaspoon ground cloves
1/4 teaspoon ground cardamom

1. Place the pears in a medium-size saucepan over medium heat. Add the remaining ingredients and bring to a boil. Reduce the heat to low and simmer, stirring occasionally, until the pears and onion are soft and the liquid is syrupy, about 30 minutes.
2. Remove from the heat and let cool. This chutney will keep, refrigerated, for several days. Serve at room temperature.

MAKES ABOUT 2 CUPS

Dried Fruit Chutney

This easy, spur-of-the-moment chutney is made with pantry ingredients. Add raisins or dried cranberries, if you like.

1 cup dried apricots

1/2 cup chopped dried apples

1/2 cup chopped pitted prunes

1/4 cup dates, pitted and chopped

1 small onion, minced

1 small dried chile, seeded and chopped

1/2 cup firmly packed light brown sugar
   or natural sweetener

1/2 cup cider vinegar

1/2 cup water

1 tablespoon peeled and minced
   fresh ginger

1 teaspoon ground allspice

1/8 teaspoon salt

The Charm of Chutney

One of the most alluring things about chutney is its versatility. Traditionally thought of as an accompaniment to curries and other Indian meals, chutney has grown beyond expectations and can be used with a variety of dishes from sandwiches to stews. Chutney is especially delicious with vegan foods because it adds zest to grain and bean dishes. The possibilities for using chutney are as varied as the ingredients that can be used to make it. At once sweet and savory, chutney can be mild or hot and made with ingredients such as fresh or dried fruits, hot chiles, crystallized ginger, onions, and spices. Add some vinegar, sugar, and water, simmer for a while, and you have chutney. After you've made your first batch, you'll be hooked. Not only does the flavor of homemade chutney far surpass most store-bought varieties, but making your own chutney can be economical as well.

1. Soak the apricots in boiling water to cover for 15 minutes. Drain and chop the apricots, then place in a medium-size saucepan over medium heat. Add the remaining ingredients and bring to a boil. Reduce the heat to low and simmer, stirring frequently, until the chutney is thick, 30 to 40 minutes.

2. Let cool to room temperature. Store in the refrigerator in a tightly sealed container, where it will keep for several weeks. Serve at room temperature.

MAKES ABOUT 2 CUPS

Fresh Mint Chutney

I've always enjoyed the fresh mint chutney at my favorite Indian restaurant, where they were kind enough to divulge the ingredients. When last summer yielded a bumper crop of fresh mint—it actually took over my garden—it was time to retrieve the ingredient list and concoct my own version of the fragrant condiment. It actually looks more like pesto than a traditional chutney, but it goes well with virtually any Indian dish. I've even used it as a dipping sauce for samosas.

2 large shallots, coarsely chopped

1 small, fresh hot green chile, seeded and chopped

1 teaspoon sugar or natural sweetener

1/4 teaspoon salt

2 cups tightly packed fresh mint leaves

1/4 cup water, or more as needed

1 tablespoon fresh lemon juice

1. Place the shallots, chile, sugar, and salt in a food processor and process until minced. Add the mint, water, and lemon juice and process until smooth, adding more water if a thinner consistency is desired.

2. Transfer to a small bowl, cover, and refrigerate for 30 minutes. Taste and adjust the seasonings before serving. Although this chutney will keep in the refrigerator for a day or so, I like to serve it shortly after making it, when the bright green color of the mint is at its best.

MAKES ABOUT 1 CUP

Summer Sunshine Salsa

This mild, sunny salsa comprises vibrant yellow vegetables, making it a striking topping for soups, stews, and chilis or a colorful addition to a taco bar. I especially like the way it looks as a garnish for black bean soup. For a hot version, add a minced fresh jalapeño or serrano chile. A little minced cilantro will add flavor and a touch of contrasting color.

1 pound ripe yellow tomatoes, peeled, seeded, and chopped

1/4 cup chopped yellow onion

1 small yellow bell pepper, seeded and chopped

Juice of 1 lemon

1/4 teaspoon salt, or more to taste

2 tablespoons minced fresh cilantro leaves (optional)

1. In a medium-size bowl, combine all the ingredients except the cilantro. Cover and refrigerate until ready to serve.

2. When ready to serve, stir in the cilantro, if using. This salsa will keep, tightly covered, in the refrigerator for 3 to 5 days.

MAKES ABOUT 2 1/2 CUPS

Peeling and Seeding Tomatoes

When fresh tomatoes are used for cooking, the skin and seeds are often removed for a more appetizing appearance.

To peel tomatoes: Use a small knife to cut out the core or stem end of each tomato, then cut an X in the bottom of the tomato and place it in boiling water for 20 to 30 seconds. Using a slotted spoon, transfer the tomato to a bowl of ice water. The skin will peel off easily.

To seed tomatoes: Cut the peeled tomato in half crosswise and use your finger or a spoon to remove the seeds. The peeled and seeded tomato is now ready to use in recipes.

Green Apple Salsa

The sweet-tart taste of Granny Smith apples is punctuated by the bite of jalapeños in this unusual salsa. Try it with grilled vegetables or as an accompaniment to grain dishes, stews, and sandwiches.

2 large Granny Smith apples, peeled,
    cored, and coarsely chopped
1 jalapeño, seeded and minced
1/3 cup minced scallions

Juice of 1 lime
Salt and freshly ground black pepper
1/4 cup minced fresh mint leaves

1. Place the apples in a medium-size bowl. Add the jalapeños, scallions, lime juice, and salt and pepper to taste and toss to combine. Cover and refrigerate until ready to use.

2. Just before serving, stir in the mint. Taste and adjust the seasonings, then serve. This salsa is best served within a few hours after it is made.

MAKES ABOUT 2¹/₂ CUPS

Fresh Tomato Salsa

This is an easy salsa to make when ripe tomatoes are plentiful. Omit the chile if you prefer a mild salsa or add a second one if you like it extra hot.

3 large, ripe tomatoes, peeled, seeded, and chopped

1 small, fresh hot red chile (optional), seeded and minced

4 scallions, minced

1 garlic clove, minced

1 tablespoon fresh lime juice

1/4 cup minced fresh cilantro leaves

Salt and freshly ground black pepper

1. Combine the tomatoes, chile (if using), scallions, and garlic in a large bowl. Add the lime juice and cilantro, season with salt and pepper to taste, and stir to combine.
2. Cover and let stand at room temperature for 1 hour before serving. If not using right away, store in the refrigerator, where it will keep for 3 to 5 days. Bring back to room temperature before serving.

MAKES ABOUT 2 1/2 CUPS

Cilantro-Green Tomato Salsa

Green tomatoes give this salsa a refreshing piquancy that is missing from salsas made with ripe tomatoes.

1 pound green tomatoes, peeled, seeded, and chopped

1/4 cup chopped onion

2 scallions, chopped

1 or 2 small, fresh hot chiles (optional), seeded and chopped, to taste

2 teaspoons fresh lime juice

1/4 teaspoon salt

1/4 cup minced fresh cilantro leaves

1. Combine all the ingredients in a medium-size bowl.

2. Cover and let stand at room temperature for 1 hour before serving. If not using right away, store in the refrigerator, where it will keep for 3 to 5 days. Bring back to room temperature before serving.

MAKES ABOUT 2¹/₂ CUPS

Cranberry-Walnut Relish

Walnuts add crunch to this colorful no-cook cranberry relish flavored with citrus. Use as a condiment with sandwiches, veggie burgers, grain dishes, or stews, as well as a refreshing alternative to traditional cranberry sauce on Thanksgiving. Chopped pecans or almonds may be used instead of the walnuts.

1 orange, peeled and white pith
   removed
One 12-ounce bag fresh cranberries,
   picked over
³/₄ cup firmly packed light brown sugar
   or natural sweetener

3 tablespoons orange marmalade
Juice of 1 lime
¹/₂ cup chopped walnuts

1. Remove the orange flesh from the membranes and place in a food processor. Add the cranberries, brown sugar, marmalade, and lime juice and process until coarsely chopped.

2. Transfer the mixture to a bowl and stir in the walnuts. Taste and adjust the seasonings. Let stand for at least 30 minutes to develop the flavors before serving. Serve cold or at room temperature. Stored tightly covered in the refrigerator, this relish will keep well for 3 to 5 days.

MAKES ABOUT 3 CUPS

Roasted Corn Relish with Smoked Chile Strips

The corn may be grilled instead of roasted, if you prefer. Cooked frozen corn kernels may be used when fresh corn is not in season, although you will not have that fresh-roasted flavor.

3 ears corn or 2 cups frozen corn
 kernels, cooked and drained
1 dried chipotle chile, soaked in very hot
 water to cover for 30 minutes
1/3 cup minced red onion

1/4 cup olive oil
2 tablespoons fresh lemon juice
2 tablespoons minced fresh cilantro
 leaves
Salt and freshly ground black pepper

1. Preheat the oven to 450 degrees F. If using fresh corn, peel back the husks from the corn, remove the corn silk, and pull the husks back up to cover the kernels. Place the ears on a baking sheet and roast until the outer husks begin to brown and the corn is fragrant, about 30 minutes. Remove from the oven and set aside to cool. Remove the husks. Using a sharp knife, remove the kernels from the cobs and place in a large bowl. Discard the cobs and husks.
2. Drain the chile and cut into thin strips. Add the chile, onion, olive oil, lemon juice, cilantro, and salt and pepper to taste to the corn. Mix well to combine, then cover and set aside to allow the flavors to blend, 15 to 20 minutes. Serve at room temperature. This relish will keep for a few days in the refrigerator, but it is best eaten the same day it is made.

MAKES ABOUT 3 CUPS

Carole's Chow-Chow

At the end of each summer, my sister, Carole, brings home bushels of fresh produce to make 30 quarts of chow-chow, a delicious mixed-vegetable relish with Pennsylvania Dutch origins. I've managed to scale down her ambitious recipe to just 12 cups (3 quarts) for those who prefer to make smaller batches. The flavor of the chow-chow improves if it's allowed to marinate for several days before use. Properly stored, it will keep for several months in the refrigerator.

2 medium-size carrots

2 celery ribs

1 large yellow onion

1 small red bell pepper, seeded

4 ounces green beans

1/2 small head green cabbage

1/2 head cauliflower

Salt

1 1/2 cups cider vinegar

1 1/4 cups sugar or natural sweetener

1 1/2 cups prepared yellow mustard

2 cups frozen lima beans

1. Peel, trim, and/or core all the fresh vegetables as needed, then cut into bite-size pieces. Place in a large bowl and salt well. Cover and let stand for several hours or overnight.

2. In a large bowl, combine the vinegar, sugar, and mustard and blend until smooth. Set aside.

3. Drain the vegetables well and place them in a large pot with just enough water to cover. Bring to a boil, then reduce the heat to medium and add the lima beans. Pour off about 2 cups of the cooking liquid, add the mustard sauce, and simmer until the vegetables are crisp-tender, about 20 minutes.

4. Let cool, then transfer the vegetables and sauce to containers with tight-fitting lids (glass jars are ideal) and store in the refrigerator until ready to use.

MAKES ABOUT 12 CUPS

Fennel Compote with Black Olives and Pine Nuts

Serve this flavorful condiment over golden fried tofu, or double the recipe, add a little extra olive oil, and use it as a pasta sauce.

1 large fennel bulb, trimmed and diced
3 tablespoons fresh lemon juice
2 shallots, minced
2 teaspoons grated lemon zest
Salt and freshly ground black pepper
1/4 cup pine nuts, toasted (page 110)

3 tablespoons chopped fresh parsley leaves
2 tablespoons pitted and halved black olives
3 tablespoons extra virgin olive oil

In a medium-size bowl, toss the fennel with the lemon juice. Stir in the shallots, lemon zest, and salt and pepper to taste. Add the pine nuts, parsley, and olives. Drizzle with the olive oil and stir to combine. Taste and adjust the seasonings, then serve at once. This compote is best served right away to fully appreciate the fresh taste and color of the ingredients.

MAKES ABOUT 2 CUPS

Three-Onion Confit

A confit is traditionally made with ingredients that are cooked slowly in animal fat. This version uses flavorful and heart-healthy olive oil to cook three kinds of onions. Use this confit as an accompaniment to sautéed seitan, or serve with hearty grain and bean dishes. It also makes a sophisticated condiment for veggie burgers.

1/2 cup olive oil
1 large red onion, chopped
3 shallots, chopped
1 bunch scallions, chopped

1 teaspoon cider vinegar
1 teaspoon light brown sugar or natural
    sweetener
Salt and freshly ground black pepper

1. In a medium-size saucepan, combine the olive oil, onion, shallots, and scallions. Cover and cook over low heat until the onions begin to soften, about 10 minutes. Stir in the vinegar, brown sugar, and salt and pepper to taste. Continue to cook until the mixture is thick and syrupy, about 30 minutes. Stir occasionally to make sure it doesn't stick to the bottom of the pan.

2. Taste and adjust the seasonings, then set aside to cool. Serve at once, or cover and refrigerate until ready to use. Bring back to room temperature before serving.

MAKES ABOUT 2 CUPS

The Entertaining Vegan

My husband and I love to entertain in our home, and the guests who share our table run the gamut from meat eaters to vegans. No one goes away hungry. My approach to vegan entertaining is to plan menus that are full of flavor and visually appealing—then relax and enjoy.

I don't usually "announce" that there's no meat or dairy on the table, because I believe that vegan food is a cuisine in its own right. Delicious food is delicious food—let it stand on its own without qualification. With nonvegans, I sometimes choose ethnic themes, pasta dishes, or one-pot vegetable and bean entrées, but I also like to expose my guests to the wonders of sautéed or roasted seitan and the versatility of soy.

Let the seasons, holidays, or other events provide inspirations for your menus. Do what many chefs do when planning their featured restaurant items: feature what's fresh and in season at the market. When planning a menu for company, try to find out whether your guests have any food allergies or aversions, say, to hot and spicy foods. If you know they have a favorite cuisine, consider choosing a theme they will enjoy.

Next, decide how many courses you want to make—from a casual one-dish supper to a formal 7-course dinner. Generally, 3 courses are enough, even for company. Begin with either a soup, salad, or appetizer as a first course (you could do 2 or even all 3 if it is a very special meal and you have the time), then follow with a main course (with sides as appropriate) and dessert. It is important to balance the courses so that there is a variety of flavors, textures, and ingredients. Pay special attention to the use of garnishes and setting a lovely table. Those little touches can raise your dining experience to the next level.

The following menus are gleaned from the recipes in this book and are provided as a guide to spur your imagination. They can be easily adapted. For example, for menus that list a salad, appetizer, and soup, don't feel that you need to make all three—choose what feels comfortable. Feel free to substitute a different dessert or side dish, for example, according to your taste preferences. Do as much of the preparation ahead of time as possible. This will allow you to spend more time with your guests, feel more relaxed, and fix a mistake if something goes wrong. It's also a good idea to try a new recipe before making it for company.

If you don't have the time or inclination for a multicourse dinner, many quick and easy one-dish recipes make great meals in themselves. Consider a thick soup served with good bread; a large salad made with raw and cooked vegetables, beans, and/or grains; a hearty stew, chili, or casserole; a quick stir-fry made with a variety of vegetables and tofu, tempeh, or seitan; or a pasta- or grain-based dish.

Use these ideas as a jumping-off point to create your own winning menu combinations for all reasons and all seasons.

MENU IDEAS

SPRINGTIME LUNCHEON

Cool Cucumber Soup with Cilantro and Lime (page 71)
Fennel, Pecan, and Watercress Salad
    with Orange Vinaigrette (page 111)
Tarragon-Scented Artichoke and Wild
    Mushroom Strudel (page 372)
Key Lime "Cheesecake" (page 492)

AUTUMN BRUNCH BUFFET

Savory Spinach Bread Pudding (page 542)
Pan-Seared Breakfast Mushrooms (page 550)
Spicy Sweet-Potato Hash (page 548)
Couscous Breakfast Cake with Pear and Dried
    Plum Compote (page 552)

WINTER SUNDAY SUPPER

Orange and Chipotle–Kissed Butternut Squash
    Bisque (page 86)
White Bean Cassoulet (page 290)
Mashed Potatoes and Company (page 204)
Balsamic-Glazed Carrots and Kale (page 200)
Chocolate Pudding Parfaits (page 506)

Summer Al Fresco

Roasted Corn Chowder (page 87)
Garlic and Herb–Marinated Vegetable Kabobs (page 336)
Rosemary-Lemon Potatoes with Black Olives and Sun-Dried Tomatoes (page 205)
Fresh Peach Crisp with Almond Butter Cream (page 501)

Company's Coming

Thyme-Scented Wild Mushroom Bisque (page 84)
Artichoke Salad Parfaits (page 109)
Yuba-Wrapped Seitan and Vegetable Rolls (page 410)
Lemon Risotto with Peas and Scallions (page 237)
Roasted Sesame Asparagus (page 192)
Coconut-Macadamia "Cheesecake" (page 490)

Holiday Dinner

Wild Mushroom Pâté (page 53)
Potato-Watercress Soup with Sesame (page 94)
Asian Pear and Baby Spinach Salad with Warm Walnut Dressing (page 103)
Seitan Roast with Chestnut and Cranberry Stuffing (page 412)
Orange-Roasted Beets and Shallots with Orange Gremolata (page 194)
Brandy-Apple Pie (page 499)

Thai One On

Thai-Style Coconut Soup (page 77)
Vegetable Spring Rolls with Spicy Peanut Dipping Sauce (page 44)
"Drunken" Noodles (page 262)
Thai-Style Papaya Salad (page 104)
Frozen Coconut "Thaiphoon" with Mango, Lime, and Peanuts (page 516)

Asian Fusion

Ginger-Scented Vegetable Pot Stickers (page 37)
Szechuan Hot and Sour Soup (page 75)
Three-Way Sesame-Coated Tofu Strips with Spicy Broccoli (page 341)
Asian Pear Tart with Toasted Almond Crust and Orange-Ginger Glaze
    (page 500)

Italian Feast

Caponata Crostini (page 56)
Tuscan White Bean Soup (page 83)
Penne Puttanesca (page 248)
Broccoli Rabe with Figs, Garlic, and Pine Nuts (page 207)
Double-Espresso Affogato (page 517) with Orange-Scented Almond Biscotti
    (page 509)

Taste of India

Curried Cauliflower Pakoras (page 47)
Three-Bean Dal (page 285)
Spicy Jasmine Rice with Carrots and Cashews (page 234)
Tofu Vindaloo (page 312)
Red Bean and Sweet Potato Curry (page 286)
Coconut-Cardamom Rice Pudding (page 505)

Knock-Their-Socks-Off International Appetizer Party

Thai-Style Leaf-Wrapped Appetizer Bites (page 38)
Sesame-Asparagus Sushi Rolls (page 41)
Baked Sweet Potato and Green Pea Samosas (page 46)
Basmati-Stuffed Grape Leaves with Pine Nuts and Dill (page 40)
Minted Baba Ganoush (page 49)
Spinach-Mushroom Phyllo Triangles (page 45)
Blushing Guacamole (page 50)
Hot and Spicy Stuffed Mushrooms (page 55)
Black Olive Bruschetta (page 58)
Roasted "Chichers" (page 281)

Roasted Garlic and Lemon Marmalade

The mellow flavor of the garlic is accented by the fresh taste of lemons. Enjoy this unusual condiment with fried tofu or grilled vegetables.

2 heads garlic
1 tablespoon olive oil
Juice and grated zest of 2 lemons
1/2 cup firmly packed light brown sugar
    or natural sweetener

1/2 teaspoon salt
1/8 teaspoon freshly ground black
    pepper

1. Preheat the oven to 375 degrees F. Place the garlic in a shallow baking pan and drizzle with the olive oil. Add a small amount of water to the pan (about 1/3 cup) and cover tightly with aluminum foil. Bake until the garlic is soft, about 1 hour. Allow to cool.

2. Peel the garlic and place the cloves in a medium-size saucepan, mashing them slightly. Add the remaining ingredients, cover, and cook over low heat until the mixture cooks down and becomes syrupy, about 20 minutes. Stir occasionally to make sure it doesn't stick to the bottom of the pan.

3. Taste and adjust the seasonings. Let cool to room temperature, then refrigerate in a tightly sealed container until ready to use. This marmalade will keep well for 2 to 3 days. Serve at room temperature.

MAKES ABOUT 1 CUP

Quick Kimchi

Made with the requisite cabbage, garlic, and chiles, this piquant Korean condiment is a good accompaniment to stir-fries and Asian-style rice dishes.

1 medium-size head napa cabbage, cored and coarsely chopped

1 medium-size carrot, cut into thin diagonal slices

1 bunch scallions, cut into thin diagonal slices

2 garlic cloves, mashed into a paste

1 tablespoon peeled and minced fresh ginger

1 teaspoon red pepper flakes, or more to taste

1/3 cup rice vinegar

2 tablespoons toasted sesame oil

2 tablespoons tamari or other soy sauce

1 tablespoon sugar or natural sweetener

1/2 teaspoon salt

1. In a large bowl, combine the cabbage, carrot, and scallions and set aside.

2. In a small bowl, combine the remaining ingredients and blend well.

3. Pour the sauce over the vegetables and stir to combine. Cover and let marinate at room temperature for at least 30 minutes before serving. If not using right away, cover and store in the refrigerator, where it will keep for several days. Serve at room temperature.

MAKES ABOUT 6 CUPS

Cucumber-Mint Raita

Cooling cucumber raita is a refreshing way to tone down the heat of a spicy Indian meal. Although it is traditionally made with yogurt, this version is made with silken tofu.

1/2 cup drained soft silken tofu
1 teaspoon fresh lemon juice
1/2 teaspoon sugar or natural
    sweetener

Salt and freshly ground black pepper
2 medium-size cucumbers, peeled,
    seeded, and thinly sliced
1/4 cup chopped fresh mint leaves

1. In a blender or food processor, combine the tofu, lemon juice, sugar, and salt and pepper to taste and process until well blended.
2. Transfer to a bowl and stir in the cucumbers. Cover and refrigerate for 30 minutes. When ready to serve, stir in the mint. Serve chilled.

SERVES 4

Tangy Tomato Ketchup

Homemade ketchup not only tastes better than bottled, but it also can be customized to suit your palate. This recipe is much less sweet than store-bought ketchups and also more complex.

1 ancho or other dried chile, soaked
    in very hot water to cover for
    30 minutes
1 tablespoon olive oil
1 small yellow onion, chopped
1 garlic clove, chopped
3 cups diced fresh tomatoes
1/4 cup tomato paste

3 tablespoons sugar or natural
    sweetener
1 teaspoon salt
1 teaspoon ground allspice
1/2 teaspoon paprika
1/2 teaspoon dry mustard
Cayenne
1/2 cup cider vinegar

1. Drain, seed, and chop the chile. Set aside.

2. Heat the olive oil in a medium-size saucepan over medium heat. Add the onion and garlic, cover, and cook until softened, about 5 minutes. Stir in the tomatoes, tomato paste, and chile and simmer for 15 minutes.

3. Put the mixture through a food mill or puree in a food processor, then push through a fine-mesh strainer back into the saucepan. Add the sugar, salt, allspice, paprika, mustard, and cayenne to taste. Cook over medium heat, stirring occasionally, until thick, about 30 minutes. Stir in the vinegar and cook, stirring occasionally, until thick, about 15 minutes. Allow to cool.

4. Refrigerate in a tightly sealed container until ready to use. The ketchup will keep for 2 weeks in the refrigerator or for several months in the freezer.

MAKES ABOUT 2 CUPS

7
veggies in the MiddLe

It has always amazed me how, with one sweeping expression, our society has relegated vegetables to a culinary afterthought with the phrase "a side of vegetables," as if to say vegetables have less importance than the meaty entrée. Few would argue that Americans would be a healthier lot if they started enjoying their vegetables "in the middle" rather than "on the side."

With the huge variety of vegetables available today, it can be a simple matter to eat the USDA-recommended "five per day" and then some. Vegetables prepared simply, especially at the peak of their season, can be the best way for you to enjoy their true flavor—lightly steamed, grilled, or roasted, with little or no adornment, perhaps a grinding or two of pepper and a squeeze of lemon. What could be easier or better tasting? Or more nutritious, since raw or lightly cooked vegetables retain the most enzymes and other nutrients.

When you consider the versatility and range of vegan ingredients, it becomes clear that there is a place for vegetables on the side, in the middle, and everywhere in between. By preparing vegetables using different cooking methods and seasonings, you can experience the full spectrum of textures and flavors. For example, *Szechuan String Beans* can be served as an entrée over rice or as an accompaniment to fried tofu or braised tempeh. Mashed potatoes can be served alongside a vegan meat loaf or seitan roast as easily as they can become the anchor of a dazzling vegetable platter. Imagine a bed of mashed potatoes surrounded by lightly steamed asparagus, crisp roasted root vegetables, and wine-braised mushrooms, or a vegetable ragout served with a raw vegetable salad or relish.

The fact is, where vegetables are concerned, there are no rules. No longer limited by the meat-potato-vegetable trinity of the past, we are free to expand our repertoires and explore vegetable preparations the world over.

Of course, it's a good idea to purchase seasonal vegetables at their peak, for that is when they are most flavorful and most economically priced. I believe that the body responds to cycles, enjoying heavier, hot, slower-cooked foods in winter and lighter foods in summer. However, since most vegetables are now available year round, when you do get a craving for that springtime asparagus in the midst of winter, you can satisfy it.

I've tried to include a broad sampling of vegetable recipes in this chapter to spur your imagination and show how particular cooking methods or ethnic nuances can transform everyday vegetables into exciting new flavor experiences. Although this chapter barely scratches the surface of ways to prepare vegetables, I hope it provides a springboard for you to explore the amazing choices at your disposal.

Roasted Sesame Asparagus

Once you begin roasting asparagus, you'll wonder why you ever prepared it any other way. Toasted sesame seeds and sesame oil give this recipe a decidedly Asian accent. For a Western approach, leave the spears whole and roast them with a small amount of olive oil instead of the sesame.

1½ to 2 pounds thin asparagus,
   bottoms trimmed
1½ tablespoons peanut oil
Salt and freshly ground black pepper

2 tablespoons sesame seeds, toasted
   (see below)
1 tablespoon toasted sesame oil

1. Preheat the oven to 450 degrees F. Cut the asparagus diagonally into 2-inch pieces and place in a bowl. Drizzle with the peanut oil and season with salt and pepper to taste. Toss to coat, then spread on a baking sheet in a single layer.
2. Roast the asparagus until just tender, 6 to 8 minutes, depending on the thickness.
3. Transfer to a bowl, sprinkle with the sesame seeds, and drizzle with the sesame oil. Toss to coat and serve hot.

SERVES 4

Toasted Sesame Seeds

Toasting brings out the nutty flavor of sesame seeds. Because they are so small, it is best to toast them in a skillet on top of the stove, where you can keep a close eye on them, rather than in the oven.

Place the sesame seeds in a skillet over medium heat and toast, stirring once or twice, until fragrant and lightly browned, 2 to 4 minutes. Once the seeds are toasted to your liking, remove them from the skillet so they don't continue to brown from the residual heat in the pan.

Sautéed Green Beans with Tomatoes and Garlic

This colorful sauté goes well with a variety of dishes. As a "side," it makes a nice pairing for sautéed tofu, tempeh, or seitan. If you cut the beans into 1- to 2-inch lengths before using, the recipe can be used as a topping for baked potatoes or rice or tossed with pasta.

1 pound green beans, ends trimmed
2 tablespoons olive oil
1/2 small red onion, chopped
3 garlic cloves, minced
One 14.5-ounce can diced tomatoes, drained

1 tablespoon chopped fresh parsley leaves
Salt and freshly ground black pepper

1. Lightly steam the green beans over boiling water until just tender. Rinse under cold running water to set the color and stop the cooking process. Drain and set aside.

2. Heat the olive oil in a large saucepan over medium heat. Add the onion, cover, and cook until softened, about 5 minutes. Add the garlic and cook until fragrant, about 30 seconds. Add the green beans, tomatoes, parsley, and salt and pepper to taste. Simmer, stirring occasionally, until the vegetables are hot and the flavors are well combined, about 10 minutes. Serve hot.

SERVES 4

Orange-Roasted Beets and Shallots with Orange Gremolata

I prefer to make this dish with small, sweet beets, but if the larger ones are all you can find, cut them into quarters to reduce the cooking time. If you prefer to omit the gremolata, you can garnish the beets with chopped fresh parsley or mint and a little grated orange zest.

2 tablespoons extra virgin olive oil

2 tablespoons frozen orange juice concentrate, thawed

8 small beets, trimmed, well scrubbed, and halved

4 large shallots, halved

Salt and freshly ground black pepper

2 tablespoons Orange Gremolata (recipe follows) for garnish

1. Preheat the oven to 450 degrees F. In a small bowl, combine the olive oil and orange juice concentrate, stirring to blend.

2. Place the beets and shallots in a lightly oiled baking dish and add the orange juice mixture, stirring to coat. Spread out in a single layer and season with salt and pepper to taste.

3. Cover the baking dish tightly and roast until the beets are soft and the shallots caramelized, stirring halfway through, about 50 minutes. The beet peels should come off easily once cooked.

4. Serve hot, garnished with a sprinkling of the gremolata.

SERVES 4

ORANGE GREMOLATA

This variation on traditional gremolata is made with oranges and mint and uses shallots instead of garlic. I especially like it as a garnish for black bean soup and roasted asparagus, but it can be used anytime you want to punch up the flavor of a dish with the sweet-fresh taste of orange and mint.

Grated zest of 1 orange

1 large shallot, chopped

1/3 cup chopped fresh mint leaves

Mince the orange zest, shallot, and mint together until well combined. Place in a tightly sealed container and refrigerate until ready to use. It is best used the same day it is made, although it will keep, tightly covered, in the refrigerator for a day or two.

MAKES ABOUT 1/3 CUP

Szechuan String Beans

My version of this classic Chinese vegetable dish is made with considerably less oil than the original, but it still has loads of flavor. Make it with regular green beans, or use Chinese long beans (also called yard-long beans), if you can find them.

1½ pounds green beans, ends trimmed

3 tablespoons tamari or other soy sauce

1 tablespoon toasted sesame oil

1 tablespoon mirin

1 teaspoon sugar or natural sweetener

2 tablespoons peanut oil

3 shallots, minced

2 garlic cloves, minced

2 teaspoons peeled and minced fresh ginger

3 tablespoons minced scallions

1 teaspoon red pepper flakes, or to taste

1. Lightly steam the green beans until just tender, about 5 minutes. Rinse under cold running water to stop the cooking process and set the color. Drain and set aside.

2. In a small bowl, combine the tamari, sesame oil, mirin, and sugar and set aside.

3. Heat the peanut oil in a wok or large skillet over medium-high heat. When the oil is hot, add the beans, a handful at a time, and stir-fry for 30 seconds, transferring the cooked beans with a slotted spoon to a platter, until all of the beans are cooked.

4. Let the oil reheat, then add the shallots, garlic, ginger, scallions, and red pepper flakes and stir-fry for 10 seconds. Return the beans to the wok and stir-fry for 30 seconds. Add the tamari mixture and stir-fry until the beans are hot and coated with sauce, about 30 seconds. Serve immediately.

SERVES 4

Hoisin-Braised Baby Bok Choy and Shiitake Mushrooms

Slow cooking over low heat allows the flavors of the sauce to permeate the bok choy and shiitakes, resulting in a satisfying and flavorful dish that is delicious over rice.

3 tablespoons hoisin sauce
1 tablespoon tamari or other soy sauce
1 tablespoon sake
1 tablespoon water
1 tablespoon peanut oil
2 dried chiles
1 teaspoon peeled and minced
    fresh ginger

1 teaspoon minced garlic
4 small baby bok choy, trimmed and
    halved lengthwise
4 ounces fresh shiitake mushrooms,
    stems removed and caps thinly
    sliced
2 tablespoons thinly sliced scallions

1. In a small bowl, combine the hoisin, tamari, sake, and water and set aside.
2. Heat the peanut oil in a wok or large skillet over medium-high heat. When the oil is hot, add the chiles and stir-fry for about 30 seconds. Discard the chiles. Add the ginger and garlic and stir-fry until the garlic is fragrant, about 30 seconds. Add the bok choy, mushrooms, scallions, and sauce and stir-fry to coat the vegetables, 2 to 3 minutes.
3. Reduce the heat to low, cover, and simmer until the vegetables are tender, about 15 minutes. Serve hot.

SERVES 4

Sesame-Broccoli Stir-Fry

Like most of the recipes in this chapter, this fragrant broccoli dish can fill the role of side dish or entrée. For a complete, well-balanced meal, add some diced firm tofu to the stir-fry and serve over brown rice.

1 large head broccoli
3 tablespoons toasted sesame oil
3 tablespoons tamari or other soy sauce
2 tablespoons hoisin sauce
1/4 cup sesame seeds, toasted (page 192)

1 tablespoon peanut oil
1/2 large red bell pepper, seeded and cut into matchsticks
2 garlic cloves, minced

1. Cut the broccoli into small florets and peel and thinly slice the stems. Steam the broccoli until barely tender, about 3 minutes. Rinse under cold running water to set the color and stop the cooking process, then drain and set aside.
2. In a small bowl, combine the sesame oil, tamari, hoisin, and sesame seeds and set aside.
3. Heat the peanut oil in a wok or large skillet over medium-high heat. When the oil is hot, add the bell pepper and garlic and stir-fry to soften slightly, about 1 minute. Add the broccoli and sauce and stir-fry, coating the vegetables with the sauce, until the vegetables are cooked to the desired doneness, about 3 minutes. Serve hot.

SERVES 4

Roasted Cauliflower with Faux Choron Sauce

What were once considered a boring vegetable and an old-fashioned sauce are given new life in this updated preparation. Roasting the cauliflower gives it an entirely new character that is complemented by the rich-tasting choron sauce.

1 head cauliflower, cut into ½-inch-
    thick slices
2 tablespoons olive oil

Salt and freshly ground black pepper
1 recipe Faux Choron Sauce (page 145),
    heated

1. Preheat the oven to 425 degrees F. Toss the cauliflower slices with the olive oil and arrange in a single layer on a lightly oiled baking sheet. Season with salt and pepper to taste. Roast until just tender, 12 to 14 minutes, turning once halfway through. Remove from the oven and transfer to a shallow serving platter.
2. Serve topped with the sauce, or serve the sauce on the side for dipping.

SERVES 4

Balsamic-Glazed Carrots and Kale

Why eat plain boiled carrots and greens? Give them a lift with this piquant balsamic glaze.

6 medium-size carrots, cut into thin
    diagonal slices
1 bunch kale, stems removed and
    coarsely chopped
2 tablespoons extra virgin olive oil

2 tablespoons balsamic vinegar
2 teaspoons tamari or other soy sauce
1/2 teaspoon sugar or natural sweetener
1/8 teaspoon cayenne

1. Place the carrots and kale in a large pot of boiling salted water and cook until the vegetables soften slightly and the kale turns bright green, 3 to 4 minutes. Drain well and set aside.

2. Heat the olive oil in a large skillet over medium heat. Add the carrots and kale along with the remaining ingredients. Bring to a simmer, then reduce the heat to low and cook, stirring occasionally, until all the liquid evaporates, about 10 minutes. Serve hot.

SERVES 4

A VEGETABLE FOR ALL SEASONS

The carrot is a vegetable for all seasons. What other vegetable satisfies throughout the year, adding its subtle sweetness, lovely color, and rich vitamins to virtually any meal? We grate carrots into summer salads, slice them into springtime stir-fries, chop them into autumn soups and stews, and roast them whole in the oven on cold winter days.

The dependable carrot can also be a shining star when transformed into a refreshing glass of bright-orange juice or a delectable moist cake, decadent in its richness. Yet carrots are also perfectly comfortable in a supporting role in vegetable medleys, salads, and side dishes. Team them with other vegetables to show off their vivid orange hue. Carrots were made to be paired with green vegetables such as broccoli, peas, and asparagus for a striking color contrast, great flavor, and, in the case of more costly vegetables such as asparagus, an economical strategy. Raw carrots also are great for healthful between-meal snacks.

High in fiber and rich in beta carotene, carrots are one of the best sources of vitamin A. They also contain healthy doses of calcium and potassium. Available in a variety of sizes, from the increasingly popular baby carrots to mammoth footlong cylinders, carrots are simple to prepare and keep well in the refrigerator for up to 2 weeks.

Although carrots are available year round, they often are thought of as winter vegetables, perhaps because they are fresh and plentiful during the cold winter months, long after the fickle vegetables of summer have faded into our memories. That is when carrots can truly work their mealtime magic. They can evoke the promise of springtime when lightly steamed and tossed with fresh herbs, or add a touch of elegance when slowly braised with a fortified wine.

Glaze carrots to bring out their natural sweetness, or combine them with other ingredients to create a warming stew of flavors. Carrots are found in virtually every cuisine and can be used to make muffins, chips, sauces, and puddings, as well as in bean, grain, and pasta dishes. They can even be incorporated into the pasta dough itself—I've noticed curried carrot pasta available in the supermarket. Still, the simplest preparation may be the best way to enjoy carrots.

My favorite way to prepare carrots is to roast them together with potatoes, onions, and other root vegetables, cooking them slowly until they are richly caramelized—their natural sweetness permeating their companions, the warmth and fragrance from the oven wafting through the house. Whereas other root vegetables such as turnips and rutabagas may not win any popularity contests, the carrot shines as a reliable ingredient that adds its bright orange rays of sunshine to meals all year long.

Cajun-Style Collards

Collard greens are popular in the southern states, where they are often boiled with a ham hock for what seems like forever. Here they have new appeal, with a different, but still southern, approach. Try this "mess of greens" with Not-So-Dirty Rice (page 232).

1½ pounds collard greens
1 tablespoon olive oil
1 small yellow onion, minced
1 celery rib, minced
½ large green bell pepper, seeded and
    minced
2 garlic cloves, minced

One 14.5-ounce can diced tomatoes,
    drained
1 teaspoon dried thyme
¼ teaspoon filé powder
¼ teaspoon cayenne
Salt and freshly ground black pepper

1. Cook the collards in a pot of boiling salted water until tender, 20 to 30 minutes. Drain, then coarsely chop and set aside.

2. Heat the olive oil in a large skillet over medium heat. Add the onion, celery, bell pepper, and garlic. Cover and cook until softened, about 7 minutes. Stir in the tomatoes, thyme, filé, and cayenne. Add the collards, season with salt and pepper to taste, and stir to coat the collards with the onion mixture. Simmer until the flavors are blended, about 10 minutes. Serve hot.

SERVES 4

Chipotle Mashed Potatoes

Pureed chipotle chiles add a smoky heat to these mashed potatoes, which can liven up the most basic meal. I like to serve them with a vegan meat loaf or grilled seitan and sautéed greens. Canned chipotles may be used instead of dried.

1 or 2 dried chipotle chiles, to your taste, soaked in very hot water to cover for 30 minutes

2 pounds Yukon Gold or russet potatoes, peeled and cut into 2-inch chunks

1/3 cup soy milk or other dairy-free milk, heated

1 tablespoon olive oil

Salt

1. Transfer the chiles to a blender along with 1 tablespoon of the soaking liquid and process until smooth. Set aside.

2. Place the potatoes in a large saucepan with cold salted water to cover. Bring to a boil over medium-high heat and continue to boil until tender, 25 to 30 minutes.

3. Drain the potatoes, return them to the saucepan, and mash with a potato masher. Mix in the chipotle puree, soy milk, olive oil, and salt to taste. Continue to mash until all the ingredients are well mixed and the potatoes are smooth. Serve hot.

SERVES 4

Mashed Potatoes and Company

Buttery Yukon Gold potatoes team up with sweet potatoes and parsnips for an unusual variation on traditional mashed potatoes. Experiment with other additions such as carrots or turnips—just be sure they're cooked until soft so they incorporate well with the potatoes.

1½ pounds Yukon Gold potatoes, peeled
1 small sweet potato, peeled
2 small parsnips, peeled and sliced
2 garlic cloves, crushed

2 tablespoons extra virgin olive oil
⅓ to ½ cup soy milk or other dairy-free milk, as needed, heated
Salt and freshly ground black pepper

1. Cut the potatoes and sweet potato into quarters and place in a large saucepan with cold salted water to cover. Add the parsnips and garlic and bring to a boil over medium-high heat. Cook until tender, about 30 minutes.

2. Drain and return to the saucepan. Add the olive oil and ⅓ cup of the milk. Using a potato masher or ricer, mash the vegetables until smooth, adding more milk, if necessary. Season with salt and pepper to taste and serve hot.

SERVES 4

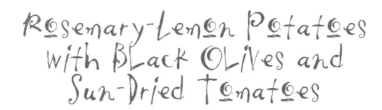

Rosemary-Lemon Potatoes with Black Olives and Sun-Dried Tomatoes

Small red potatoes offer a perfect backdrop for a wide range of Mediterranean flavors, from fragrant rosemary and refreshing lemon to the salty depth of black olives and the smoky richness of sun-dried tomatoes.

1¹/₂ pounds small red potatoes
1 tablespoon olive oil
2 shallots, minced
1 teaspoon chopped fresh rosemary
    leaves

¹/₂ teaspoon salt
2 tablespoons fresh lemon juice
¹/₄ cup black olives, pitted and halved
¹/₄ cup oil-packed or rehydrated
    sun-dried tomatoes, chopped

1. Place the potatoes in a large saucepan with salted water to cover. Bring to a boil over medium-high heat and continue to boil until tender, about 30 minutes. Drain well. Cut the potatoes into halves or quarters, depending on their size, place in a large bowl, and set aside.

2. Heat the olive oil in a large skillet over medium heat. Add the shallots, cover, and cook until softened, 3 to 5 minutes. Add the potatoes and cook until browned, 5 to 7 minutes. Sprinkle with the rosemary, salt, and lemon juice, then add the olives and sun-dried tomatoes and stir gently to combine. Serve hot.

SERVES 4

Grilled Radicchio and Fennel

It's no wonder grilled vegetables have become so popular—the flavor is incredible. I like to experiment with grilling different vegetables just to see how delicious the results might be, and I haven't been disappointed yet. Fennel and radicchio might be considered two unusual choices for the grill, but they are commonly grilled in Italy—a country where cooks know how to coax the most flavor out of their ingredients. If you don't have a grill, use the broiler instead.

2 medium-size fennel bulbs, trimmed
Olive oil as needed
2 large heads radicchio, wilted outer leaves removed

Salt and freshly ground black pepper
Chopped fresh herb leaves for garnish (optional)
Lemon wedges for serving (optional)

1. If using a gas or electric grill or a broiler, preheat it until it is hot (about 500 degrees F). If using charcoal, let the fire burn until the coals are hot and covered with white ash. Cook your vegetables about 4 inches above or below the heat source, depending on whether you're grilling or broiling.
2. Cut the fennel into wedges, toss with enough olive oil to coat, and grill on both sides until soft and lightly browned, about 10 minutes per side.
3. Meanwhile, cut the radicchio heads into quarters, cutting through the root end, and place them in a bowl of cold water for 5 minutes.
4. Coat the radicchio with olive oil and place on the grill, turning frequently and brushing with more oil, if necessary. Watch carefully to be sure it does not burn. Grill until soft and browned, about 10 minutes total.
5. Serve the fennel and radicchio hot, sprinkled with salt and pepper to taste and a drizzle of olive oil, if desired. Garnish with chopped herbs and serve with lemon wedges, if you like.

SERVES 4

Broccoli Rabe with Figs, Garlic, and Pine Nuts

Southern Italian cooking often combines bitter greens such as broccoli rabe, also known as rapini, or escarole with dried fruits such as figs or raisins. The garlic and olive oil add depth, and the pine nuts provide a bit of crunch. Use fresh figs when they are in season; otherwise, dried are fine.

2 bunches broccoli rabe, stems trimmed and coarsely chopped

2 tablespoons olive oil

3 garlic cloves, minced

1/3 cup coarsely chopped fresh or dried figs

1/4 cup pine nuts

Salt and freshly ground black pepper

1. Bring a large pot of salted water to a boil. Add the broccoli rabe and boil for 5 minutes. Drain well and set aside.

2. Heat the olive oil in a large skillet over medium heat. Add the garlic and cook until fragrant, about 30 seconds. Add the figs and pine nuts and cook until the pine nuts are lightly toasted, about 1 minute. Stir in the broccoli rabe and season with salt and pepper to taste. Cook, stirring occasionally, until tender, about 5 minutes. Serve hot.

SERVES 4

Did You Know...

Dark green vegetables should be cooked uncovered to prevent discoloration? Covering green vegetables while they cook causes a buildup of acids that react with the chlorophyll and turn the vegetables a brownish color.

Brandy-Glazed Winter Squash with Apple-Pecan Topping

I like to make this dish just for the lovely aroma that permeates the house while it bakes.

1 large winter squash, such as butter-
    cup or butternut
1 small yellow onion, chopped
1/3 cup brandy
3 tablespoons firmly packed light
    brown sugar or natural sweetener

2 tablespoons olive oil
1 tablespoon water
Salt and freshly ground black pepper
1 large Granny Smith apple, peeled,
    cored, and chopped
1/2 cup chopped pecans

1. Preheat the oven to 400 degrees F. Halve, seed, and peel the squash, then cut into 2-inch chunks. Place in a lightly oiled baking dish large enough for the squash to fit in a single layer.

2. Sprinkle the onion over the squash and pour on the brandy. Add 1 tablespoon of the brown sugar, 1 tablespoon of the olive oil, and the water. Season with salt and pepper to taste. Seal tightly with a lid or aluminum foil and bake until soft, 30 to 40 minutes. Gently turn the squash at least once during cooking for even browning. Uncover and remove from the oven.

3. In a bowl, combine the apple, pecans, remaining 1 tablespoon olive oil, and remaining 2 tablespoons brown sugar. Sprinkle the apple mixture over the squash, return to the oven, and bake, uncovered, until the top is bubbly and golden brown, about 15 minutes. Serve hot.

SERVES 4

Watercress-Walnut Stir-Fry

Infused with the flavors of ginger and walnuts, the watercress is cooked just long enough to lose its raw taste while retaining its texture and freshness. I like to think of this as a cooked salad and often use it as a bed for sautéed portobello mushroom or seitan strips.

2 teaspoons peanut oil

1 teaspoon peeled and minced fresh
ginger

Leaves from 2 bunches watercress,
coarsely chopped

1/4 teaspoon red pepper flakes

1 tablespoon tamari or other soy sauce

1/2 cup chopped walnuts

2 teaspoons walnut oil (optional)

1. Heat the peanut oil in a large skillet or wok over medium-high heat. When the oil is hot, add the ginger and cook until fragrant, about 30 seconds. Add the watercress, red pepper flakes, tamari, and walnuts and stir-fry until wilted but not overcooked, about 3 minutes.

2. Serve hot, drizzled with the walnut oil, if desired.

SERVES 4

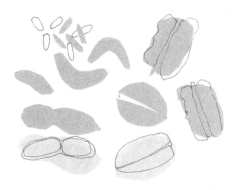

Golden Ratatouille

Using the many golden-hued vegetables now available gives a new lift to this classic vegetable stew from the Provence region of France. Fresh herbs provide a green color accent. If you want to turn this into a glowing main course, add a 15-ounce can of chickpeas, drained and rinsed, and serve over rice that has been cooked with a pinch of turmeric.

2 tablespoons olive oil

1 small yellow onion, diced

1 small yellow bell pepper, seeded and
  cut into 1/2-inch dice

1 small eggplant, peeled and cut into
  1/2-inch dice

2 garlic cloves, minced

Salt and freshly ground black pepper

2 small yellow squash, cut into
  1/2-inch-thick rounds

4 large, ripe yellow tomatoes, peeled,
  seeded, and chopped

1 tablespoon minced fresh thyme
  leaves

1 tablespoon chopped fresh parsley
  leaves

1. Heat the olive oil in a large saucepan over medium heat. Add the onion, cover, and cook until softened, about 5 minutes. Add the bell pepper, eggplant, garlic, and salt and pepper to taste and stir gently to combine. Cook, covered, until the vegetables are slightly softened, about 10 minutes. Stir in the squash, tomatoes, and thyme and cook until all the vegetables are tender, about 20 minutes.

2. Sprinkle with the parsley and serve hot.

SERVES 4 TO 6

Maple-Baked Root Vegetables

Oven baking and root vegetables were made for each other, especially during the chilly winter months when their warm fragrance fills the house. Cutting the vegetables into similar-size pieces helps ensure even cooking, and a small amount of maple syrup brings out their natural sweetness.

4 medium-size carrots, cut into 1-inch chunks

6 shallots, halved

2 medium-size parsnips, peeled and cut into 1-inch chunks

2 small turnips, peeled and cut into 1-inch chunks

1 small rutabaga, peeled and cut into 1-inch chunks

2 tablespoons olive oil

2 to 3 tablespoons pure maple syrup, to your taste

Salt and freshly ground black pepper

1. Preheat the oven to 450 degrees F. Place the carrots, shallots, parsnips, turnips, and rutabaga in a large bowl. Add the olive oil, maple syrup, and salt and pepper to taste and toss to combine well.

2. Transfer the vegetables to a large lightly oiled roasting pan or baking dish and bake until soft on the inside and caramelized on the outside, about 1 hour, stirring gently every 20 minutes to ensure even browning. Serve hot.

SERVES 4

Rootin' for Root Vegetables

In addition to the ever-popular carrots, root vegetables include turnips, beets, rutabagas, celery root (celeriac), parsley root, and parsnips. Root vegetables make wonderful additions to soups, stews, and vegetable medleys. In addition, they are all delicious glazed, pureed, and roasted. Carrots are especially rich in vitamin A and potassium, beets are loaded with iron, and parsley root is high in B complex vitamins. Parsnips, celery root, rutabagas, and turnips are all high in potassium and vitamin C.

In Search of Antioxidants

Antioxidants are special compounds present in certain vitamins and minerals that protect against oxidation, or cellular damage, caused by free radicals. This damage can lead to chronic diseases, including many cancers and diseases associated with aging. Among the best-known antioxidant vitamins are beta carotene and vitamins C and E.

- Beta carotene can be found in orange, red, yellow, and dark green vegetables and fruits. Among the best sources are apricots, broccoli, cantaloupe, prunes, raisins, carrots, kale, mustard greens, spinach, beets, sweet potatoes, onions, and winter squash.
- Vitamin C is found in abundance in citrus fruits (especially grapefruit), as well as broccoli, cantaloupe, cherries, bell peppers, kiwifruit, potatoes, strawberries, blueberries, blackberries, raspberries, red grapes, tomatoes, alfalfa sprouts, cauliflower, Brussels sprouts, and cabbage.
- Vitamin E is found in almonds, oats, olive oil, peanuts, sunflower seeds, and wheat germ, as well as blackberries, cantaloupe, corn, black currants, and grapefruit.

Shredded-Vegetable Fritters

You can vary the vegetables and seasonings in these fritters according to your preference. A dash of curry powder or cumin will change their character, as will substituting cilantro for the parsley or a hot chile for the red bell pepper. Serve with vegan sour cream, applesauce, chutney, or salsa.

1 small red onion, peeled

1 large sweet potato, peeled

1 small carrot, peeled

1/2 small red bell pepper, seeded and minced

1 tablespoon minced fresh parsley leaves

1/2 cup unbleached all-purpose flour

Egg replacer for 1 egg (page 509)

1 teaspoon salt

1/4 teaspoon freshly ground black pepper

Peanut oil for frying

1. Preheat the oven to 250 degrees F. Using a hand grater or the shredding disk of a food processor, shred the onion, sweet potato, and carrot and place in a colander. Press out the liquid and transfer the vegetables to a large bowl.

2. Stir in the bell pepper, parsley, flour, egg replacer, salt, and pepper and mix well.

3. Pour a thin layer of peanut oil in a large nonstick skillet and heat over medium-high heat. Scoop out a large spoonful of the vegetable mixture and press against it with your hand to tightly pack. Place the fritter in the hot pan and cook until golden brown on both sides, about 5 minutes per side. Repeat until all the vegetable mixture is used. Drain the cooked fritters on paper towels, then transfer to the oven to keep warm until all the fritters are cooked, adding more oil to the pan as needed. Serve hot.

SERVES 4 TO 6

8

Going with the Grain

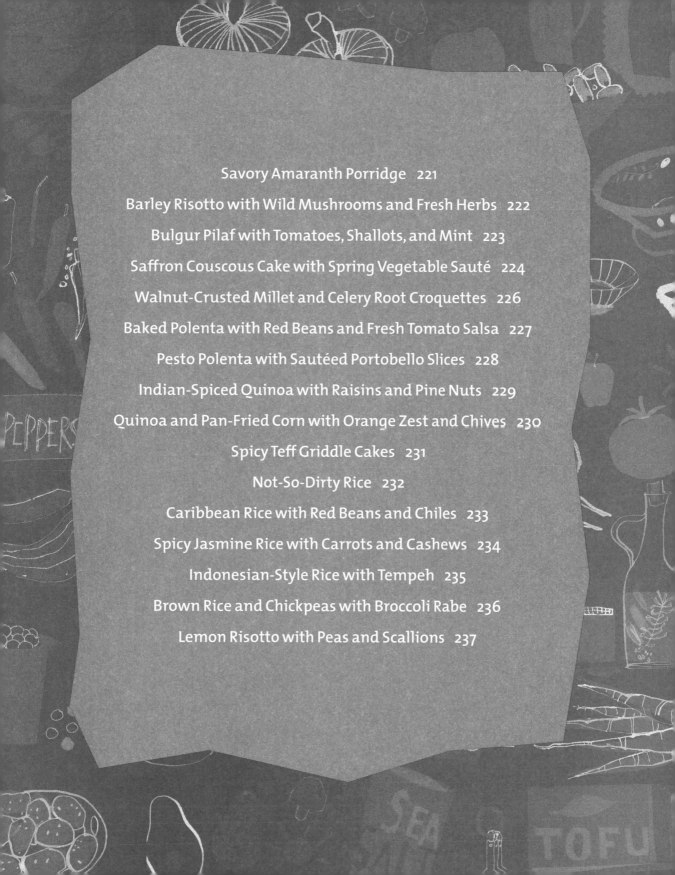

Grains are finally receiving the attention they deserve, as basmati and jasmine rice now occupy shelves where only Uncle Ben's once stood, and ancient grains such as quinoa and kamut appear on trendy restaurant menus. Until recent years, the only exposure to grains for many Americans, beyond the occasional serving of white rice, was in the form of processed breakfast cereals, breads, and pasta.

Many people now enjoy nutritious whole grains as the foundation of a well-balanced meal. Spoon some brown rice or quinoa onto a plate, top it with a generous serving of a bean and vegetable stew, and dinner is served. Grains can also be used to make everything from soups to desserts and to add substance to burgers, loaves, and stuffings.

This chapter offers recipes using several varieties of rice, including brown, basmati, and jasmine. You will also find recipes that use cornmeal (polenta), quinoa, barley, and millet, as well as couscous—that great grain impostor that is actually milled semolina wheat. These and other grains, such as spelt, amaranth, and kamut, which are extremely high in protein and loaded with flavor, provide immense versatility in menu planning. Best of all, you can now find these formerly remote grains in natural food stores.

A world of exciting flavors awaits you with each grain you try. I encourage you to experiment with some of the whole grains used in this chapter and to explore further by substituting grains or perhaps making a grain medley, using two or more grains in the same recipe. Although grains such as quinoa, kamut, and even millet might be unfamiliar to you, they are staple grains elsewhere in the world. Their widely divergent textures and generally neutral flavors make them fun to incorporate into your cooking repertoire.

GRAINS

Grains are considered staples throughout the world because they are an economical source of high-quality nutrition. Whole grains are rich in protein, B complex vitamins, vitamin E, and other nutrients and are good sources of fiber and carbohydrates. Refined grains are less nutritious because they have had part or all of the germ and bran removed. To compensate, many refined grain products are enriched with vitamins and minerals.

Here is a list of the some of the grains in the world's pantry.

- *Amaranth:* Considered a sacred grain of the Incas, this tiny grain is high in lysine, which boosts its value as a protein source. It has a distinctive, nutty flavor and can be used in baking or as a hot breakfast cereal.
- *Barley:* A flavorful, chewy grain, barley is frequently used in soups, pilafs, and salads or cooked as a breakfast cereal. Pearl barley, which has had its hard outer layers removed, is less nutritious than unrefined whole barley.
- *Buckwheat:* A traditional ingredient in eastern Europe, buckwheat groats, or kasha, as they are called when cooked, have a deep, nutty flavor that combines well with other grains.
- *Bulgur:* Sometimes called cracked wheat, bulgur is partially cooked whole-grain wheat that has been dried and cracked. It comes in small, medium, and coarse grinds and has a nutty flavor and a fluffy texture when cooked. Bulgur is used to make tabbouleh salad.
- *Corn:* Often treated as a vegetable, corn is in reality a grain that can be ground into different textures, called cornmeal or grits, and used to make breakfast porridge and polenta, as well cornbread and other baked goods.
- *Couscous:* Usually classified as a grain, couscous is actually a tiny pasta made from semolina wheat. But since it looks and acts like a grain, it is included here. Popular

in North African and Middle Eastern cooking, couscous is most widely available in a precooked, or instant, form and takes just five minutes to cook.

- *Kamut:* This ancient member of the wheat family has its origins in Egypt. Its grains are extremely large, chewy, and dense when cooked. Kamut is an interesting and nutritious addition to grain medleys. Because of its large size and long cooking time, kamut benefits from soaking overnight to reduce the cooking time by several minutes.
- *Millet:* A tiny, nutritious grain, millet is high in protein and rich in iron, calcium, B vitamins, and potassium. This highly digestible grain cooks fairly quickly and works well in stuffings, patties, and pilafs.
- *Oats:* Available steel-cut, rolled, or quick-cooking, oats are predominantly used as a breakfast cereal in the United States, and their flour is used in baking. Oats contain calcium, iron, and B vitamins and are a good source of protein and carbohydrates.
- *Quinoa:* Pronounced "KEEN-wah," this small, quick-cooking grain is extremely high in protein and has a good balance of amino acids. It also contains calcium, B vitamins, vitamin E, and iron. This sand-colored, disk-shaped grain is from the Andes, where it is known as "the mother grain." Quinoa has a mild, nutty flavor and fluffy texture when cooked.
- *Rice:* See the next section.
- *Spelt:* Also called farro, spelt is one of the oldest cultivated grains. Related to wheat, it has a mild, nutty flavor and is usually tolerated well by people with wheat allergies. As is the case with kamut, because of its large size and long cooking time, spelt benefits from soaking overnight.
- *Teff:* This grain is so small that several uncooked teff kernels can fit on the head of a pin. Cooked teff has a sweet flavor and a somewhat gelatinous consistency. It is best used in puddings and baked goods. The Ethiopian flatbread called *injera* is made with teff.

RICE

There's more to rice than the refined, starchy white variety, and many of the more exotic varieties are also more nutritious. Here are the main varieties widely available in supermarkets and natural, ethnic, and specialty food stores.

- *Arborio rice:* A short-grain rice from Italy's Po Valley, Arborio rice is the star ingredient in creamy risottos.

- *Basmati rice:* This aromatic long-grain rice from India comes in white and brown varieties. It has long grains that remain separate and firm when cooked.
- *Brown rice:* This whole-grain form of rice is available in short-, medium-, and long-grain varieties. It is nutritionally superior to white rice because it has not been stripped of its nutrients through polishing.
- *Jasmine rice:* This fragrant Thai favorite has a delicate, flowery bouquet. Its texture is slightly sticky when cooked.
- *Sticky rice:* This short-grain rice is used to make desserts and other Asian dishes and is also called glutinous rice. Japanese sticky rice is used to make sushi and is sometimes sold as sushi rice.
- *White rice:* This is brown rice that has been stripped of its nutrients through polishing, which removes the hull, bran, and germ. Because of this, white rice is often enriched with vitamins and minerals. Long-grain white rice is the most widely used variety.
- *Wild rice:* Not really a rice but the seed of a tall, aquatic grass of North America, wild rice is high in amino acids and B vitamins and has double the protein of white rice. It is often paired with other grains in pilafs.

STORING AND COOKING GRAINS

Most whole grains can be stored, unrefrigerated, in tightly covered containers away from heat, light, and humidity. Grains that have been ground, cracked, or flaked should be refrigerated, as the natural oils in the grains have been exposed and are more prone to becoming rancid. As a general rule, I store all grains in the refrigerator or freezer.

Although soaking grains is not necessary, it can significantly reduce their cooking times. In all cases, grains should be rinsed before using to remove loose hulls, dust, and other impurities.

To intensify the flavor of grains, you can lightly toast them in a dry skillet before cooking.

Most grains can be cooked in a pot with about two times as much water as grain, or more depending on the cooking time. Bring the water to a boil, cover, reduce the heat to low, and simmer until tender. The water will be absorbed into the grain. For 1 cup of uncooked grain, the average yield will be about 3 cups of cooked grain. Besides cooking on top of the stove, grains may be baked in the oven in a tightly covered pot. To do this, bring the water to a boil on top of the stove, then add the grain, cover tightly, and bake in a preheated 325 degree F oven for approximately the same amount of time as for stovetop cooking. Longer-cooking grains benefit from cooking in a pressure cooker, while grains with shorter cooking times taste great prepared pilaf style, which begins with sautéing the grains in oil, then adding liquid to finish the cooking.

Following is a table of average cooking times for several grains using the stovetop cooking method. Be sure to salt the water after it comes to a boil. Let the grains stand, covered, for 5 minutes after cooking, then fluff with a fork before serving.

STOVETOP COOKING TIMES FOR GRAINS

Grain (1 cup)	Water	Cooking Time
Amaranth	2 cups	20 minutes
Barley (pearl)	3 cups	30 minutes
Basmati rice	$1^3/_4$ cups	15 to 20 minutes
Brown rice (long-grain)	2 cups	30 minutes
Brown rice (short- or medium-grain)	3 cups	45 minutes
Buckwheat (kasha)	2 cups	20 minutes
Bulgur	2 cups	15 minutes
Couscous	$1^1/_4$ cups	5 minutes
Kamut	4 cups	2 hours
Millet	2 cups	30 minutes
Quinoa	2 cups	15 minutes
Spelt	$2^3/_4$ cups	1 hour
Teff	3 cups	15 minutes
White rice (long-grain)	$1^3/_4$ cups	15 to 20 minutes
Wild rice	$3^3/_4$ cups	45 minutes

Savory Amaranth Porridge

This ancient grain of the Aztecs has a strong flavor that is at once sweet and savory—some say "nutty"—and that people either love or hate. Extremely high in protein, iron, and calcium, the tiny amaranth grains cook up slightly gelatinous and are often ground into flour and combined with other flours to make baked goods such as muffins, cookies, and quick breads. This porridge is similar in texture to a restorative Chinese congee and may be eaten at any time of day, including breakfast. To prepare this as a more traditional hot breakfast cereal, omit the last four ingredients and top as you would oatmeal—with soy milk, sweetener, and a sprinkling of granola or raisins.

1 cup amaranth

3 cups water

Salt

3 scallions, minced

1 tablespoon tamari or other soy sauce

1 teaspoon olive oil

2 tablespoons roasted pumpkin seeds
    or pepitas

1. In a medium-size saucepan over medium-high heat, combine the amaranth and water and bring to a boil. Reduce the heat to low, add salt to taste, and simmer until the water is absorbed, about 30 minutes. During the last 5 minutes of cooking time, stir in the scallions, tamari, and olive oil.

2. Spoon the porridge into serving bowls, sprinkle with the pumpkin seeds, and serve hot.

SERVES 4

Barley Risotto with Wild Mushrooms and Fresh Herbs

Both fresh and dried mushrooms are used to amplify the woodsy mushroom flavor, which is complemented by the barley and fresh herbs. Another layer of mushroom flavor is added with the Mushroom Stock, but you may use Basic Vegetable Stock (page 68) instead, if you prefer. Although Arborio rice is traditionally used to make risotto, barley provides a hearty change of pace.

1/4 cup dried porcini mushrooms,
    soaked in 1 cup very hot water
    for 20 minutes
4 cups Mushroom Stock (page 69)
1/2 cup white wine
2 tablespoons olive oil
1/4 cup minced shallots
1 large garlic clove, minced

1 cup pearl barley
2 cups chopped cremini mushrooms
2 teaspoons minced fresh marjoram
    leaves
2 teaspoons minced fresh parsley leaves
2 teaspoons minced fresh chives
Salt and freshly ground black pepper

1. Drain the porcinis, reserving the soaking liquid. Strain the liquid and set aside. Chop the mushrooms and set aside.

2. Combine the stock, reserved mushroom liquid, and wine in a medium-size saucepan over medium heat and bring to a simmer.

3. In a large skillet or saucepan, heat the olive oil over medium heat. Add the shallots and garlic and cook, stirring, until fragrant and slightly softened, about 1 minute. Add the barley and both kinds of mushrooms and stir until coated with oil.

4. Add 1/2 cup of the hot liquid and simmer, uncovered and stirring frequently, until the liquid is almost absorbed. Continue adding the stock mixture 1/2 cup at a time, stirring until the liquid is absorbed, until the barley is tender, about 30 minutes. You may not need to use all of the stock mixture.

5. About 5 minutes before the risotto is finished, stir in the marjoram, parsley, chives, and salt and pepper to taste.

6. To serve, spoon the risotto into shallow bowls and serve hot.

SERVES 4

Bulgur Pilaf with Tomatoes, Shallots, and Mint

Also called cracked wheat, bulgur is a quick-cooking grain with a hearty, nut-like flavor that is used to make the popular Middle Eastern salad tabbouleh. Fresh or canned tomatoes may be used for this recipe. Cooked chickpeas or another type of bean may be added for substance. I like to serve this pilaf with a cooked green vegetable such as string beans or sautéed spinach.

2 tablespoons olive oil

3 shallots, finely chopped

1 cup medium bulgur

2 cups Basic Vegetable Stock (page 68)

Salt and freshly ground black pepper

1 cup finely diced fresh or canned
    tomatoes

1 tablespoon chopped fresh mint leaves

1. Heat the olive oil in a large skillet over medium heat. Add the shallots, cover, and cook until softened, about 3 minutes. Add the bulgur and stir to combine. Stir in the stock and bring to a boil. Reduce the heat to low and season with salt and pepper to taste. Cover and simmer until the bulgur is tender and the liquid is absorbed, about 15 minutes.

2. Remove from the heat and stir in the tomatoes. Cover and let stand for 5 minutes. Stir in the mint, cover, and let stand for 5 minutes more before serving.

SERVES 4

Saffron Couscous Cake with Spring Vegetable Sauté

Whether this dish is saffron flavored or saffron colored will depend on your budget. Made with either saffron or turmeric, it's lovely served for a spring lunch or light supper. To serve as a first course, you can cut the couscous cake into smaller wedges or place the couscous mixture into small ring molds or individual tart pans instead of the large springform pan.

2 tablespoons olive oil, plus more for brushing
2 large shallots, minced
2 cups instant couscous
3 cups Basic Vegetable Stock (page 68), heated
Pinch of ground saffron or turmeric
1/8 teaspoon cayenne
Salt
1/2 small yellow bell pepper, seeded and cut into matchsticks

8 ounces thin asparagus, bottoms trimmed and cut diagonally into 1-inch pieces
1 medium-size carrot, shredded
3 scallions, minced
1/2 cup frozen baby green peas, thawed
1 cup grape or cherry tomatoes, cut in half
Freshly ground black pepper
2 tablespoons minced fresh parsley or other herb leaves

1. Heat 1 tablespoon of the olive oil in a medium-size saucepan over medium heat. Add the shallots, cover, and cook until softened, about 5 minutes. Add the couscous and stir to coat with the oil. Stir in the hot stock and bring to a boil. Reduce the heat to low and stir in the saffron, cayenne, and salt to taste. Cover and cook until all the liquid is absorbed, 5 to 7 minutes.

2. Transfer the couscous to a lightly oiled 9-inch springform pan and smooth the top. Refrigerate until firm, at least 1 hour or up to 4 hours.

3. Preheat the oven to 350 degrees F. Remove the cake from the refrigerator, release the springform pan, and cut the cake into 6 wedges. Place on a lightly oiled baking sheet and brush lightly with olive oil. Bake until just hot, 12 to 15 minutes.

4. Meanwhile, heat the remaining 1 tablespoon olive oil in a large skillet over medium heat. Add the bell pepper and asparagus and cook, stirring, until slightly softened, about 5 minutes. Add the carrot, scallions, peas, tomatoes, and salt and pepper to taste. Cook until the vegetables are tender, about 3 minutes. Stir in the parsley.

5. Arrange the couscous wedges on individual plates, top with a large spoonful of the vegetables, and serve immediately.

SERVES 6

Did You know...

The shallot was considered an aphrodisiac in ancient Rome? One wonders if this was because the subtle-tasting shallot, unlike its odoriferous relatives, garlic and onions, does not cause bad breath.

Walnut-Crusted Millet and Celery Root Croquettes

These croquettes can be served as a side dish or light entrée and are a delicious way to enjoy millet, a very nourishing grain that is an infrequent visitor to dinner tables in the United States. Celery root, or celeriac, is an often overlooked vegetable that resembles a large, dusky brown knob. It tastes like regular celery but with a subtler flavor. For an elegant presentation, serve these croquettes in a pool of Basic Brown Sauce (page 148) or Yellow Pepper Coulis (page 156).

1 cup millet
1 small celery root (celeriac), peeled and shredded
1 medium-size yellow onion, minced
3 cups water

Salt
Freshly ground black pepper
1 cup ground walnuts
1/2 cup dry bread crumbs
Olive oil for frying

1. Combine the millet, celery root, onion, and water in a medium-size saucepan over medium-high heat and bring to a boil. Reduce the heat to low, salt the water, cover, and simmer until the ingredients are soft and all the water is absorbed, about 30 minutes.

2. Transfer the millet mixture to a medium-size bowl. Season with salt and pepper to taste and refrigerate until chilled.

3. In a shallow bowl, combine the walnuts and bread crumbs. Shape the millet mixture into patties and coat evenly with the walnut mixture.

4. Heat 2 tablespoons of the olive oil in a large skillet over medium heat. Working in batches if necessary, add the croquettes and cook until well browned on both sides, 3 to 5 minutes per side. Add more oil as needed. Serve immediately.

SERVES 4

Baked Polenta with Red Beans and Fresh Tomato Salsa

The polenta may be made a few days ahead and refrigerated until needed. Then simply cut it into serving-size portions and finish in the oven. If you prefer, you may pan-fry the polenta in a little olive oil instead of baking it.

3½ cups water

1 teaspoon salt, plus more for seasoning

1 cup medium-ground yellow cornmeal

2 tablespoons minced fresh cilantro leaves

3 tablespoons olive oil

Freshly ground black pepper

4 scallions, chopped

1½ cups cooked or one 15-ounce can dark red kidney or other red beans, drained and rinsed

1 cup Fresh Tomato Salsa (page 174)

1. Bring the water to a boil in a large saucepan over high heat. Reduce the heat to medium, add the salt, and slowly whisk in the cornmeal, stirring constantly. Reduce the heat to low and continue to cook, stirring frequently, until thick, 30 to 40 minutes. Stir in 1 tablespoon of the cilantro and 1 tablespoon of the olive oil and season with salt and pepper to taste.

2. Spoon the polenta into a lightly oiled, shallow 10-inch square baking dish and spread it evenly over the bottom. Refrigerate until firm, at least 30 minutes.

3. Heat 1 tablespoon of the olive oil in a medium-size skillet over medium heat. Add the scallions and cook until slightly softened, about 1 minute. Stir in the beans, the remaining 1 tablespoon cilantro, and the salsa. Season with salt and pepper to taste. Simmer until the mixture is hot and the flavors are blended, about 5 minutes. Keep warm over very low heat.

4. Preheat the oven to 375 degrees F. Cut the polenta into 4 squares and place on a lightly oiled baking sheet. Brush the tops with the remaining 1 tablespoon olive oil and bake until hot and golden brown, about 20 minutes.

5. To serve, transfer the polenta to individual plates, spoon some of the salsa on top, and serve hot.

SERVES 4

Pesto Polenta with Sautéed Portobello Slices

Slices of juicy portobello mushrooms complement the pesto-infused polenta for an intriguing flavor. This is a great company dish because the polenta may be made a day or so in advance and then cut and baked when needed.

3¹/₂ cups water

1 teaspoon salt, plus more for
  seasoning

1 cup medium-ground yellow cornmeal

¹/₄ cup vegan pesto, homemade
  (page 157) or store-bought

3 tablespoons olive oil

Freshly ground black pepper

2 garlic cloves, chopped

4 large portobello mushrooms,
  stems removed and caps cut into
  ¹/₄-inch-thick slices

1. Bring the water to a boil in a large saucepan over high heat. Reduce the heat to medium, add the salt, and slowly whisk in the cornmeal, stirring constantly. Reduce the heat to low and continue to cook, stirring frequently, until thick, about 30 minutes. Near the end of the cooking time, thin the pesto with 1 tablespoon of the olive oil and stir it into the polenta. Season with salt and pepper to taste.

2. Spoon the polenta into a lightly oiled, shallow 10-inch square baking dish and spread it evenly over the bottom. Refrigerate until firm, at least 30 minutes.

3. Heat 1 tablespoon of the olive oil in a large skillet over medium heat. Add the garlic and cook until fragrant, about 30 seconds. Add the mushroom slices, season with salt and pepper to taste, and cook until the mushrooms are tender, about 5 minutes. Keep warm over very low heat.

4. Preheat the oven to 375 degrees F. When the polenta is firm, cut into 4 squares. Place on a lightly oiled baking sheet and brush with the remaining 1 tablespoon olive oil. Bake until hot and golden brown, about 30 minutes.

5. To serve, transfer the polenta to individual plates, spoon some of the mushrooms on top, and serve hot.

SERVES 4

Indian-Spiced Quinoa with Raisins and Pine Nuts

Despite the fact that quinoa hails from South America, it adapts deliciously to the flavors of Indian spices and the Middle Eastern pilaf-style cooking method. Quinoa is available in natural food stores.

1 1/2 cups quinoa

2 tablespoons olive oil

2 large shallots, minced

1 teaspoon peeled and minced fresh ginger

1/2 teaspoon ground cardamom

1/2 teaspoon ground coriander

1/4 teaspoon ground cumin

1/8 teaspoon cayenne

3 cups Basic Vegetable Stock (page 68) or water, heated

Salt and freshly ground black pepper

1/3 cup golden raisins

1/4 cup pine nuts, toasted (page 110)

2 tablespoons minced fresh parsley leaves

1. Rinse the quinoa well to remove the bitter white coating. Drain thoroughly and set aside.

2. Heat the olive oil in a large skillet over medium heat. Add the shallots and ginger and cook, stirring, until the shallots are slightly softened, about 1 minute. Add the quinoa along with the cardamom, coriander, cumin, and cayenne and stir to coat with the oil. Stir in the hot stock and bring to a boil. Reduce the heat to low and season with salt and pepper to taste. Cover and cook until all the water is absorbed, about 10 minutes.

3. Remove from the heat and stir in the raisins, pine nuts, and parsley. Serve hot.

SERVES 4

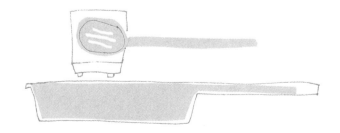

Quinoa and Pan-Fried Corn with Orange Zest and Chives

The sweetness of the corn, accented by the orange zest, complements the nutty flavor of the quinoa.

1 1/2 cups quinoa
3 cups Basic Vegetable Stock (page 68)
2 tablespoons olive oil
1 1/2 cups fresh or frozen corn kernels
3 scallions, minced

1 tablespoon grated orange zest
Salt and freshly ground black pepper
2 tablespoons minced fresh chives for garnish

1. Rinse the quinoa well to remove the bitter white coating. Drain and set aside.
2. Bring the stock to a simmer in a large saucepan over medium heat. Stir in the quinoa, cover, and reduce the heat to low. Simmer until all the water is absorbed, about 15 minutes.
3. Heat the olive oil in a skillet over medium heat. Add the corn and scallions and cook, stirring, until fragrant, about 3 minutes. Add the contents of the skillet to the quinoa. Stir in the orange zest and salt and pepper to taste. Set aside for 5 minutes so the flavors can blend.
4. To serve, spoon the quinoa into a shallow serving bowl, garnish with the chives, and serve hot.

SERVES 4

Spicy Teff Griddle Cakes

This tiniest of grains is used to make *injera*, the traditional Ethiopian flatbread. High in protein and calcium, teff can be enjoyed as a breakfast cereal or used in baked goods. Serve these griddle cakes with any of a variety of sauces, including Faux Choron Sauce (page 145) and Spicy Peanut Dipping Sauce (page 160). If you'd like to try these cakes for breakfast, omit the scallions and cayenne and top with pure maple syrup. Look for teff in natural food stores.

1/2 cup teff
3 cups water (approximately)
1 cup unbleached all-purpose flour
1/2 cup minced scallions

1 teaspoon baking powder
1/8 teaspoon cayenne, or to taste
Salt

1. In a medium-size saucepan over medium heat, combine the teff and 1 1/2 cups of the water. Cover and bring to a boil. Reduce the heat to low and simmer, stirring occasionally, until all the water is absorbed, about 15 minutes.
2. Transfer the teff to a large bowl and add the flour, scallions, baking powder, cayenne, and salt to taste. Stir in as much of the remaining 1 1/2 cups water as needed to make a batter and mix until smooth.
3. Preheat the oven to 200 degrees F. Lightly oil a griddle or large skillet and place over medium-high heat. For each cake, ladle about 1/4 cup of the batter onto the hot griddle and cook until it is browned on both sides, 3 to 4 minutes per side. Repeat until all the batter is used, re-oiling the griddle as needed and keeping the cooked cakes warm in the oven.

SERVES 4

Not-So-Dirty Rice

Traditional dirty rice is so named because the white rice is flecked with brown pieces of chopped chicken livers. In this version, vegetarian burger crumbles are used instead and are combined with onion, bell pepper, garlic, and spices. If vegetarian burger crumbles are unavailable, thaw two veggie burgers (Original Vegan Boca Burger is a good choice), chop finely, and proceed with recipe.

1 tablespoon olive oil

1 medium-size onion, finely chopped

1 small green bell pepper, seeded and
    finely chopped

2 garlic cloves, minced

2 cups vegetarian burger crumbles
    (see headnote)

1 teaspoon Tabasco sauce

1 teaspoon dried thyme, crumbled

1/2 teaspoon salt

1/8 teaspoon cayenne

3 cups freshly cooked long-grain
    white rice

Heat the olive oil in a large saucepan over medium heat. Add the onion and bell pepper, cover, and cook until softened, about 5 minutes. Add the garlic, burger crumbles, Tabasco, thyme, salt, and cayenne. Stir to combine and heat through, about 5 minutes. Stir in the rice and cook until hot, 5 to 7 minutes. Taste and adjust the seasonings, then serve hot.

SERVES 4

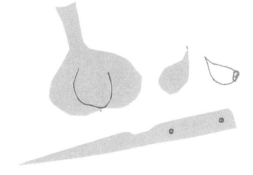

Caribbean Rice with Red Beans and Chiles

As in many other areas of the world, rice and beans are a popular combination in the Caribbean islands, where cooks often jazz things up with hot chiles and fragrant spices.

1 tablespoon olive oil

1 small red onion, minced

1 small red bell pepper, seeded and chopped

1 or 2 small, fresh hot chiles, to your taste, seeded and minced

2 garlic cloves, minced

1/2 teaspoon peeled and minced fresh ginger

1 cup basmati rice

1/2 teaspoon light brown sugar, palm sugar, or natural sweetener

1/2 teaspoon salt

1/2 teaspoon ground allspice

1/4 teaspoon dried thyme

1/4 teaspoon freshly grated nutmeg

2 cups hot water

11/2 cups cooked or one 15-ounce can dark red kidney or other red beans, drained and rinsed

1. Heat the olive oil in a saucepan over medium heat. Add the onion, bell pepper, chiles, garlic, and ginger. Cover and cook, stirring, until the onion is softened, about 5 minutes. Stir in the rice to coat with the oil. Add the brown sugar, salt, allspice, thyme, and nutmeg, stirring to combine. Stir in the water, reduce the heat to medium-low, cover, and cook until the rice is tender, about 20 minutes.

2. Stir in the beans and cook until hot, about 5 minutes. Taste and adjust the seasonings, then serve hot.

SERVES 4

Spicy Jasmine Rice with Carrots and Cashews

In this quick and easy dish, fragrant jasmine rice is stir-fried with vegetables, fresh ginger, and minced hot chile pepper. The sweet crunch of cashews adds textural contrast. If you like, add some thawed green peas for a color accent. Thai basil, with its haunting anise-like flavor, is also a good addition, stirred in at the end.

2 tablespoons peanut oil

1 small red onion, finely chopped

1 small, fresh hot red chile, seeded and minced

1 large carrot, grated

2 garlic cloves, minced

1 tablespoon peeled and grated fresh ginger

2 scallions, minced

2 tablespoons tamari or other soy sauce

1/2 teaspoon light brown sugar, palm sugar, or natural sweetener

3 cups cold cooked jasmine rice, broken up into small pieces

1/2 cup chopped unsalted dry-roasted cashews

1. Heat the peanut oil in a large skillet or wok over medium-high heat. Add the onion and stir-fry until softened, about 5 minutes. Add the chile, carrot, garlic, ginger, and scallions and stir-fry until soft and fragrant, about 2 minutes.

2. Add the tamari, brown sugar, and rice and stir-fry until the ingredients are blended and the rice is heated through, about 10 minutes.

3. To serve, place the rice in a shallow bowl, sprinkle with the chopped cashews, and serve immediately.

SERVES 4

Did You Know...

Ginger is known for its healing properties as well as its fragrant spiciness? It is said to have a positive effect on the heart and blood circulation and is also used to prevent nausea. Hot ginger tea is sometimes used to relieve symptoms of the common cold.

Indonesian-Style Rice with Tempeh

Inspired by the spicy-sweet Indonesian fried rice dish called *nasi goreng*, this can be made using alternative ingredients. For example, omit the tempeh, use broccoli and bell pepper instead of carrot and cabbage, or garnish with bean sprouts or diced tomato instead of cucumber and peanuts. The traditional accompaniment is a hot and spicy relish called *sambal*, which can be found in Asian markets.

3 shallots, peeled

1 or 2 small, fresh hot red chiles, to your taste, seeded

1 garlic clove, peeled

1/4 teaspoon salt

2 tablespoons peanut oil

1 large carrot, shredded

2 cups finely chopped napa cabbage

1 cup crumbled poached tempeh (page 14)

3 tablespoons tamari or other soy sauce

2 1/2 teaspoons light brown sugar, palm sugar, or molasses

3 cups cold cooked basmati or other long-grain white or brown rice, broken up into small pieces

1 medium-size cucumber, peeled, seeded, and shredded, for garnish

1/2 cup chopped unsalted dry-roasted peanuts for garnish

1. In a food processor or blender, combine the shallots, chiles, garlic, and salt and process until smooth. Set aside.

2. Heat the peanut oil in a large skillet or wok over medium heat. Add the carrot and cabbage and stir-fry until slightly softened, about 1 minute. Add the tempeh, 1 1/2 tablespoons of the tamari, and the sugar and cook until the tempeh is lightly browned, about 2 minutes. Stir in the reserved shallot mixture and cook until fragrant, about 30 seconds. Add the rice and the remaining 1 1/2 tablespoons tamari and stir-fry to combine all the ingredients and heat through, about 10 minutes.

3. To serve, place the rice mixture in a shallow serving bowl or on a large platter and garnish with the cucumber and peanuts.

SERVES 4

Brown Rice and Chickpeas with Broccoli Rabe

This nourishing and wholesome recipe makes a great one-dish meal that you can put together in minutes when you start with cooked rice and canned chickpeas. Broccoli rabe, also called rapini, looks sort of like "skinny" broccoli, with long slender stems, tiny buds, and leaves. It has a pleasant, slightly bitter flavor and is available in well-stocked supermarkets.

2 bunches broccoli rabe,
   stems trimmed

2 tablespoons olive oil

1 small yellow onion, finely chopped

2 garlic cloves, minced

1½ cups cooked or one 15-ounce can
   chickpeas, drained and rinsed

3 cups cold cooked brown rice,
   broken up into small pieces

Salt and freshly ground black pepper

1. Cook the broccoli rabe in a pot of boiling salted water until tender, about 5 minutes. Drain and coarsely chop. Set aside.

2. Heat the olive oil in a large skillet over medium heat. Add the onion and garlic, cover, and cook until softened, about 5 minutes. Add the broccoli rabe and cook for 2 minutes, stirring to combine. Stir in the chickpeas, rice, and salt and pepper to taste. Cook, stirring, until heated through, about 10 minutes. Serve hot.

SERVES 4

"The greatness of a nation and its moral progress can be judged by the way its animals are treated."
—MAHATMA GANDHI

Lemon Risotto with Peas and Scallions

The sparkling taste of fresh lemon makes this risotto ideal springtime fare. I like to accompany it with roasted asparagus and warm crusty bread.

4 cups Basic Vegetable Stock
   (page 68)
1/4 cup fresh lemon juice
2 tablespoons olive oil

1 1/2 cups Arborio rice
1/2 cup minced scallions
2/3 cup frozen baby green peas, thawed
Salt and freshly ground black pepper

1. Bring the stock and lemon juice to a simmer in a medium-size saucepan over medium heat. Reduce the heat to low and continue to simmer.

2. In a large skillet or saucepan, heat the oil over medium heat. Add the rice and scallions and stir until coated with oil. Add 1/2 cup of the hot liquid and simmer, uncovered and stirring frequently until the liquid is almost absorbed. Continue adding the stock mixture 1/2 cup at a time, stirring until the liquid is absorbed, until the rice is tender but firm and the mixture is thick and creamy, about 25 minutes.

3. About 10 minutes before the risotto is finished, stir in the peas and salt and pepper to taste.

4. To serve, spoon into shallow bowls and serve hot.

SERVES 4

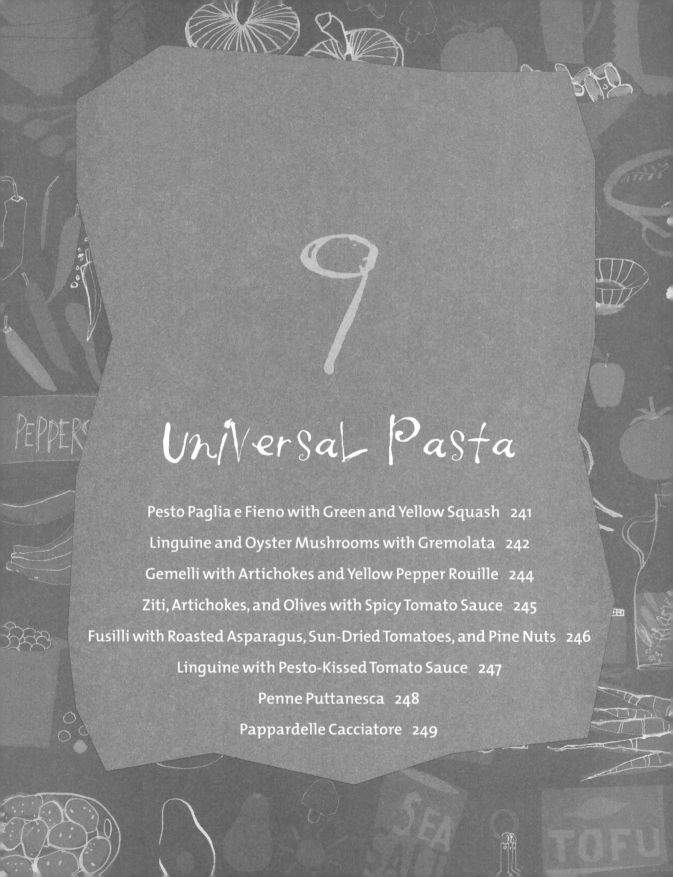

9

Universal Pasta

Everyone loves pasta. What's not to like? It's delicious and versatile, fun to eat, and easy to prepare. Pasta is an especially popular choice for vegan meals because of the seemingly endless variety of plant-based toppings. From the traditional tomato marinara sauce to basil pesto to the vegetable showcase pasta primavera, you could eat a different pasta meal every night. Add the international noodle dishes to pasta's repertoire, and your pasta world becomes a pasta universe.

You may already be familiar with naturally vegan pasta dishes—sauces that do not include meat or dairy. But there are easy ways to transform favorite meat- and dairy-based sauces into vegan originals. In this chapter, you will discover *Alfredo-Style Fettuccine*, made creamy with almonds and soy, and *Mac and "Cheese"* casserole, which works magic using tofu, miso, and nutritional yeast. Veggie burgers, eggplant, and mushrooms provide meaty substance in several tomato-based sauces. There's also a selection of hearty eastern European recipes, including *Potato Pierogi with Savoy Cabbage and Pear and Dried Plum Compote*, as well as a number of flavorful Asian dishes that pair soba, udon, and rice sticks with vegetables, soy foods, and exotic seasonings.

Vegans, take note: whereas most dried pasta is made without eggs, most fresh pasta is made with them. However, a few brands of fresh vegan pasta can be found in some natural food stores and through mail-order sources. (This goes for egg-free "egg" noodles as well.) It is also possible to make fresh pasta at home without using eggs. The simplest approach, however, is to rely on dried pasta.

Pesto Paglia e Fieno with Green and Yellow Squash

Tuscany's "straw and hay" pasta dish is so named for its green and yellow noodles. This theme is elaborated on here with the addition of green and yellow squash, cut into long strips with a mandoline, sharp knife, or vegetable peeler.

8 ounces spinach linguine

8 ounces regular linguine

1/4 cup olive oil

1 medium-size zucchini, cut lengthwise into thin strips

1 medium-size yellow squash, cut lengthwise into thin strips

Salt and freshly ground black pepper

1/3 cup vegan pesto, homemade (page 157) or store-bought

1. Cook both types of linguine in a large pot of boiling salted water, stirring occasionally, until *al dente*, 8 to 10 minutes.

2. While the pasta is cooking, heat the olive oil in medium-size skillet over medium heat, add the squash, and cook until softened, 3 to 4 minutes. Season with salt and pepper to taste. Reduce the heat to low and keep warm.

3. Drain the pasta and place in a large, shallow serving bowl. Add the squash and pesto and toss gently to combine. Serve at once.

SERVES 4

Linguine and Oyster Mushrooms with Gremolata

Gremolata, sometimes spelled gremolada, is a zesty mixture of garlic, lemon, and parsley that brings out the slightly sweet flavor of the oyster mushrooms in this recipe. A garnish often sprinkled on Italian stews such as *osso buco*, this Milanese seasoning is paired here with pasta to good effect.

1 pound linguine

1/4 cup extra virgin olive oil

1/4 cup minced shallots

2 1/2 cups sliced oyster mushrooms

Salt and freshly ground black pepper

1/3 cup Gremolata (recipe follows)

1. Cook the linguine in a large pot of boiling salted water, stirring occasionally, until *al dente*, 8 to 10 minutes.

2. While the pasta is cooking, heat 1 tablespoon of the olive oil in a large skillet over medium heat. Add the shallots, cover, and cook until softened, about 5 minutes. Add the mushrooms and cook, stirring frequently, until they begin to soften, about 3 minutes. Season with salt and pepper to taste.

3. Drain the pasta and place in a large, shallow serving bowl. Add the mushroom mixture, the remaining 3 tablespoons olive oil, and the Gremolata and toss gently to combine. Serve at once.

SERVES 4

GREMOLATA

Gremolata is a flavorful garnish made with lemon, garlic, and parsley. It can be used to enhance certain stews, pastas, and sautéed dishes. I sometimes add 2 tablespoons of ground nuts or seeds for extra flavor and substance.

1/3 cup chopped fresh parsley leaves
2 large garlic cloves, chopped

Grated zest of 1 lemon

Mince the parsley, garlic, and lemon zest together until well combined. Cover tightly and refrigerate until ready to use. For the best flavor, use the same day it is made, but it will keep for a day or so in the refrigerator.

MAKES ABOUT 1/3 CUP

Gemelli with Artichokes and Yellow Pepper Rouille

A rouille is a thick Provençal sauce usually made with roasted red peppers and thickened with bread. This version uses yellow peppers that are sautéed rather than roasted, resulting in a much lighter flavor.

1/3 cup extra virgin olive oil
2 large yellow bell peppers, seeded and coarsely chopped
1 slice firm white bread
1/2 teaspoon salt
1/8 teaspoon cayenne

1 pound gemelli
2 garlic cloves, pressed
One 15-ounce can artichoke hearts, drained and quartered
2 tablespoons chopped fresh basil leaves

1. Heat 2 tablespoons of the olive oil in a large skillet over medium-low heat. Add the bell peppers, cover, and cook until soft, about 15 minutes. Remove from the heat.

2. Trim the crust from the bread and soak in water to cover for 5 minutes. Squeeze out the water and place the bread in a food processor along with the bell peppers, salt, and cayenne. Process until smooth, then set the rouille aside.

3. Cook the gemelli in a large pot of boiling salted water, stirring occasionally, until *al dente*, 8 to 10 minutes.

4. While the pasta is cooking, heat the remaining olive oil in a medium-size skillet over medium heat. Add the garlic and cook until fragrant, about 30 seconds. Add the artichoke hearts and cook, stirring to coat with the garlic and oil, until heated through, about 5 minutes.

5. Drain the pasta and place in a large, shallow serving bowl. Add the artichokes and toss to combine. Top with the rouille, sprinkle with the basil, and serve immediately.

SERVES 4

Ziti, Artichokes, and Olives with Spicy Tomato Sauce

Plum tomatoes are a good choice for making tomato sauce because they are meatier than regular tomatoes, with less water and seeds. Canned tomatoes may be used if fresh ones are unavailable or out of season.

2 tablespoons olive oil

1 small yellow onion, chopped

3 garlic cloves, chopped

2 tablespoons tomato paste

2 pounds ripe plum tomatoes, chopped, or one 28-ounce can plum tomatoes, drained and chopped

One 9-ounce package frozen artichoke hearts, cooked according to package directions and drained

2 tablespoons dry red wine

1/2 teaspoon red pepper flakes

1/2 cup Kalamata or other brine-cured black olives, pitted and chopped

Salt and freshly ground black pepper

1 pound ziti

1/4 cup chopped fresh basil or parsley leaves

1. Heat the olive oil in a large saucepan over medium heat. Add the onion, cover, and cook until softened, about 5 minutes. Stir in the garlic and tomato paste and cook, stirring, until the garlic is fragrant, about 30 seconds. Add the tomatoes, artichokes, wine, and red pepper flakes. Reduce the heat to low and stir in the olives. Season with salt and pepper to taste and simmer while you cook the ziti.

2. Cook the ziti in a pot of boiling salted water, stirring occasionally, until *al dente*, about 10 minutes.

3. Drain the pasta and place in a large, shallow serving bowl. Add the sauce and basil and toss to combine. Serve hot.

SERVES 4

Fusilli with Roasted Asparagus, Sun-Dried Tomatoes, and Pine Nuts

The smoky flavor of sun-dried tomatoes teams with roasted asparagus and toasted pine nuts against a backdrop of chewy fusilli tossed in garlicky olive oil for a wonderful combination of textures and flavors.

12 ounces thin asparagus, bottoms trimmed and cut diagonally into 2-inch pieces
3 tablespoons extra virgin olive oil, plus more for drizzling, if desired
1/2 cup oil-packed or rehydrated sun-dried tomatoes

1 pound fusilli
1 large garlic clove, minced
Salt and freshly ground black pepper
1/4 cup chopped fresh basil or parsley leaves
3 tablespoons pine nuts, toasted (page 110)

1. Preheat the oven to 450 degrees F. Toss the asparagus with 1 tablespoon of the olive oil and place on a lightly oiled baking sheet. Roast until just tender, 6 to 8 minutes. Remove from the oven and set aside.

2. Cut the tomatoes into 1/4-inch-wide strips and set aside.

3. Cook the fusilli in a large pot of boiling salted water, stirring occasionally, until *al dente*, 8 to 10 minutes.

4. While the pasta is cooking, heat the remaining 2 tablespoons olive oil in a large skillet over medium heat. Add the garlic and cook, stirring, until fragrant, about 30 seconds. Add the roasted asparagus, tomatoes, and salt and pepper to taste. Reduce the heat to low and keep warm.

5. Drain the pasta and place in a large, shallow serving bowl. Add the asparagus mixture, basil, and pine nuts. Toss to combine, drizzle on a little more olive oil, if desired, and serve hot.

SERVES 4

Linguine with Pesto-Kissed Tomato Sauce

Basil pesto is swirled into the tomato sauce just before serving to add an extra dimension of flavor. For a "meaty" sauce with more protein, add some chopped or crumbled veggie burgers or vegetarian burger crumbles near the end of the cooking time.

1 tablespoon olive oil

1 small yellow onion, chopped

2 garlic cloves, minced

1/4 cup tomato paste

One 28-ounce can crushed tomatoes

Salt and freshly ground black pepper

1/4 cup vegan pesto, homemade (page 157) or store-bought

1 pound linguine

1. Heat the olive oil in a large skillet over medium heat. Add the onion, cover, and cook until softened, about 5 minutes. Add the garlic and cook, stirring, until fragrant, about 30 seconds. Stir in the tomato paste, crushed tomatoes, and salt and pepper to taste. Reduce the heat to low and simmer to reduce slightly and blend the flavors, 10 to 15 minutes. Shortly before serving, blend the pesto into the sauce.
2. As the sauce simmers, cook the linguine in a large pot of boiling salted water, stirring occasionally, until *al dente*, 8 to 10 minutes.
3. Drain the pasta and place in a large, shallow serving bowl. Add the sauce and toss to coat evenly. Serve hot.

SERVES 4

Fried Spaghetti

Fried spaghetti, made with cold leftover pasta, is a delicious reason to make more pasta than you need. When I was a child, my father enjoyed this dish even more than when the pasta was served fresh the night before. If you don't have leftover spaghetti, you can cook some ahead, toss it with tomato sauce, and allow to cool. Like fried rice, which gets mushy if made with hot rice, it's best to start this dish with cold spaghetti, which is then fried in a skillet with a small amount of olive oil until the pasta becomes crispy on the bottom. Be careful not to burn.

Penne Puttanesca

The name of this piquant pasta sauce means "streetwalker style," supposedly because ladies of the evening often prepared it at the end of a long night's work. Flavorful Gaeta olives are available in Italian markets and well-stocked super-markets and are especially good in this sauce. If unavailable, substitute another high-quality olive.

2 tablespoons olive oil
3 large garlic cloves, finely chopped
One 28-ounce can crushed tomatoes
1/2 cup pitted and sliced black Gaeta
    olives
1/4 cup pitted and sliced green olives
2 tablespoons capers, drained and
    chopped

1/2 teaspoon red pepper flakes
Salt and freshly ground black pepper
1 pound penne
2 tablespoons minced fresh parsley
    leaves

1. Heat the olive oil in a large saucepan over medium heat. Add the garlic and cook, stirring, until fragrant, about 30 seconds. Stir in the tomatoes, black and green olives, capers, red pepper flakes, and salt and pepper to taste. Reduce the heat to low and simmer, stirring occasionally, for 10 to 15 minutes to blend the flavors.
2. While the sauce is simmering, cook the penne in a large pot of boiling salted water, stirring occasionally, until *al dente*, 8 to 10 minutes.
3. Drain the pasta and place in a large, shallow serving bowl. Add the sauce and toss gently to combine. Sprinkle with the parsley and serve hot.

SERVES 4

Pappardelle Cacciatore

As a child, when my mom made chicken cacciatore, I'd skip the chicken and enjoy the tender stewed vegetables and pappardelle that went with it. Now I enjoy Mom's recipe made with tempeh and still savor the pasta and vegetables. If pappardelle, a wide ribbon pasta, is unavailable, use fettuccine instead.

2 tablespoons olive oil

One 8-ounce package tempeh, cut into
    1-inch pieces

1/2 cup dry white wine

1 celery rib, coarsely chopped

1 small carrot, coarsely chopped

1 small green bell pepper, seeded and
    coarsely chopped

1 garlic clove, minced

One 28-ounce can diced tomatoes,
    undrained

1 teaspoon minced fresh rosemary
    leaves or 1/2 teaspoon dried

1 teaspoon minced fresh marjoram
    leaves or 1/2 teaspoon dried

Salt and freshly ground black pepper

1 pound pappardelle or fettuccine

1. Heat 1 tablespoon of the olive oil in a large skillet over medium heat. Add the tempeh and cook, stirring, until lightly browned on all sides, about 5 minutes. Remove from the skillet and set aside.

2. Deglaze the pan with the wine, stirring to scrape up any browned bits of tempeh from the bottom. Reduce the wine by one-half and set aside.

3. Heat the remaining 1 tablespoon olive oil in a large saucepan over medium heat. Add the celery, carrot, bell pepper, and garlic. Cover and cook until softened, about 10 minutes. Add the tomatoes and juice, rosemary, marjoram, and salt and pepper to taste and simmer for 15 minutes. Add the reserved tempeh and reduced wine and simmer for 15 minutes to blend the flavors. Reduce the heat to low and keep warm.

4. Cook the pasta in a large pot of boiling salted water, stirring occasionally, until *al dente*, about 10 minutes. Drain and divide among 4 individual plates or shallow bowls. Top with the sauce and serve at once.

SERVES 4

Tuscan-Style Pasta with Chickpeas, Zucchini, and Rosemary

Beans are so prevalent in Tuscan cooking that the people of Tuscany are called bean eaters. For variety, fresh basil or another fragrant herb may be substituted for the rosemary.

2 tablespoons olive oil

2 small zucchini, halved lengthwise and cut into 1/4-inch-thick half-moons

2 garlic cloves, minced

1 tablespoon chopped fresh rosemary leaves

One 14.5-ounce can plum tomatoes, drained and chopped

1 1/2 cups cooked or one 15-ounce can chickpeas, drained and rinsed

1/4 teaspoon red pepper flakes

Salt and freshly ground black pepper

1 pound penne or other short, tubular pasta

1. Heat the olive oil in a medium saucepan over medium heat. Add the zucchini and cook until slightly softened, about 2 minutes. Add the garlic and cook until fragrant, about 30 seconds. Stir in the rosemary, tomatoes, chickpeas, red pepper flakes, and salt and pepper to taste. Cook, stirring occasionally, for 10 minutes to blend the flavors.

2. Meanwhile, cook the penne in a large pot of boiling salted water, stirring occasionally, until *al dente*, 8 to 10 minutes. Drain and place in a large, shallow serving bowl. Add the sauce and toss gently to combine. Serve at once.

SERVES 4

Fettuccine with Red Lentil Sauce

Although lentils are more prominent in Indian and Middle Eastern cooking, they are also used in Italian cuisine. This thin, lens-shaped legume is rich in protein, calcium, iron, and B complex vitamins. Use red lentils if you can find them. Otherwise, brown are fine. Since lentils do not require soaking and cook quickly in 30 minutes, this recipe doesn't require a lot of planning to get dinner on the table.

3/4 cup dried red or brown lentils, picked over and rinsed

2 carrots, cut into thin diagonal slices

1 celery rib, diced

3 tablespoons olive oil

1 garlic clove, minced

One 6-ounce can tomato paste

Salt and freshly ground black pepper

1 pound fettuccine

2 tablespoons chopped fresh Italian parsley leaves

1. Place the lentils, carrots, and celery in a pot of boiling salted water. Reduce the heat to medium-low and simmer until tender, about 30 minutes. Drain, reserving 2 cups of the cooking liquid. Toss the lentil mixture with 1 tablespoon of the olive oil and set aside.

2. Heat the remaining 2 tablespoons olive oil in a large skillet over medium heat. Add the garlic and cook until fragrant, about 30 seconds. Stir in the tomato paste and cook for 2 minutes to mellow the flavor of the paste. Stir in the reserved lentil cooking liquid, blending until smooth. Add the lentil mixture and season with salt and pepper to taste. Reduce the heat to low and simmer to blend the flavors while you cook the pasta. If too much liquid evaporates, add some water.

3. Cook the fettuccine in a large pot of boiling salted water, stirring occasionally, until *al dente*, about 10 minutes. Drain and divide among 4 individual plates or shallow bowls. Top with the sauce, sprinkle with the parsley, and serve at once.

SERVES 4

Linguine with Sage and White Bean Sauce

Cannellini beans flavored with sage are a popular Tuscan combination. Here they are pureed into a creamy pasta sauce enlivened with a splash of balsamic vinegar, a slightly sweet and syrupy aged vinegar from Modena, Italy.

2 tablespoons olive oil

1 small yellow onion, minced

1/4 cup torn fresh sage leaves

1 1/2 cups cooked or one 15-ounce can cannellini beans, drained and rinsed

1 tablespoon balsamic vinegar

1/2 teaspoon salt

Freshly ground black pepper

1/2 cup hot Basic Vegetable Stock (page 68) or water, or more as needed, heated

1 pound linguine

Whole fresh sage leaves for garnish

1. Heat the olive oil in a large skillet over medium heat. Add the onion, cover, and cook until softened, about 5 minutes. Add the torn sage leaves and cook for 1 minute. Add the beans, vinegar, salt, and pepper to taste and stir to blend the flavors.
2. Transfer to a food processor or blender, add the stock, and process until smooth, adding more stock, if necessary. Transfer to a small saucepan over low heat and keep warm, adding more stock if the sauce is too thick.
3. Cook the linguine in a large pot of boiling salted water, stirring occasionally, until *al dente*, about 10 minutes. Drain and place in a large, shallow serving bowl. Add the sauce and toss to combine. Garnish with the whole sage leaves and serve at once.

SERVES 4

Alfredo-Style Fettuccine

Inspired by the Roman classic made with grated cheese and heavy cream, this version relies on soy and blanched almonds to create a creamy, protein-rich sauce.

1 tablespoon olive oil

1 small yellow onion, chopped

1 tablespoon dry white wine

1/3 cup blanched almonds

4 ounces soft silken tofu, drained

1 tablespoon mellow white miso paste

1 1/2 cups soy milk or other dairy-free milk, or as needed

1/2 teaspoon salt, or more to taste

Pinch of freshly grated nutmeg

Pinch of cayenne

1 pound fettuccine

2 tablespoons minced fresh parsley leaves

Grated vegan Parmesan cheese (optional)

1. Heat the olive oil in a small skillet over medium heat. Add the onion, cover, and cook until softened, about 5 minutes. Stir in the wine and set aside.

2. Finely grind the almonds in a blender or food processor. Add the onion mixture and process until smooth. Add the tofu and miso and process until blended. Add 1 cup of the soy milk, the salt, nutmeg, and cayenne and process until smooth. Slowly add as much of the remaining 1/2 cup soy milk as necessary until a sauce-like consistency is achieved.

3. Transfer to a medium-size saucepan over low heat and heat gently. Taste and adjust the seasonings and keep warm.

4. Cook the fettuccine in a large pot of boiling salted water, stirring occasionally, until *al dente*, about 10 minutes. Drain and place in a large, shallow serving bowl. Add the sauce and toss. Sprinkle with the parsley and vegan Parmesan (if using). Serve hot.

SERVES 4

Tahini Rotini with Broccoli and Lemon

Tahini, or sesame paste, is loaded with protein and calcium, while broccoli is a good source of calcium, vitamin C, and other nutrients. It's hard to believe that a dish that's so good for you could taste this rich and creamy. Typically used in Middle Eastern cuisine, tahini is available in well-stocked supermarkets, natural food stores, and specialty food shops.

2 large garlic cloves, peeled

1 cup cooked or canned chickpeas, drained and rinsed

1/4 cup tahini (sesame paste)

Juice and zest of 1 lemon

2 tablespoons tamari or other soy sauce

1/8 teaspoon cayenne

1 cup Basic Vegetable Stock (page 68) or water, heated

1 pound rotini

2 cups broccoli florets

2 tablespoons sesame seeds, toasted (page 192)

1. In a food processor, combine the garlic, chickpeas, tahini, lemon juice (reserve the zest), tamari, and cayenne and process until smooth. Transfer the mixture to a medium-size saucepan over low heat, stir in the hot stock, and keep warm.

2. Cook the rotini in a large pot of boiling salted water, stirring occasionally, until *al dente*, 8 to 10 minutes. During the last 5 minutes of cooking time, add the broccoli florets to the pot.

3. Drain the pasta and broccoli and place in a large, shallow serving bowl. Add the warm tahini sauce and toss gently. Sprinkle with the reserved lemon zest and sesame seeds and serve at once.

SERVES 4

Did You Know...

Broccoli is an excellent source of calcium, potassium, and folic acid and contains more vitamin C than oranges? In addition, like other crucifers, broccoli contains beta carotene, which is believed to fight cancer.

Ravioli Without Borders

Some restaurants now serve what is called "open" ravioli, where the pasta and stuffing are layered rather than sealed shut. This recipe was inspired by that concept, but I take it a step further. To my thinking, true borderless ravioli should use ingredients that traverse the globe.

2 tablespoons extra virgin olive oil

2 garlic cloves, minced

2 tablespoons minced onion

8 ounces fresh shiitake mushrooms, stems removed and caps finely chopped

8 ounces firm tofu, drained and crumbled

1/2 large roasted red bell pepper (page 143), finely chopped

Salt and freshly ground black pepper

24 wonton wrappers, thawed if frozen

24 baby spinach leaves, lightly steamed and kept warm

1/4 cup vegan pesto, homemade (page 157) or store-bought

1/4 cup black olive tapenade (page 58)

1/4 cup Fresh Tomato Salsa (page 174) or your favorite salsa

Whole fresh basil leaves or minced fresh parsley leaves for garnish

1. Heat 1 tablespoon of the olive oil in a large skillet over medium heat. Add the garlic, onion, and mushrooms. Cover and cook until softened, about 5 minutes. Add the tofu, roasted pepper, and salt and pepper to taste, stirring to combine. Reduce the heat to low and keep warm.

2. Working in batches, cook the wonton wrappers in a large pot of gently boiling salted water until they rise to the surface and are tender, about 3 minutes. Using a slotted spoon, transfer the cooked wonton wrappers to a dry kitchen towel to drain.

3. To serve, arrange 3 wonton wrappers on each of 4 plates in a spoke-like fashion. Top each wrapper with 2 spinach leaves. Top the spinach with a spoonful of the warm filling mixture and top the filling with the remaining wonton wrappers. Place a spoonful of the pesto on one of the assembled ravioli on each plate, a spoonful of the tapenade on another of the ravioli on each plate, and a spoonful of the salsa on the remaining ravioli on each plate. Drizzle with the remaining 1 tablespoon olive oil and garnish with the basil.

SERVES 4

Udon-Shiitake Stir-Fry with Sake and Ginger

This noodle stir-fry features udon, the chewy noodles from Japan, combined with woodsy shiitake mushrooms and a flavorful sauce laced with sake and ginger. If sake is unavailable, dry white wine may be substituted. I like to precede this dish with an appetizer of edamame, fresh soybeans in the pod. Frozen edamame can be found in Asian markets and some supermarkets.

12 ounces udon noodles

2 teaspoons toasted sesame oil

3 tablespoons sake

3 tablespoons tamari or other soy sauce

2 tablespoons brown rice syrup or other natural liquid sweetener

2 tablespoons peanut oil

2 shallots, finely chopped

8 ounces fresh shiitake mushrooms, stems removed and caps thinly sliced

1 tablespoon peeled and minced fresh ginger

1. Cook the udon noodles according to the package directions. Drain and place in a medium-size bowl. Add the sesame oil and toss to combine. Set aside.

2. In a small bowl, combine the sake, tamari, and brown rice syrup until well blended. Set aside.

3. Heat the peanut oil in a large skillet or wok over medium-high heat. Add the shallots, mushrooms, and ginger and stir-fry until the mushrooms are tender, about 3 minutes.

4. Stir in the sake mixture and udon noodles and cook, stirring, until heated through, 3 to 5 minutes. Serve hot.

SERVES 4

Pad Thai

Slightly sweet and sour and mildly spiced, *pad thai* is the most popular Thai noodle dish in the West. For a colorful addition, add bite-size pieces of steamed broccoli or green beans.

12 ounces fresh or dried rice noodles

2 tablespoons plus 1 teaspoon peanut oil

8 ounces extra-firm tofu, drained and cut into 1/2-inch-wide strips

2 tablespoons tamari or other soy sauce

1/2 small red bell pepper, seeded and cut into thin strips

4 scallions, minced

1 garlic clove, minced

1 medium-size, ripe tomato, peeled, seeded, and chopped

2 tablespoons firmly packed light brown sugar or natural sweetener

2 tablespoons rice vinegar

1/2 cup fresh bean sprouts

1/4 cup chopped unsalted dry-roasted peanuts

1. Prepare the rice noodles. If fresh, rinse under very hot water and place in a large bowl, separating them into individual strands. If dried, plunge into a large pot of boiling water to soften. Drain and place in a large bowl. Toss the noodles with the 1 teaspoon peanut oil and set aside.

2. Heat 1 tablespoon of the peanut oil in a large skillet or wok over medium-high heat. Add the tofu and stir-fry until lightly browned, about 5 minutes. Add 1 tablespoon of the tamari, stirring to coat. Transfer to a platter and set aside.

3. Heat the remaining 1 tablespoon peanut oil in the same skillet or wok over medium heat. Add the bell pepper, scallions, and garlic and stir-fry until softened, about 5 minutes. Add the tomato, brown sugar, vinegar, and remaining 1 tablespoon tamari. Cook for about 3 minutes to blend the flavors. Add the reserved noodles and tofu and toss gently to combine and heat through, about 5 minutes.

4. Divide among 4 individual plates, sprinkle with the bean sprouts and peanuts, and serve at once.

SERVES 4

Rice Noodles and Tofu with Asian Pesto

Fresh and dried rice noodles are available at Asian markets in a variety of sizes, from narrow vermicelli to 1/4-inch-wide rice sticks. Some stores carry rice noodle sheets that you can cut to any width you prefer. As a flavor variation, you could use Thai basil or mint leaves instead of the cilantro.

2 large garlic cloves, peeled

1 small, fresh hot chile (optional), seeded

1/3 cup unsalted dry-roasted peanuts

1 teaspoon peeled and minced fresh ginger

1 1/2 cups loosely packed fresh cilantro leaves

1/2 cup loosely packed fresh parsley leaves

3 tablespoons toasted sesame oil

3 tablespoons peanut oil

8 ounces extra-firm tofu, drained and cut into 1/2-inch dice

1 tablespoon tamari or other soy sauce

1 pound fresh or dried rice noodles

1. In a food processor, combine the garlic, chile (if using), peanuts, and ginger and process until minced. Add the cilantro and parsley and process into a paste. With the machine running, add 2 tablespoons of the sesame oil and 2 tablespoons of the peanut oil through the feed tube and process until smooth. Set aside.

2. Heat the remaining 1 tablespoon peanut oil in a large skillet over medium-high heat. Add the tofu and cook until golden brown all over, about 5 minutes. Sprinkle with the tamari, tossing to coat. Reduce the heat to low and keep warm.

3. Prepare the rice noodles. If fresh, rinse under very hot water and place in a large, shallow serving bowl, separating them into individual strands. If dried, plunge into a large pot of boiling water to soften. Drain and place in a large, shallow serving bowl. Toss the noodles with the pesto to coat evenly. Top with the tofu, drizzle with the remaining 1 tablespoon sesame oil, and serve hot.

SERVES 4

Sesame Soba Noodles

Soba, or Japanese buckwheat noodles, have a nutty flavor that matches well with the creamy sesame sauce, which is also rich in protein and calcium. Colorful vegetables add textural variety as well as nutrients.

1/2 cup tahini (sesame paste)

3 garlic cloves, peeled

3 tablespoons tamari or other soy sauce

2 tablespoons toasted sesame oil

1 tablespoon brown rice vinegar

2 teaspoons sugar or natural sweetener

1/2 to 3/4 cup water, as needed

1 tablespoon peanut oil

1 large carrot, cut into small matchsticks

1/2 red bell pepper, seeded and cut into small matchsticks

1/2 cup frozen green peas, thawed

12 ounces soba noodles

1 tablespoon sesame seeds, toasted (page 192)

1. In a food processor or blender, process the tahini, garlic, tamari, 1 tablespoon of the sesame oil, the vinegar, sugar, and enough water to obtain a smooth, sauce-like consistency. Transfer the sauce to a small saucepan and heat over low heat, stirring until hot. Keep the sauce warm.

2. Heat the peanut oil in a medium-size skillet over medium-high heat. Add the carrot and bell pepper and stir-fry until tender, 3 to 5 minutes. Add the peas and stir-fry until hot, about 1 minute. Reduce the heat to low and keep the vegetables warm.

3. Cook the soba noodles according to the package directions. Drain and place in a large, shallow serving bowl. Drizzle on the remaining 1 tablespoon sesame oil and toss to coat evenly. Add the vegetables and sauce and toss to combine. Sprinkle with the sesame seeds and serve hot.

SERVES 4

Three-Flavor Pancit

Pancit is a Filipino noodle dish that usually includes a variety of meat and seafood. This recipe calls for tofu, tempeh, and seitan, but you can simplify it by using just one of them in an increased quantity. Either wheat or rice vermicelli may be used.

8 ounces wheat or rice vermicelli

1 tablespoon toasted sesame oil

2 tablespoons peanut oil

8 ounces extra-firm tofu, drained and cut into 1/2-inch dice

4 ounces seitan, cut into thin strips

1 cup crumbled poached tempeh (page 14)

1 tablespoon peeled and minced fresh ginger

1/2 small red bell pepper, seeded and chopped

1 bunch scallions, chopped

1 cup frozen green peas, thawed

3 tablespoons tamari or other soy sauce

2 tablespoons minced fresh cilantro leaves for garnish

Lemon wedges for garnish

1. Cook the vermicelli according to the package directions. Drain and place in a medium-size bowl. Toss with the sesame oil and set aside.

2. Heat 1 tablespoon of the peanut oil in a large skillet over medium heat. Add the tofu and cook until golden brown, about 5 minutes. Remove from the skillet and set aside. Add the seitan to the same skillet and cook until browned, about 5 minutes. Remove from the skillet and set aside with the tofu. Add the tempeh and cook until browned, about 5 minutes. Remove from the skillet and set aside with the tofu and seitan.

3. Heat the remaining 1 tablespoon peanut oil in the same skillet over medium-high heat. Add the ginger, bell pepper, and scallions and cook, stirring, until softened, about 3 minutes. Add the peas, tofu, tempeh, and seitan. Add 1 tablespoon of the tamari and stir to coat. Add the noodles and the remaining 2 tablespoons tamari and cook until hot, about 5 minutes, tossing gently to combine.

4. Serve hot, garnished with the cilantro and lemon wedges.

SERVES 4

Tofu and Vegetable Lo Mein

Traditional Chinese lo mein noodles may contain eggs, so be sure to check the ingredient list before you buy them. Regular linguine is a good substitute.

12 ounces egg-free Chinese noodles or linguine

2 teaspoons toasted sesame oil

2 tablespoons peanut oil

8 ounces extra-firm tofu, drained and cut into 1/2-inch dice

4 scallions, chopped

2 1/2 cups shredded napa cabbage or trimmed and shredded bok choy

1 small carrot, shredded

1 1/2 cups snow peas, strings removed

1 garlic clove, minced

2 teaspoons peeled and minced fresh ginger

3 tablespoons tamari or other soy sauce

1. Cook the noodles according to the package directions. Drain and place in a large bowl. Add the sesame oil and toss to coat evenly. Set aside.

2. Heat 1 tablespoon of the peanut oil in a large skillet or wok over medium-high heat. Add the tofu and stir-fry until golden brown all over, 3 to 5 minutes. Remove from the skillet and set aside.

3. Reheat the skillet over medium-high heat with the remaining 1 tablespoon peanut oil. Add the scallions and cabbage and stir-fry for 1 minute to soften slightly. Add the carrot, snow peas, garlic, and ginger and stir-fry for 1 minute. Add 1 tablespoon of the tamari and stir-fry until the vegetables are tender, about 3 minutes. Add the noodles, tofu, and remaining 2 tablespoons tamari, tossing to combine. Serve hot.

SERVES 4

"Drunken" Noodles

Some say this Thai dish is so named because it features hot chiles, which are believed to be a cure for hangovers. Whatever the reason for the name, it is one of my favorite dishes. I used to order it every week at my favorite Thai restaurant. When that restaurant closed, I began making the dish at home. The distinctive, licorice-like flavor of fresh Thai basil (available at Asian markets) is essential, but if Thai chiles are unavailable, any hot chile will do. Look for dark soy sauce, vegetarian oyster sauce, and palm sugar at Asian markets as well.

12 ounces fresh or dried rice noodles, about 1/4-inch wide

2 tablespoons plus 1 teaspoon peanut oil

1/4 cup dark soy sauce or tamari

2 tablespoons vegetarian oyster sauce

1 teaspoon palm sugar or other natural sweetener

2 cups drained and diced extra-firm tofu

1 small red onion, halved and cut into thin half-moons

3 garlic cloves, minced

2 Thai chiles, or to taste, seeded and minced

2 cups broccoli florets, blanched for 1 minute in boiling water and drained

1 1/2 cups loosely packed fresh Thai basil leaves

1/2 cup fresh bean sprouts

1. Prepare the noodles. If fresh, rinse under very hot water and place in a large bowl, separating them into individual strands. If dried, plunge into a large pot of boiling water to soften. Drain and place in a large bowl. Toss the noodles with the 1 teaspoon peanut oil and set aside.

2. In a small bowl, combine the soy sauce, oyster sauce, and sugar and set aside.

3. Heat the peanut oil in a large skillet or wok over medium-high heat. Add the tofu and cook, stirring, until golden, about 1 minute. Remove from the skillet and set aside.

4. Add the onion to the skillet and stir-fry to soften slightly, about 2 minutes. Add the garlic and chiles and stir-fry until fragrant, about 30 seconds. Add the sauce mixture, broccoli, noodles, tofu, and basil and stir-fry until hot, about 4 minutes. Taste and adjust the seasonings.

5. Transfer to a serving platter, sprinkle with the sprouts, and serve hot.

SERVES 4

PASTA: FRESH VS. DRIED

Both fresh and dried pasta are enjoyed for their unique tastes and textures. Although both can produce delicious results, commercially made fresh pasta is generally not vegan, since it is usually prepared with eggs, which are combined with all-purpose flour to make a soft dough that is then rolled through a pasta machine. By contrast, dried pasta is made by an extrusion process using semolina flour and water—no eggs. The good news is that if you really prefer fresh pasta, you can easily make fresh egg-free pasta at home. In addition, a few commercial egg-free brands are available in natural food stores or from mail-order outlets.

Dried pasta takes longer to cook than fresh, usually 3 to 15 minutes, depending on the shape, and the preferred outcome is *al dente*, or "firm to the bite." Fresh pasta cooks in 2 to 3 minutes, with more tender results. Dried pasta will keep for up to a year when stored in a tightly sealed container in a cool, dry place. Fresh pasta will keep in the refrigerator for up to 1 week or in the freezer for up to 1 month.

Vermicelli, Chickpeas, and Vegetables with Creamy Curry Sauce

In India, vermicelli noodles are often used to make a sweet pudding, but I prefer to prepare them with a savory curry sauce and lots of vegetables. At Indian markets, you can find a variety of curry seasoning blends in powder or paste form, from mild to extra hot. If the Madras curry powder sold in supermarkets is all that is available, that will work, too. Accompany this dish with Three-Fruit Chutney (page 168) or another chutney of your choice.

2 tablespoons corn oil

1 small yellow onion, minced

1 small carrot, thinly sliced

1 small green or red bell pepper, seeded and chopped

2 garlic cloves, minced

2 tablespoons Indian curry powder or paste

One 14.5-ounce can diced tomatoes, undrained

1/2 cup frozen green peas, thawed

1 1/2 cups cooked or one 15-ounce can chickpeas, drained and rinsed

One 14-ounce can unsweetened coconut milk

4 ounces soft silken tofu, drained

Salt and freshly ground black pepper

12 ounces vermicelli

1/2 cup chopped unsalted dry-roasted peanuts

2 scallions, minced

1. Heat the corn oil in a large skillet over medium heat. Add the onion, carrot, and bell pepper. Cover and cook until softened, about 5 minutes. Add the garlic and curry and stir to blend. Stir in the tomatoes and juice, simmer to blend the flavors, and reduce the liquid by one half, 5 to 7 minutes. Add the peas and chickpeas, reduce the heat to low, and keep warm.

2. In a food processor or blender, combine the coconut milk, tofu, and salt and pepper to taste. Process until smooth, then stir into the vegetable mixture and simmer gently.

3. Cook the vermicelli in a large pot of boiling salted water, stirring occasionally, until *al dente*, about 3 minutes. Drain and place in a large, shallow serving bowl. Add the vegetables and sauce and toss well to combine. Sprinkle with the peanuts and scallions and serve hot.

SERVES 4

Sweet Noodle Kugel with Apples and Almonds

For convenience, you can assemble the kugel the day before and refrigerate it until needed. For best results, return it to room temperature before baking. Served with a salad, this makes a good lunch or brunch entrée.

8 ounces fettuccine, broken into thirds

1 large Delicious apple, peeled, cored, and shredded

1/2 cup golden raisins, soaked in boiling water to cover and drained

2 teaspoons fresh lemon juice

One 12-ounce package soft silken tofu, drained

1/4 cup almond butter

1/2 cup plus 1 tablespoon sugar or natural sweetener

2 teaspoons ground cinnamon

2 cups soy milk or other dairy-free milk

1 teaspoon pure vanilla extract

1/2 cup ground almonds

1/2 cup fresh bread crumbs

2 tablespoons corn oil

1. Cook the fettuccine in a large pot of boiling salted water, stirring occasionally, until *al dente*, about 10 minutes. Drain and place in a large bowl. Add the apple, raisins, and lemon juice. Toss well to mix and set aside.

2. Preheat the oven to 350 degrees F. In a food processor or blender, combine the tofu, almond butter, the 1/2 cup sugar, 1 teaspoon of the cinnamon, the soy milk, and vanilla and process until smooth. Stir into the noodle mixture and mix well.

3. Transfer to a lightly oiled, shallow 9 x 13-inch baking dish. Bake, covered, for 30 minutes.

4. While the kugel is baking, combine the almonds, bread crumbs, corn oil, the 1 tablespoon sugar, and the remaining 1 teaspoon cinnamon in a small bowl.

5. Remove the kugel from the oven, top evenly with the almond-crumb mixture, and bake, uncovered, until lightly browned, about 10 minutes. Let stand for 15 minutes before serving. Serve warm or at room temperature.

SERVES 6

Potato Pierogi with Savoy Cabbage and Pear and Dried Plum Compote

When my mother made homemade pierogi, she always made three kinds: potato, cabbage, and prune. It was then up to everyone in the family to discern his or her favorite by the slight color variation the different filling would impart through the dough. As luck would have it, I enjoyed all three. My updated and streamlined interpretation of Mom's recipe is only for potato pierogi (most people's favorite), but I like to serve them with sautéed cabbage and a dried plum compote. That way, I can still enjoy the flavors of all three varieties.

Filling:
1¹/₂ pounds all-purpose potatoes
Salt and freshly ground black pepper
2 tablespoons olive oil
1 small yellow onion, minced

Dough:
3 cups unbleached all-purpose flour
1 cup water
1 tablespoon olive oil
1 teaspoon salt

Topping:
2 tablespoons olive oil
¹/₂ small head Savoy cabbage, cored and
     thinly sliced
Salt and freshly ground black pepper

1 tablespoon olive oil for frying
Pear and Dried Plum Compote
     (page 553)

1. To make the filling, peel the potatoes and cut them into 2-inch chunks. Place in a large pot with cold salted water to cover. Bring to a boil over medium-high heat and continue to boil until tender, about 20 minutes. Drain and mash, then season with salt and pepper to taste and set aside.

2. Heat the olive oil in a medium-size skillet over medium heat. Add the onion, cover, and cook until softened, about 5 minutes. Add the onion to the potatoes and set aside to cool completely.

3. To make the dough, place the flour in a large bowl and make a well in the center. Add the water, olive oil, and salt and mix until combined. Knead until smooth, then divide in half.

4. On a floured work surface, roll out one piece of the dough into a rectangle about ¹/₈ inch thick. Cut into 4-inch-wide strips, then cut crosswise to make 4-inch squares.

5. To assemble the pierogi, place a heaping tablespoon of the filling on one half of each dough square. Moisten the edges and fold over into triangles. To seal, press the edges together with your fingers or the tines of a fork. Repeat with the remaining dough and filling.

6. Working in batches, cook the pierogi in a large pot of salted boiling water until they float, 2 to 3 minutes. Drain well and set aside until all the pierogi are cooked.

7. To make the topping, heat the olive oil in a large skillet over medium heat. Add the cabbage and salt and pepper to taste. Cook, stirring occasionally, until tender, 8 to 10 minutes. Keep warm.

8. To fry the pierogi, heat the olive oil in a large skillet over medium heat. Working in batches, cook the pierogi until lightly browned on both sides, about 3 minutes total.

9. To serve, arrange the cabbage on a serving platter and top with the pierogi. Serve with the compote on the side.

SERVES 6

Buckwheat with Buttons and Bow Ties

The eastern European favorite known as *kasha varnishkas* is made with buckwheat groats, or kasha, combined with bow-tie pasta, or farfalle. I like to add carrot "buttons" for color, as well as to further embellish the whimsical name. The homey nature of this naturally vegan dish makes it ideal winter fare. Look for kasha in well-stocked supermarkets and natural food stores.

2 tablespoons olive oil

1 cup coarse buckwheat groats (kasha)

2 small carrots, cut into thin rounds

2 cups Basic Vegetable Stock (page 68), heated

8 ounces farfalle or bow-tie pasta

1 small yellow onion, chopped

Salt and freshly ground black pepper

2 tablespoons minced fresh parsley leaves for garnish

1. Heat 1 tablespoon of the olive oil in a medium-size saucepan over medium heat. Stir in the groats and carrots and cook for 2 minutes, stirring to coat with the oil. Add the stock and bring to a boil. Reduce the heat to low, cover, and simmer until the groats are cooked and the carrots are tender, about 15 minutes. Set aside.
2. Cook the pasta in a large pot of boiling salted water, stirring occasionally, until *al dente*, 8 to 10 minutes. Drain, combine with the groats and carrots, and set aside.
3. Heat the remaining 1 tablespoon olive oil in a small skillet over medium heat. Add the onion and cook, stirring, until tender and lightly browned, about 10 minutes. Stir the onion into the groats mixture and season with salt and pepper to taste. Set over low heat, stirring gently, to heat through, about 5 minutes. Garnish with the parsley and serve hot.

SERVES 4

Pesto-Tossed Golden Potato Gnocchi

A bit of turmeric adds a light golden hue to the gnocchi to make a colorful contrast to the green pesto. For best results, make sure the potatoes are still warm when making the dough. Be judicious in your use of turmeric, using only enough to impart a light golden color—too much will turn the gnocchi bright yellow and add a slightly bitter flavor. If you won't be using the gnocchi right away, place the raw gnocchi on cookie sheets and freeze for several hours or overnight. Transfer them to plastic bags and store in the freezer, where they will keep for a month or so.

2 large baking potatoes
1 cup unbleached all-purpose flour,
   or more as desired
1 teaspoon salt
1/4 teaspoon turmeric, or more as
   needed

1/2 cup vegan pesto, homemade
   (page 157) or store-bought,
   at room temperature

1. Preheat the oven to 400 degrees F. Puncture the potatoes in a few places and bake until soft, about 1 hour. Reduce the oven temperature to 275 degrees F.

2. Place the flour in a large bowl and sprinkle with the salt. Make a well in the center of the flour and set aside.

3. Peel the potatoes while they are still hot and mash them using a potato masher or ricer. Sprinkle on the turmeric, stirring gently to incorporate it. Place the potatoes in the center of the flour. Using a spoon, slowly draw the flour into the potatoes to form a slightly sticky dough, adding more flour, if necessary. If a deeper yellow color is desired, sprinkle on a little more turmeric. Knead the dough until smooth, 3 to 4 minutes. Divide the dough into 6 pieces.

4. On a floured board, roll each piece of dough into a 1/2-inch-thick rope with the palms of your hands. Cut into 3/4-inch pieces, then roll each piece briefly between your fingers to smooth the edges. Press one side of each gnocchi against the tines of a fork.

5. Working in batches, cook the gnocchi in a large pot of salted boiling water until they rise to the top, about 3 minutes. Remove with a slotted spoon and drain well. Transfer to a rimmed baking sheet and keep warm in the oven while you cook the rest.

6. Once all the gnocchi are cooked, place in a large, shallow serving bowl, add the pesto, and toss gently to combine. Serve hot.

SERVES 4

Mac and "Cheese"

Reminiscent of traditional macaroni and cheese, this version is made with a creamy soy-based sauce that receives its cheese-like flavor from miso paste and nutritional yeast. Since most vegan cheeses don't melt well, I don't use any here, relying instead on the crumb topping and flavorful sauce to carry the dish. Some vegans add nutritional yeast to dishes because they think it imparts a "cheesy" taste. Others find the flavor too strong. I've made it an optional ingredient so that you can decide for yourself. If you don't use it, however, be sure to check the seasoning—you may need to add more salt.

8 ounces elbow macaroni

2 tablespoons olive oil

1 large yellow onion, chopped

2 cups soy milk or other dairy-free milk

One 12-ounce package soft silken tofu,
  drained

1 tablespoon fresh lemon juice

2 teaspoons mellow white miso paste

2 teaspoons nutritional yeast (optional)

1/4 teaspoon dry mustard

1/4 teaspoon cayenne

Pinch of freshly grated nutmeg

Salt

1/2 cup dry bread crumbs

1. Cook the macaroni in a pot of salted boiling water, stirring occasionally, until *al dente*, about 8 minutes. Drain and set aside in a large bowl.

2. Preheat the oven to 375 degrees F. Heat 1 tablespoon of the olive oil in a medium-size skillet over medium heat. Add the onion, cover, and cook until softened, about 5 minutes.

3. Place the onion in a blender or food processor. Add the soy milk, tofu, lemon juice, miso, nutritional yeast (if using), mustard, cayenne, nutmeg, and salt to taste.

Process until smooth. Pour the sauce over the macaroni and mix well. Transfer the mixture to a lightly oiled 2¹/₂-quart baking dish and set aside.

4. In a small bowl, combine the bread crumbs with the remaining 1 tablespoon olive oil, stirring to coat. Sprinkle the crumb mixture evenly over the macaroni mixture, cover, and bake until hot and bubbly, about 25 minutes. Uncover and bake until the top is lightly browned, about 10 minutes more. Remove from the oven and let sit for 5 minutes before serving.

SERVES 4

10

The World of Beans

As a major protein source for much of the world, beans are among the most important ingredients on the planet. Countless varieties exist in a wide range of colors and sizes. In addition to being high in protein, beans are also chock-full of fiber and B vitamins and low in fat. Among the best known are black beans, black-eyed peas, chickpeas, kidney beans, lentils, split peas, lima beans, navy beans, pinto beans, and soybeans.

Bean dishes have long played key roles in the cuisines of many cultures, but the same has not been true in the United States. Thanks to the recent interest in global cuisines and healthy eating, all that is changing. More Americans are realizing what vegetarians and much of the world have known for centuries—that beans can be enjoyed as a versatile and economical protein source. As more people look for alternatives to meat, beans are finding their way onto restaurant menus and dinner tables throughout the United States.

Because of their importance in the vegan diet, beans are used in many of the chapters throughout this book, often to add protein and substance to recipes that would otherwise be lacking in both, such as soups or pasta dishes. This chapter features a selection of recipes in which beans play the starring role. Among the global delights that await preparation are *White Bean Cassoulet, Three-Bean Dal,* and *Black Bean Croquettes with Yellow Pepper Coulis.* In many instances, beans combine with grains and vegetables to make well-balanced one-dish meals. Because of their versatility, beans can be an inspiration to the creative cook.

SOAKING BEANS

Soaking dried beans is an important step in the bean-cooking process, since it rehydrates the dried beans and shortens their cooking time. Because soaking helps dissolve some of the complex sugars in beans that cause digestive gas, it also aids digestion. Before soaking or cooking, dried beans must be picked over and washed to remove dust, small stones, and other debris. With the exception of lentils and split peas, all beans require soaking.

To soak beans, place them in a bowl and add water to cover by about 3 inches. Soak the beans overnight and drain before cooking.

For a quick-soak method, place the beans in a pot with water to cover by 2 or 3 inches and bring to a boil for 2 minutes. Remove the pot from the heat, cover, and let stand for 2 hours. Drain the beans before cooking.

Don't be deterred by the long soaking and cooking times required for dried beans. All you need is a little planning. To save time, however, you can cook beans in a pressure cooker or a slow cooker, both of which are enjoying renewed popularity. The new generation of pressure cookers are safer and easier to use than the old-fashioned variety, and slow cookers, with their larger capacity and sleek new lines, have come a long way from the avocado green and harvest gold Crock-Pots of the early 1970s.

COOKING BEANS

To cook beans, simmer them in a pot over low heat in about 3 cups of water per 1 cup of beans. Cook with the lid on, stirring occasionally. Salt and acidic foods such as tomatoes should be added midway through or near the end of the cooking time, as adding them during the earlier cooking stages will toughen the beans and lengthen the cooking time. Generally, 1 cup of dried beans will yield 2 to 2$^1/_2$ cups of cooked beans. Cooking times may vary depending on the type, quality, and age of the bean; the altitude; and even the water quality. The following cooking times are provided for conventional stovetop cooking, since that is what the majority of people use.

STOVETOP COOKING TIMES FOR SOAKED BEANS

Beans (1 cup dried)	Water	Cooking Time
Adzuki	3 cups	50 minutes
Anasazi	3 1/2 cups	1 1/2 hours
Black	3 1/2 cups	1 1/2 to 2 hours
Black-eyed peas	3 cups	1 hour
Borlotti	3 cups	1 1/2 hours
Cannellini	3 1/2 cups	1 1/2 to 2 hours
Chickpeas	4 cups	3 hours
Great Northern	3 1/2 cups	1 1/2 to 2 hours
Kidney	3 1/2 cups	2 hours
Lentils*	3 cups	35 to 45 minutes
Navy	3 1/2 cups	1 1/2 to 2 hours
Pinto	3 1/2 cups	2 hours
Split peas*	3 cups	45 minutes

*Note: Lentils and split peas do not require soaking.

To give you more options, most of the bean recipes in this book call for "cooked or canned" beans. While canned beans are great to keep on hand for sheer convenience, dried beans that you cook yourself taste better and are more economical. To give dried beans the same convenience as canned, cook up a large batch and then divide and freeze them for later use.

Adzuki Beans and Winter Squash Sauté

The naturally sweet adzuki bean and winter squash complement each other in flavor and texture, while the deep burgundy color of the beans makes a striking contrast with the vivid orange squash. Adzuki beans are available at natural food stores, but another red bean can be substituted if you can't find them. For a nourishing meal, serve over freshly cooked brown rice and an accompanying dark green vegetable such as kale.

1 medium-size winter squash, such as
    butternut, buttercup, or kabocha
2 tablespoons olive oil
3 shallots, halved and sliced
1/4 cup water

1 tablespoon tamari or other soy sauce
1 1/2 cups cooked or one 15-ounce can
    adzuki beans, drained and rinsed
Salt and freshly ground black pepper

1. Halve, peel, and seed the squash. Cut into bite-size pieces and set aside.
2. Heat the olive oil in a large skillet over medium heat. Add the shallots and cook, stirring, until slightly softened, about 3 minutes. Add the squash, stirring to coat. Add the water and tamari, cover, and cook until the squash is tender, about 20 minutes.
3. Gently stir in the beans and season with salt and pepper to taste. Cook until the beans are hot, about 5 minutes. Serve hot.

SERVES 4

Cuban-Style Black Beans

This spicy bean dish is sometimes called "Moors and Christians" when served with white rice. It's also quite tasty served over cornbread.

1 tablespoon olive oil

1 medium-size red onion, finely chopped

1 small carrot, finely chopped

1 small red bell pepper, seeded and finely chopped

2 garlic cloves, minced

1¹/₂ teaspoons chili powder

¹/₄ teaspoon cayenne

One 14.5-ounce can diced tomatoes, drained and finely chopped

1¹/₂ cups cooked or one 15-ounce can black beans, drained and rinsed

Salt and freshly ground black pepper

¹/₄ cup minced scallions for garnish

1 tablespoon chopped fresh parsley leaves for garnish

1. Heat the olive oil in a large skillet over medium heat. Add the onion, carrot, bell pepper, and garlic. Cover and cook until softened, about 7 minutes. Stir in the chili powder, cayenne, tomatoes, and beans, and salt and pepper to taste. Cover and simmer, stirring occasionally, until the vegetables are tender and the tomatoes are saucy, about 10 minutes. Taste and adjust the seasonings.
2. Serve hot, garnished with the scallions and parsley.

SERVES 4

Black Bean Croquettes with Yellow Pepper Coulis

You can change the character of these versatile croquettes by varying the herbs or spices by accompanying them with a different sauce, such as chutney, salsa, or Spicy Peanut Dipping Sauce (page 160).

1 1/2 cups cooked or one 15-ounce can black beans, drained and rinsed
1 large all-purpose potato, peeled, diced, cooked in water until tender, and drained
1/4 cup grated onion
1/4 cup grated carrots
2 tablespoons minced fresh parsley leaves

1 teaspoon salt
1/2 teaspoon freshly ground black pepper
1 cup dry bread crumbs
1/4 cup olive oil
1 cup Yellow Pepper Coulis (page 156)

1. Place the beans, potato, onion, carrots, parsley, salt, and pepper in a food processor and process until well blended. Divide the mixture into 4 equal mounds and shape into patties. Coat each evenly with the bread crumbs and set on a baking sheet, flattening the bottoms. Refrigerate for 30 minutes.
2. Heat the olive oil in a large skillet over medium heat. Cook the croquettes until golden brown all over, about 5 minutes. Drain on paper towels and serve hot, surrounded by the coulis.

SERVES 4

Simmered Borlotti Beans and Tomatoes

Dried or canned borlotti beans, also called cranberry or Roman beans, can be found in Italian markets. If unavailable, use pinto, cannellini, or fava beans. This dish is terrific served over noodles or rice. It is also good made with the addition of diced potatoes.

1 tablespoon olive oil

3 shallots, chopped

2 garlic cloves, chopped

1 teaspoon dried marjoram

$1/8$ teaspoon cayenne

$1\frac{1}{2}$ cups cooked or one 15-ounce can borlotti beans, drained and rinsed

One 14.5-ounce can diced tomatoes, drained

Salt and freshly ground black pepper

3 tablespoons chopped fresh parsley leaves for garnish

1. Heat the olive oil in a large saucepan over medium heat. Add the shallots, cover, and cook until softened, about 5 minutes. Add the garlic, marjoram, and cayenne and cook, stirring, until fragrant, about 1 minute. Stir in the beans, tomatoes, and salt and pepper to taste. Cover and cook until the flavors are blended and the tomatoes are saucy, about 10 minutes.

2. To serve, transfer to a large serving bowl and garnish with the parsley.

SERVES 4

Roasted "Chichers"

Roasted chickpeas, called "chichers" in my family, were one of my grandmother's favorite snacks. When I was a child, my father and I would go to the Italian market to purchase treats for Grandmom. Chichers were always at the top of the list. Much like roasted peas, a popular Asian snack food, roasted chickpeas are crunchy and nut-like and can be eaten out of hand or used as a salad garnish.

1½ cups cooked or one 15-ounce can chickpeas, drained and rinsed	2 tablespoons olive oil Salt

1. Preheat the oven to 400 degrees F. Place the chickpeas and olive oil in a shallow baking dish big enough to accommodate the chickpeas in a single layer. Toss gently to coat, then season with salt to taste.

2. Roast the chickpeas, stirring occasionally, until they begin to brown, about 20 minutes. Remove from the oven and allow to cool. Sprinkle with a little more salt, if desired. Serve at room temperature.

SERVES 4

Chickpea and Green Bean Tagine

A tagine is a delectable Moroccan stew redolent of fragrant fruits and spices. The word *tagine* refers to both the dish itself and the pot it is cooked in. Try it served over couscous, quinoa, or rice.

1½ cups mixed dried fruit
1 tablespoon olive oil
1 large yellow onion, chopped
2 garlic cloves, minced
½ teaspoon ground cinnamon
¼ teaspoon turmeric
⅛ teaspoon ground allspice
8 ounces green beans, ends trimmed
    and cut into 1-inch pieces
One 14.5-ounce can diced tomatoes,
    undrained

1½ cups Basic Vegetable Stock
    (page 68)
1 teaspoon light brown sugar or natural
    sweetener
Salt and freshly ground black pepper
1½ cups cooked or one 15-ounce can
    chickpeas, drained and rinsed
¼ cup slivered blanched almonds
2 tablespoons minced fresh parsley
    leaves
1 teaspoon grated lemon zest

1. Place the dried fruit in a small heatproof bowl. Add boiling water to cover and soak for 20 minutes to soften. Drain, coarsely chop, and set aside.

2. Heat the olive oil in a large saucepan over medium heat. Add the onion, cover, and cook until softened, about 5 minutes. Stir in the garlic, cinnamon, turmeric, and allspice and cook, stirring, for 30 seconds. Add the green beans, tomatoes and juice, stock, brown sugar, and salt and pepper to taste. Reduce the heat to low and simmer until the green beans are tender, about 20 minutes.

3. Add the reserved fruit and the chickpeas and cook for 5 to 10 minutes to blend the flavors. Stir in the almonds, parsley, and lemon zest. Taste and adjust the seasonings, then serve hot.

SERVES 4

Chickpea and Eggplant Kibbeh

Kibbeh is a traditional Lebanese dish usually made with bulgur and ground lamb. In this version, chickpeas and eggplant, two popular Middle Eastern ingredients, are used to replace the meat. The result is a hearty one-dish meal that can be assembled ahead of time and baked just before serving. I like to serve this with a sesame sauce that is made by thinning hummus with a little soy milk.

1/2 cup fine bulgur

2 cups boiling water

1 1/2 cups cooked or one 15-ounce can
    chickpeas, drained and rinsed

1 teaspoon ground allspice

1/2 teaspoon ground cinnamon

1/4 teaspoon ground cumin

Salt and freshly ground black pepper

2 tablespoons olive oil

1 cup chopped onion

1 medium-size eggplant, peeled and
    chopped

1/3 cup pine nuts

1 teaspoon fresh lemon juice

1. Place the bulgur in a medium-size heatproof bowl. Add the boiling water and let stand for 20 minutes. Drain well and squeeze to remove any excess water. Place the bulgur in a large bowl.

2. Coarsely chop the chickpeas and add to the bulgur. Add the allspice, cinnamon, cumin, and salt and pepper to taste. Stir to combine and set aside.

3. Heat the olive oil in a large skillet over medium heat. Add the onion, cover, and cook until softened, about 5 minutes. Add the eggplant and continue to cook, stirring a few times, until tender, 5 to 7 minutes. Stir in the pine nuts and lemon juice and season with salt and pepper to taste. Set aside.

4. Preheat the oven to 350 degrees F. Press half the bulgur-chickpea mixture into the bottom of a lightly oiled 10-inch square baking dish, smoothing the top. Add the eggplant mixture, then cover with the remaining bulgur-chickpea mixture, pressing down to smooth.

5. Bake until hot and lightly browned, about 30 minutes. Remove from the oven and let stand for 10 minutes before serving. Serve warm or at room temperature.

SERVES 6

Middle Eastern Lentils and Rice with Caramelized Shallots

The traditional Middle Eastern combination of lentils and rice flavored with shallots and fragrant spices makes a well-balanced meal when accompanied by a green vegetable or salad.

1 cup dried brown lentils, picked over
    and rinsed
2 tablespoons olive oil
4 large shallots, chopped
1 teaspoon ground cumin

1 teaspoon ground coriander
1/2 teaspoon sweet paprika
Salt and freshly ground black pepper
1 cup basmati rice
3 cups water

1. Partially cook the lentils in a medium-size saucepan of salted boiling water for 15 minutes. Drain and set aside.

2. Heat 1 tablespoon of the olive oil in a large skillet over medium heat. Add the shallots and cook, stirring frequently, until lightly browned, about 10 minutes. Remove half of the shallots from the skillet and set aside.

3. Add the lentils to the skillet and stir in the cumin, coriander, paprika, and salt and pepper to taste. Add the rice and water, bring to a boil, and cook, uncovered, until the lentils are tender and the rice is cooked, about 30 minutes. Remove from the heat, cover, and set aside for 10 to 15 minutes while you finish cooking the reserved shallots.

4. Heat the remaining 1 tablespoon olive oil in a small skillet over medium heat. Add the reserved shallots and cook until browned and caramelized, about 5 minutes.

5. Place the rice and lentil mixture in a large serving bowl and top with the crisp shallots. Serve hot.

SERVES 4

Did You Know...

Dried beans and lentils will keep well for up to a year if stored in airtight containers in a cool, dry place?

Three-Bean Dal

This is my interpretation of a creamy dal recipe shared by Ashok Arora, owner of Nawab, my favorite Indian restaurant in Virginia Beach. The original dish, called *dal makhani*, is made with three kinds of dried beans, and the preparation time is often more than I can spare. By using a combination of canned beans and dried split peas, I manage to achieve that creamy, slow-cooked flavor in a fraction of the time.

1/2 cup dried yellow split peas,
   picked over and rinsed
3 cups water
1 teaspoon turmeric
1 1/2 cups cooked or one 15-ounce can
   black beans, drained and rinsed
1 1/2 cups cooked or one 15-ounce can
   kidney or other red beans,
   drained and rinsed
Salt
2 tablespoons corn oil
1 medium-size yellow onion, chopped

1 large garlic clove, minced
2 teaspoons peeled and minced fresh
   ginger
1 teaspoon ground cumin
1/2 teaspoon ground coriander
1/2 teaspoon cayenne
1/4 teaspoon ground cardamom
One 14.5-ounce can diced tomatoes,
   drained and finely chopped
2 tablespoons chopped fresh cilantro
   leaves for garnish

1. Place the split peas and water in a large saucepan over medium-high heat. Bring to a boil, reduce the heat to low, add the turmeric, and simmer, partially covered and stirring occasionally, for 20 minutes. Add the black and red beans, season with salt to taste, and simmer, uncovered, until the sauce thickens and the beans are very soft, about 20 minutes.

2. Heat the corn oil in a large skillet over medium heat. Add the onion, cover, and cook until softened, about 5 minutes. Add the garlic and ginger and cook, stirring, until fragrant, about 30 seconds. Add the cumin, coriander, cayenne, cardamom, and tomatoes, stirring constantly for about 30 seconds. Pour the contents of the skillet over the simmering bean mixture and stir well to combine. Taste and adjust the seasonings.

3. Serve hot, garnished with the chopped cilantro.

SERVES 6

Red Bean and Sweet Potato Curry

Vibrant in color and flavor, this curry is delicious served over freshly cooked basmati rice, accompanied by a green salad and your favorite chutney.

1 tablespoon corn oil
1 small yellow onion, chopped
1 tablespoon curry powder
1 teaspoon ground coriander
3/4 teaspoon ground cumin
1/2 teaspoon turmeric
1/4 teaspoon cayenne
1 small green bell pepper, seeded and
    coarsely chopped
2 garlic cloves, minced
1 tablespoon peeled and grated fresh
    ginger

1 3/4 cups Basic Vegetable Stock
    (page 68)
One 14.5-ounce can diced tomatoes,
    undrained
1 1/2 cups cooked or one 15-ounce can
    dark red kidney beans, drained
    and rinsed
2 medium-size sweet potatoes, peeled
    and diced
Salt and freshly ground black pepper

1. Heat the corn oil in a large saucepan over medium heat. Add the onion, cover, and cook until softened, about 5 minutes. Stir in the curry powder, coriander, cumin, turmeric, and cayenne. Add the bell pepper, garlic, and ginger and cook, stirring, for 30 seconds. Add the stock and tomatoes and juice and bring to a boil. Reduce the heat to low and add the beans and sweet potatoes. Season with salt and pepper to taste, cover, and simmer until the vegetables are tender, about 20 minutes.
2. For a thicker, creamier sauce, puree up to 2 cups of the mixture and stir back into the pot. Serve hot.

SERVES 4

Know Beans About Beans

- Purchase dried beans that are of uniform size and brightly colored. Avoid beans that are dull, cracked, or have pinholes.
- Dried beans should be stored in airtight containers in a cool, dry place.
- Beans should be cooked until tender to aid in their digestion.
- A piece of kombu sea vegetable added to the cooking water helps tenderize beans and adds flavor and nutrients.
- To keep beans from toughening, add salt at the end of the cooking time.
- Add dried herbs to beans during the final 30 minutes of cooking. Add fresh herbs after the beans are cooked.
- Cool cooked beans in their cooking water to keep them moist.
- When cooking beans, make extra for another use. Cooked beans will keep in the refrigerator for up to 1 week or in the freezer for up to 6 months.

Red Bean Cakes with Creamy Coconut Sauce

Red beans and rice are a popular pair in many regions of the world. Here they are blended with spicy seasonings and formed into cakes that are served with a rich coconut sauce.

2 tablespoons olive oil
1 small red onion, chopped
1 small red bell pepper, seeded and
  chopped
1/2 cup chopped celery
1 large garlic clove, minced
1/2 teaspoon sweet paprika
1/2 teaspoon dried thyme
1/4 teaspoon cayenne, or to taste
Salt and freshly ground black pepper

11/2 cups cooked or one 15-ounce can
  pinto, kidney, or other red beans,
  drained and rinsed
1/2 cup cold cooked white or brown rice
2 tablespoons minced fresh parsley
  leaves
1/4 cup blanched almonds
1 tablespoon minced shallots
1/2 cup unsweetened coconut milk

1. Heat 1 tablespoon of the olive oil in a large skillet over medium heat. Add the onion, bell pepper, celery, garlic, paprika, thyme, and cayenne. Cover and cook, stirring occasionally, until softened, about 10 minutes. Season with salt and pepper to taste and set aside to cool.

2. In a food processor, combine the beans, rice, parsley, salt and pepper to taste, and sautéed onion mixture. Pulse to blend, leaving some texture intact. Shape into patties and set aside.

3. Heat the remaining 1 tablespoon olive oil in a large skillet over medium heat. Add the bean cakes and cook, turning once, until browned on both sides, 7 to 10 minutes total. Reduce the heat to low and keep warm while you prepare the sauce.

4. Place the almonds and shallots in a blender and grind into a paste. Add the coconut milk and salt and pepper to taste and blend until smooth. Transfer to a small saucepan over low heat and cook, stirring, until hot.

5. Transfer the hot bean cakes to a platter, pour the sauce over them, and serve.

SERVES 4

Tuscan White Beans with Garlic and Sage

The people of Tuscany have a prolific bean preparation repertoire. Among their classic recipes is a simple sauté of white beans, garlic, and sage in olive oil. This is delicious as a topping for bruschetta or pasta. You may add cooked chopped greens such as escarole or broccoli rabe (rapini) to the sauté, if you like.

2 tablespoons extra virgin olive oil, plus more for drizzling, if desired
2 garlic cloves, minced
10 fresh sage leaves, minced, or 1 teaspoon dried

3 cups cooked or two 15-ounce cans cannellini or other white beans, drained and rinsed
Salt and freshly ground black pepper

1. Heat the olive oil in a large skillet over medium-low heat. Add the garlic and cook, stirring, until fragrant, about 30 seconds. Add the sage and cook, stirring, until fragrant, 30 seconds more.

2. Add the beans, stirring to coat. Simmer over low heat until hot, about 10 minutes. Season with salt and pepper to taste and drizzle with a little olive oil, if desired. Serve hot.

SERVES 4

White Bean Cassoulet

This adaptation of a French country classic features white beans, an important component of the original made with meat. You can use dried beans in this recipe, if you like, but it will take several hours to make, not counting soaking time. By using canned beans, it can be ready within an hour from start to finish.

2 tablespoons olive oil
1 large red onion, chopped
2 medium-size carrots, thinly sliced
2 small parsnips, peeled and chopped
3 garlic cloves, minced
2 teaspoons Dijon mustard
1 tablespoon mellow white miso paste
    dissolved in 2 tablespoons hot
    (not boiling) water
1/2 teaspoon dried marjoram
1/2 teaspoon dried thyme
1 large bay leaf

Salt and freshly ground black pepper
3 cups cooked or two 15-ounce cans
    Great Northern, navy, or other
    white beans, drained and rinsed
One 14.5-ounce can diced tomatoes,
    drained and chopped
2 cups Basic Vegetable Stock (page 68),
    or as needed
1/2 cup dry toasted bread crumbs
2 tablespoons chopped fresh parsley
    leaves

1. Preheat the oven to 350 degrees F. Heat the olive oil in a large skillet over medium heat. Add the onion, carrots, and parsnips. Cover and cook until slightly softened, about 5 minutes. Stir in the garlic and cook, stirring, until fragrant, about 30 seconds.
2. Blend the mustard into the miso mixture and stir it into the vegetables. Add the thyme, marjoram, bay leaf, and salt and pepper to taste and set aside.
3. Place the beans and tomatoes in a lightly oiled casserole dish. Add the vegetable mixture and enough stock just to cover the ingredients, stirring to combine.
4. Cover and bake until the vegetables are tender, about 45 minutes. Remove and discard the bay leaf. Sprinkle with the bread crumbs and parsley and serve hot.

SERVES 4 TO 6

Mediterranean Bean Ragout

Bean dishes can be found throughout the Mediterranean countryside. This one features creamy and meaty cannellini beans in a brothy ragout enriched with the sweet flavor of fennel. It is delicious served over freshly cooked flat noodles.

2 tablespoons olive oil

1 large yellow onion, chopped

2 medium-size carrots, thinly sliced

1 large all-purpose potato, peeled
    and diced

1 fennel bulb, trimmed and thinly sliced

2 garlic cloves, minced

2 tablespoons tomato paste

2 cups Basic Vegetable Stock (page 68)

$1/2$ cup dry white wine

1 teaspoon dried thyme

2 bay leaves

3 cups cooked or two 15-ounce cans
    cannellini or other white beans,
    drained and rinsed

Salt

1. Heat the olive oil in a large saucepan over medium heat. Add the onion and carrots, cover, and cook until slightly softened, about 5 minutes. Add the potato, fennel, and garlic and cook, stirring, until the garlic is fragrant, about 30 seconds. Stir in the tomato paste, stock, wine, thyme, and bay leaves. Bring to a boil, then reduce the heat to low and simmer until the vegetables are tender, about 20 minutes.
2. Add the beans and salt to taste. Simmer until heated through and the flavors are blended, about 10 minutes. Remove and discard the bay leaves. If a thicker ragout is desired, puree about 1 cup of the mixture in a blender or food processor and stir back into the pot. Serve hot.

SERVES 4 TO 6

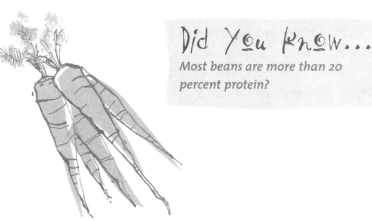

Did You know...
Most beans are more than 20 percent protein?

Old-Fashioned Baked Beans

The quintessential American bean dish drenched in a spicy-sweet tomato sauce can be enjoyed as more than a side dish for hot dogs. Try it as a main course, spooned over cornbread and accompanied by a salad or slaw.

1 tablespoon olive oil
1 small yellow onion, minced
1 garlic clove, minced
1 teaspoon chili powder
1/8 teaspoon cayenne
One 14.5-ounce can tomato puree
2 tablespoons light brown sugar or
    natural sweetener
2 tablespoons molasses

1 tablespoon prepared yellow mustard
1 1/2 tablespoons tamari or other soy
    sauce
1 1/2 tablespoons white wine vinegar
Salt and freshly ground black pepper
3 cups cooked or two 15-ounce cans
    Great Northern or butter beans,
    drained and rinsed

1. Preheat the oven to 350 degrees F. Heat the olive oil in a medium-size saucepan over medium heat. Add the onion and garlic, cover, and cook until softened, about 5 minutes. Stir in the chili powder and cayenne. Add the tomato puree, sugar, molasses, mustard, tamari, and vinegar and bring to a boil. Reduce the heat to low and simmer until slightly reduced, about 15 minutes. Season with salt and pepper to taste.

2. Place the beans in a lightly oiled 1 1/2-quart baking dish. Add the sauce, stirring to combine. Cover and bake until hot and bubbly, about 20 minutes. Serve hot.

SERVES 4

Smoky Refried Beans

Chipotle chiles add smoke and heat to these cumin-spiced refried beans. Gauge the number of chiles and the amount of cumin used according to your taste. Refried beans are traditionally cooked in lard, but this healthier version is cooked in olive oil. I like to serve it over rice or use it as a burrito filling.

1 or 2 dried chipotle chiles, to your taste, soaked in very hot water to cover for 30 minutes

2 tablespoons olive oil

1 small yellow onion, minced

1 teaspoon ground cumin, or to taste

3 cups cooked or two 15-ounce cans pinto beans, drained and rinsed

Salt and freshly ground black pepper

1. Drain the chiles and puree in a food processor or blender. Set aside.

2. Heat the olive oil in a large skillet over medium heat. Add the onion, cover, and cook until softened, about 5 minutes. Add the cumin and stir to coat the onion. Add the chipotle puree, beans, and salt and pepper to taste. Coarsely mash the beans, stirring to incorporate the other ingredients. Cook until heated through, 7 to 10 minutes. Taste and adjust the seasonings, then serve hot.

SERVES 4

11

From the Stew & Chili Pot

Stews are one of my favorite choices for dinner. For one reason, they are easy to prepare—most stews require little more than combining several ingredients in a pot that simmers until done. This same ease of preparation is what helps build the rich, complex flavors of most stews, as the essence of the vegetables, seasonings, and other ingredients commingle into one delicious whole. When beans or soy products are added to the pot, a stew can become a delectable, well-balanced meal, especially when it is served over cooked whole grains.

In addition, stews can be economical and are a great way to stretch your dollar when cooking for a crowd. Among their other virtues, stews taste better when reheated, so leftovers become something to look forward to. Whether preparing a nourishing weeknight meal for the family or a sumptuous main course for guests, you can use stews ranging from humble to "haute" to fill the bill.

Is it any wonder that stews are enjoyed the world over? In this chapter, you will find recipes from virtually every corner of the globe—some authentically vegan stews and others made vegan with the change of a few ingredients. Sample such diverse dishes as *Indonesian-Inspired Tempeh Stew* and *Belgian-Style Seitan Stew with Dark Beer*, or choose from the wide variety of America's favorite stew—chili. Vegetarian chili is one of the most popular ways for vegans to enjoy a wholesome and hearty one-dish meal loaded with protein and flavor. If you've been making the same old chili recipe time and again, you're in luck—this chapter features a dozen different ways to make "a bowl of red."

Farm Stand Vegetable Stew with Basil Pesto

Although stews are more often enjoyed during the fall and winter months, don't overlook the opportunity to create a late-summer stew made with fresh seasonal vegetables. Prepare it early in the day, when the kitchen is still cool, and simply reheat it later on. Vary the vegetables according to your preference or what's plentiful. You may use chopped fresh herbs instead of the pesto, if you prefer. I like to serve this stew in shallow bowls accompanied by grilled bread.

2 ears corn
1 tablespoon olive oil
1 large red onion, chopped
1 small red bell pepper, seeded and
    cut into 1/4-inch pieces
8 ounces green beans, ends trimmed
    and cut into 1-inch pieces
2 large, ripe tomatoes, peeled, seeded,
    and chopped

2 cups Basic Vegetable Stock (page 68),
    or more as needed
Salt and freshly ground black pepper
1 medium-size zucchini, diced
1 small yellow squash, halved
    lengthwise and cut into
    1/4-inch-thick half-moons
1/4 cup vegan pesto, homemade
    (page 157) or store-bought

1. Using a sharp knife, cut the kernels from the corn and set aside.

2. Heat the olive oil in a large saucepan over medium heat. Add the onion, cover, and cook until softened, about 5 minutes. Add the bell pepper, green beans, tomatoes, stock, and salt and pepper to taste and bring to a boil. Reduce the heat to low and simmer, partially covered, until the vegetables are tender, about 20 minutes. Add the zucchini, yellow squash, and corn kernels and cook until tender, about 10 minutes, adding more stock if the stew becomes too dry.

3. When ready to serve, remove from the heat and stir in the pesto. Taste and adjust the seasonings, then serve.

SERVES 4

Autumn Vegetable Stew

Each fall, when I feel that first nip in the air, I yearn for a fragrant pot of stew brimming with all the colors and flavors of autumn. That's when I head to the nearest farmers' market, where summer's fragile offerings have been replaced by sturdy root vegetables, winter squash, collards, and other autumn produce. Dark red kidney beans add a lovely color accent, along with protein and substance, to this stew.

2 tablespoons olive oil

1 medium-size yellow onion, finely
   chopped

1 large yellow turnip or small rutabaga,
   peeled and diced

1 large carrot, halved lengthwise and
   cut into 1/4-inch-thick half-moons

1 large parsnip, peeled, halved
   lengthwise, and cut into
   1/4-inch-thick half-moons

1 large sweet potato, peeled and diced

2 cups peeled, seeded, and diced
   winter squash

1/2 cup dry white wine

2 cups Basic Vegetable Stock (page 68),
   or more if desired

1 teaspoon chopped fresh thyme leaves
   or 1/2 teaspoon dried

1 teaspoon salt

1/4 teaspoon freshly ground black
   pepper

2 cups chopped collard greens or
   other dark leafy greens, cooked
   until tender and drained

1 1/2 cups cooked or one 15-ounce can
   dark red kidney beans, drained
   and rinsed

2 tablespoons chopped fresh parsley
   leaves

1. Heat the olive oil in a large saucepan over medium heat. Add the onion, turnip, carrot, parsnip, sweet potato, and squash. Cover and cook, stirring occasionally, until slightly softened, about 10 minutes. Stir in the wine, stock, thyme, salt, and pepper and bring to a boil. Reduce the heat to low and simmer until the vegetables soften and the liquid is reduced, about 30 minutes. If a thinner stew is desired, add more stock. If a thick stew is preferred, puree about $1^1/2$ cups of the stew in a blender or food processor and stir back into the pot.

2. Stir in the collards and kidney beans. Taste and adjust the seasonings. Simmer to heat through and allow the flavors to mingle, about 10 minutes. Sprinkle with the parsley and serve hot.

SERVES 6

Portobello and Green Bean Ragout with Madeira

I especially like the way the mushrooms absorb the flavor of the Madeira, adding a lusty richness to the stew. If Madeira is unavailable, you could try another fortified wine such as Marsala or port, or use a regular dry red or white wine, if you prefer. Serve over rice or noodles.

2 tablespoons olive oil

1 pound large portobello mushrooms, stems removed and caps cut into $^1/2$-inch dice

$^1/2$ cup dry Madeira

3 shallots, chopped

1 celery rib, minced

2 cups Basic Vegetable Stock (page 68), reduced over medium-high heat to 1 cup

Salt and freshly ground black pepper

8 ounces green beans, ends trimmed and cut into 1-inch pieces

1 tablespoon cornstarch dissolved in 2 tablespoons water

1 tablespoon minced fresh tarragon or parsley leaves

1. Heat 1 tablespoon of the olive oil in a large skillet over medium heat. Add the mushrooms and cook until browned all over, about 5 minutes. Add $^1/4$ cup of the Madeira, tossing to coat. Set aside.

2. Heat the remaining 1 tablespoon olive oil in a large saucepan over medium heat. Add the shallots and celery, cover, and cook, stirring occasionally, until tender, about 10 minutes. Stir in the remaining $1/4$ cup Madeira, the stock, and salt and pepper to taste and bring to a boil over medium-high heat. Add the green beans, reduce the heat to medium, and simmer until the beans are tender and the liquid is reduced slightly, about 20 minutes.

3. Whisk in the cornstarch mixture and cook, stirring, until thickened, about 2 minutes. Add the mushrooms and tarragon, reduce the heat to low, and simmer for 5 minutes to blend the flavors. Serve hot.

SERVES 4

Winter Squash and Burdock Root Stew

Burdock root is a long, slender root that is widely used in macrobiotic cooking to increase vitality. It is also considered a blood purifier. The plant grows wild throughout the United States, and the root is available in Asian markets and specialty food shops. It has a thin, edible skin and oxidizes quickly when cut. To prevent browning, soak cut burdock in water and lemon juice. This will also help eliminate its earthy, slightly bitter taste. Its texture is chewy and somewhat fibrous, but it softens when cooked. This gentle stew, which combines burdock with sweet-tasting kabocha squash and chewy shiitake mushrooms, is ideal winter fare served over brown rice or soba noodles.

Barley miso is made from barley, soybeans, and sea salt. One of the darker, saltier misos, it is aged longer and made with more soybeans than mellow white miso. As with all misos, don't let the stew boil after the miso is added, or all its beneficial enzymes will be destroyed.

1 small kabocha or other winter squash, peeled, seeded, and diced

3 medium-size burdock roots, trimmed, well scrubbed, and thinly sliced

1 1/2 cups carrots cut into diagonal slices

1 small yellow onion, chopped

2 1/2 cups Basic Vegetable Stock (page 68)

1 tablespoon barley miso paste

1 tablespoon tamari or other soy sauce

2 cups chopped napa cabbage

4 fresh shiitake mushrooms, stems removed and caps sliced

2 teaspoons toasted sesame oil

1. Place the squash, burdock, carrots, onion, and stock in a large saucepan over medium-high heat and bring to a boil. Reduce the heat to low, cover, and simmer until the vegetables begin to soften, about 20 minutes.

2. In a small bowl, blend the miso, tamari, and 1/4 cup of the broth. Stir back into the pot. Add the cabbage and mushrooms and simmer until the vegetables are tender, about 15 minutes.

3. Just before serving, drizzle the sesame oil into the stew. Taste and adjust the seasonings, then serve hot.

SERVES 4

African Sweet Potato and Peanut Stew

If you've never had a dish that combined sweet potatoes and peanuts, you're in for a treat. Even people who claim not to like sweet potatoes enjoy this stew. Serve it over rice or couscous.

1 tablespoon olive oil

1 medium-size yellow onion, chopped

1 medium-size green bell pepper, seeded and chopped

1 large garlic clove, minced

2 teaspoons light brown sugar or natural sweetener

1 teaspoon peeled and grated fresh ginger

1/2 teaspoon ground cumin

1/2 teaspoon ground cinnamon

1/4 teaspoon cayenne

1 1/2 pounds sweet potatoes, peeled and cut into 1/2-inch dice

One 14.5-ounce can crushed tomatoes

1 1/2 cups Basic Vegetable Stock (page 68)

Salt

1 1/2 cups cooked or one 15-ounce can dark red kidney beans, drained and rinsed

2 tablespoons smooth natural peanut butter

1/2 cup chopped unsalted dry-roasted peanuts

1. Heat the olive oil in a large saucepan over medium heat. Add the onion, cover, and cook until softened, about 5 minutes. Add the bell pepper and garlic, cover, and cook until softened, about 5 minutes. Stir in the brown sugar, ginger, cumin, cinnamon, and cayenne and cook, stirring, for 30 seconds. Add the sweet potatoes and stir to coat. Stir in the tomatoes, stock, and salt to taste. Bring to a boil, then reduce the heat to low and simmer until the vegetables are soft, about 30 minutes.

2. About 10 minutes before the end of the cooking time, stir in the kidney beans and simmer until heated through.

3. Place the peanut butter in a small bowl and blend in about 1/4 cup of the broth, stirring until smooth, then stir it into the stew. If a thicker consistency is desired, puree 1 cup of the stew in a blender or food processor and stir back into the pot.

4. Taste and adjust the seasonings. Sprinkle with the chopped peanuts and serve.

SERVES 4 TO 6

Marjoram-Scented Artichoke and Chickpea Stew

Two Mediterranean favorites, artichokes and chickpeas, are combined in a flavorful stew redolent of fresh herbs. Frozen artichoke hearts and canned chickpeas make short work of the preparation, resulting in a dish special enough for company when served with a green salad and hearty bruschetta or focaccia.

2 tablespoons olive oil

1 large sweet yellow onion, chopped

1 small red bell pepper, seeded and cut into 1-inch pieces

2 garlic cloves, minced

1 bay leaf

1 1/2 teaspoons minced fresh marjoram leaves or 3/4 teaspoon dried

1/2 cup dry white wine

2 cups Super-Rich Vegetable Stock (page 70)

1 pound Yukon Gold or other all-purpose potatoes, peeled and cut into 1-inch chunks

Salt and freshly ground black pepper

One 9-ounce package frozen artichoke hearts, cooked according to package directions and drained

1 1/2 cups cooked or one 15-ounce can chickpeas, drained and rinsed

1. Heat the olive oil in a large skillet over medium heat. Add the onion, cover, and cook until softened, about 5 minutes. Add the bell pepper and garlic, cover, and cook until softened, about 5 minutes. Add the bay leaf and dried marjoram (if using). Stir in the wine. Add the stock and bring to a boil. Add the potatoes and salt and pepper to taste, reduce the heat to low, and simmer until the potatoes are fork tender, about 20 minutes.

2. Stir in the artichoke hearts, chickpeas, and fresh marjoram (if using). If a thicker stew is desired, puree 1 cup of the mixture in a blender or food processor and stir back into the pot. Simmer gently until heated through, about 5 minutes.

SERVES 4

Tuscan White Bean and Fennel Stew with Orange and Rosemary

Among other things, Tuscany is known for its olive oil, wine, and sun-ripened produce, as well as meaty beans such as the creamy cannellini. This stew incorporates many of these ingredients in a salute to the Tuscan countryside. A light, dry Pinot Grigio and some grilled Italian bread make ideal accompaniments.

2 tablespoons olive oil

1 large sweet yellow onion, chopped

2 medium-size carrots, halved lengthwise and cut into 1/4-inch-thick half-moons

2 garlic cloves, minced

1 large fennel bulb, trimmed and diced

1/2 cup dry white wine

1 1/2 cups Basic Vegetable Stock (page 68)

1 pound small red potatoes, unpeeled and quartered

One 14.5-ounce can diced tomatoes, undrained

Salt and freshly ground black pepper

2 small zucchini, cut into 1/4-inch-thick rounds

1 1/2 cups cooked or one 15-ounce can cannellini or other white beans, drained and rinsed

1 tablespoon minced orange zest

2 teaspoons minced fresh rosemary leaves or 1 teaspoon dried

1. Heat the olive oil in a large saucepan over medium-high heat. Add the onion and carrots, cover, and cook until softened, about 5 minutes. Add the garlic and cook, stirring, for 30 seconds. Add the fennel and wine and bring to a boil. Reduce the heat to medium and simmer, uncovered and stirring, until the wine is reduced by one-half, about 5 minutes. Add the stock, potatoes, tomatoes and juice, and salt and pepper to taste. Bring to a boil, then reduce the heat to low and simmer, stirring occasionally, until the potatoes soften, about 20 minutes.

2. Add the zucchini, beans, and salt and pepper to taste. Simmer until the ingredients are tender and the desired consistency is achieved, about 15 minutes. If a thicker stew is desired, puree 1 cup of the stew in a blender or food processor and stir back into the pot.

3. A few minutes before serving, stir in the orange zest and rosemary. Serve hot.

SERVES 4 TO 6

Moroccan-Spiced Fava Bean Stew

Fragrant spices and dried fruits lend a Moroccan flavor to this hearty stew made with meaty fava beans. Fresh favas can be difficult to find and are time-consuming to prepare, since they need to be blanched and peeled before cooking. Dried, frozen, or canned fava beans may be found in specialty markets and some supermarkets. If favas are unavailable, substitute butter beans or lima beans. Serve over couscous or rice.

1/2 cup mixed dried fruit

1/4 cup raisins or dried currants

1 tablespoon olive oil

1 large sweet yellow onion, chopped

1 large carrot, diced

1 large garlic clove, minced

1 teaspoon ground cumin

1 teaspoon ground cinnamon

One 14.5-ounce can diced tomatoes, drained and chopped

8 ounces green beans, ends trimmed and cut into 1-inch pieces

2 cups Basic Vegetable Stock (page 68)

1 1/2 cups cooked or one 15-ounce can fava beans, drained and rinsed

1/2 cup frozen green peas, thawed

Salt and freshly ground black pepper

1 tablespoon minced fresh cilantro or parsley leaves

1. Place the dried fruit and raisins in a small heatproof bowl. Add boiling water to cover and soak for 20 minutes to soften. Drain and set aside.

2. Heat the olive oil in a large saucepan over medium heat. Add the onion and carrot, cover, and cook until softened, about 5 minutes. Add the garlic, cumin, and cinnamon and cook, stirring, for 30 seconds. Add the tomatoes, green beans, and stock and bring to a boil. Reduce the heat to low, cover, and simmer until the vegetables are tender, about 20 minutes.

3. Add the favas, peas, fruit, and salt and pepper to taste. Simmer, uncovered, until the flavors are blended and the desired consistency is achieved, about 10 minutes.

4. Sprinkle with the cilantro and serve.

SERVES 4

Curried Lentils with Carrots and Peas

Aromatic spices and coconut milk turn everyday lentils into a richly flavored stew. If a smoother texture is desired, puree up to two cups in a blender or food processor and stir back into the pot. Serve over freshly cooked basmati rice.

1 large yellow onion, cut into pieces
2 garlic cloves, peeled
1 teaspoon peeled and chopped fresh
    ginger
2 tablespoons olive oil
1 tablespoon curry powder
1/2 teaspoon ground cardamom
1/2 teaspoon ground cinnamon
1/2 teaspoon dry mustard
1/4 teaspoon cayenne

1/4 teaspoon ground allspice
1/4 teaspoon turmeric
3 cups water
1 1/4 cups dried brown lentils, picked
    over and rinsed
2 medium-size carrots, halved length-
    wise and cut into thin half-moons
3/4 cup frozen green peas, thawed
1 cup unsweetened coconut milk
Salt and freshly ground black pepper

1. In a food processor, puree the onion, garlic, and ginger.
2. Heat the olive oil in a large saucepan over low heat. Add the onion puree, cover, and cook to mellow the flavor, about 5 minutes, stirring a few times. Stir in the spices and cook, stirring, for 30 seconds. Add the water and bring to a simmer. Add the lentils, cover, and cook until tender, 30 to 40 minutes. After 10 minutes, add the carrots.
3. When the lentils and carrots are tender, add the peas, coconut milk, and salt and pepper to taste. Simmer, uncovered, to incorporate the flavors, about 10 minutes. Serve hot.

SERVES 4 TO 6

Belgian-Style Seitan Stew with Dark Beer

This adaptation of the hearty Belgian stew *carbonnade à la flamande* is made with seitan, which absorbs all the flavors of the rich sauce. Serve over noodles and wash it down with more of the beer that you use in the stew.

3 tablespoons olive oil

1 pound seitan, cut into thin strips

1 large yellow onion, chopped

1 tablespoon light brown sugar or natural sweetener

2 tablespoons unbleached all-purpose flour

1 cup dark beer

1 tablespoon molasses

2 teaspoons Dijon mustard

2 teaspoons white wine vinegar

1 teaspoon dried thyme, crumbled

1 bay leaf

1 cup Basic Vegetable Stock (page 68)

Salt and freshly ground black pepper

1. Heat 1 tablespoon of the olive oil in a large skillet over medium-high heat. Add the seitan and cook until browned on all sides, about 10 minutes. Set aside.

2. Heat the remaining 2 tablespoons olive oil in a large saucepan over medium heat. Add the onion, cover, and cook until softened, about 5 minutes.

3. Stir in the brown sugar and cook, uncovered and stirring frequently, until the onion is caramelized, about 10 minutes. Add the flour and cook, stirring, for 1 to 2 minutes to remove the raw taste. Stir in the beer, molasses, mustard, vinegar, thyme, and bay leaf. Add the stock, season with salt and pepper to taste, and simmer, stirring occasionally, until thickened, 10 to 15 minutes.

4. Add the seitan and simmer until the flavors are blended, about 10 minutes. Remove the bay leaf and taste and adjust the seasonings. Serve hot.

Did You know...

Seitan is a cholesterol-free food that is high in protein and a good source of iron? This "meat from wheat" also is low in calories, carbohydrates, and fat.

SERVES 4

Wheat-Meat Stroganoff

The meaty texture and appearance of seitan, or wheat-meat, make it a natural stand-in for beef in this creamy eastern European classic made with vegan sour cream. Serve over wide noodles.

2 tablespoons olive oil

12 ounces seitan, cut into 1/2-inch dice

2 tablespoons tomato paste

2 cups Basic Vegetable Stock (page 68)

1 large yellow onion, chopped

1 large green bell pepper, seeded and chopped

8 ounces small white mushrooms, quartered

2 tablespoons unbleached all-purpose flour

1 1/2 tablespoons sweet Hungarian paprika

Salt and freshly ground black pepper

1/2 cup vegan sour cream, homemade (page 139) or store-bought

1. Heat 1 tablespoon of the olive oil in a large skillet over medium heat. Add the seitan and brown on all sides, 7 to 8 minutes. Set aside.

2. In a small bowl, combine the tomato paste and 1/4 cup of the stock, blending until smooth. Set aside.

3. Heat the remaining 1 tablespoon olive oil in a large saucepan over medium heat. Add the onion and bell pepper, cover, and cook until softened, about 5 minutes. Add the mushrooms and cook, uncovered, until the liquid evaporates, about 3 minutes. Stir in the flour and paprika and cook, stirring, for about 1 minute to remove the raw taste from the flour. Add the tomato paste mixture, stirring until smooth. Stir in the remaining 1 3/4 cups stock and bring to a boil, then reduce the heat to low. Season with salt and pepper to taste and simmer until the flavors are blended and the sauce thickens somewhat, about 25 minutes.

4. Slowly whisk in the vegan sour cream until well blended. Add the seitan and simmer until heated through, about 5 minutes. Serve hot.

SERVES 4

Tempeh Goulash

Tempeh and sauerkraut, both fermented foods, are a natural pair in this new take on Hungarian goulash. Serve over wide noodles.

2 cups sauerkraut

3 tablespoons olive oil

Two 8-ounce packages tempeh, poached (page 14) and cut into 1-inch chunks

1 small yellow onion, chopped

2 garlic cloves, minced

2 tablespoons sweet Hungarian paprika

1/2 cup dry white wine

1 teaspoon caraway seeds

2 tablespoons tomato paste

2 cups Basic Vegetable Stock (page 68)

1/2 cup vegan sour cream, homemade (page 139) or store-bought

Salt and freshly ground black pepper

1. Rinse the sauerkraut under cold running water and drain well. Transfer to a medium-size bowl and set aside.

2. Heat 1 tablespoon of the olive oil in a large skillet over medium heat. Add the tempeh and brown on all sides, 6 to 8 minutes. Set aside.

3. Heat the remaining 2 tablespoons olive oil in a large saucepan over medium heat. Add the onion, cover, and cook until softened, about 5 minutes. Stir in the garlic and paprika and cook for 1 minute. Stir in the wine and bring to a boil. Add the tempeh, sauerkraut, and caraway seeds.

4. In a small bowl, blend the tomato paste and 1/2 cup of the stock. Add to the goulash along with the remaining 1 1/2 cups stock. Bring to a boil, reduce the heat to low, and simmer, uncovered and stirring occasionally, until the liquid is reduced and the flavors are blended, 20 to 30 minutes.

5. Pour about 1/3 cup of the simmering broth into a small bowl and whisk in the vegan sour cream until blended. Stir the sour cream mixture back into the goulash, season with salt and pepper to taste, and simmer to blend the flavors, about 5 minutes. Serve hot.

SERVES 4

Indonesian-Inspired Tempeh Stew

This flavorful stew is made with Indonesian ingredients, including tempeh, coconut milk, and pungent seasonings. Serve over freshly cooked rice.

2 tablespoons olive oil

One 12-ounce package tempeh, poached (page 14) and cubed

3 shallots, chopped

3 garlic cloves, minced

1 small, fresh hot chile, seeded and minced

1 teaspoon peeled and minced fresh ginger

1 large sweet potato, peeled and diced

1 cup water

One 14.5-ounce can crushed tomatoes

1 tablespoon tamari or other soy sauce

1 cup unsweetened coconut milk

Salt and freshly ground black pepper

2 tablespoons minced fresh cilantro leaves

1 teaspoon minced lime zest

1. Heat 1 tablespoon of the olive oil in a large skillet over medium-high heat. Add the tempeh and brown on all sides, about 5 minutes. Set aside.

2. Heat the remaining 1 tablespoon olive oil in a large saucepan over medium heat. Add the shallots, garlic, chile, and ginger. Cover and cook until softened, about 5 minutes. Add the sweet potato, water, tomatoes, and tamari. Cover and cook, stirring occasionally, until the vegetables are tender, about 20 minutes. Uncover and reduce the heat to low. Add the coconut milk, salt and pepper to taste, and tempeh. Simmer, stirring occasionally, until thickened, about 10 minutes.

3. Just before serving, stir in the cilantro and lime zest. Serve hot.

SERVES 4

Chipotles: Smokin' Good

The popularity of smoky hot chipotle chiles is spreading like wildfire. Their distinctive, earthy flavor adds spice to salsas and dips, chilis and stews, and even breads and potatoes. At one time, these dried jalapeños were found only in ethnic markets, either plain or canned in adobo sauce (a rich tomato sauce). These days, chipotles can be found on many supermarket shelves. McIlhenny Company of Tabasco fame even makes a chipotle sauce.

Tempeh and Red Bean Jambalaya with Chipotle Chiles

The chipotle chiles add smoky heat to this spicy stew, which is best served over freshly cooked rice. Filé powder, made from sassafras leaves, thickens the stew and adds flavor. It can be found in specialty food shops and well-stocked supermarkets. For a milder version, decrease or omit the chiles.

2 dried chipotle chiles, soaked in very
    hot water to cover for 30 minutes
2 tablespoons olive oil
One 8-ounce package tempeh, poached
    (page 14) and cut into 1/2-inch dice
1 large onion, chopped
1 large green bell pepper, seeded and
    chopped
2 garlic cloves, minced

1 1/2 cups cooked or one 15-ounce can
    dark red kidney beans, drained
    and rinsed
One 28-ounce can crushed tomatoes
1 cup water
1 teaspoon filé powder
1 teaspoon dried thyme, crumbled
Salt
Cayenne

1. Drain the chiles, chop, and set aside.

2. Heat 1 tablespoon of the olive oil in a large skillet over medium-high heat. Add the tempeh and cook, stirring occasionally, until browned on all sides, about 5 minutes. Set aside.

3. Heat the remaining 1 tablespoon olive oil in a large saucepan over medium heat. Add onion and bell pepper, cover, and cook, stirring occasionally, until tender, about 10 minutes. Stir in the garlic and cook for 1 minute. Add the beans, tomatoes, water, filé powder, thyme, and salt and cayenne to taste. Stir in the tempeh and chiles and simmer until the liquid cooks down and the flavors have blended, about 30 minutes. Serve hot.

SERVES 4

Tofu Vindaloo

Vegetable vindaloo is a spicy favorite in Indian restaurants and is easy to make at home. In this version, I feature tofu because it takes on the surrounding flavors while adding protein and substance. You may use chickpeas instead, if you prefer. Serve over freshly cooked basmati rice.

3 garlic cloves, peeled

1½ tablespoons peeled and chopped fresh ginger

½ teaspoon ground cardamom

½ teaspoon ground coriander

½ teaspoon ground cumin

½ teaspoon dry mustard

½ teaspoon cayenne

¼ teaspoon ground cinnamon

¼ teaspoon turmeric

3 tablespoons olive oil

One 16-ounce package extra-firm tofu, drained and diced

Salt and freshly ground black pepper

1 large yellow onion, chopped

1 large carrot, halved lengthwise and cut into ¼-inch-thick half-moons

1 small red bell pepper, seeded and diced

One 14.5-ounce can diced tomatoes, undrained

½ cup frozen green peas, thawed

1 cup water, or more as needed

1. In a blender or food processor, combine the garlic, ginger, cardamom, coriander, cumin, mustard, cayenne, cinnamon, turmeric, and 1 tablespoon of the olive oil. Process until smooth and set aside.

2. Heat 1 tablespoon of the olive oil in a large skillet over medium-high heat. Add the tofu and cook until golden brown on all sides, 6 to 8 minutes. Season with salt and pepper to taste. Transfer to a medium-size bowl and set aside.

3. Heat the remaining 1 tablespoon olive oil in a large saucepan over medium heat. Add the onion and carrot, cover, and cook until softened, about 5 minutes. Add the bell pepper, cover, and cook until slightly softened, about 5 minutes. Add the spice paste and cook, stirring, for 1 minute. Stir in the tomatoes and juice, peas, and water and bring to boil. Reduce the heat to low and season with salt and pepper to taste. Cover and simmer until the vegetables are tender, about 10 minutes.

4. Add the tofu and cook, uncovered, for 10 minutes so that the tofu can absorb the flavors of the sauce. Taste and adjust the seasonings. If the stew is too thick, add a little more water. Serve hot.

SERVES 4

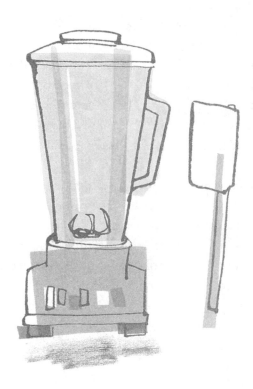

Three-Bean Chili

Vegetarian chili has become widely viewed as a great way to introduce meatless meals to nonvegetarians because it's hearty and robust—things many people do not usually associate with vegetarian cuisine. This version features three kinds of beans, but you may substitute chopped or crumbled veggie burgers or vegetarian burger crumbles for all or part of the beans. Serve with crackers or cornbread, or ladled over rice or noodles.

1 tablespoon olive oil

1 large sweet yellow onion, chopped

1/2 small green bell pepper, seeded and chopped

2 garlic cloves, minced

1 small, fresh hot chile (optional), seeded and minced

3 tablespoons tomato paste

2 tablespoons chili powder, or to your taste

One 28-ounce can crushed tomatoes

1 1/2 cups cooked or one 15-ounce can black beans, drained and rinsed

1 1/2 cups cooked or one 15-ounce can pinto beans, drained and rinsed

1 1/2 cups cooked or one 15-ounce can dark red kidney beans, drained and rinsed

1 1/2 cups water

1 teaspoon salt

1/4 teaspoon freshly ground black pepper

Heat the olive oil in a large saucepan over medium heat. Add the onion and bell pepper, cover, and cook, stirring occasionally, until tender, about 10 minutes. Add the garlic and chile (if using) and cook for 1 minute. Stir in the tomato paste, chili powder, and tomatoes until well blended. Add all the beans, the water, salt, and pepper and simmer, stirring occasionally, until the liquid is reduced and the flavors are blended, 30 to 40 minutes. Taste and adjust the seasonings, then serve hot.

SERVES 6

Did You Know...

It's a good idea to eat beans in combination with foods high in vitamin C, such as cruciferous vegetables or bell peppers? Doing so will increase the body's absorption of the iron in the beans.

Very Veggie Chili

This chili is loaded with a variety of vegetables that harmonize well with the zesty seasonings. For a change of pace, serve it over freshly cooked couscous or quinoa.

1/4 cup tomato paste

2 tablespoons chili powder

1 teaspoon ground allspice

1 tablespoon molasses

1 tablespoon tamari or other soy sauce

2 tablespoons olive oil

1 large red onion, chopped

1 celery rib, minced

1 medium-size eggplant, peeled and chopped

1 small red bell pepper, seeded and chopped

1 small, fresh hot chile (optional), seeded and minced

1 garlic clove, minced

One 14.5-ounce can diced tomatoes, undrained

1 1/2 cups cooked or one 15-ounce can chickpeas, drained and rinsed

1 1/2 cups water

Salt and freshly ground black pepper

1. In a small bowl, combine the tomato paste, chili powder, allspice, molasses, and tamari, stirring to blend. Set aside.

2. Heat the olive oil in a large saucepan over medium heat. Add the onion and celery, cover, and cook until softened, about 5 minutes. Add the eggplant, bell pepper, chile (if using), and garlic. Cover and cook, stirring occasionally, until softened, about 10 minutes.

3. Stir in the tomato paste mixture. Add the tomatoes and juice, chickpeas, water, and salt and pepper to taste. Simmer, stirring occasionally, until the liquid is reduced and the vegetables are tender, about 30 minutes. Serve hot.

SERVES 6

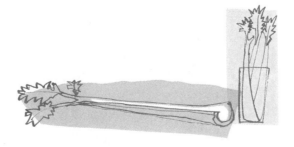

Black Bean and Butternut Squash Chili

This chili recipe has become a tradition at Halloween parties because of the vivid color contrast between the black beans and bright orange squash. Serve it in a large, hollowed-out pumpkin to add to the festivities, accompanied by your choice of garnishes or toppings.

1 tablespoon olive oil

1 medium-size yellow onion, chopped

1 garlic clove, minced

1 jalapeño (optional), seeded and minced

One 14.5-ounce can plum tomatoes, drained and chopped

1 cup water

1 cup apple juice

1/4 cup tomato paste

2 tablespoons chili powder, or to your taste

1 teaspoon salt

1 medium-size butternut squash, peeled, seeded, and cut into 1/2-inch dice

3 cups cooked or two 15-ounce cans black beans, drained and rinsed

1. Heat the olive oil in a large pot over medium heat. Add the onion, garlic, and jalapeño (if using). Cover and cook until softened, about 5 minutes. Add the tomatoes, water, apple juice, tomato paste, chili powder, salt, and squash and stir to combine. Bring to a boil, then reduce the heat to low. Cover and simmer until the squash is tender, about 30 minutes.

2. Add the beans, then taste and adjust the seasonings. Simmer, uncovered, for about 15 minutes to blend the flavors. Serve hot.

SERVES 6

Roasted Root Vegetable Chili

The rich, mellow flavor of roasted root vegetables makes this a perfect choice for a late autumn meal, accompanied by warm cornbread, fresh from the oven. You may peel or not peel the carrots, parsnips, and potato, but as with all vegetables, be sure to wash them thoroughly if left unpeeled.

2 tablespoons olive oil
1 large sweet yellow onion, chopped
2 large carrots, diced
2 medium-size parsnips, peeled and diced
1 large Yukon Gold potato, diced
Salt and freshly ground black pepper
1 garlic clove, minced

1 jalapeño (optional), seeded and minced
One 6-ounce can tomato paste
2 tablespoons chili powder
2 cups water
3 cups cooked or two 15-ounce cans pinto beans, drained and rinsed

1. Preheat the oven to 400 degrees F. Use 1 tablespoon of the olive oil to coat the bottom of a shallow baking pan. Distribute the onion, carrots, parsnips, and potato in the pan, tossing to coat. Sprinkle with salt and pepper to taste and roast, turning once, until softened and lightly browned, about 30 minutes.
2. Heat the remaining 1 tablespoon olive oil in a large pot over medium heat. Add the garlic and jalapeño (if using) and cook, stirring, until fragrant, about 3 minutes. Add the tomato paste, chili powder, water, and salt to taste and stir well. Bring to a boil, reduce the heat to low, and simmer for 15 minutes.
3. When the roasted vegetables are tender, add them to the pot along with the beans and simmer for 15 minutes to blend the flavors. Serve hot.

SERVES 6

Black Bean Chili with Cilantro Pesto

The Cilantro Pesto adds a special touch to this chili, but it's flavorful enough to stand on its own if you prefer to omit the pesto.

1 tablespoon olive oil
1 large onion, chopped
$1/3$ cup chopped celery
2 garlic cloves, minced
One 6-ounce can tomato paste
One 14.5-ounce can plum tomatoes, drained and chopped
2 tablespoons chili powder

$1/2$ teaspoon ground cumin
2 cups water
Salt and freshly ground black pepper
1 tablespoon fresh lemon juice
3 cups cooked or two 15-ounce cans black beans, drained and rinsed
$1/3$ cup Cilantro Pesto (recipe follows)

1. Heat the olive oil in a large pot over medium heat. Add the onion, celery, and garlic. Cover and cook until softened, about 5 minutes. Add the tomato paste, tomatoes, chili powder, cumin, water, and salt and pepper to taste. Reduce the heat to low and simmer for 30 minutes.

2. Add the lemon juice and beans and simmer for about 15 minutes. Taste and adjust the seasonings. Just before serving, swirl in the pesto.

SERVES 6

"I am in favor of animal rights as well as human rights. That is the way of a whole human being."
—ABRAHAM LINCOLN

CILANTRO PESTO

1 cup tightly packed fresh cilantro leaves

¼ cup raw almonds

2 large garlic cloves, peeled

½ teaspoon salt

¼ cup olive oil

Combine the cilantro, almonds, garlic, and salt in a food processor and process until smooth. With the machine running, add the olive oil through the feed tube and process into a smooth paste. Store, tightly covered, in the refrigerator with a thin layer of olive oil on top to prevent discoloration.

MAKES ABOUT 1 CUP

Anasazi Chili with Quinoa

The anasazi is a sweet, meaty bean, whose name means "ancient stranger" in the Navajo language. Paired with quinoa, the high-protein grain of the ancient Incas, it becomes a dish steeped in Native American heritage. If anasazi beans are unavailable, pinto or kidney beans may be used. Cook anasazi beans the same way you would cook pinto beans (page 276).

1 tablespoon olive oil

1 medium-size yellow onion, finely chopped

1 small red bell pepper, seeded and chopped

2 tablespoons chili powder

1/2 teaspoon ground cumin

1/2 teaspoon dried oregano

1 teaspoon salt

Freshly ground black pepper

One 28-ounce can plum tomatoes, drained and chopped

3 cups cooked anasazi beans, drained and rinsed

1 1/2 cups water

4 to 6 cups freshly cooked quinoa (page 220)

1. Heat the olive oil in a large pot over medium heat. Add the onion and bell pepper, cover, and cook until softened, about 5 minutes. Stir in the chili powder, cumin, oregano, salt, and pepper to taste. Add the tomatoes, beans, and water and stir to combine. Bring to a boil, reduce the heat to low, and simmer for 30 minutes, stirring occasionally. Taste and adjust the seasonings.

2. To serve, spoon the chili over the quinoa.

SERVES 4 TO 6

Sweet and Spicy Chili

The slivered almonds add an interesting twist to this chili. Accompany it with an aromatic rice such as jasmine or basmati to complement the hint of sweetness in the chili.

1 tablespoon olive oil

1 small sweet yellow onion, chopped

2 garlic cloves, minced

2 tablespoons chili powder

2 teaspoons light brown sugar or
    natural sweetener

1/2 teaspoon ground cumin

1/2 teaspoon ground cinnamon

1 teaspoon salt

1/8 teaspoon cayenne

One 28-ounce can diced tomatoes,
    undrained

One 6-ounce can tomato paste

2 cups apple juice

One 4-ounce can diced hot green chiles,
    drained

3 cups cooked or two 15-ounce cans
    kidney beans, drained and rinsed

2 cups vegetarian burger crumbles

6 cups freshly cooked aromatic rice
    (see headnote)

1/4 cup slivered almonds, toasted
    (page 110), for garnish

1. Heat the olive oil in a large pot over medium heat. Add the onion and garlic, cover, and cook until softened, about 5 minutes. Stir in the chili powder, brown sugar, cumin, cinnamon, salt, and cayenne. Add the tomatoes and juice, tomato paste, apple juice, chiles, and beans. Stir to combine and bring to a boil. Reduce the heat to low, stir in the burger crumbles, and simmer for 30 minutes, stirring occasionally. Taste and adjust the seasonings.

2. Serve over the rice, garnished with the almonds.

SERVES 6

East Coast Chili

This chili is typical of those I've encountered in homes and restaurants in the eastern United States, where it's often served over cooked elbow macaroni.

1 tablespoon olive oil

1 large yellow onion, chopped

2 tablespoons chili powder, or to your taste

1/2 teaspoon dried oregano

1/8 teaspoon cayenne

One 28-ounce can crushed tomatoes

One 6-ounce can tomato paste

2 cups water

2 cups vegetarian burger crumbles

3 cups cooked or two 15-ounce cans kidney beans, drained and rinsed

Salt and freshly ground black pepper

1. Heat the olive oil in a large pot over medium heat. Add the onion, cover, and cook until softened, about 5 minutes. Stir in the chili powder, oregano, cayenne, tomatoes, tomato paste, and water. Bring to a boil, reduce the heat to low, cover, and simmer for 15 minutes.

2. Stir in the burger crumbles, beans, and salt and pepper to taste. Simmer for about 30 minutes to blend the flavors. Serve hot.

SERVES 6

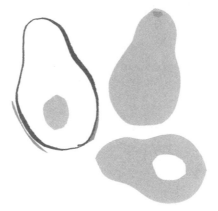

West Coast Chili

California olives and avocados, combined with vibrant fresh vegetables, contribute to the West Coast influence of this chili. To complete the picture, serve with a bottle of good California wine and some San Francisco sourdough bread. Be sure to prepare the avocado at the last minute to avoid discoloration.

1 tablespoon olive oil

1 medium-size yellow onion, chopped

1 small red bell pepper, seeded and chopped

1 small yellow bell pepper, seeded and chopped

1 garlic clove, minced

8 ripe plum tomatoes, diced

1/4 cup tomato paste

2 tablespoons chili powder

1 teaspoon minced fresh oregano leaves or 1/2 teaspoon dried

1/2 cup dry red wine

1 1/2 cups water

3 cups cooked or two 15-ounce cans kidney beans, drained and rinsed

Salt and freshly ground black pepper

2 ripe avocados, peeled, pitted, and diced

1/2 cup pitted and sliced brine-cured black olives

1. Heat the olive oil in a large pot over medium heat. Add the onion, bell peppers, and garlic. Cover and cook until softened, about 10 minutes. Add the tomatoes, tomato paste, chili powder, oregano, wine, water, beans, and salt and pepper to taste. Simmer until the flavors are blended and the desired consistency is achieved, about 30 minutes.

2. Serve hot, topped with the avocados and olives.

SERVES 4 TO 6

Did You Know...

The avocado is rich in potassium, folic acid, vitamin B_6, and other nutrients? Though high in fat, it contains enzymes that help break down fat in the body.

Backyard Barbecue Chili

The smoky sweetness of the barbecue sauce permeates this flavorful chili. To keep in the backyard barbecue spirit, serve it with cole slaw, corn chips, and other picnic fare, even if it's snowing outside.

1 tablespoon olive oil

1 medium-size yellow onion, chopped

1 small red bell pepper, seeded and chopped

One 28-ounce can diced tomatoes, undrained

1 cup water

1/2 cup bottled spicy barbecue sauce

2 tablespoons tomato paste

2 tablespoons chili powder

1 teaspoon light brown sugar or natural sweetener

Salt and freshly ground black pepper

2 cups vegetarian burger crumbles

3 cups cooked or two 15-ounce cans kidney beans, drained and rinsed

1. Heat the olive oil in a large pot over medium heat. Add the onion and bell pepper, cover, and cook until softened, about 5 minutes. Stir in the tomatoes and juice, water, barbecue sauce, tomato paste, chili powder, brown sugar, and salt and pepper to taste. Bring to a boil, reduce the heat to low, and simmer, covered, for 20 minutes, stirring occasionally.

2. Stir in the burger crumbles and beans and cook for 15 minutes to blend the flavors. Add a little water if the mixture becomes too dry. Serve hot.

SERVES 6

Orange and Thyme-Scented White Bean and "Sausage" Chili

This rich, aromatic chili is sophisticated enough for company. Serve over basmati rice and accompanied by a crisp white wine.

1 tablespoon olive oil

1 large yellow onion, chopped

1 small red bell pepper, seeded and chopped

1 jalapeño (optional), seeded and minced

3 tablespoons chili powder

1 tablespoon minced fresh thyme leaves or 1 teaspoon dried

1 tablespoon light brown sugar or natural sweetener

One 14.5-ounce can diced tomatoes, undrained

1 cup Fresh Tomato Salsa (page 174) or your favorite salsa

3 cups cooked or two 15-ounce cans cannellini or other white beans, drained and rinsed

2 cups chopped or crumbled soy sausage

1 cup water

1/2 cup orange juice

2 tablespoons orange-flavored liqueur (optional)

2 teaspoons chopped orange zest

Salt and freshly ground black pepper

Orange slices and fresh thyme sprigs for garnish

1. Heat the olive oil in a large pot over medium heat. Add the onion, bell pepper, and jalapeño (if using). Cover and cook until softened, about 5 minutes. Stir in the chili powder, thyme, and brown sugar. Add the tomatoes and juice, salsa, beans, soy sausage, and water, and simmer for 30 minutes.

2. Stir in the orange juice, liqueur (if using), orange zest, and salt and pepper to taste. Cook for 10 minutes to blend the flavors.

3. Serve hot, garnished with orange slices and thyme sprigs.

SERVES 6

Quick-as-Lightning Chili

This chili tastes as if it took all day to make, but it actually goes together in a flash with ingredients from your pantry. The vegetables in the chunky salsa add substance, making chopping vegetables unnecessary, while the chopped or crumbled veggie burgers give a meaty texture and are ideal when there are no other meat alternatives in the house. Serve over pasta or rice, accompanied by your favorite toppings.

1 tablespoon olive oil

2 or 3 frozen veggie burgers, thawed and chopped or crumbled

2 tablespoons chili powder

One 16-ounce jar chunky salsa

One 14.5-ounce can crushed tomatoes

3 cups cooked or two 15-ounce cans pinto beans, drained and rinsed

1/2 cup water, or more as needed

Salt and freshly ground black pepper

Heat the olive oil in a large pot over medium heat and add the chopped or crumbled veggie burgers. Stir in the remaining ingredients and bring to a boil. Reduce the heat to low and simmer until the flavors are blended and the desired consistency is achieved, about 30 minutes. If the chili becomes too thick, add more water. Serve hot.

SERVES 4 TO 6

Beyond Stew

In addition to warming the body and soul, vegan stews can be delicious, healthful, and economical. Stews are also simple to prepare. In most cases, all that is required is to chop a few vegetables, toss them into a pot with some vegetable stock or water, add some seasonings, and simmer for an hour or more.

Don't be afraid to be creative when you cook: stews are meant to be seasoned to taste. If you don't like an ingredient, substitute another that you do like. For example, try green beans instead of broccoli or thyme instead of oregano. And while we're on the subject of spices, add spices to taste—a little at a time. Slow simmering tends to bring out the flavor of spices, so you want to be careful not to add too much at the beginning.

When you make a large pot of stew, it can last for several meals. If your family hates "leftovers," transform the remaining stew into a potpie with the simple addition of a crust made out of biscuit or pie dough. By crowning a humble stew with a golden, flaky crust, you can elevate it to company fare, especially when served with a salad and light dessert. You also can make shepherd's pie by spooning some stew into a casserole and topping it with a layer of mashed potatoes. Just pop it into the oven and bake until bubbly.

Another way to get more mileage out of your stew is to serve it over rice or couscous one day and over pasta a couple of days later, seasoned in a different way. If the first version of stew is mildly seasoned, you can give it a lift (and new life) by adding some curry paste and coconut milk to the second incarnation. Or try adding a swirl of pesto or maybe some salsa.

12

Food that Sizzles: Grilling, Sautéing, and Stir-Frying

Whatever you're making for dinner, chances are good that you will use a skillet for all or part of the preparation. I can think of no other single cooking vessel that commands such importance in the kitchen. A good skillet can become your best friend. The type of skillet you use is a matter of personal preference, whether it's Grandma's cast-iron frying pan or a shiny new wok. There are a wide variety of materials, sizes, and types of pans to choose from, but if I could have only one skillet, it would be a 12-inch sauté pan, for its versatility and ease of use.

From Asian stir-fries to French sautés to old-fashioned simmered dishes, the recipes in this chapter run the gamut of skillet-cooked entrées using tofu, tempeh, seitan, and vegetables. Many skillet dishes, especially stir-fries and sautés, can be ready in 15 minutes or less.

Even in oven-cooked dishes, a skillet is often used to partially cook or sear some of the ingredients to improve the flavor, texture, or color of the dish. At the same time, recipes that might normally be prepared in the oven are sometimes simmered on top of the stove to save time or to avoid heating up the kitchen by turning on the oven.

Having good skillet sense doesn't mean you can't also enjoy the thrill of the grill. Many modern kitchens now have a grill built right into the stovetop for convenient grilling all year round. For that reason, this chapter includes suggestions for adapting certain recipes for the grill, as well as a few recipes designed specifically for grilling, whether indoors or out.

Za'tar-Spiced Bean Patties with Coconut-Curry Sauce

My friend and former neighbor Samantha Ragan came up with this dish and brought over a plateful to share her creation. After one bite, I was hooked. The creamy richness of the sauce is an ideal complement to the spicy bean patties. You can vary the size of the patties according to your preference, from bite-size on up. You also can shape them into balls or logs, if you prefer, and serve them over basmati rice. Za'tar herb blend is usually made up of sumac, thyme, oregano, and hyssop and can be found in gourmet shops or specialty markets. The name also can refer to a wild oregano grown in the Middle East. If you cannot find za'tar, substitute a blend of dried thyme, mint, and oregano.

1 large all-purpose potato, peeled and
    diced
1 medium-size carrot, chopped
1 cup cooked brown lentils, well drained
1 cup cooked or canned chickpeas,
    drained and rinsed
1 garlic clove, peeled
2 tablespoons dried za'tar
    (see headnote)
Salt

3 tablespoons olive oil
1 small yellow onion, chopped
1 heaping tablespoon curry powder
$1/2$ teaspoon light brown sugar or
    natural sweetener
$1/2$ teaspoon cayenne, or to taste
$3/4$ cup diced fresh or canned tomatoes
One 14-ounce can unsweetened
    coconut milk, or as needed

1. Steam the potato and carrot until tender, about 10 minutes. Set aside to cool.
2. Blot the lentils and chickpeas dry and place in a food processor. Add the potato and carrot mixture, garlic, za'tar, and salt to taste. Pulse to combine, being careful not to overprocess, so that some of the texture remains. Shape into patties.

3. Preheat the oven to 275 degrees F. Heat 2 tablespoons of the olive oil in a large skillet over medium-high heat. Working in batches, add the patties and cook, turning once, until they are browned on both sides, about 3 minutes per side. Place the browned patties on a baking sheet and keep warm in the oven.

4. Heat the remaining 1 tablespoon olive oil in a medium-size saucepan over medium heat. Add the onion, cover, and cook until softened, about 5 minutes. Stir in the curry powder, brown sugar, and cayenne, then add the tomatoes. Simmer until the tomatoes break up and become saucy, about 5 minutes. Reduce the heat to low and stir in about half of the coconut milk.

5. Place the sauce mixture in a blender and process until smooth. Return to the saucepan and add as much of the remaining coconut milk as needed to achieve the desired consistency. Heat over low heat, then taste and adjust the seasonings. Serve the patties topped with the sauce.

SERVES 4

Getting Enough Iron?

A well-balanced vegan diet can provide ample iron for most people. Iron-rich vegan foods include blackstrap molasses, leafy greens, sea vegetables, beans, nuts, nutritional yeast, wheat germ, dried fruits, prune juice, and fortified cereals. If you take an iron supplement, here are some tips.

- Look for a supplement that contains ferrous fumarate—it is easier on the stomach.
- Do not take iron supplements at the same time as calcium supplements, because the iron may inhibit calcium absorption.
- To increase the absorption of iron, take vitamin C or drink juice high in vitamin C when you take your iron supplement.

Mahogany Eggplant

Tender slices of Japanese eggplant are steeped in a flavorful tamari broth, which imbues it with a rich mahogany color. Serve this dish over freshly cooked rice. Small Japanese eggplants are used, but regular eggplants may be substituted, if necessary. To prepare this dish on the grill, brush the eggplant with a small amount of the sauce, then heat the remaining sauce separately to top the grilled eggplant.

3 tablespoons peanut oil

3 Japanese eggplants, cut into
    1/4-inch-thick diagonal slices

2 garlic cloves, minced

3 scallions, chopped

1 tablespoon peeled and minced fresh
    ginger

3 tablespoons tamari or other soy sauce

1 tablespoon sake or dry white wine

1 teaspoon light brown sugar or natural
    sweetener

1 teaspoon Asian chili paste

1/4 cup water

1. Heat 2 tablespoons of the peanut oil in a large skillet over medium-high heat. Add the eggplant in batches and cook until browned on both sides, about 10 minutes total. Transfer to a plate and set aside.

2. Heat the remaining 1 tablespoon peanut oil in the same skillet over medium heat. Add the garlic, scallions, and ginger and cook, stirring, until fragrant, about 30 seconds. Stir in the tamari, sake, brown sugar, chili paste, and water and simmer for 2 to 3 minutes, stirring to blend. Return the eggplant to the pan, tossing to coat it with the sauce. Cover and simmer until tender, about 10 minutes. Serve hot.

SERVES 4

Grilled Portobellos with Rosemary-Roasted Vegetables

This colorful dish is full of flavor, thanks to the plethora of diced roasted vegetables that make up the topping for the juicy portobello mushrooms. This is one of those recipes that can be adapted for stovetop, grill, or oven—or any combination. In this version, I grill the mushrooms and roast the vegetables for the topping, but the other cooking methods are interchangeable, with delicious results.

1 large red onion, chopped

1 large yellow bell pepper, seeded and chopped

1 medium-size zucchini, chopped

1/3 cup olive oil

2 tablespoons coarsely chopped fresh rosemary or other herb leaves

Salt and freshly ground black pepper

1 large, ripe tomato, chopped

4 large portobello mushrooms, stems removed

1. Preheat the oven to 425 degrees F and heat your grill or get a charcoal fire going. In a large bowl, combine the onion, bell pepper, zucchini, 1/4 cup of the olive oil, the rosemary, and salt and pepper to taste. Toss to coat the vegetables with the oil, then spread them in a single layer in a rimmed baking sheet. Roast until tender and lightly browned, about 25 minutes.

2. Reduce the oven temperature to 275 degrees F. Add the tomato to the roasted vegetables, stirring to combine, and return to the oven to keep warm.

3. Brush the mushrooms with the remaining olive oil and grill until tender and lightly charred on the outside, about 5 minutes per side.

4. To serve, arrange the portobello caps gill side down on 4 individual plates and top with the roasted vegetable mixture.

SERVES 4

VARIATION: For a more substantial entrée, grill 4 veggie burgers along with the mushrooms. To serve, place the burgers on the plate, top each with a mushroom cap, and top with the roasted vegetables.

Jerk-Spiced Portobello Steaks

Zesty jerk seasonings enhance the meaty texture of the mushrooms. They are pan-fried in this recipe but are also delicious cooked on the grill or under the broiler. Green Apple Salsa (page 173) is a good accompaniment. These succulent 'shrooms can be served over rice or on toasted burger rolls.

2 teaspoons light brown sugar or
    natural sweetener
1 teaspoon ground cumin
1 teaspoon ground allspice
1 teaspoon dried oregano
1 teaspoon sweet paprika

1 teaspoon salt
1/2 teaspoon cayenne
1/4 teaspoon freshly grated nutmeg
4 large portobello mushrooms, stems
    removed
1/4 cup extra virgin olive oil

1. In a shallow bowl, combine the brown sugar, cumin, allspice, oregano, paprika, salt, cayenne, and nutmeg. Set aside.

2. Coat the mushroom caps with 2 tablespoons of the olive oil, then coat them evenly with the spice mixture. Heat the remaining 2 tablespoons olive oil in a large skillet over medium heat. Add the mushrooms and cook until tender, about 5 minutes per side. Serve hot.

SERVES 4

Thrill of the Grill

Little compares with the flavor of vegetables cooked on the grill. Most vegetables can be grilled, as long as you account for their size and shape. For large pieces, simply place lightly oiled vegetables over hot coals and cook until slightly charred on the outside and tender on the inside. Smaller vegetables or cut vegetable pieces can be threaded onto bamboo skewers or placed on a mesh rack or in a perforated basket before grilling. Place longer-cooking vegetables, such as onions, on the grill first, then add the quick-cooking ones, such as tomatoes, later.

Garlic and Herb-Marinated Vegetable Kabobs

If you're using wooden bamboo skewers, you'll need to soak them in water for 30 minutes before using to prevent them from burning. Cooking on an outdoor grill is ideal, but an indoor grill, broiler, or hot oven will do the job nicely as well. Serve over freshly cooked rice.

4 shallots, halved lengthwise
1 fennel bulb, trimmed, quartered,
    and separated into 8 pieces
1 large red bell pepper, seeded and
    cut into 8 pieces

2 small yellow squash or zucchini,
    cut into 8 chunks
8 small white mushrooms
1 cup Garlicky Herb Marinade
    (page 161)

1. Place the shallots, fennel, bell pepper, squash, and mushrooms in a medium-size bowl. Pour the marinade over all, turning the vegetables to coat with the marinade. Set aside for 30 minutes to marinate, or cover and refrigerate for several hours or overnight.

2. Preheat the grill, broiler, or oven. Thread one piece of each vegetables on 8 skewers and cook on an indoor or outdoor grill, or place on a lightly oiled baking sheet and cook under the broiler or in a preheated 450 degree F oven. Cook until the vegetables are tender, about 10 minutes, turning once. Serve hot.

SERVES 4

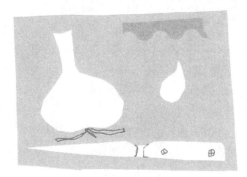

Pan-Fried Tofu and Watercress with Lemon-Caper Sauce

The piquant flavor of the lemon-caper sauce is absorbed by the crisply fried tofu and enhanced by the peppery bite of the watercress. Oven-browned potatoes make a particularly good accompaniment.

One 16-ounce package extra-firm tofu, drained and cut into 1/4-inch-thick slices

Salt and freshly ground black pepper

2 tablespoons olive oil

1/4 cup dry white wine

3 tablespoons fresh lemon juice

2 tablespoon capers, drained and chopped

1 large garlic clove, minced

2 bunches watercress, tough stems removed

1. Pat the tofu dry and season with salt and pepper to taste. Set aside.

2. Heat 1 tablespoon of the olive oil in a large skillet over medium-high heat. Add the tofu and cook in batches until golden brown on both sides, 2 to 4 minutes per side. Add the wine, lemon juice, and capers and simmer until the sauce is slightly reduced, about 2 minutes. Reduce the heat to low and keep warm.

3. Heat the remaining 1 tablespoon olive oil in a large skillet over medium heat. Add the garlic and cook, stirring, until fragrant, about 30 seconds. Add the watercress and cook, stirring, until just wilted, 2 to 3 minutes. Season with salt and pepper to taste.

4. Transfer the watercress to a serving platter or 4 individual plates and arrange the tofu on top. Drizzle the sauce over the tofu and serve hot.

SERVES 4

Meat Alternatives on the Grill

Like most vegetables, meat alternatives such as seitan, tempeh, and tofu are great on the grill, as are commercial meat alternative products such as burgers and hot dogs. For best results, keep these things in mind.

1. Most meat alternatives contain little fat and are more delicate than meat, so it's important to start with a clean, well-oiled grill to ensure that they won't fall apart or stick to the grill.

2. Because of their naturally neutral flavors, tofu, tempeh, and seitan all take well to marinating and basting and are good choices for grilling. If you don't have time to marinate, be sure to brush them with a small amount of oil (or a mixture of oil and tamari) for easier grilling.

3. Since meat alternatives are precooked, they need very little time on the grill—just enough to heat them through and impart that great grilled taste and appearance. Cook for no more than 5 minutes per side over a medium-hot fire.

4. Tempeh, seitan, and tofu may be grilled in slices or slabs, or cut into bite-size pieces and threaded onto skewers or placed on a mesh rack or in a perforated basket (especially useful for the more delicate tofu).

5. To prepare tofu for the grill, use only extra firm tofu and press out all the moisture (page 12) before marinating or grilling.

6. As a rule, use $1/2$ to $3/4$ cup marinade per pound of ingredients to be marinated—more if you plan to serve extra at the table as a dipping sauce. Marinate your ingredients for about 1 hour, turning once. Following are some good marinade combinations. Note: Marinades that contain solid ingredients such as garlic or chiles should be pureed in a food processor or blender.

   - *Ragin' Cajun Marinade:* 2 garlic cloves, chopped; $1/3$ cup olive oil; 3 tablespoons white wine vinegar; 1 tablespoon tamari or other soy sauce; 1 teaspoon dried thyme; $1/2$ teaspoon cayenne; $1/2$ teaspoon paprika; $1/4$ teaspoon celery salt; $1/4$ teaspoon salt

   - *Smoky Hot Southwest Marinade:* 2 garlic cloves, chopped; 2 canned chipotle chiles in adobo sauce; $1/3$ cup orange juice; 2 tablespoons fresh lime juice; 1 tablespoon tamari or other soy sauce; $1/2$ teaspoon ground cumin

- *Whatta Jerk Caribbean Marinade:* 1 jalapeño, seeded and chopped; 3 scallions, chopped; 1 garlic clove, chopped; $1/4$ cup olive oil; 2 tablespoons tamari or other soy sauce; $1/4$ cup fresh lime juice; 1 tablespoon firmly packed light brown sugar or natural sweetener; 2 teaspoons dried thyme; 1 teaspoon ground allspice; $1/4$ teaspoon ground cinnamon; $1/4$ teaspoon dried oregano
- *Asian Barbecue Marinade:* 1 garlic clove, chopped; 1 tablespoon peeled and minced fresh ginger; $1/4$ cup tamari or other soy sauce; 2 tablespoons toasted sesame oil; 2 tablespoons hoisin sauce; 2 tablespoons rice vinegar
- *Tempting Teriyaki Marinade:* 2 garlic cloves, chopped; 1 teaspoon peeled and grated fresh ginger; $1/4$ cup tamari or other soy sauce; $1/4$ cup orange juice; 2 tablespoons toasted sesame oil; 2 tablespoons rice vinegar; $1^{1}/_{2}$ tablespoons firmly packed light brown sugar or natural sweetener
- *Fragrant Thai Marinade:* 2 garlic cloves, chopped; 1 teaspoon peeled and minced fresh ginger; 2 teaspoons minced fresh cilantro leaves; $1/4$ cup tamari or dark soy sauce; $1/4$ cup vegetarian oyster sauce; 2 tablespoons fresh lime juice; 2 tablespoons palm sugar or other natural sweetener

The following recipes can also be used as marinades or bastes for your favorite meat alternatives (or vegetables).
- Spicy Peanut Dipping Sauce (page 160)
- Ginger-Lime Dipping Sauce (page 160)
- Garlicky Herb Marinade (page 161)
- Mango Sunburst Sauce (page 156)
- Bourbon-Spiked Barbecue Sauce (page 153)
- Gloria's Glorious Garlic Sauce (page 154)

Sautéed Tofu with Shallots, Almonds, and Amaretto

I love to cook with wine and spirits—just a splash adds excitement and sophistication to a quick sauté. Amaretto, an almond-flavored liqueur, adds a decidedly decadent touch to thinly sliced tofu sautéed to a crisp golden brown. The crunch of toasted almonds amplifies the flavor of the liqueur. As an alternative, you could make this dish with hazelnuts and Frangelico, a hazelnut-flavored liqueur.

One 16-ounce package extra-firm tofu, drained and cut into 1/4-inch-thick slices
1/4 cup unbleached all-purpose flour
Salt and freshly ground black pepper
3 tablespoons olive oil
4 shallots, thinly sliced lengthwise

1/2 cup Basic Vegetable Stock (page 68)
1/4 cup amaretto or other almond-flavored liqueur
1/2 cup slivered almonds, toasted (page 110)
1 tablespoon minced fresh parsley leaves

1. Dredge the tofu in the flour, tapping off any excess. Season with salt and pepper to taste.
2. Heat the olive oil in a large skillet over medium-high heat. Add the tofu and cook until browned on both sides, 2 to 4 minutes per side. Remove from the skillet, transfer to a plate, and set aside.
3. Add the shallots to the skillet, cover, and cook until tender, about 5 minutes. Add the stock and liqueur and heat almost to boiling. Reduce the heat to low, return the tofu to the pan, add the almonds and parsley, and simmer to infuse the tofu with the flavor of the sauce and to heat through, about 5 minutes. Serve hot.

SERVES 4

Three-Way Sesame-Coated Tofu Strips with Spicy Broccoli

If you're looking for ways to get more calcium in your diet, this recipe is for you. Tofu, broccoli, and sesame seeds are loaded with calcium. Sesame lovers will delight in the three layers of sesame flavor—from the creamy tahini to the toasted sesame seeds and oil.

2 1/2 cups broccoli florets

1/4 cup tahini (sesame paste)

2 tablespoons tamari or other soy sauce

1/3 cup water, or as needed

1 cup sesame seeds

One 16-ounce package extra-firm tofu, drained and cut into 1/2-inch-wide x 1/2-inch-thick strips

2 tablespoons peanut oil

1/2 teaspoon red pepper flakes

2 teaspoons toasted sesame oil

1. Steam the broccoli until crisp-tender, 2 to 3 minutes, then plunge into a bowl of ice water. Drain and set aside.

2. In a small, shallow bowl, combine the tahini, 1 tablespoon of the tamari, and enough water to make a smooth sauce. Place the sesame seeds on a plate. Dredge the tofu strips in the tahini mixture, then coat with the sesame seeds.

3. Heat 1 tablespoon of the peanut oil in a large skillet over medium heat. Working in batches, add the tofu strips and cook until lightly browned on both sides, about 5 minutes total. Transfer to a serving platter and keep warm.

4. Heat the remaining 1 tablespoon peanut oil in the same skillet over medium heat. Add the red pepper flakes and broccoli and stir-fry until hot, about 2 minutes. Splash with the remaining 1 tablespoon tamari and spoon the broccoli over the tofu. Drizzle the sesame oil over all and serve hot.

SERVES 4

To-Fu Yung

In addition to featuring many vegan menu items, Chinese and other Asian restaurants often will substitute tofu for meat or leave the egg out of some dishes when asked. But in dishes where eggs dominate, such as *egg foo yung*, it may be easier simply to make this soy-based version at home.

One 12-ounce package firm silken tofu, drained and mashed

2 tablespoons tamari or other soy sauce

1/4 teaspoon turmeric

2 tablespoons peanut oil

1 1/2 cups fresh bean sprouts

1 cup chopped white mushrooms

1/2 cup chopped scallions

1 tablespoon toasted sesame oil

1 cup Basic Brown Sauce (page 148), heated

1. In a blender or food processor, process the tofu, tamari, and turmeric until well blended. Set aside.

2. Heat 1 tablespoon of the peanut oil in a large skillet over medium-high heat. Add the bean sprouts, mushrooms, and scallions and stir-fry until tender, 3 to 5 minutes. Remove from the heat and stir in the tofu mixture.

3. Preheat the oven to 250 degrees F. Heat the remaining 1 tablespoon peanut oil in a small nonstick skillet over medium heat. Spoon about 3/4 cup of the tofu mixture into the pan and cook until lightly browned, about 5 minutes. Carefully turn over to cook the other side until browned, then place on a baking sheet to keep warm in the oven while you cook the rest. Repeat until all the mixture is used.

4. When ready to serve, drizzle with the sesame oil and top with the sauce.

SERVES 4

Cajun Spice-Rubbed Tempeh

Spice rubs, popular in meat dishes, also work well for tofu, tempeh, and seitan, as well as vegetables such as portobello mushrooms and sliced eggplant. In addition to cooking in a skillet, spice-rubbed foods are terrific cooked on the grill. Serve with Not-So-Dirty Rice (page 232) and a side of slaw. Filé powder is traditionally used to help thicken and season gumbo. It is made from ground sassafras leaves and is available in gourmet shops and well-stocked supermarkets.

1 teaspoon sweet paprika

1 teaspoon dried thyme

1 teaspoon garlic powder

1 teaspoon onion powder

1 teaspoon light brown sugar or natural sweetener

1 teaspoon salt

¹/₂ teaspoon cayenne

¹/₂ teaspoon filé powder (optional)

Two 8-ounce packages tempeh, poached (page 14) and cut into ¹/₂-inch-thick slices

¹/₄ cup extra virgin olive oil

1. Combine the paprika, thyme, garlic powder, onion powder, brown sugar, salt, cayenne, and filé powder in a small, shallow bowl and set aside.

2. Lightly brush the tempeh with some of the olive oil, then dredge it in the spice mixture, gently rubbing the spices into the tempeh with your hands.

3. Heat the remaining oil in a large skillet over medium-high heat. Cook the tempeh in batches until crisp and well browned, about 5 minutes per side. Serve hot.

SERVES 4

Tempeh and Sweet Peppers with Bourbon-Spiked Barbecue Sauce

This yummy sauce is a great way to make tempeh tempting. The sweet bell peppers add a delicious flavor and color accent. Serve as an entrée with oven-roasted potatoes, or spoon into a crusty roll and serve as a sandwich.

2 tablespoons olive oil

Two 8-ounce packages tempeh, poached (page 14) and cut into 1/2-inch-wide x 1/2-inch-thick strips

1 large red bell pepper, seeded and cut into thin strips

1 small green bell pepper, seeded and cut into thin strips

3/4 cup Bourbon-Spiked Barbecue Sauce (page 153), or more as needed

1. Heat the olive oil in a large skillet over medium heat. Cook the tempeh in batches until browned on all sides, about 5 minutes. Remove from the skillet with a slotted spoon and set aside.

2. Add the bell peppers to the skillet. Cover and cook over medium heat until softened, about 5 minutes. Return the tempeh to the pan and reduce the heat to low. Add the barbecue sauce, stirring to coat the tempeh. Cook, stirring occasionally, for about 10 minutes to allow tempeh to absorb the sauce. If the sauce becomes too thick, add a little water or more barbecue sauce. Serve hot.

SERVES 4

Did You Know...

Bell peppers are a good source of potassium and vitamins A and C? In fact, they contain more vitamin C than oranges.

Teriyaki-Glazed Tempeh

A sweet and savory teriyaki glaze gives the tempeh a lovely golden brown color while filling it with flavor. This sauce is also good on sautéed or grilled tofu, seitan, or eggplant. Or you can use it as a dipping sauce for vegetable tempura.

Two 8-ounce packages tempeh,
    poached (page 14) and cut into
    1/2-inch-wide x 1/2-inch-thick strips
3 tablespoons tamari or other soy sauce
3 tablespoons orange juice

1 garlic clove, minced
2 tablespoons toasted sesame oil
1 tablespoon pure maple syrup
Salt and freshly ground black pepper
2 tablespoons peanut oil

1. Place the tempeh in a large, shallow dish and set aside.
2. In a small bowl, combine the tamari, orange juice, garlic, sesame oil, maple syrup, and salt and pepper to taste. Blend well, then pour over the tempeh and set aside for at least 1 hour, turning halfway through. If marinating for longer than 1 hour, cover and refrigerate.
3. Using a slotted spoon, transfer the tempeh to a platter, reserving the marinade.
4. Heat the peanut oil in a large skillet over medium heat. Cook the tempeh in batches until browned all over, about 5 minutes. Add the reserved marinade and simmer until the tempeh is hot and well glazed, about 10 minutes. Serve hot.

SERVES 4

How to Season Your Cast-Iron Skillet or Wok

The key to enjoying a long and happy relationship with your cast-iron skillet or wok is to condition it well. First, wash, rinse, and dry the pan. Next, generously oil the inside surface with a light, neutral-tasting cooking oil such as peanut oil. Then place the pan in a preheated 350 degree F oven for 1 hour. Turn the heat off and allow the pan to cool in the oven (this will take about 4 hours). Wipe out any excess oil, and your pan is ready to use.

Be sure to dry your pan well after each use to prevent rust.

Tempeh Simmered with Tomatoes and Sauerkraut

Perhaps it's because they're both fermented foods, but tempeh and sauerkraut seem to be made for each other. Serve with a coarse, dark bread or spoon over wide noodles.

1 tablespoon olive oil

Two 8-ounce packages tempeh, poached (page 14) and cut into ¹/₂-inch-wide x ¹/₂-inch-thick strips

2 cups sauerkraut, drained

One 14.5-ounce can diced tomatoes, drained

1 teaspoon light brown sugar or natural sweetener

Salt and freshly ground black pepper

1 tablespoon minced fresh parsley leaves

1. Heat the olive oil in a large saucepan over medium heat. Add the tempeh and cook until browned all over, 5 to 7 minutes.

2. Gently stir in the sauerkraut, tomatoes, brown sugar, and salt and pepper to taste. Reduce the heat to low and simmer, stirring occasionally, until the flavors blend and the tomatoes are saucy, about 15 minutes.

3. Sprinkle with the parsley and serve hot.

SERVES 4

Pan-Seared Seitan with Cremini Mushrooms and Red Wine

The red wine sauce is absorbed by both the seitan and the mushrooms, resulting in a full-flavored dish that goes well with noodles, rice, or potatoes.

1 tablespoon olive oil

1 pound seitan, cut into 1/2-inch-wide x 1/4-inch-thick strips

2 shallots, minced

6 ounces cremini mushrooms, sliced

1/2 cup dry red wine

1 cup Basic Vegetable Stock (page 68)

1 teaspoon minced fresh thyme leaves or 1/2 teaspoon dried

Salt and freshly ground black pepper

1. Heat the olive oil in a large skillet over medium-high heat. Add the seitan and cook until browned on all sides, about 5 minutes. Using a slotted spoon, transfer to a plate and set aside.

2. To the same skillet, add the shallots and cook, stirring, until softened, about 2 minutes. Add the mushrooms and wine and simmer, stirring, to reduce the liquid slightly, 2 to 3 minutes. Using a slotted spoon, transfer the mushrooms to the plate with the seitan.

3. Add the stock and thyme to the skillet, increase the heat to high, and bring to a boil. Reduce the heat to medium and simmer until the liquid is reduced by one-half, about 5 minutes. Return the seitan and mushrooms to the skillet and season with salt and pepper to taste. Cook until heated through, 2 to 3 minutes. Serve hot.

SERVES 4

Shredded Seitan with Green Beans and Shallots

A splash of sherry and tamari combines with a swirl of mustard to provide a flavorful backdrop for seitan and green beans sautéed with shallots. Serve over rice.

8 ounces green beans, ends trimmed
    and halved
2 tablespoons olive oil
2 large shallots, minced
1 large garlic clove, minced
1 pound seitan, shredded

Salt and freshly ground black pepper
$1/3$ cup dry sherry
1 tablespoon Dijon mustard
1 cup Basic Vegetable Stock (page 68)
2 tablespoons tamari or other soy sauce

1. Steam the green beans until just tender, about 5 minutes. Rinse under cold running water to stop the cooking. Transfer to a large bowl and set aside.
2. Heat the olive oil in a large skillet over medium-high heat. Add the shallots, garlic, seitan, and salt and pepper to taste and cook until the seitan is browned all over, about 5 minutes. Using a slotted spoon, transfer the seitan to a plate and set aside.
3. Deglaze the skillet with the sherry, stirring to dislodge any browned bits from the pan. Stir in the mustard. Add the stock and tamari and bring to boil. Reduce the heat to low and simmer, uncovered, until the liquid is reduced, about 10 minutes. Add the seitan and green beans, stirring to heat through and coat with the sauce, about 5 minutes. Serve hot.

SERVES 4

Hoisin-Drenched Garlic Seitan with Baby Bok Choy

The sweet and sassy hoisin sauce permeates the seitan and enlivens the bok choy. Baby bok choy is more tender than the larger version and is visually appealing when served cut in half lengthwise. Look for it in Asian markets and well-stocked supermarkets. Serve over rice.

4 small baby bok choy, trimmed and
   halved lengthwise
2 tablespoons peanut oil
2 large garlic cloves, minced

12 ounces seitan, thinly sliced
Salt and freshly ground black pepper
1/2 cup hoisin sauce
3 tablespoons water

1. Lightly steam the bok choy until just tender, 3 to 4 minutes. Transfer to a plate and set aside.

2. Heat 1 tablespoon of the peanut oil in a large skillet over medium heat. Add the garlic and seitan and cook until the seitan is browned all over, about 5 minutes. Season with salt and pepper to taste. Stir in the hoisin sauce and water, blending well. Add the bok choy and spoon the sauce over all to coat. Reduce the heat to low and simmer until tender, about 10 minutes. Serve hot.

SERVES 4

Soy-Encased Vegetable Patties

These versatile parcels lend themselves to a variety of sauces, from a fruity chutney or peanut sauce to a spicy salsa or mushroom sauce. You may alter the seasonings to complement the sauce you are using. For example, you might add some minced fresh ginger if using an Asian sauce or a little minced thyme if serving with a mushroom sauce. Use a leftover baked potato, if available. If not, peel, dice, and sauté or bake a medium-size potato until tender. (Cooking in water will add too much moisture to the patties.)

1 cup diced cooked potato (see
   headnote)
1 cup cooked or canned Great Northern
   beans, drained and rinsed
1/2 cup cauliflower florets, steamed
   until crisp-tender
1/2 cup sliced carrots, steamed until
   crisp-tender
2 tablespoons minced fresh parsley
   leaves

1 teaspoon salt
1/8 teaspoon cayenne
1/4 cup ground pecans
1/4 cup dry bread crumbs
1/4 cup olive oil
2 large sheets yuba (bean curd skin;
   see right)

1. In a food processor, process the potato, beans, cauliflower, carrots, parsley, salt, and cayenne until smooth. Shape the mixture into 4 balls of equal size and flatten into patties about 1/2 inch thick.

2. Combine the pecans and bread crumbs in a small, shallow bowl. Dredge the patties in the mixture to coat evenly. Place on a plate and refrigerate for 30 minutes.

3. Heat 1 tablespoon of the olive oil in a large skillet over medium heat. Add the patties and cook until golden brown on both sides, 3 to 4 minutes per side. Remove the patties from the skillet and set aside on paper towels to cool.

4. Cut the yuba sheets in half to make 4 pieces. Soften with a little water, if necessary, to make pliable. Place a vegetable patty on the lower third of each yuba piece. Fold the sides over onto the patty and roll up to enclose the patty and create a flat parcel.

5. Heat the remaining 3 tablespoons olive oil in a large skillet over medium heat. Add the parcels and cook until golden brown and crispy on both sides, about 3 minutes per side. Serve at once.

SERVES 4

Yuba Is Only Skin-Deep

Yuba, also known as bean curd skin, is an unusual yet versatile ingredient used widely in Asian cooking. Made from the skin that forms on the surface of hot soy milk as it cools, yuba is available in Asian markets and is sold in fresh, partially dried, and dried sheets. The partially dried and dried versions need to be moistened or soaked just long enough to become pliable. Yuba can be used as dumpling or spring roll wrappers or to encase other ingredients. It fries up crisp and golden brown. Fresh yuba is sometimes cut into strips and used like noodles.

13

The Global Oven

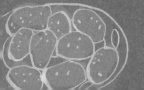

Throughout the world's cuisines can be found a variety of delicious oven-baked specialties, from gratins to casseroles to potpies. Some are naturally vegan, and those that are not can often be easily adapted by changing a few ingredients. Consider the quiche.

In its traditional state, a quiche is made with eggs and cream. The *Provençal Vegetable Quiche* in this chapter uses tofu to replace those ingredients, resulting in a finished product that is every bit as delicious as its traditional counterpart. The same holds true for other classic recipes. Here you'll find a fresh take on old favorites such as shepherd's pie, eggplant Parmesan, and spanakopita. There are also intriguing new creations, such as *Tarragon-Scented Artichoke and Wild Mushroom Strudel* and *Black Bean and Sweet Potato Enchiladas*.

Despite the fact that gratins often garner more respect than casseroles, the two have quite a lot in common. First, both the serving dish and the finished product have the same name. Second, both gratins and casseroles are usually topped with cheese or a bread crumb mixture. Whereas casseroles are thought of as home-style weekday fare and are decidedly heartier, gratins are often reserved for guests. Contrary to popular belief, neither has to be smothered in cheese or drowning in heavy cream to succeed. You'll be pleasantly surprised to find some light and lovely gratins and casseroles here that are completely vegan and thoroughly delicious.

Artichoke and Root Vegetable Gratin

The artichokes provide texture and flavor in this satisfying gratin, while at the same time adding a sophisticated touch. Frozen artichoke hearts work fine and are more convenient than fresh.

1 pound all-purpose potatoes, peeled and thinly sliced

1 large carrot, thinly sliced

1 medium-size parsnip, peeled and thinly sliced

1/4 cup olive oil

1 leek (white part only), washed well and thinly sliced

2 garlic cloves, minced

One 9-ounce package frozen artichoke hearts, cooked according to package directions, drained, and chopped

Salt and freshly ground black pepper

1/2 cup Basic Vegetable Stock (page 68)

1 teaspoon minced fresh thyme leaves or 1/2 teaspoon dried

1 cup fresh bread crumbs

1/4 teaspoon sweet Hungarian paprika

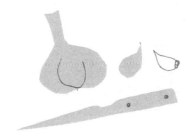

1. Preheat the oven to 375 degrees F. Parboil the potato, carrot, and parsnip slices in boiling salted water for 5 minutes. Drain well and set aside.

2. Heat 2 tablespoons of the olive oil in a large skillet over medium heat. Add the leek, garlic, and artichokes, and salt and pepper to taste. Cover and cook, stirring occasionally, until the leek is tender, about 5 minutes. Stir in the stock and thyme and set aside.

3. Lightly oil a 2-quart gratin dish. Layer half of the potato, carrot, and parsnip slices in the bottom of the dish. Top with half of the arti-

Did You Know...

Artichokes are believed to have a number of medicinal properties, including blood cleanser and diuretic? This vegetable, which is actually the flower bud of a plant, is also a good source of potassium and magnesium.

choke mixture and season with salt and pepper to taste. Top with the remaining potato, carrot, and parsnip slices, the remaining artichoke mixture, and salt and pepper to taste.

4. In a small bowl, combine the bread crumbs, the remaining 2 tablespoons olive oil, and the paprika. Blend gently with a fork and sprinkle on top of the gratin.

5. Bake until the vegetables are tender and the top is golden brown, about 45 minutes. Let rest for 5 minutes before serving.

SERVES 4

Love from the Oven

I hate to admit it, but I think there may be something to that old TV jingle "Nothing says lovin' like something from the oven"—especially during the cold winter months when any excuse for extra heat is appreciated. But it's more than that. When we bake foods in the oven, the fragrance broadcasts comfort throughout the house. Whether it's a slow-cooking entrée or a quick batch of cookies, the cozy warmth emanating from the kitchen sets the tone in the house. I find myself planning oven-baked meals just so I can experience the nurturing feeling they provide.

Basil-Scented Fennel and Tomato Gratin

Although this gratin is heavenly in the summer when fresh tomatoes and fennel are at their peak, I sometimes prepare it in the middle of winter when I crave the fresh flavors of the warmer months. Fennel can usually be found in supermarkets year round, but if the only fresh tomatoes available are rock hard and pink, use canned. Every year I try to freeze enough pesto to get me through the winter, but store-bought vegan pesto (available at some natural food stores) may be used if homemade is unavailable.

1/4 cup olive oil
2 leeks (white parts only), washed well
   and chopped
1 large or 2 small fennel bulbs, trimmed
   and thinly sliced
2 garlic cloves, minced
1/4 cup vegan pesto, homemade (page
   157) or store-bought

1/2 cup Basic Vegetable Stock (page 68)
3 large, ripe tomatoes, thinly sliced
Salt and freshly ground black pepper
1 cup fresh bread crumbs
1/4 cup chopped pine nuts

1. Preheat the oven to 375 degrees F. Heat 2 tablespoons of the olive oil in a large skillet over medium heat. Add the leeks, fennel, and garlic. Cover and cook until softened, about 5 minutes. Remove from the heat and set aside.

2. In a small bowl, combine the pesto and stock until blended. Set aside.

3. Lightly oil a 2-quart gratin dish. Arrange half of the fennel mixture in the bottom of the dish. Top with half of the tomato slices and season with salt and pepper to taste. Top with the remaining fennel mixture, the remaining tomato slices, and salt and pepper to taste. Pour the pesto mixture over the top.

4. In a small bowl, combine the bread crumbs, pine nuts, and remaining 2 table-spoons olive oil. Blend gently with a fork and sprinkle on top of the gratin.

5. Bake until the vegetables are tender and the top is golden brown, about 40 minutes. Let rest for 5 minutes before serving.

SERVES 4

Spring Vegetable Gratin

Roasting vegetables—even delicate spring vegetables such as asparagus—at high temperature brings out their full flavor. Here, instead of roasting individual vegetables, I combine them into a gratin that can be served as a light entrée or side dish. As an accompaniment, I like to serve bruschetta, topped with garlicky white beans or another hearty topping.

1 pound small new red or white
    potatoes, unpeeled and thinly
    sliced
1/4 cup olive oil
3 scallions, chopped
2 garlic cloves, minced
1 small yellow squash, halved
    lengthwise and cut into
    1/4-inch-thick half-moons

1 cup cherry or grape tomatoes,
    cut in half
8 ounces thin asparagus, bottoms
    trimmed
1/4 cup Basic Vegetable Stock (page 68)
1 tablespoon minced fresh dill
Salt and freshly ground black pepper
3/4 cup fresh bread crumbs
1/4 cup slivered blanched almonds

1. Preheat the oven to 400 degrees F. Parboil the potato slices in boiling salted water for 5 minutes. Drain well and set aside.

2. Heat 2 tablespoons of the olive oil in a large skillet over medium heat. Add the scallions and garlic and cook, stirring, until fragrant, about 30 seconds.

3. Lightly oil a 2-quart gratin dish. Arrange the potatoes in the bottom of the dish. Top with the scallion, garlic, and olive oil mixture. Add a layer of squash and a layer of tomatoes, then arrange the asparagus on top in a spoke-like fashion. Pour on the stock, sprinkle with the dill, and season with salt and pepper to taste.

4. In a small bowl, combine the bread crumbs and remaining 2 tablespoons olive oil. Blend gently with a fork to combine and sprinkle evenly on top of the gratin. Sprinkle with the almonds.

5. Bake until the vegetables are tender and the top is golden brown, about 45 minutes. Let rest for 5 minutes before serving.

SERVES 4

Cheesy Potato-Chili Gratin

All this casserole needs as an accompaniment is a salad or green vegetable for a satisfying dinner. I prefer Yukon Gold potatoes for their buttery, rich flavor, but you may use another variety, if you wish.

3 large Yukon Gold potatoes, peeled
    and thinly sliced
1 small yellow onion, thinly sliced
One 4-ounce can diced hot green chiles,
    drained
1 teaspoon salt
1 teaspoon dried basil
1 teaspoon chili powder

1/8 teaspoon cayenne
1 cup vegan sour cream, homemade
    (page 139) or store-bought
2 cups prepared vegetarian chili,
    homemade (pages 314–326) or
    store-bought
1 cup shredded vegan mozzarella
    cheese

1. Preheat the oven to 375 degrees F.

2. In a lightly oiled 9 x 13-inch baking dish, layer the potatoes, onion, and chiles, sprinkling each layer with some of the salt, basil, chili powder, and cayenne. Cover and bake until the vegetables are tender, 30 to 40 minutes.

3. Remove from the oven and spread the vegan sour cream over the top. Spread the chili over the sour cream and sprinkle evenly with the vegan cheese. Return to the oven and bake, uncovered, until heated through and bubbly, about 15 minutes.

SERVES 6

Sweet Potato Gratin with Pineapple and Coconut Milk

This is a delicious way to prepare sweet potatoes around the holidays, especially for those finicky family members who say they don't like sweet potatoes. This opulent gratin, laced with coconut milk and pineapple, may just win them over.

1 1/2 pounds sweet potatoes, peeled
    and thinly sliced
1 tablespoon olive oil
2 shallots, chopped
1 cup chopped fresh or canned
    pineapple
1/2 cup unsweetened coconut milk

1/2 teaspoon ground cardamom
1/8 teaspoon cayenne
Salt
Freshly ground black pepper
1/2 cup ground unsalted dry-roasted
    peanuts

1. Preheat the oven to 375 degrees F. Parboil the potato slices in boiling salted water for 5 minutes. Drain well and set aside.

2. Heat the olive oil in a large skillet over medium heat. Add the shallots, cover, and cook until tender, about 5 minutes. Stir in the pineapple, coconut milk, cardamom, cayenne, and salt to taste. Set aside.

3. Lightly oil a 2-quart gratin dish. Arrange half of the sweet potatoes in the bottom of the dish. Season with salt and pepper to taste. Top with half of the pineapple mixture, followed by the remaining sweet potatoes and then the remaining pineapple mixture. Sprinkle the peanuts on top.

4. Bake until the sweet potatoes are tender, about 40 minutes. Let rest for 5 minutes before serving.

SERVES 4 TO 6

Black Bean and Sweet Potato Enchiladas

Sweet potatoes can pop up in unusual places, such as this enchilada casserole made with black beans and spicy salsa. Easy to prepare ahead of time, this is a colorful and tasty way to enliven a weeknight meal. Roasting the sweet potatoes gives them a greater depth of flavor.

2 large sweet potatoes, peeled and diced

1 tablespoon olive oil

1 large garlic clove, minced

1 small, fresh hot chile, seeded and minced

1 1/2 cups cooked or one 15-ounce can black beans, drained and rinsed

One 14.5-ounce can diced tomatoes, drained

1 tablespoon chili powder

Salt and freshly ground black pepper

2 cups Fresh Tomato Salsa (page 174) or your favorite salsa

8 large flour tortillas

1/4 cup finely chopped red onion

1. Preheat the oven to 400 degrees F. Arrange the sweet potatoes in a single layer on a lightly oiled baking sheet and roast until tender, turning once, about 20 minutes. Remove from the oven and set aside.

2. Reduce the oven temperature to 350 degrees F. Heat the olive oil in a large skillet over medium heat. Add the garlic and chile and cook, stirring, until fragrant, about 30 seconds. Add the beans, tomatoes, chili powder, and salt and pepper to taste. Stir in the sweet potatoes and simmer for 5 minutes. Set aside.

3. Spread a thin layer of salsa over the bottom of a lightly oiled 9 x 13-inch baking dish and set aside.

4. Place a tortilla on a flat work surface. Spoon a portion of the sweet potato mixture down the center of the tortilla and roll it up. Place the filled tortilla in the baking dish seam side down and repeat with the remaining tortillas and filling mixture. Spoon any remaining filling mixture on top of the enchiladas, top with the remaining salsa, and sprinkle with the onion. Cover and bake until hot and bubbly, about 20 minutes. Serve hot.

SERVES 8

Parmesan-Style Eggplant

Eggplant Parmesan has always been one of my favorite dishes, so I was determined to make a vegan version that I could enjoy. As long as I was cutting out the cholesterol and fat of the cheese, I decided to make this dish even healthier by baking the eggplant slices rather than breading and frying them, resulting in a decidedly lighter dish than Mom used to make, but delicious nonetheless. Since vegan cheese does not usually melt well, you may prefer to use homemade or store-bought gomasio, a sesame seed and sea salt condiment, which adds a great nutty-salty flavor, as well as calcium.

1 large eggplant, cut into 1/4-inch-thick
    slices
2 tablespoons olive oil
1 small onion, minced
2 garlic cloves, minced
One 28-ounce can crushed tomatoes
2 cups vegetarian burger crumbles or
    3 frozen veggie burgers, thawed
    and chopped or crumbled

2 tablespoons minced fresh parsley
    leaves
1 tablespoon minced fresh basil leaves
    or 1 1/2 teaspoons dried
1 teaspoon minced fresh oregano
    leaves or 1/2 teaspoon dried
Salt and freshly ground black pepper
1/4 cup grated vegan Parmesan cheese
    or Gomasio (recipe follows)

1. Preheat the oven to 375 degrees F. Place the eggplant on a lightly oiled baking sheet and bake until tender, 12 to 15 minutes, turning once. Remove from the oven and set aside. Leave the oven on.

2. Heat the olive oil in a large skillet over medium heat. Add the onion and garlic, cover, and cook until softened, about 5 minutes. Stir in the tomatoes, burger crumbles, herbs, and salt and pepper to taste. Simmer for 10 minutes to blend the flavors.

3. Spoon a layer of the tomato sauce over the bottom of a 2 1/2-quart baking dish. Top with a layer of eggplant slices and sprinkle with a small amount of the vegan cheese or gomasio. Continue layering until all of the eggplant slices are used. To finish, top with a layer of the sauce and sprinkle with the remaining cheese or gomasio.

4. Bake until hot and bubbly, about 40 minutes. Let rest for 5 minutes before serving.

SERVES 4

Gomasio

Gomasio is a Japanese condiment made with ground sesame seeds and sea salt that imparts a delicious salty-nutty flavor to vegetable, grain, and pasta dishes. It can be purchased ready-made in Asian markets and natural food stores or made easily at home. I like to keep some gomasio in a shaker to sprinkle on pasta instead of Parmesan cheese.

7 tablespoons sesame seeds, toasted (page 192)   **1 tablespoon sea salt**

Place the sesame seeds and sea salt in a food processor or blender and process until well ground but with some texture remaining. Transfer to an airtight container and store in the refrigerator, where it will keep for several weeks.

MAKES ½ CUP

Pistachio-Dusted Saffron Potatoes

The creamy white bean puree and crunchy pistachio topping provide added protein, making this a satisfying entrée as well as a side dish. As long as I have the oven on, I like to roast some asparagus to serve with it. If the pricey saffron is not within your culinary budget, substitute a pinch of turmeric to give the gratin a lovely golden color.

1 tablespoon olive oil
1 large yellow onion, thinly sliced
1 medium-size yellow bell pepper, seeded and chopped
1 1/2 pounds Yukon Gold potatoes, peeled and thinly sliced
Salt and freshly ground black pepper

1 cup Basic Vegetable Stock (page 68)
Pinch of saffron threads
1 cup cooked or canned cannellini or other white beans, drained and rinsed
1/2 cup chopped unsalted dry-roasted pistachios

1. Preheat the oven to 400 degrees F. Heat the olive oil in a large skillet over medium heat. Add the onion and bell pepper, cover, and cook until softened, about 5 minutes.
2. In a large bowl, combine the onion mixture, potatoes, and salt and pepper to taste. Transfer to a lightly oiled 2 1/2-quart baking dish and set aside.
3. Heat the stock in a small saucepan and add the saffron. Set aside.
4. In a food processor or blender, puree the beans. Add the stock mixture and process until smooth. Pour over the potato mixture, cover, and bake until the potatoes are tender, about 1 hour.
5. Remove the cover, sprinkle with the pistachios, and bake for 10 minutes to lightly toast the pistachios. Let rest for 5 minutes before serving.

SERVES 6

Ultimate Shepherd's Pie

Since leftover mashed potatoes are often the inspiration for making a shepherd's pie, I thought that the ultimate version should feature filling ingredients that are readily available and easy to use—hence the use of veggie burgers. Simply thaw them long enough so that you can chop or crumble them. They work like a charm, adding great taste and texture, enhanced by the ground walnuts. Use the extra-rich Mashed Potatoes and Company (page 204) or your favorite mashed potato recipe.

2 tablespoons olive oil

1 large yellow onion, chopped

1 large carrot, chopped

4 ounces white mushrooms, chopped

1 tablespoon tomato paste

2 tablespoons tamari or other soy sauce

1 cup Basic Vegetable Stock (page 68)

1 teaspoon minced fresh thyme leaves
 or 1/2 teaspoon dried

1 teaspoon minced fresh marjoram
 leaves or 1/2 teaspoon dried

Salt and freshly ground black pepper

1 tablespoon cornstarch dissolved in
 2 tablespoons water

3 frozen veggie burgers, thawed and
 chopped or crumbled

1/2 cup frozen green peas, thawed

1/4 cup ground walnuts

3 cups mashed potatoes
 (see headnote)

1/4 teaspoon sweet Hungarian paprika

1. Preheat the oven to 375 degrees F. Heat 1 tablespoon of the olive oil in a large skillet over medium heat. Add the onion and carrot, cover, and cook until tender, about 5 minutes. Add the mushrooms and cook, stirring occasionally, for 3 minutes. Stir in the tomato paste, tamari, stock, thyme, marjoram, and salt and pepper to taste. Stir in the cornstarch mixture and simmer to thicken slightly, about 1 minute.

2. Spoon the filling mixture into a lightly oiled 2 1/2-quart baking dish. Stir in the chopped burgers, peas, and walnuts. Taste and adjust the seasonings. Spread the mashed potatoes over the top. Sprinkle with the paprika and drizzle with the remaining 1 tablespoon olive oil.

3. Bake until the potatoes are hot and bubbly and the top is golden brown, about 30 minutes. Serve hot.

SERVES 4

Winter Vegetable Potpie

Potpies are old-fashioned comfort food at its best, and this version, made with chewy seitan and a variety of vegetables, is as comforting as they come. Feel free to vary the filling ingredients according to your preference or what you have on hand. For example, you could use corn instead of peas, or tofu or tempeh in place of the seitan.

Filling:
1 large all-purpose potato, peeled and
  diced
1 large carrot, chopped
1 parsnip, peeled and chopped
1 1/4 cups Super-Rich Vegetable Stock
  (page 70)
2 tablespoons tamari or other soy sauce
1 tablespoon cornstarch dissolved in
  2 tablespoons water
1 tablespoon olive oil

1 medium-size yellow onion, chopped
12 ounces seitan, coarsely chopped
Salt and freshly ground black pepper
1/2 cup frozen green peas, thawed

Crust:
1 1/4 cups unbleached all-purpose flour
1/4 teaspoon salt
1/3 cup chilled corn oil
2 tablespoons ice water

1. To make the filling, cook the potato, carrot, and parsnip in a pot of boiling salted water until tender, about 10 minutes. Drain, rinse, and set aside.
2. In a small saucepan, bring the stock and tamari to a boil over medium-high heat. Reduce the heat to low and whisk in the cornstarch mixture. Simmer, stirring, until thickened, 2 to 3 minutes. Remove from the heat and set aside.
3. Heat the olive oil in a medium-size skillet over medium heat. Add the onion, cover, and cook until softened, about 5 minutes. Using a slotted spoon, transfer the onion to a lightly oiled 2-quart casserole dish.
4. Reheat the skillet and add the seitan. Season with salt and pepper to taste and cook, stirring, until browned, about 5 minutes. Transfer to the casserole dish. Stir in the peas, potato-carrot-parsnip mixture, and sauce and set aside.
5. Preheat the oven to 350 degrees F.
6. To make the crust, in a food processor, combine the flour and salt, pulsing to blend. Add the corn oil and process until the mixture is crumbly. With the machine

running, slowly add the water and process until the mixture forms a ball. On a lightly floured surface, roll out the dough until it is slightly larger than the casserole dish. Place the crust over the casserole and crimp the edges.

7. Bake until the filling is hot and bubbly and the crust is browned, about 45 minutes. Let rest for 5 minutes before serving.

SERVES 6

VEGETABLES "FALL" INTO WINTER

Long after the last tomato of summer has been picked from the vine, autumn vegetables take the spotlight, pleasing the eye as well as the palate. Whether it's the sturdy winter squash in their brilliant hues, the lush green collards and kale, or the rugged earthiness of freshly dug potatoes, fall vegetables call us home to supper and gently nurture us as the weather turns colder. The very sight of them can make us crave simmering stews and the smell of fragrant casseroles baking in the oven.

It is widely known that fresh, locally grown produce tastes better and is more nutritious than that trucked or shipped in from somewhere else. In this age when supermarkets carry South American grapes, Australian oranges, and pencil-thin asparagus in the dead of winter, it's hard to tell what is in season and what is not. For that kind of information, go to the source: patronize your local farmers' markets and roadside stands. When you do, chances are you'll come home with a carload of culinary inspiration. And getting there can be half the fun. Little compares to driving down a country road on a cool autumn day to a produce stand where rows of field pumpkins stand at attention and the sweet scent of freshly picked apples perfumes the air. Filling your kitchen with fall vegetables—from cabbage to collards, potatoes to pumpkins—is a delicious way to make the transition into winter.

In-a-Jiffy Chili-Couscous Pie

This casserole can be assembled in advance and popped in the oven less than an hour before serving. While it bakes, you can make a salad and set the table—and suddenly dinner's ready. I like to put out bowls of salsa and sliced black olives as toppings. Sweet and Spicy Chili (page 321) is especially good in this recipe.

2¼ cups water

1½ cups instant couscous

1 teaspoon olive oil

½ teaspoon salt

1 cup shredded vegan cheddar
   cheese

3 cups prepared vegetarian chili,
   homemade (pages 314–326) or
   store-bought

⅓ cup minced onion

One 4-ounce can diced hot green chiles,
   drained

1. Preheat the oven to 350 degrees F.

2. Bring the water to a boil in a large saucepan. Stir in the couscous, olive oil, and salt. Cover and remove from the heat. Let stand for 10 minutes, then spread the couscous over the bottom of a lightly oiled 10-inch baking dish or pie plate.

3. Sprinkle the couscous with ½ cup of the vegan cheese, then top with the chili. Sprinkle evenly with the onion, chiles, and remaining ½ cup cheese.

4. Bake until bubbly, about 30 minutes. Let rest for 5 minutes before serving.

SERVES 4 TO 6

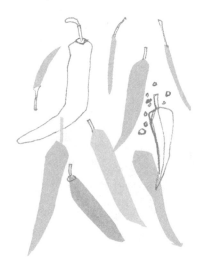

Hot Tamale Vegetable Pie

Studded with chiles, corn, and pimientos, this colorful casserole is a crowd pleaser and easy to make to boot. Top with salsa, as recommended here, or use as a zesty base for your favorite chili.

2 cups frozen corn kernels, thawed

1/4 cup minced red onion

One 4-ounce can diced hot green chiles, drained

3 tablespoons chopped canned pimientos

8 ounces soft tofu, drained and crumbled

1/4 cup yellow cornmeal

2 tablespoons unbleached all-purpose flour

1 teaspoon chili powder

1 teaspoon sugar or natural sweetener

3/4 teaspoon salt

3/4 teaspoon baking powder

Freshly ground black pepper

Fresh Tomato Salsa (page 174) or your favorite salsa, to your taste

1. Preheat the oven to 375 degrees F.

2. In a large bowl, combine the corn, onion, chiles, and pimientos. Set aside.

3. In a blender or food processor, combine the tofu, cornmeal, flour, chili powder, sugar, salt, baking powder, and black pepper to taste and process until smooth. Fold into the vegetable mixture, stirring to combine. Transfer to a lightly oiled 10-inch pie plate and smooth the top.

4. Bake until firm and golden brown on top, 30 to 35 minutes. Let rest for 5 minutes before cutting into wedges. Serve topped with the salsa.

SERVES 4 TO 6

Provençal Vegetable Quiche

Silken tofu is used instead of eggs and cream in this light and luscious quiche. Mediterranean-spiced vegetables and a flaky crust make it a good choice for a light lunch or supper entrée served with a crisp green salad.

Crust:
1 cup unbleached all-purpose flour
1/4 cup chilled corn oil
1/4 teaspoon salt
1 tablespoon cold water, or more as needed

Filling:
1 tablespoon olive oil
1 leek (white part only), washed well and chopped
1 garlic clove, minced
1 1/2 cups chopped zucchini
1 cup chopped white mushrooms
1 cup finely chopped fresh or canned tomatoes, well drained
1/4 cup pitted black olives, chopped
1 teaspoon minced fresh marjoram leaves
1 teaspoon minced fresh basil leaves
1 teaspoon minced fresh tarragon leaves
1 teaspoon minced fresh parsley leaves
Salt and freshly ground black pepper
2 cups drained and crumbled firm silken tofu
1 cup soy milk or other dairy-free milk
1 tablespoon Dijon mustard
1/8 teaspoon cayenne
1/2 cup grated vegan Parmesan cheese (optional)

1. To make the crust, combine the flour, corn oil, and salt in a food processor and pulse until crumbly. With the machine running, add the water and process until the mixture forms a ball. Flatten the dough, wrap in plastic, and refrigerate for at least 30 minutes. On a lightly floured work surface, roll out the dough to fit into a 10-inch quiche pan or pie plate. Line the pan or plate with the dough and trim the edges.
2. Preheat the oven to 375 degrees F.
3. To make the filling, heat the olive oil in a large skillet over medium heat. Add the leek, garlic, zucchini, mushrooms, and tomatoes and cook, stirring occasionally, until the vegetables soften and the liquid evaporates, about 7 minutes. Stir in the olives, herbs, and salt and pepper to taste. Set aside.

4. In a food processor or blender, combine the tofu, soy milk, mustard, cayenne, and salt to taste. Blend well.

5. Spoon the vegetable mixture into the crust and sprinkle with the vegan cheese, if using. Pour the tofu mixture over all, distributing it evenly.

6. Bake until the filling is set and the top is golden brown, about 45 minutes. Let rest for 5 minutes before cutting.

SERVES 4 TO 6

"Say 'Cheese'" Alternatives

A number of vegan alternatives to cheese are available, but read the labels carefully to be sure they do not contain casein, whey, or other animal ingredients. Vegan cheese can be used instead of Parmesan or mozzarella, and crumbled tofu can replace ricotta cheese in lasagna and other recipes. Also available are vegan cream cheese, vegan yogurt, and vegan sour cream. But even if it says "soy" on the package, unless it specifically indicates that it's vegan, check the ingredients.

Tarragon-Scented Artichoke and Wild Mushroom Strudel

This elegant dish makes a terrific entrée for a special meal, preceded by a crisp green salad and served with grilled asparagus or tomatoes. A dry white wine is a good beverage choice.

1 tablespoon olive oil, plus more for
  brushing
3 shallots, chopped
2 garlic cloves, minced
8 ounces cremini or other mushrooms,
  chopped
Salt and freshly ground black pepper
8 ounces extra-firm tofu, drained
  and crumbled
One 9-ounce package frozen artichoke
  hearts, cooked according to
  package directions, drained,
  and coarsely chopped

2 tablespoons chopped fresh tarragon
  leaves
One 16-ounce package phyllo pastry,
  thawed overnight in the
  refrigerator
1 cup Double Mushroom Sauce
  (page 149)

1. Heat the 1 tablespoon olive oil in a large skillet over medium heat. Add the shallots and garlic and cook, stirring, until tender, about 5 minutes. Add the mushrooms and salt and pepper to taste. Cook, stirring occasionally, until the mushrooms release their liquid. Continue cooking until the liquid has evaporated, about 5 minutes. Set aside to cool.

2. Place the tofu in a large bowl. Add the artichokes, tarragon, and mushroom mixture. Season with salt and pepper to taste and stir well to combine. Set aside.

3. Preheat the oven to 350 degrees F. Lightly oil a large baking sheet. Remove 6 phyllo pastry sheets from the package. Tightly seal the remaining sheets and reserve for another use. Place 1 sheet on a flat work surface with a long side facing you and brush lightly with olive oil. Lay another sheet on top and brush with oil. Repeat the layering with the remaining 4 sheets.

4. Spoon the artichoke mixture evenly on top of the phyllo sheets, leaving a 3-inch border around the edges. Fold the short ends over the filling, then roll lengthwise into a cylinder to encase the filling. Place the strudel seam side down on the prepared baking sheet and brush with oil.

5. Bake until hot inside and golden brown outside, 30 to 40 minutes. While the strudel bakes, heat the mushroom sauce in a small saucepan over medium heat. If serving family style, pass the sauce on the side. If serving on plates, spoon the sauce onto each plate and top with a slice of strudel.

SERVES 4 TO 6

Layered Polenta-Chili Casserole

The natural marriage of cornmeal and chili will make this casserole a family favorite. Instant polenta, as well as packaged cooked polenta, is available at specialty food stores or in the gourmet section of many supermarkets, if you prefer a quick alternative to making polenta from scratch.

4 cups water

1 1/2 teaspoons salt

1 tablespoon corn oil

1 1/2 cups yellow cornmeal

2 1/2 cups vegetarian chili, homemade (pages 314–326) or store-bought

1 cup Fresh Tomato Salsa (page 174) or your favorite salsa

1 1/2 cups shredded vegan mozzarella cheese

1. In a large saucepan, combine the water, salt, and corn oil over high heat and bring to a boil. Reduce the heat to medium and gradually whisk in the cornmeal, stirring constantly to avoid lumps. Cook, stirring, until the polenta begins to pull away from the sides of the pan, about 20 minutes.

2. Preheat the oven to 350 degrees F. Spoon half of the polenta into a lightly oiled 9 x 13-inch baking dish and smooth the surface with a wet rubber spatula. Spread the chili on top. Spoon the remaining polenta on top of the chili, top with the salsa, and sprinkle evenly with the vegan mozzarella.

3. Bake until hot, about 30 minutes.

SERVES 4 TO 6

Mushroom-Soy Pastitsio

This fresh take on the classic Greek casserole uses mushrooms and tofu instead of ground meat. The special noodles used to make pastitsio can be found in ethnic markets, but I prefer a more unconventional shape, such as radiatore ("little radiators"). Like many of the recipes in this chapter, you can assemble it ahead of time and bake just before serving. A crisp green salad is all you need for a complete meal.

1 pound radiatore or other small pasta

1 tablespoon olive oil

1 large yellow onion, chopped

2 garlic cloves, chopped

One 16-ounce package firm tofu, drained and crumbled

8 ounces white mushrooms, chopped

1/2 teaspoon dried oregano

1/2 teaspoon ground cinnamon

1/4 cup dry red wine

2 cups tomato sauce, homemade (pages 150–152) or store-bought

1/4 cup chopped fresh parsley leaves

3/4 cup drained soft silken tofu

2 cups soy milk or other dairy-free milk

1/2 teaspoon salt

1/8 teaspoon freshly ground black pepper

Pinch of freshly grated nutmeg

1/2 cup grated vegan Parmesan cheese or Gomasio (page 363)

1. Cook the pasta in a pot of boiling salted water, stirring occasionally, until *al dente*, about 8 minutes. Drain and set aside.

2. Heat the olive oil in a large skillet over medium heat. Add the onion, cover, and cook until softened, about 5 minutes. Stir in the garlic, firm tofu, mushrooms, oregano, cinnamon, and wine and simmer to reduce a bit, about 3 minutes. Stir in the tomato sauce and parsley, reduce the heat to low, and cook to reduce the liquid and blend the flavors, about 10 minutes.

3. Preheat the oven to 375 degrees F. Combine the silken tofu, soy milk, salt, pepper, and nutmeg in a blender or food processor and process until smooth.

4. Spread half of the pasta over the bottom of a lightly oiled 9 x 13-inch baking dish and sprinkle with half of the vegan cheese. Spread all of the tomato mixture over the top and layer the remaining pasta on top. Spread the pureed tofu mixture over the pasta and sprinkle with the remaining cheese.

5. Bake until hot and bubbly and the top is lightly browned, about 45 minutes. Let rest for 10 to 15 minutes before serving.

SERVES 6 TO 8

Chili-Macaroni Bake

A variation on the "chili mac" popular in Kansas City, this dish combines chili with everyone's favorite, macaroni and cheese. I like to use East Coast Chili (page 322) in this recipe.

12 ounces elbow macaroni

2 tablespoons olive oil

1/2 cup minced onion

2 tablespoons unbleached all-purpose
   flour

2 cups soy milk or other dairy-free milk,
   heated

1 teaspoon salt

1/8 teaspoon cayenne

1 cup shredded vegan cheddar cheese

3 cups vegetarian chili, homemade
   (pages 314–326) or store-bought

1. Cook the elbows in a pot of boiling salted water, stirring occasionally, until *al dente*, about 8 minutes. Drain and set aside. Preheat the oven to 375 degrees F.

2. Heat the olive oil in a medium-size saucepan over medium heat. Add the onion, cover, and cook until softened, about 5 minutes. Add the flour and cook, stirring, for 1 minute. Reduce the heat to low and slowly whisk in the soy milk. Continue to cook, stirring, until the mixture thickens, about 2 minutes. Add the salt and cayenne.

3. In a large bowl, combine the sauce, pasta, and 1/2 cup of the vegan cheese. Spoon into a 9 x 13-inch baking dish and spread the chili on top. Sprinkle the remaining 1/2 cup cheese over the chili and bake until hot and bubbly, about 30 minutes.

SERVES 6

Linguine Tetrazzini

Based on the early-20th-century gratin made with turkey and noodles, this version uses tofu with the requisite sherry and almonds. Although it is named for the famous opera star Luisa Tetrazzini, most authorities agree that it is doubtful she ever tasted the dish. Steamed green beans, warm dinner rolls, and a fruity white wine round out the meal.

12 ounces linguine

2 tablespoons olive oil

3 shallots, minced

One 16-ounce package firm tofu,
    drained and cut into 1/2-inch dice

8 ounces white mushrooms, sliced

1/4 cup dry sherry

1/4 teaspoon salt

1/8 teaspoon freshly ground black
    pepper

1 cup Basic Vegetable Stock (page 68)

1 tablespoon cornstarch dissolved in
    2 tablespoons water

1 cup soy milk or other dairy-free milk

3/4 cup slivered almonds, toasted
    (page 110)

1 cup grated vegan mozzarella cheese

1/2 cup dry bread crumbs

1. Cook the linguine in a pot of boiling salted water, stirring occasionally, until *al dente*, 8 to 10 minutes. Drain and set aside. Preheat the oven to 375 degrees F.
2. Heat the olive oil in large skillet over medium heat. Add the shallots, cover, and cook until softened, about 5 minutes. Add the tofu and mushrooms and cook until the tofu is lightly browned and the mushrooms are softened, about 5 minutes. Add the sherry, salt, and pepper, stirring for 1 minute. Remove from the heat and set aside.
3. In a medium-size saucepan, heat the stock to a boil over medium-high heat. Whisk in the cornstarch mixture, stirring until thickened. Reduce the heat to low, then slowly stir in the soy milk. Set aside.
4. In a large bowl, combine the pasta, tofu mixture, almonds, and 1/2 cup of the vegan cheese. Stir in the sauce and mix well.
5. Transfer the mixture to a lightly oiled 9 x 13-inch baking dish. Sprinkle the top with the remaining 1/2 cup cheese and the bread crumbs, then bake until hot and bubbly, about 30 minutes.

SERVES 6

Lasagna Primavera

When you see "primavera" in a recipe title, you know it means lots of colorful spring vegetables, and this lasagna won't disappoint. Layers of chewy noodles and a tofu-vegetable filling are blanketed with a creamy vegan white sauce topped with garlicky fresh bread crumbs. For variety, broccoli or asparagus may be substituted for the zucchini.

12 ounces lasagna noodles
3 tablespoons olive oil
3 shallots, chopped
1 medium-size carrot, chopped
1 large zucchini, chopped
4 ounces white mushrooms, chopped
1/2 cup frozen green peas, thawed
Salt and freshly ground black pepper

Two 16-ounce packages firm tofu,
    drained and crumbled
1/4 cup minced fresh parsley leaves
3 cups Vegan Béchamel Sauce
    (page 146)
1 garlic clove, minced
1 cup fresh bread crumbs

1. Preheat the oven to 350 degrees F. Cook the lasagna noodles in a large pot of salted boiling water, stirring occasionally, until *al dente*, about 10 minutes. Drain the noodles and spread out on a work surface to prevent them from sticking together.
2. Heat 1 tablespoon of the olive oil in a large skillet over medium heat. Add the shallots and carrot, cover, and cook until softened, about 5 minutes. Add the zucchini and mushrooms and cook, stirring occasionally, until softened, about 5 minutes. Add the peas and salt and pepper to taste. Set aside to cool.
3. In a large bowl, combine the tofu, parsley, sautéed vegetables, and salt and pepper to taste. Mix well.
4. Spread a thin layer of the sauce over the bottom of a 9 x 13-inch baking dish. Add a layer of noodles and top with half of the tofu-vegetable mixture, spreading it evenly. Repeat the layering with the noodles, tofu-vegetable mixture, and sauce, ending with a layer of sauce.

5. Heat the remaining 2 tablespoons olive oil in a small skillet over medium heat. Add the garlic and cook, stirring, until fragrant, about 30 seconds. Remove from the heat, add the bread crumbs, and season with salt and pepper to taste. Toss to coat. Sprinkle on top of the lasagna.

6. Bake until hot and bubbly, 40 to 45 minutes. Let rest for 10 minutes before serving.

SERVES 6 TO 8

Eggplant and Spinach Lasagna

Adding cooked chopped eggplant to the tomato sauce gives this dish substantial texture. Since vegan mozzarella doesn't melt well, I make it an optional ingredient. Other topping ideas include vegan Parmesan cheese or a sprinkling of Gomasio (page 363).

12 ounces lasagna noodles

2 tablespoons olive oil

1 medium-size eggplant, peeled and chopped

3 cups tomato sauce, homemade (pages 150–152) or store-bought

Two 16-ounce packages firm tofu, drained and crumbled

One 10-ounce package frozen chopped spinach, cooked according to package directions and well drained

Salt and freshly ground black pepper

1/2 cup shredded vegan mozzarella cheese (optional)

1. Preheat the oven to 350 degrees F. Cook the lasagna noodles in a large pot of salted boiling water, stirring occasionally, until *al dente*, about 10 minutes. Drain the noodles and spread out on a work surface to keep them from sticking together.

2. Heat the olive oil in a large skillet over medium heat. Add the eggplant and cook, stirring occasionally, until tender, about 10 minutes. Stir in the tomato sauce and set aside.

3. In a large bowl, combine the tofu and spinach, blending well. Season with salt and pepper to taste. Set aside.

4. Spread a thin layer of the sauce over the bottom of a 9 x 13-inch baking dish. Add a layer of noodles and top with half of the tofu mixture, spreading it out evenly. Top with another layer of noodles, a layer of sauce, and the remaining tofu mixture. Finish with a layer of noodles and the remaining sauce.

5. Bake for 30 minutes. Remove from the oven and sprinkle with the vegan cheese, if using. Continue to bake until hot and bubbly, about 15 minutes more. Let rest for 10 to 15 minutes before serving.

SERVES 6 TO 8

Butternut Squash and Wild Mushroom Lasagna

Flavorful mushrooms, butternut squash, and pecans make this out-of-the-ordinary lasagna extraordinary. Use a variety of fresh wild mushrooms, if available, or include a small amount of reconstituted dried porcinis or morels for extra flavor. Cremini or portobello mushrooms may be used as well. When assembled ahead of time, this makes a great weeknight supper. Serve with steamed broccoli or another green vegetable.

1 tablespoon olive oil
1 small yellow onion, minced
1 small butternut squash, peeled, seeded, and coarsely grated
1 garlic clove, minced
3 cups mixed sliced wild mushrooms, such as chanterelle, shiitake, and oyster mushrooms
1 teaspoon dried thyme
Salt and freshly ground black pepper
12 ounces lasagna noodles

1/4 teaspoon turmeric
One 16-ounce package soft tofu, drained
1 cup soy milk or other dairy-free milk
1/2 cup chopped pecans, toasted (page 110)
1 cup shredded vegan mozzarella cheese
1/4 cup minced fresh Italian parsley leaves

1. Preheat the oven to 375 degrees F. Cook the lasagna noodles and turmeric in a large pot of boiling salted water, stirring occasionally, until *al dente*, about 10 minutes. Drain the noodles and spread out on a work surface to prevent them from sticking together.

2. Heat the olive oil in a large saucepan over medium heat. Add the onion, squash, and garlic. Cover and cook, stirring occasionally, until softened, about 10 minutes. Add the mushrooms, thyme, and salt and pepper to taste and cook until softened, about 5 minutes. Transfer to a large bowl and set aside.

3. Combine the tofu, soy milk, and salt to taste in a food processor and process until smooth.

4. Spread a thin layer of the tofu mixture over the bottom of a 9 x 13-inch baking dish. Add a layer of noodles and top with half of the squash mixture. Sprinkle with half of the pecans. Repeat the layering with the remaining squash, noodles, and tofu. Top with the vegan cheese and remaining pecans.

5. Bake until hot and bubbly, about 30 minutes. Let rest for 5 minutes. Garnish with the parsley and serve.

SERVES 8

Tomato-Basil Lasagna Spirals

Here lasagna noodles are used to create spirals of pasta for a lovely presentation. Serve with a salad or roasted, pencil-thin asparagus and warm focaccia.

2 tablespoons olive oil

4 shallots, minced

1 garlic clove, minced

One 16-ounce package firm tofu, drained and crumbled

3 oil-packed or rehydrated sun-dried tomatoes, chopped

1/4 cup vegan pesto, homemade (page 157) or store-bought

1/3 cup fresh bread crumbs

1 teaspoon salt

1/8 teaspoon cayenne

2 tablespoons tomato paste

1/4 cup dry red wine

One 14.5-ounce can plum tomatoes, drained and finely chopped

Salt and freshly ground black pepper

1/4 cup minced fresh basil leaves

12 lasagna noodles

Whole fresh basil leaves for garnish

1. Heat 1 tablespoon of the olive oil in a small skillet over medium heat. Add half of the shallots and all of the garlic, cover, and cook until softened, about 5 minutes. Transfer to a food processor and add the tofu, sun-dried tomatoes, pesto, bread crumbs, salt, and cayenne. Process until smooth. Transfer to a medium-size bowl and refrigerate for 30 minutes.

2. Meanwhile, heat the remaining 1 tablespoon olive oil in a medium-size saucepan over medium-low heat. Add the remaining shallots and cook for 5 minutes, stirring frequently. Stir in the tomato paste, then add the wine, tomatoes, and salt and pepper to taste. Simmer for 10 minutes, then stir in the minced basil. Reduce the heat to low and keep warm.

3. Cook the lasagna noodles in a large pot of boiling salted water, stirring occasionally, until *al dente*, about 10 minutes. Drain the noodles and spread out on a work surface to prevent them from sticking together. Pat dry.

4. Preheat the oven to 350 degrees F. Divide the chilled filling among the noodles, spreading it evenly over the surface of each noodle. Roll each up tightly into a spiral-shaped roll. Place seam side down in a lightly oiled shallow baking dish. Lightly nap the pasta rolls with 1 cup of the sauce. Cover with aluminum foil and bake until hot, about 20 minutes.

5. To serve, spread a small amount of warm sauce on each individual plate and stand 2 or 3 of the rolls upright on the sauce. Spoon the remaining sauce over the rolls and garnish with the whole basil leaves.

SERVES 4 TO 6

Tempeh and Eggplant Moussaka

This traditional Greek casserole made with eggplant lends itself well to a vegan interpretation.

1 large or 2 medium eggplants, peeled

3 tablespoons olive oil

8 ounces poached tempeh (page 14), chopped

1 yellow onion, chopped

3 garlic cloves, minced

1 tablespoon minced fresh oregano or 1 teaspoon dried

1/2 teaspoon ground nutmeg

1/2 teaspoon ground cinnamon

1 (14.5-ounce) can crushed tomatoes

1/2 cup white wine

Salt and freshly ground black pepper

1 cup soft tofu

1 cup soy milk

1 cup vegetable stock

1 tablespoon fresh lemon juice

1/2 teaspoon salt

1/4 teaspoon black pepper

1/4 cup bread crumbs

1. Preheat the oven to 400 degrees F. Cut the eggplant into 1/4-inch slices and place on a lightly oiled baking sheet. Cover with foil and bake until softened, about 15 minutes, turning once. Set aside. Reduce oven temperature to 375 degrees F.

2. Heat 2 tablespoons of the oil in a large skillet over medium heat. Add the tempeh and cook until golden, about 10 minutes. Remove from the skillet and set aside.

3. Heat the remaining oil in the same skillet over medium heat. Add the onion, cover, and cook until softened, about 10 minutes. Add the garlic, oregano, nutmeg, and cinnamon. Stir in the crushed tomatoes and wine. Add the reserved tempeh and season to taste with salt and pepper. Simmer until the mixture thickens slightly and the flavors are blended, 10 to 15 minutes. Set aside.

4. In a blender or food processor, combine the tofu, soy milk, vegetable stock, lemon juice, salt, and black pepper. Process until smooth and set aside.

5. Arrange a layer of the reserved eggplant slices in the bottom of a 10-inch square baking dish, then top with half of the reserved tempeh mixture. Add another layer of eggplant, followed by the remaining tempeh mixture and the remaining eggplant slices. Pour the sauce over all and sprinkle with the bread crumbs.

6. Bake until hot and bubbly, about 30 minutes. Let rest for at least 10 minutes before serving.

SERVES 4 TO 6

"Until he extends the circle of his compassion to all living things, man will not himself find peace."
—ALBERT SCHWEITZER

Tofu and Kale Spanakopita

This variation on the classic spanakopita is made with calcium-rich kale and firm tofu instead of the traditional spinach and feta cheese. Olive oil is used instead of butter to brush the layers of flaky pastry.

1 pound kale, stems removed
1 tablespoon olive oil, plus more for
    brushing
1 medium-size yellow onion, minced
2 garlic cloves, minced
One 16-ounce package firm tofu,
    drained and crumbled
1 tablespoon fresh lemon juice

1 teaspoon salt
1/4 teaspoon freshly ground black
    pepper
Pinch of freshly grated nutmeg
One 16-ounce package phyllo pastry,
    thawed overnight in the
    refrigerator

1. Cook the kale in a pot of boiling salted water until tender, about 15 minutes. Drain well, squeezing out any excess moisture. Coarsely chop and set aside.

2. Heat the olive oil in a large skillet over medium heat. Add the onion, cover, and cook until softened, about 5 minutes. Add the garlic and cook, stirring, until softened, about 1 minute. Add the kale and cook until all the liquid is absorbed, about 3 minutes.

3. Transfer to a food processor and add the tofu, lemon juice, salt, pepper, and nutmeg. Process until smooth and set aside.

4. Preheat the oven to 375 degrees F. Unwrap the phyllo pastry and remove 10 sheets. Cover with plastic wrap, then a damp towel. Tightly seal the remaining sheets and reserve for another use. Place 1 sheet in a lightly oiled, shallow 10-inch square baking dish, pressing it gently into the bottom and sides of the dish. Using a pastry brush, lightly brush a small amount of olive oil on the pastry. Top with another sheet of pastry and brush with a little more oil. Repeat this layering procedure with 4 more sheets and oil. Spread the filling on the pastry and smooth the top.

5. Place a sheet of phyllo over the filling, gently pressing to smooth the top. Brush a small amount of oil on the pastry and repeat with the remaining 3 sheets, brushing each layer with oil. Trim the excess pastry to within 1 inch of the baking dish. Roll the trimmed edges inward and tuck into the rim of the dish to make a neat edge. Brush the rolled edge with oil.

6. Bake until golden brown, about 30 minutes. Let rest for 15 minutes, then cut into squares. Serve warm or at room temperature.

SERVES 6

Eat Your Greens: Collards and Kale

Sturdy, dark, leafy greens such as collards and kale are high in vitamins A and C, iron, calcium, and potassium. These hardy greens keep well in the refrigerator for a week or longer and are especially delicious boiled, steamed, or braised. They go well with grains and can be added to casseroles and stews. Pair collards or kale with carrots, sweet potatoes, or kidney beans for a colorful combination that is full of flavor and nutrition.

Simply Stuffed

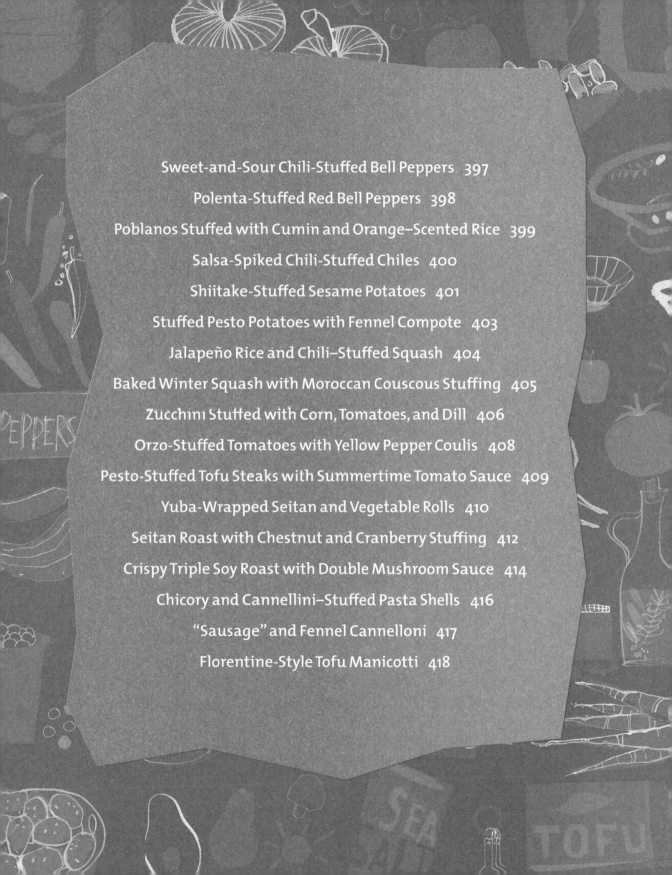

When I look at a mushroom, bell pepper, or squash, I see more than a vegetable; I see edible containers.

Whether it is tiny cherry tomatoes filled with creamy hummus or large beefsteak tomatoes overflowing with rice and vegetables, fresh produce used as receptacles for other foods is a delicious and practical way to cook. In addition to tomatoes, consider stuffing mushrooms, peppers, squash, eggplants, and even cabbage. You can also stuff onions, artichokes, and, everyone's favorite, potatoes. When I'm in the mood to stuff, few vegetables are safe. One time I even stuffed carrots with a mushroom-shallot mixture and baked them in red wine. Fried stuffed zucchini flowers are an old family favorite. Stuffed vegetables can be served as the main course of a meal, depending on the heartiness of the stuffing.

When you stuff vegetables, you can savor a delicious combination of ingredients that is made more flavorful by the permeating essence of the vegetable holding it. Adding to the enjoyment is the artful presentation and the fact that you get to eat the container. Once you start thinking of vegetables as containers, you may never look at produce the same way again.

But why stop with vegetables? As this chapter shows, not only is there more than one way to stuff a pepper, but you also can stuff tofu, seitan, and, of course, pasta. With all these choices, you'll be simply stuffed in no time.

Tomato-Simmered Cabbage Packets Stuffed with Barley and Tempeh

These flavorful cabbage bundles are typically served in eastern European countries, where they are called *halupki*. I especially like the barley in the stuffing, but the packets can be made with another grain, such as rice, bulgur, or quinoa. The tempeh combines especially well with the flavors of the cabbage and the sweet-and-sour tomato broth. You may prepare this dish on top of the stove, if you wish. Simply layer the cabbage packets in a large saucepan or Dutch oven and simmer over low heat. I prefer the oven method because I can arrange the *halupki* in one layer, pop them in the oven, and serve them in the same dish.

1 large head green cabbage, cored
1 tablespoon olive oil
1 cup grated onion
1 medium-size carrot, grated
3 cups water
Salt
1¼ cups pearl barley
One 8-ounce package tempeh, poached (page 14) and chopped

2 tablespoons minced fresh parsley leaves
¼ teaspoon ground allspice
Freshly ground black pepper
¼ cup red wine vinegar
¼ cup firmly packed light brown sugar or natural sweetener
One 28-ounce can crushed tomatoes

1. Place the cabbage in a large pot with a steamer rack. Add 2 to 3 inches of water, cover, and bring to a boil over high heat. Reduce the heat to medium and cook until the outer leaves are softened, about 10 minutes. Remove from the pot and let cool. Carefully remove the tender leaves and set aside.

2. Return of the cabbage head to the steamer and cook, covered, to soften the remaining leaves, about 5 minutes. Remove from the steamer and let cool. Peel off the leaves and set aside with the others. You will need about 18 leaves total.

3. Heat the olive oil in a large skillet over medium heat. Add the onion and carrot and cook, covered, until tender, about 10 minutes.

4. Meanwhile, bring the water to a boil in a medium-size saucepan over high heat. Salt the water, then add the barley. Reduce the heat to medium and simmer, uncovered, until just tender, about 10 minutes. Drain well and place in a large bowl. Add the tempeh, onion mixture, parsley, allspice, and salt and pepper to taste. Mix well.

5. Preheat the oven to 350 degrees F. Place 1 cabbage leaf rib side down on a flat work surface. Place approximately $1/3$ cup of the stuffing mixture in the center of the leaf. Roll up the leaf around the stuffing, tucking in the sides as you roll. Repeat the process with the softened leaves until all the filling is used. Arrange the cabbage rolls seam side down in a lightly oiled shallow baking dish.

6. In a medium bowl, combine the vinegar, brown sugar, and tomatoes. Pour over the cabbage rolls and season with salt and pepper to taste. Cover and bake until tender, about 45 minutes. Serve hot.

SERVES 6 TO 8

Versatile Cabbage

A member of the mustard family (Cruciferae), which also includes broccoli, cauliflower, and Brussels sprouts, cabbage is rich in potassium, folic acid, and vitamins B6 and C. It is enjoyed raw, fermented, or cooked in a variety of ways, from stuffed to soups to stir-fries. It is also good braised and goes well with potatoes, root vegetables, and sliced apples.

Turkish-Style Stuffed Eggplant with Walnut Sauce

To get the most juice from a fresh pomegranate, bring it to room temperature and roll it back and forth between a flat work surface and the palm of your hand. Look for bottled pomegranate juice in Middle Eastern grocery stores and gourmet shops. Note: This dish may be prepared ahead of time, with the final baking done just before you're ready to serve it.

2 medium-size eggplants, halved lengthwise

3 tablespoons olive oil

1 large yellow onion, chopped

1/2 teaspoon turmeric

1 cup ground walnuts

1 cup Basic Vegetable Stock (page 68)

Salt and freshly ground black pepper

2 tablespoons tomato paste

1/4 cup firmly packed light brown sugar or natural sweetener

1/4 cup fresh or bottled pomegranate juice

2 tablespoons fresh lemon juice

1 small green bell pepper, seeded and chopped

1 cup cooked basmati rice

2 tablespoons minced fresh mint leaves

2 tablespoons minced fresh parsley leaves

1. Preheat the oven to 400 degrees F. Place the eggplant halves cut side down on a lightly oiled baking sheet and bake until partially softened, about 15 minutes. Remove from the oven and set aside to cool.

2. When cool enough to handle, scoop out the inside of the eggplant, leaving 1/4-inch-thick shells intact. Coarsely chop the eggplant flesh and set aside along with the shells.

3. Heat 1 tablespoon of the olive oil in a medium-size saucepan over medium heat. Add half of the onion, cover, and cook until softened, about 5 minutes. Add the turmeric, 1/2 cup of the walnuts, the stock, and salt and pepper to taste. Bring to a boil, then reduce the heat to medium-low and simmer, stirring occasionally, until the sauce begins to thicken, about 15 minutes.

4. In a small bowl, combine the tomato paste, brown sugar, pomegranate juice, and lemon juice and blend well. Add to the sauce, reduce the heat to low, and simmer while you prepare the rest of the dish.

5. Heat the remaining 2 tablespoons olive oil in a large skillet over medium heat. Add the remaining onion and the bell pepper, cover, and cook until softened, about 5 minutes. Stir in the chopped eggplant and salt and pepper to taste. Continue cooking to blend the flavors, about 5 minutes, then transfer the eggplant mixture to a large bowl and stir in the rice, remaining $1/2$ cup walnuts, the mint, and parsley. Season with salt and pepper to taste.

6. Divide the stuffing among the eggplant shells and arrange them in a lightly oiled baking dish. Bake until the shells are tender and the filling is hot, 15 to 20 minutes. Serve topped with the walnut sauce.

SERVES 4

"*Non-violence leads to the highest ethics, which is the goal of all evolution. Until we stop harming all other living beings, we are still savages.*"
—THOMAS A. EDISON

Stir-Fried Watercress in Japanese Eggplants

Be sure not to overcook the watercress. It should retain a slight crunch without tasting raw. For a dish with more substance, stir-fry some diced extra-firm tofu with a splash of tamari and add it to the stuffing. Add the red pepper flakes if you like a spicier dish.

4 Japanese eggplants, halved lengthwise

1 tablespoon peanut oil

3 scallions, chopped

1 large garlic clove, minced

2 bunches watercress, tough stems removed

2 tablespoons tamari or other soy sauce

1/2 teaspoon red pepper flakes (optional)

Salt and freshly ground black pepper

4 to 5 cups freshly cooked rice

2 tablespoons toasted sesame oil

1 tablespoon sesame seeds, toasted (page 192)

1. Preheat the oven to 400 degrees F. Arrange the eggplant halves cut side down in a lightly oiled baking dish and bake until just tender, about 15 minutes. Reduce the temperature to 250 degrees F. Let the eggplant cool slightly, then scoop out the inside, being careful not to pierce the skin and leaving a 1/3-inch-thick shell. Coarsely chop the flesh and set aside. Return the eggplant shells to the oven to keep warm.

2. Heat the peanut oil in a large skillet over low heat. Add the scallions, garlic, and chopped eggplant and cook until fragrant, about 30 seconds. Add the watercress, tamari, and red pepper flakes (if using). Stir-fry until the watercress is slightly limp, about 30 seconds. Season with salt and pepper to taste.

3. To serve, spoon a bed of rice on a large platter or 4 individual plates. Arrange the eggplant shells on the rice and divide the watercress mixture between them. Drizzle with the sesame oil, then sprinkle with the sesame seeds.

SERVES 4

Portobello Mushrooms Stuffed with Chipotle Mashed Potatoes and Fried Leeks

There are a lot of flavors and textures going on in this deceptively simple dish. The earthy flavor of the mushrooms is enhanced by the spicy creaminess of the potatoes, and the crispy fried leeks add a surprising crunch. It's a great way to use up leftover mashed potatoes but delicious enough that you may want to prepare the potatoes especially for this recipe

4 large portobello mushrooms, stems removed
3 tablespoons olive oil
1 tablespoon tamari or other soy sauce
Salt and freshly ground black pepper

2 cups Chipotle Mashed Potatoes (page 203)
2 leeks (white parts only), washed well and slivered lengthwise

1. Using a knife or a spoon, scrape out and discard the brown gills from the underside of the mushroom caps. Heat 1 tablespoon of the olive oil in a large skillet over medium-high heat. Add the mushrooms cut side up and sear until browned, about 30 seconds. Add the tamari, turn over the mushrooms, season with salt and pepper to taste, and cook for 30 seconds. Remove the mushrooms from the skillet and set aside.

2. Preheat the oven to 375 degrees F. Spoon 1/2 cup of the mashed potatoes into each mushroom cap and smooth the top. Drizzle the stuffed mushrooms with 1 tablespoon of the olive oil and place in a lightly oiled baking dish. Bake until hot, about 10 minutes.

3. While the mushrooms are baking, heat the remaining 1 tablespoon olive oil in a large skillet over medium-high heat. Add the leeks and cook, stirring, until crisp, about 5 minutes. Transfer to paper towels to drain.

4. To serve, place the mushrooms on a plate and top with the fried leeks.

SERVES 4

Sweet-and-Sour Chili-Stuffed Bell Peppers

The zesty filling makes a nice change from traditional stuffed peppers. Virtually any chili works well in this recipe.

4 medium-size green bell peppers
2 cups vegetarian chili, homemade
   (pages 314–326) or store-bought
1 cup cooked rice
1 cup shredded vegan cheddar cheese

1 cup tomato juice
1 tablespoon cider vinegar
1 tablespoon light brown sugar or
   natural sweetener
1 teaspoon chili powder

1. Cut the tops off the peppers and remove the seeds and membranes. Parboil the peppers in boiling water for 5 minutes. Drain and set aside.
2. Preheat the oven to 350 degrees F. In a large bowl, combine the chili, rice, and vegan cheese until well mixed. Fill the peppers with the chili mixture, place them upright in a baking dish, and set aside.
3. In a small bowl, combine the tomato juice, vinegar, brown sugar, and chili powder until well blended. Pour around the peppers and bake until hot, about 30 minutes. Serve hot.

SERVES 4

Polenta-Stuffed Red Bell Peppers

The striking color contrast of the peppers and polenta is just the first thing about this dish that demands attention. The next, of course, is the great taste. If you don't have time to make polenta from scratch, you can use instant polenta or the ready-to-use polenta now available in the produce section of many supermarkets.

4 cups water

1½ teaspoons salt, plus more for seasoning

1 tablespoon corn oil

1½ cups yellow cornmeal

4 large red bell peppers

⅓ cup oil-packed or rehydrated sun-dried tomatoes

3 tablespoons olive oil

½ cup minced onion

1 garlic clove, minced

1 tablespoon minced fresh parsley leaves

1 teaspoon minced fresh basil leaves

Freshly ground black pepper

1. In a large saucepan, combine the water, salt, and corn oil and bring to a boil over high heat. Reduce the heat to medium and gradually whisk in the cornmeal, stirring constantly to avoid lumps. Cook, stirring, until the polenta begins to pull away from the sides of the pan, about 20 minutes. Remove from the heat and set aside.

2. Preheat the oven to 350 degrees F. Slice off the tops of the peppers and remove the seeds and ribs. Plunge the peppers into a pot of boiling water and cook until slightly softened, about 3 minutes. Remove from the water with tongs and set aside, cut side down, to drain.

3. Drain the sun-dried tomatoes, chop, and set aside.

4. Heat the olive oil in a large skillet over medium heat. Add the onion, cover, and cook until softened, about 5 minutes. Add the garlic and cook, stirring, until fragrant, about 30 seconds.

5. In a large bowl, combine the polenta, onion mixture, tomatoes, parsley, basil, and salt and pepper to taste. Mix well. Fill the peppers with the polenta mixture and place upright in a baking dish. Add a few tablespoons of water to the baking dish, cover, and bake until the peppers are tender and the stuffing is hot, about 30 minutes. Serve hot.

SERVES 4

Poblanos Stuffed with Cumin and Orange-Scented Rice

The symphony of flavors is sure to make this dish the center of attention at the dinner table. Poblanos are the flavorful, dark green chiles used to make *chiles rellenos*. They are available in well-stocked supermarkets and Hispanic grocery stores.

2 oranges, well scrubbed

8 poblano chiles

2 tablespoons olive oil

1 small yellow onion, minced

1 small carrot, grated

1 tablespoon ground cumin

2 cups cooked white or brown rice

Salt and freshly ground black pepper

1/4 cup chopped almonds

1. Preheat the oven to 350 degrees F. Grate 2 tablespoons of zest from the oranges and set aside in a small bowl. Remove the remaining peel and pith from the oranges and discard. Coarsely chop the oranges, removing any seeds, if necessary, and add to the zest along with any juice. Set aside.

2. Lightly roast the poblanos according to the directions on page 143. Make a lengthwise cut in the chiles and remove the seeds. Place cut side up in a lightly oiled baking dish and set aside.

3. Heat 1 tablespoon of the olive oil in a large skillet over medium heat. Add the onion and carrot, cover, and cook until softened, about 5 minutes. Add the cumin, rice, orange mixture, and salt and pepper to taste. Mix well.

4. Spoon the stuffing mixture into the chiles and sprinkle with the almonds. Drizzle with the remaining 1 tablespoon olive oil and bake until hot, about 30 minutes. Serve hot.

SERVES 4

Salsa-Spiked Chili-Stuffed Chiles

A ny variety of large chile may be used in this recipe—or even bell peppers, if you prefer. I especially like the great taste of poblanos that can range from mild to hot. Serve them over rice.

8 poblano or other long green chiles
2 cups vegetarian chili, homemade
    (pages 314–326) or store-bought
1 cup Fresh Tomato Salsa (page 174) or
    your favorite salsa

1 cup vegan sour cream, homemade
    (page 139) or store-bought
Shredded vegan cheddar cheese

1. Lightly roast the chiles according to the directions on page 143.
2. Preheat the oven to 350 degrees F. Cut a slit in each chile and remove the seeds. Stuff with 1/4 cup of the chili. Arrange the stuffed chiles in a single layer in a lightly oiled baking dish and set aside.
3. In a small bowl, combine the salsa and vegan sour cream until well blended. Spread on top of the stuffed chiles and sprinkle evenly with the vegan cheese. Bake until heated through and bubbly, about 30 minutes. Serve hot.

SERVES 4

Shiitake-Stuffed Sesame Potatoes

Asian flavors abound in these rich and satisfying stuffed potatoes. Although they make a terrific side dish with a teriyaki- or hoisin-sauced entrée, they also are substantial enough to be enjoyed as the main event of a meal.

4 large baking potatoes, well scrubbed
1 tablespoon peanut oil
8 ounces fresh shiitake mushrooms, stems removed and caps chopped
1 tablespoon tamari or other soy sauce

4 ounces soft silken tofu, drained and mashed
1 tablespoon toasted sesame oil
Salt and freshly ground black pepper

1. Preheat the oven to 400 degrees F. Prick the potatoes with a fork and bake until soft, about 1 hour. Remove from the oven.

2. Heat the peanut oil in a large skillet over medium heat. Add the mushrooms and cook, stirring, until the mushrooms are tender and the liquid evaporates, about 5 minutes. Stir in the tamari and set aside.

3. When the potatoes are cool enough to handle, cut in half lengthwise and, leaving the shells intact, carefully scoop out the flesh into a large bowl. Add the tofu, sesame oil, and salt and pepper to taste and mash until well combined. Add the mushroom mixture and mix well. Spoon the stuffing into the potato shells and arrange in a lightly oiled baking pan. Bake until hot, 15 to 20 minutes. Serve hot.

SERVES 4

One Potato, Two Potato

Potatoes are among the most popular vegetables, and there are seemingly infinite ways to prepare them. Rich in potassium, niacin, vitamins C and B_6, and iron, potatoes can be paired with root vegetables, squash, and dark leafy greens in soups, stews, and braised or roasted dishes. For a healthy alternative to French fries, cut potatoes into strips, arrange on a lightly oiled baking sheet, and bake at 425 degrees F until soft and browned, turning once, 20 to 30 minutes. Then season with salt and pepper to taste.

Sweet potatoes also taste great prepared this way, as well as baked, mashed, fried, or sautéed. They are delicious in soups and stews, and because they are naturally sweet, they can be used in pies, cookies, and other desserts. An excellent source of vitamin A, sweet potatoes also contain potassium, vitamins C and B_6, and riboflavin.

The best way to store potatoes and sweet potatoes is in a cool, dark, dry place.

Stuffed Pesto Potatoes with Fennel Compote

I love potatoes stuffed with everything from spinach to chili, but the aromatic combination of vegan pesto and fennel makes this version extra special. In addition to adding creaminess to the stuffing, the silken tofu provides protein and helps make these potatoes hearty enough to serve as an entrée, allowing two halves per person.

4 large baking potatoes, well scrubbed

8 ounces soft silken tofu, drained and mashed

1/2 cup vegan pesto, homemade (page 157) or store-bought

1 tablespoon tamari or other soy sauce

Salt and freshly ground black pepper

Olive oil for drizzling

1 cup Fennel Compote with Black Olives and Pine Nuts (page 178)

1. Preheat the oven to 400 degrees F. Pierce the potatoes with a fork and bake until soft, about 1 hour. Remove from the oven and allow to cool. When cool enough to handle, cut in half lengthwise and, leaving the shells intact, scoop out the flesh into a large bowl.

2. Add the tofu, vegan pesto, tamari, and salt and pepper to taste, blending until well combined. Spoon the stuffing back into the potato skins and arrange in a lightly oiled baking pan. Drizzle with a small amount of olive oil and bake until hot, 15 to 20 minutes.

3. To serve, arrange the potato halves on a platter or 4 individual plates and top each with a spoonful of the fennel compote and another drizzle of olive oil, if desired.

SERVES 4

Jalapeño Rice and Chili-Stuffed Squash

The complementary flavors of spicy chili and mellow squash join forces in this hearty and wholesome entrée. If you can find the sweet, orange-fleshed kabocha squash, also called Hokkaido pumpkin, you're in for a special treat.

1 medium-size butternut or other winter squash, halved and seeded
1 tablespoon olive oil
1 medium-size yellow onion, minced
1 jalapeño, seeded and minced

2 cups vegetarian chili, homemade (pages 314–326) or store-bought
1 cup cooked rice
1/2 teaspoon salt

1. Preheat the oven to 375 degrees F. Place the squash halves cut side down in a lightly oiled baking dish and bake until just tender, about 30 minutes. Remove from the oven and set aside.

2. Heat the olive oil in a large skillet over medium heat. Add the onion and jalapeño, cover, and cook until softened, about 5 minutes. Transfer to a large bowl and add the chili, rice, and salt. Mix well to combine.

3. Fill the squash cavities with the stuffing. Add 1/4 inch of water to the baking pan, cover, and bake until the squash are tender and the filling is hot, about 20 minutes. Serve hot.

SERVES 2

A Squash by Any Other Name: Winter Squash

Among the varieties of winter squash are acorn, butternut, buttercup, hubbard, and turban, as well as the pumpkin. Most varieties are interchangeable in recipes. Winter squash is an excellent source of potassium and vitamins A and C. It can be steamed, braised, or baked and is especially good stuffed with a savory filling.

Baked Winter Squash with Moroccan Couscous Stuffing

If kabocha squash is unavailable, substitute any sweet winter squash, such as butternut or acorn. The sweetness of the squash is enhanced by the aromatic spices.

1 large or 2 medium-size kabocha
 squash
2 cups water, plus more as needed
Salt
1 cup instant couscous
$1/4$ teaspoon ground cinnamon
$1/4$ teaspoon ground cardamom
$1/8$ teaspoon ground cloves
2 tablespoons olive oil

1 large yellow onion, chopped
1 garlic clove, minced
2 cups chopped white mushrooms
2 teaspoons peeled and minced fresh
 ginger
Freshly ground black pepper
$1/2$ cup raisins
$1/2$ cup chopped unsalted dry-roasted
 peanuts

1. Preheat the oven to 375 degrees F. Cut the squash in half and scoop out the seeds. Place the squash halves cut side down in a shallow baking dish. Add $1/4$ inch of water, cover tightly, and bake until just tender, about 30 minutes. Carefully turn the halves over and set aside.
2. While the squash is baking, bring the water to a boil in a medium-size saucepan over high heat. Salt the water, then add the couscous, cinnamon, cardamom, and cloves. Reduce the heat to very low, cover, and simmer for 8 to 10 minutes, or until the water is absorbed. Remove from the heat and set aside.
3. Heat the olive oil in a large skillet over medium heat. Add the onion and garlic, cover, and cook until softened, about 5 minutes. Add the mushrooms, ginger, and salt and pepper to taste. Cook, stirring a few times, until the mushrooms are soft, about 3 minutes. Remove from the heat.
4. Fluff the couscous with a fork and transfer to a large bowl. Add the onion mixture, raisins, and peanuts. If the mixture seems too dry, add a little water to moisten. Divide the stuffing equally among the squash halves and, using the same baking dish, cover and bake until hot, about 20 minutes. Serve hot.

SERVES 4

Zucchini Stuffed with Corn, Tomatoes, and Dill

After a trip to the farmers' market, these stuffed zucchini will help solve your dilemma of which vegetables to cook up first, since they use a little bit of everything. When fresh corn and ripe tomatoes are out of season, frozen corn and canned tomatoes work well. Despite its appellation as a "summer" squash, fresh zucchini seems to be available year round.

4 medium-size zucchini, halved
    lengthwise
2 tablespoons olive oil
2 shallots, minced
2 tablespoons seeded and minced red
    bell pepper
2 garlic cloves, minced
Salt and freshly ground black pepper
3 large, ripe tomatoes, finely chopped,
    or one 14.5-ounce can diced
    tomatoes, drained and finely
    chopped

1 cup fresh or frozen corn kernels
2 teaspoons light brown sugar or
    natural sweetener
2 teaspoons fresh lemon juice
3 tablespoons minced fresh dill

1. Use a sharp knife or melon baller to remove the zucchini flesh, leaving a 1/3-inch-thick shell. Chop the flesh well and set aside.
2. Steam the zucchini shells over boiling water until tender, about 5 minutes. Set aside to cool.
3. Heat 1 tablespoon of the olive oil in a medium-size skillet over medium heat. Add the shallots, bell pepper, garlic, chopped zucchini, and salt and pepper to taste. Cover and cook until tender, about 10 minutes. Add the tomatoes, corn, brown sugar, lemon juice, and 2 tablespoons of the dill. Simmer, uncovered and stirring occasionally, until the liquid is absorbed, about 10 minutes. Remove from the heat and set aside to cool.

4. Preheat the oven to 350 degrees F. Spoon the stuffing mixture into the zucchini shells and arrange in a lightly oiled baking dish. Cover and bake until hot, about 30 minutes.

5. To serve, sprinkle with the remaining 1 tablespoon dill, drizzle with the remaining 1 tablespoon olive oil, and finish with a few grindings of pepper.

SERVES 4

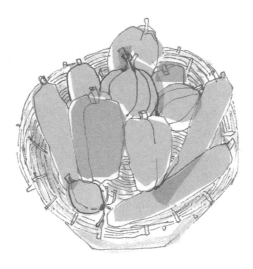

Orzo-Stuffed Tomatoes with Yellow Pepper Coulis

This is a great way to use orzo, a small rice-shaped pasta usually reserved for soup. But keep this recipe in mind whenever you have a small amount of any leftover cooked grain and an abundance of firm, ripe tomatoes.

1/2 cup orzo

4 large, ripe tomatoes

1/3 cup pine nuts, toasted (page 110)

1 large garlic clove, minced

2 tablespoons minced fresh parsley
    leaves

2 tablespoons minced fresh basil leaves

Salt and freshly ground black pepper

Extra virgin olive oil for drizzling

1 cup Yellow Pepper Coulis (page 156)

1. Cook the orzo in boiling salted water, stirring occasionally, until tender, 8 to 10 minutes. Drain and set aside.

2. Preheat the oven to 375 degrees F. Cut a 1/2-inch-thick slice off the top of each tomato. Scoop out the pulp, leaving a 1/2-inch-thick shell. Set aside.

3. Chop the tomato pulp and place in a large bowl. Add the orzo, pine nuts, garlic, parsley, basil, and salt and pepper to taste and mix well. Stuff the tomato shells with the mixture. Place them in a lightly oiled baking dish, drizzle with the olive oil, and bake until hot, about 20 minutes.

4. To serve, spoon a small amount of the coulis onto 4 individual plates or a serving platter and carefully place the tomatoes on top.

SERVES 4

Pesto-Stuffed Tofu Steaks with Summertime Tomato Sauce

The tofu readily absorbs the flavors of the pesto and tomato sauce in this light and luscious dish. It makes a great dinner entrée served with pasta and a salad. Note: If buying pesto at the store, be sure to check the ingredients—most brands contain cheese.

One 16-ounce package extra-firm tofu, drained and cut into four ³/₄-inch-thick slices

¹/₂ cup vegan pesto, homemade (page 157) or store-bought

Salt and freshly ground black pepper

1¹/₂ cups Summertime Tomato Sauce (page 150)

2 tablespoons olive oil

2 small roasted red bell peppers (page 143), cut into strips, for garnish

Fresh basil leaves for garnish

1. Cut a slit in the side of each tofu slice and stuff 1 tablespoon of the vegan pesto into each pocket. Season with salt and pepper to taste and set aside.

2. Heat the tomato sauce in a small saucepan over low heat and keep warm.

3. Heat 1 tablespoon of the olive oil in a large skillet over medium heat. Add the tofu and cook until golden brown on both sides, about 5 minutes. Reduce the heat to low and keep warm.

4. In a small bowl, combine the remaining ¹/₄ cup pesto and the remaining 1 tablespoon olive oil, blending well.

5. To serve, spoon a small amount of the warm tomato sauce on 4 individual plates. Top with a tofu steak. Drizzle 1 tablespoon of the pesto over one-third of each tofu slice. Spoon a small amount of the tomato sauce over another third and leave the remaining portion un-sauced. Garnish with the roasted pepper strips and basil leaves.

SERVES 4

Yuba-Wrapped Seitan and Vegetable Rolls

Yuba, or bean curd skin, is a versatile ingredient in Asian cooking that is often used as a dumpling wrapper. Here it is used as a crispy outer wrapper for a flavorful seitan roll stuffed with julienned vegetables. These rolls can be served with a wide range of sauces, including Faux Choron Sauce (page 145), Spicy Peanut Dipping Sauce (page 160), or Double Mushroom Sauce (page 149).

One 1-pound piece raw seitan
   (page 16)
1/4 cup tamari or other soy sauce
3 tablespoons peanut oil
1 large red bell pepper, seeded and
   cut into thin strips
4 ounces fresh shiitake mushrooms,
   stems removed and caps cut into
   thin strips

1 large yellow squash, cut lengthwise
   into thin strips
4 scallions, sliced lengthwise
2 teaspoons toasted sesame oil
Salt and freshly ground black pepper
2 large yuba sheets (bean curd skin;
   see page 351)

1. Cut the seitan into 4 slices and, using a rolling pin, roll out to about 1/4 inch thick. Place in a shallow bowl, cover with the tamari, and set aside.

2. Heat 1 tablespoon of the peanut oil in a skillet over medium heat. Add the bell pepper, cover, and cook until slightly softened, about 5 minutes. Add the mushrooms, squash, and scallions and cook until tender, about 5 minutes. Drizzle with the sesame oil, season with salt and pepper to taste, and set aside to cool.

3. Remove the seitan pieces from the marinade and place on a flat work surface. Divide the vegetable mixture among the slices, arranging the vegetable strips at one end of each slice, and roll up. Secure each roll with a toothpick or kitchen twine and place seam side down on a platter.

4. Heat 1 tablespoon of the peanut oil in a large skillet over medium-high heat. Add the seitan rolls and sear all over. Remove from the pan and set aside to cool.

5. Cut the yuba sheets in half and soak in a shallow bowl of water to soften for about 5 seconds, if necessary, then drain. Place a seitan roll on the lower third of each yuba sheet. Fold the sides of the yuba onto the seitan and roll up. Repeat with the remaining seitan rolls and yuba sheets.

6. Heat the remaining 1 tablespoon peanut oil in a large skillet over medium heat. Add the rolls and cook until golden brown and crispy on both sides, 5 to 7 minutes total. Serve hot.

SERVES 4

THINKING OUTSIDE THE STUFFING BOX

To me, my mother's chestnut stuffing was always the best part of Thanksgiving dinner. Even as a child, I bypassed the turkey in favor of the trimmings. These days, my mother's stuffing recipe finds its way into many a vegan seitan roast and stuffed winter squash. Just as stuffing doesn't have to be reserved for one day a year, neither does your stuffing recipe—or, for that matter, what you stuff it in. Cube cornbread or multigrain bread in place of white bread. Consider using leftover rice, millet, or other grains in place of bread. Experiment with different herbs, fruits, nuts, and chopped cooked vegetables. How about some pesto or sun-dried tomatoes?

Now that you have your stuffing, where should it go? It can, of course, stand on its own baked in a casserole or loaf pan. The seitan roast (page 412) is my personal favorite for holiday meals. And then there are vegetables: winter squash, summer squash, bell peppers, portobello mushrooms, eggplants, onions, and tomatoes— all of which make winning receptacles. So what are you waiting for? Get stuffing!

Seitan Roast with Chestnut and Cranberry Stuffing

For meat-free holiday dining, it doesn't get much better than this. Even the skeptics at your dinner table will be impressed with the chewy wheat-meat surrounding a savory stuffing studded with chestnuts and cranberries. Serve with mashed potatoes and all the trimmings.

One 1-pound piece raw seitan
  (page 16)
1/2 cup tamari or other soy sauce
2 tablespoons olive oil
1 cup minced onion
1/2 cup minced celery
1 teaspoon dried thyme
1 teaspoon dried sage
2 tablespoons brandy

6 cups cubed bread
8 ounces cooked chestnuts (page 413)
1/3 cup sweetened dried cranberries
1/2 cup minced fresh parsley leaves
1 cup water
1 teaspoon salt
1/2 teaspoon freshly ground black
  pepper
1 1/2 cups Basic Brown Sauce (page 148)

1. In a zipper-top plastic bag, marinate the seitan in the tamari for 1 hour or overnight, turning it several times.
2. Heat the olive oil in a medium skillet over medium heat. Add the onions and celery, cover, and cook until softened, about 5 minutes. Add the thyme, sage, and brandy and cook for 1 minute. Remove from the heat and set aside.
3. Place the bread in a large bowl. Add the chestnuts, cranberries, parsley, water, salt, and pepper. Stir in the onion mixture and mix well. Taste and adjust the seasonings, adding more water if the mixture is too dry. Set aside.
4. Using a rolling pin, roll out the marinated seitan to about 1/4 inch thick. Spread the surface with the stuffing and roll up. Place seam side down in a lightly oiled shallow baking pan. Bake, uncovered, until the surface is firm and golden brown, 30 to 40 minutes.
5. Let stand at room temperature for 10 minutes. Using a serrated knife, cut the roast into 1/2-inch-thick slices and serve with the brown sauce.

SERVES 8

Chestnuts, Roasted and Otherwise

Chestnuts have been eaten since ancient times, primarily in Italy, Spain, China, and Japan. They are especially popular in France, Italy, and North Africa, where they are usually eaten roasted or boiled. In many cities, street vendors sell hot roasted chestnuts on cold winter days.

George Washington and Thomas Jefferson were interested in growing chestnut trees during the late 1700s. Despite our forefathers' efforts, our country's once flourishing chestnut trees were nearly wiped out by a blight in the early twentieth century. For that reason, we import most of our chestnuts from Europe.

Chestnuts have a crumbly texture and a sweet, mild flavor. Unlike other nuts, they are low in fat. They have a fair amount of protein, are high in carbohydrates, and are a good source of calcium, potassium, B complex vitamins, magnesium, and iron.

In addition to eating them out of hand, you can use chestnuts in a variety of sweet and savory recipes, from soups to stuffings to desserts. Canned and bottled peeled chestnuts are available year round. Though expensive, they eliminate the labor-intensive job of peeling them yourself. Sweetened chestnuts, called *marrons glacés*, are also available, as are pureed chestnuts, dried chestnuts, and chestnut flour. Many of these items can be found in gourmet or specialty food shops.

When shopping for chestnuts, look for firm, heavy nuts with dark brown, shiny shells. If you can hear them rattling around in their shells, they are old and dried out. Unpeeled chestnuts can be stored in a cool, dry place for 1 to 2 weeks. It is important to note that the crisp, white water chestnuts used in Chinese stir-fries are not a substitute for regular chestnuts.

Both the shell and thin brown skin of the chestnut need to be removed before eating. Boiling or roasting the chestnuts beforehand makes them easier to peel. To cook chestnuts, pierce the shells with a sharp knife, cutting an X in the shell. Then boil or roast them at 375 degrees F and peel them while still fairly hot, using a sharp knife to remove the outer shell and the inner skin. They are then ready to eat or use in recipes. Boiling is recommended if the chestnuts are to be used in another recipe, but for peeling and eating out of hand, roast them for maximum flavor.

Crispy Triple Soy Roast with Double Mushroom Sauce

This protein-rich seitan roast uses soy in three ways: it is seasoned with a tamari-miso paste, stuffed with tofu, and encased in crispy yuba. This roast lends itself to a variety of seasonings. Add a little peeled and minced fresh ginger when you sauté the garlic, or add some thyme or another herb when you throw in the parsley.

One 1-pound piece raw seitan
    (page 16)
1/2 cup tamari or other soy sauce
2 tablespoons olive oil
12 ounces white mushrooms, chopped
1 garlic clove, minced
8 ounces extra-firm tofu, drained and
    crumbled
Salt and freshly ground black pepper

4 cups cubed bread
1 tablespoon minced fresh parsley
    leaves
2 teaspoons mellow white miso paste
1 large sheet yuba (bean curd skin;
    page 351)
1 cup Double Mushroom Sauce
    (page 149)

1. In a zipper-top plastic bag, marinate the seitan in the tamari for 1 hour or overnight, turning it several times.

2. Heat 2 tablespoons of the olive oil in medium-size skillet over medium heat. Add the mushrooms and garlic and cook, stirring, until tender, about 5 minutes. Stir in the tofu, season with salt and pepper to taste, and cook until the liquid is evaporated, about 10 minutes. Transfer to a large bowl, mix in the bread cubes and parsley, and let cool.

3. In a small bowl, combine the tamari marinade and miso, stirring to blend well. Set aside.

4. Using a rolling pin, roll out the marinated seitan to about 1/4 inch thick. Brush the surface with the tamari-miso mixture and spread the stuffing over all, to within 1 inch of the edge. Roll up the seitan to encase the stuffing and place seam side down on a platter.

5. Preheat the oven to 350 degrees F. Soak the yuba in a shallow bowl of water to soften for 5 seconds, if necessary, then drain. Spread out the yuba on a flat work surface, place the seitan at one end, and roll up, tucking in the sides as you roll. Place seam side down in a lightly oiled shallow baking pan. Bake, uncovered, until hot inside and golden brown and crisp outside, 30 to 40 minutes.

6. Let stand at room temperature for 10 minutes. Using a serrated knife, cut into $1/2$-inch-thick slices and serve with the mushroom sauce.

SERVES 6 TO 8

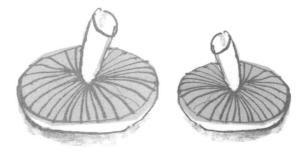

Chicory and Cannellini-Stuffed Pasta Shells

Chicory, also known as curly endive, is a slightly bitter green widely used in Italian cooking. It can be very sandy, however, so be sure to wash it well before using.

1 large head chicory, washed well and coarsely chopped

8 ounces large pasta shells

2 tablespoons olive oil

2 large garlic cloves, minced

1½ cups cooked or one 15-ounce can cannellini or other white beans, drained and rinsed

Salt and freshly ground black pepper

2 cups Vegan Béchamel Sauce (page 146)

One 12-ounce package soft silken tofu, drained and mashed

2 tablespoons minced fresh parsley leaves

1. Cook the chicory in a pot of boiling salted water until tender, about 10 minutes. Drain well and set aside.

2. Cook the pasta shells in a large pot of boiling salted water, stirring occasionally, until *al dente*, about 10 minutes. Drain well and set aside.

3. Heat the olive oil in a large skillet over medium heat. Add the garlic and cook, stirring, until fragrant, about 30 seconds. Add the chicory, beans, and salt and pepper to taste. Simmer until the flavors are well combined, about 5 minutes. Set aside to cool.

4. Preheat the oven to 350 degree F. Spoon a thin layer of the sauce over the bottom of a lightly oiled shallow baking dish and set aside.

5. In a medium-size bowl, combine the chicory-bean mixture, tofu, and salt and pepper to taste. Mix until well blended, then spoon the mixture into the pasta shells. Arrange the stuffed shells on top of the sauce and spoon the remaining sauce on top. Cover and bake until hot and bubbly, about 30 minutes. Sprinkle with the parsley and serve.

SERVES 4

"Sausage" and Fennel Cannelloni

Although cannelloni is virtually indistinguishable from manicotti, the difference usually lies in the filling. Whereas manicotti usually contains a cheese filling, cannelloni is usually made with a meat filling.

12 cannelloni tubes

2 medium-size fennel bulbs, trimmed and coarsely chopped

1 tablespoon olive oil

1 small yellow onion, minced

One 14.5-ounce can plum tomatoes, drained and chopped

3 cups chopped or crumbled soy sausage

1/2 teaspoon red pepper flakes

1/2 teaspoon dried oregano

1/2 teaspoon dried basil

Salt and freshly ground black pepper

1 cup fresh bread crumbs

1 cup grated vegan mozzarella cheese

3 cups tomato sauce, homemade (pages 150–152) or store-bought

1. Cook the cannelloni in a pot of boiling salted water, stirring occasionally, until *al dente*, about 8 minutes. Drain and rinse under cold running water, then set aside.

2. Lightly steam the fennel until tender, about 5 minutes. Set aside.

3. Heat the olive oil in a large skillet over medium heat. Add the onion, cover, and cook until softened, about 5 minutes. Add the tomatoes, soy sausage, red pepper flakes, oregano, basil, and salt and pepper to taste. Cook for 10 minutes, stirring to blend the flavors. Stir in the fennel.

4. Transfer to a large bowl, add the bread crumbs and 1/2 cup of the vegan cheese, and stir to blend well. Set aside. Preheat the oven to 350 degrees F.

5. Spread a layer of the tomato sauce over the bottom of a lightly oiled 9 x 13-inch baking dish. Using a teaspoon, fill the cannelloni, arranging the stuffed tubes in a single layer in the baking dish. Spoon the remaining sauce over the cannelloni, top with the remaining 1/2 cup cheese, and cover with aluminum foil. Bake until hot, about 20 minutes. Uncover and bake until the top is golden brown, about 10 minutes more. Serve hot.

SERVES 4

Florentine-Style Tofu Manicotti

This lovely dish is a good choice to prepare in advance for a dinner party. You can just pop it in the oven when needed. With soy milk and two kinds of tofu, it's a delicious way to enjoy good-for-you soy.

12 manicotti tubes

3 tablespoons olive oil

2 scallions, minced

Two 10-ounce packages frozen chopped spinach, cooked according to package directions and drained well

1/4 teaspoon freshly grated nutmeg

Salt and freshly ground black pepper

One 16-ounce package firm tofu, drained and crumbled

1 tablespoon fresh lemon juice

One 12-ounce package soft silken tofu, drained

2 cups soy milk or other dairy-free milk

1 cup fresh bread crumbs

1 cup grated vegan mozzarella cheese

1. Cook the manicotti in a pot of boiling salted water, stirring occasionally, until *al dente*, about 8 minutes. Drain and rinse under cold running water, then set aside.

2. Heat 1 tablespoon of the olive oil in a large skillet over medium heat. Add the scallions, cover, and cook until softened, about 5 minutes.

3. Squeeze the spinach to remove as much liquid as possible and add to the skillet. Add the nutmeg and salt and pepper to taste and cook for 2 minutes, stirring to blend the flavors.

4. Transfer to a large bowl, add the firm tofu and lemon juice, and stir to blend well. Add salt and pepper to taste and set aside.

5. In a blender or food processor, combine the silken tofu, soy milk, and salt and pepper to taste. Process until smooth. Spread a layer of this sauce over the bottom of a lightly oiled 9 x 13-inch baking dish. Preheat the oven to 350 degrees F.

6. Using a teaspoon, fill the manicotti until well packed. Arrange the stuffed tubes in a single layer in the baking dish. Spoon the remaining sauce on top.

7. In a small bowl, combine the bread crumbs and remaining 2 tablespoons olive oil with a fork. Sprinkle over the manicotti. Top with the vegan cheese and cover with aluminum foil. Bake for 20 minutes, then uncover and bake until the top is golden brown, about 10 minutes more. Let rest for a few minutes, then serve.

SERVES 4

15

New World Pizza

Americans consume pizza at a rate of 350 slices per second, so it's hard to believe that it has been only 100 years since the first American pizzeria opened in New York. This savory pie became popular in 18th-century Italy, where it was topped with tomatoes, olive oil, garlic, and oregano. Mozzarella cheese was added later, when a patriotic pizza depicting the colors of the Italian flag (red tomato sauce, green basil, and white cheese) was made to honor Queen Margherita. However, long before Naples became the birthplace of the pizza we know today, ancient civilizations, including the Greeks and Egyptians, were enjoying savory baked flatbreads, often seasoned with oil, garlic, and herbs.

Inspired by pizza's ancient global history, this chapter sets out to explore a variety of ways pizza can be enjoyed without cheese, since vegan cheese products are not known for their melting ability—a trait one naturally associates with the popular cheese pizza. Of course, you can always load your pizza with vegan cheese and even vegan pepperoni, if you like. But with savory toppings that include tomatoes, mushrooms, fresh herbs, beans, eggplant, and even cabbage, you may not miss those traditional pizza trappings. In this chapter, you'll see that when you "hold the cheese," it doesn't mean you have to hold back on flavor.

Traditional Pizza Dough

This basic dough recipe can be enhanced by the addition of a small amount of fresh or dried herbs. You also can replace up to one-half of the flour with whole wheat flour, if you like. I like to use a food processor to make the dough, but you can make it by hand, if you wish.

1¹/₂ teaspoons active dry yeast
³/₄ cup warm water
2¹/₄ cups unbleached all-purpose flour
1 teaspoon salt

Pinch of sugar or natural sweetener
1 tablespoon olive oil, plus more for
   spreading

1. Place the yeast in a small bowl. Add ¹/₄ cup of the water and stir to dissolve. Set aside for 5 to 10 minutes.
2. To make the dough in a food processor, combine the flour, salt, and sugar, pulsing to blend. With the machine running, add the yeast mixture through the feed tube, along with the olive oil and as much of the remaining ¹/₂ cup water as necessary to make the dough hold together.
   To make the dough by hand, combine the flour, salt, and sugar in a large bowl. Stir in the yeast mixture, olive oil, and the remaining ¹/₂ cup water until combined.
3. Turn the dough out onto a lightly floured work surface and knead until smooth and elastic, about 3 minutes. Transfer to a large oiled bowl. Spread a small amount of oil on top of the dough, cover with plastic wrap, and set aside in a warm place to rise until doubled in bulk, about 1 hour.
4. Use immediately or store for up to 8 hours in the refrigerator or for 3 to 4 weeks in the freezer. Make sure it is tightly wrapped in plastic.

MAKES ONE 12-INCH PIZZA

Enriched Pizza Dough

The addition of soy flour and sesame seeds provides extra protein and calcium in this pizza dough, along with a slightly nutty flavor. The texture is slightly coarser than that of Traditional Pizza Dough (page 423) and is ideal for some of the more nontraditional toppings in this chapter.

1 1/2 teaspoons active dry yeast
3/4 cup warm water
2 cups unbleached all-purpose flour
1/4 cup soy flour
1 1/2 tablespoons ground sesame seeds

1 teaspoon salt
Pinch of sugar or natural sweetener
1 tablespoon olive oil, plus more for spreading

1. Place the yeast in a small bowl. Add 1/4 cup of the water and stir to dissolve. Set aside for 5 to 10 minutes.

2. To make the dough in a food processor, combine the flours, sesame seeds, salt, and sugar, pulsing to blend. With the machine running, add the yeast mixture through the feed tube, along with the olive oil and as much of the remaining 1/2 cup water as necessary to make the dough hold together.

To make the dough by hand, combine the flours, sesame seeds, salt, and sugar in a large bowl. Stir in the yeast mixture, olive oil, and remaining 1/2 cup water until combined.

3. Turn the dough out onto a lightly floured work surface and knead until smooth and elastic, about 3 minutes. Transfer to a large oiled bowl. Spread a small amount of oil on top of the dough, cover with plastic wrap, and set aside in a warm place to rise until doubled in bulk, about 1 hour.

4. Use immediately or store for up to 8 hours in the refrigerator or for 3 to 4 weeks in the freezer. Make sure it is tightly wrapped in plastic.

MAKES ONE 12-INCH PIZZA

Fresh Tomato Pizza with Basil Pesto

Fragrant vegan pesto combines with diced plum tomatoes for a fresh-tasting variation of the basic "tomato pie." If fresh, ripe tomatoes are out of season, use canned tomatoes, or even a canned pizza sauce. If you're in the mood for a more traditional pie, sprinkle with some vegan cheese.

1 recipe Traditional Pizza Dough
   (page 423)
1/2 cup vegan pesto, homemade (page
   157) or store-bought

2 tablespoons olive oil
4 ripe plum tomatoes, peeled, seeded,
   and diced
Salt and freshly ground black pepper

1. Preheat the oven to 450 degrees F.

2. Punch the dough down. On a lightly floured work surface, roll out into a circle about 1/4 inch thick. Transfer to a lightly oiled pizza pan or baking sheet and bake on the bottom oven rack for 10 minutes.

3. In a medium size bowl, combine the pesto and olive oil, stirring to blend. Add the tomatoes and salt and pepper to taste. Toss gently to combine.

4. Remove from the oven and top with the tomato-pesto mixture, spreading to within 1/2 inch of the edge. Bake until the crust is golden brown, 5 to 10 minutes. Serve hot.

SERVES 4

The First Pizza Delivery

When pizza first became popular in Naples, bakers prepared it to sell to sailors as they returned from a day at sea. This classic "marinara" pizza was made with fresh tomatoes, garlic, oil, and oregano. At that time, pizza was baked in ovens and then sold in the streets by boys who would bring the pizza directly to the fishermen in tin stoves called *stufas*, which they balanced on their heads, to keep the pizza warm.

Broccoli Rabe and White Bean Pizza

The combination of sautéed beans, greens, and garlic makes a great topping. Sprinkle some red pepper flakes into the sauté for a spicy accent. Broccoli rabe, also known as rapini, is available in well-stocked supermarkets.

1 bunch broccoli rabe, stems trimmed
   and coarsely chopped
2 tablespoons olive oil, plus more
   for drizzling
2 garlic cloves, minced
1 1/2 cups cooked or one 15-ounce can
   cannellini or other white beans,
   drained and rinsed

Salt and freshly ground black pepper
1 recipe Traditional Pizza Dough
   (page 423)

1. Preheat the oven to 450 degrees F.
2. Cook the broccoli rabe in boiling salted water until tender, about 10 minutes. Drain very well and set aside.
3. Heat the olive oil in a large skillet over medium heat. Add the garlic and cook until fragrant, about 30 seconds. Add the broccoli rabe, beans, and salt and pepper to taste. Cook for about 5 minutes to blend the flavors. Set aside.
4. Punch the dough down. On a lightly floured work surface, roll out into a circle about 1/4 inch thick. Transfer to a lightly oiled pizza pan or baking sheet and bake on the bottom oven rack for 10 minutes.
5. Remove from the oven and drizzle with a little olive oil. Spread the broccoli rabe mixture on top, to about 1/2 inch of the edge. Bake until the crust is golden brown, about 10 minutes. Serve hot.

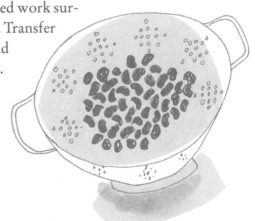

SERVES 4

Wild Mushroom Pizza with Garlic and Fresh Thyme

This is a mushroom pizza with a touch of class, topped with loads of juicy wild mushrooms redolent of garlic and thyme. Serve with white wine and a crisp green salad for a sophisticated meal.

8 ounces fresh wild mushrooms, such as oyster, shiitake, and/or chanterelle mushrooms
2 tablespoons olive oil
3 garlic cloves, minced

1 teaspoon minced fresh thyme leaves
Salt and freshly ground black pepper
1 recipe Traditional Pizza Dough (page 423)

1. Preheat the oven to 450 degrees F.

2. Trim and slice the mushrooms. Heat the olive oil in a large skillet over medium heat. Add the mushrooms and garlic and cook, stirring, until softened, about 5 minutes. Add the thyme and salt and pepper to taste. Continue to cook, stirring occasionally, until the liquid evaporates, 7 to 10 minutes.

3. Punch the dough down. On a lightly floured work surface, roll out into a circle about 1/4 inch thick. Transfer to a lightly oiled pizza pan or baking sheet and bake on the bottom oven for 5 minutes.

4. Remove from the oven and top with the mushroom mixture, spreading it to within 1/2 inch of the edge. Bake until the crust is golden brown, 12 to 15 minutes. Serve hot.

SERVES 4

Pizza Bandiera

Like pizza Margherita, which uses tomatoes, basil, and cheese to depict the colors of the Italian flag, this pizza is topped with sautéed tomatoes, green bell peppers, and onion. Like many Italian preparations, these vegetables are cooked until very soft. The word *bandiera* is Italian for "flag."

1 tablespoon olive oil

1 medium-size yellow onion, chopped

2 small green bell peppers, seeded and chopped

3 large, ripe tomatoes, peeled, seeded, and diced

1 tablespoon dry white wine

Pinch of sugar or natural sweetener

Salt and freshly ground black pepper

1 recipe Traditional Pizza Dough (page 423)

1 tablespoon finely chopped fresh basil leaves

1. Preheat the oven to 450 degrees F.

2. Heat the olive oil in a large skillet over medium heat. Add the onion, cover, and cook until softened, about 5 minutes. Add the bell peppers, cover, reduce the heat to medium-low, and cook until tender, 5 to 7 minutes. Add the tomatoes, wine, sugar, and salt and pepper to taste. Cook for 10 minutes, stirring occasionally, to blend the flavors. Add the basil, then taste and adjust the seasonings.

3. Punch the dough down. On a lightly floured work surface, roll out into a circle about 1/4 inch thick. Transfer to a lightly oiled pizza pan or baking sheet and bake on the bottom oven rack for 5 minutes.

4. Remove from the oven and top with the vegetable mixture, spreading it to within 1/2 inch of the edge. Bake until the crust is golden brown, 12 to 15 minutes. Serve hot.

SERVES 4

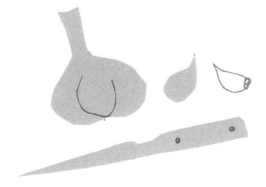

Pizza Puttanesca

The classic pasta sauce made with capers and two kinds of olives is so delicious it deserves to be spread around—on pizza. Assemble a quick version of the sauce, as provided here, or use the recipe on page 248.

1 cup seasoned tomato or pizza sauce

1/4 cup pitted and sliced black olives

3 tablespoons pitted and sliced
   green olives

1 1/2 tablespoons capers, drained and
   chopped

1 recipe Traditional Pizza Dough
   (page 423)

1. Preheat the oven to 450 degrees F.

2. Combine the sauce, olives, and capers in a small bowl. Set aside.

3. Punch the dough down. On a lightly floured work surface, roll out into a circle about 1/4 inch thick. Transfer to a lightly oiled pizza pan or baking sheet and bake on the bottom oven rack for 10 minutes.

4. Remove from the oven and top with the sauce mixture, spreading it to within 1/2 inch of the edge. Bake until the crust is golden brown, 8 to 10 minutes. Serve hot.

SERVES 4

Pizza Variations

Pizza as we know it—a yeasty flatbread topped with tomato sauce and other toppings—became popular a couple of hundred years after Christopher Columbus brought the tomato back to Italy from the New World. Long before that time, however, ancient civilizations such as the Greeks and Etruscans were turning out their own versions of the delectable flatbread seasoned with oil, herbs, and spices that we know as focaccia, or "fireplace floor bread." Other regional Italian flatbreads include *ciabatta*, named for its "slipper" shape, and *pane carasau*, also known as *carta da musica*, or "music paper," since this Sardinian bread is thin, dry, and crisp.

Roasted Eggplant and Sesame Pizza

The combination of sesame and eggplant lends a Middle Eastern flavor to this pizza. Slender Japanese eggplant or small regular eggplant are used. If only a larger eggplant is available, chop it instead of slicing it into rounds and proceed with the recipe.

2 small eggplants (see headnote)
2 shallots, thinly sliced
3 tablespoons toasted sesame oil
Salt and freshly ground black pepper

1 recipe Enriched Pizza Dough
  (page 424)
1 tablespoon sesame seeds
1/2 teaspoon dried oregano

1. Preheat the oven to 450 degrees F.

2. Slice the eggplants into 1/4-inch-thick rounds and place in a medium-size bowl. Add the shallots, sesame oil, and salt and pepper to taste and mix to combine. Arrange the eggplant-shallot mixture on a lightly oiled baking sheet and roast, turning once, until tender but not browned, about 10 minutes. Remove from the oven and set aside.

3. Punch the dough down. On a lightly floured work surface, roll out into a circle about 1/4 inch thick. Transfer to a lightly oiled pizza pan or baking sheet and bake on the bottom oven rack for 5 minutes.

4. Remove from the oven and top with the eggplant-shallot mixture, spreading it to within 1/2 inch of the edge. Sprinkle with the sesame seeds and oregano. Bake until the crust is golden brown, 12 to 15 minutes. Serve hot.

SERVES 4

Spicy Black Bean and Salsa Pizza

This nontraditional pizza has a taste of the Southwest. The topping would feel right at home on a tortilla, but I prefer the more substantial pizza crust.

1 dried chipotle chile, soaked in very
   hot water to cover for 30 minutes
1 cup Fresh Tomato Salsa (page 174) or
   your favorite salsa
1 cup cooked or canned black beans,
   drained and rinsed

2 tablespoons minced fresh cilantro
   leaves
Salt and freshly ground black pepper
1 recipe Traditional Pizza Dough
   (page 423)

1. Preheat the oven to 450 degrees F.

2. Drain the chile, reserving a few tablespoons of the soaking liquid. Puree the chile in a blender or food processor with the liquid. Transfer to a medium-size bowl and add the salsa, beans, cilantro, and salt and pepper to taste. Stir to blend and set aside.

3. Punch the dough down. On a lightly floured work surface, roll out into a circle about 1/4 inch thick. Transfer to a lightly oiled pizza pan or baking sheet and bake on the bottom oven rack for 10 minutes.

4. Remove from the oven. Top with the salsa-bean mixture, spreading it to within 1/2 inch of the edge. Bake until the crust is golden brown, 8 to 10 minutes. Serve hot.

SERVES 4

Pizza with Sautéed Cabbage and Onion

A Polish pizza is no joke. In many eastern European countries, a yeasted flatbread is served topped with sautéed cabbage, onions, and sometimes potatoes. Pizza is truly a universal food.

2 tablespoons olive oil
1 medium-size Vidalia or other sweet
    yellow onion, chopped
3 cups cored and finely shredded
    Savoy cabbage

Salt and freshly ground black pepper
1 recipe Enriched Pizza Dough
    (page 424)

1. Preheat the oven to 450 degrees F.

2. Heat the olive oil in a large skillet over medium heat. Add the onion, cover, and cook until softened, about 5 minutes. Add the cabbage, cover, reduce the heat to medium-low heat, and cook until tender, about 5 minutes. Season with salt and pepper to taste and continue to cook until the vegetables are slightly caramelized, 5 to 7 minutes. Set aside.

3. Punch the dough down. On a lightly floured work surface, roll out into a circle about 1/4 inch thick. Transfer to a lightly oiled pizza pan or baking sheet and bake on the bottom oven rack for 8 minutes.

4. Remove from the oven and top with the cabbage mixture, spreading it to within 1/2 inch of the edge. Bake until the crust is golden brown, 10 to 12 minutes. Serve hot.

SERVES 4

Pizza Bombay

I sometimes use Indian flatbread as a delicious stand-in for pizza crust, so I decided to turn the tables and use regular pizza dough to host an Indian-spiced topping made with spinach and lentils.

1 tablespoon olive oil

1 medium-size yellow onion, chopped

1 tablespoon curry powder

1 pound fresh spinach, tough stems removed, washed well, and coarsely chopped

Salt and freshly ground black pepper

1 cup cooked brown lentils, well drained

1 recipe Traditional Pizza Dough (page 423)

1. Preheat the oven to 450 degrees F.

2. Heat the olive oil in a large skillet over medium heat. Add the onion, cover, and cook until softened, about 5 minutes. Add the curry powder, stirring to coat the onion. Add the spinach and salt and pepper to taste. Cook until the spinach is wilted and just tender, 2 to 4 minutes. Stir in the lentils, then taste and adjust the seasonings. Set aside.

3. Punch the dough down. On a lightly floured work surface, roll out into a circle about 1/4 inch thick. Transfer to a lightly oiled pizza pan or baking sheet and bake on the bottom oven rack for 8 minutes.

4. Remove from the oven and top with the spinach-lentil mixture, spreading it to within 1/2 inch of the edge. Bake until the crust is golden brown, 10 to 12 minutes. Serve hot.

SERVES 4

Did You Know...

If you add salt to the water when washing vegetables, it will help remove any insects, sand, and other particles?

Cheesy Chili-Topped Pizza

Two of America's favorite foods combine for a hearty pizza with loads of flavor. Additional toppings may include chopped jalapeños, salsa, sliced olives, or chopped onion.

1 recipe Traditional Pizza Dough
    (page 423)
2 cups vegetarian chili, homemade
    (pages 314–326) or store-bought

1 cup shredded vegan mozzarella or
    cheddar cheese
Additional toppings (see headnote;
    optional)

1. Preheat the oven to 450 degrees F.

2. Punch the dough down. On a lightly floured work surface, roll out into a circle about $1/4$ inch thick. Transfer to a lightly oiled pizza pan or baking sheet and bake on the bottom oven rack for 10 minutes.

3. Remove from the oven and top with the chili, spreading it to within $1/2$ inch of the edge. Sprinkle on the vegan cheese and additional toppings (if using). Bake until the crust is golden brown, 8 to 10 minutes. Serve hot.

SERVES 4

Freeform Caramelized Onion Tart

This French pizza, known as a *pissaladière*, is a savory specialty from Nice. Traditionally, the topping is caramelized onions, niçoise olives, and anchovies. For this version, we "hold the anchovies."

1/4 cup extra virgin olive oil
2 large Vidalia or other sweet yellow
   onions, thinly sliced
Salt and freshly ground black pepper

1 recipe Enriched Pizza Dough
   (page 424)
1/2 cup pitted and halved niçoise olives

1. Heat 2 tablespoons of the olive oil in a large skillet over medium-low heat. Add the onions, cover, and cook until softened, about 5 minutes. Season with salt and pepper to taste, reduce heat to low, and continue to cook, stirring a few times, until the onions are very soft, golden brown, and caramelized, 30 to 40 minutes. Remove from the heat and allow to cool.

2. Punch the dough down. On a lightly floured work surface, roll out into a rectangular shape about 1/4 inch thick. Transfer to a lightly oiled baking sheet, cover with a cloth, and let rise in a warm place for 30 minutes. Meanwhile, preheat the oven to 400 degrees F.

3. Drizzle the dough with the remaining 2 tablespoons olive oil. Spread the onions on top and dot with the olives. Bake on the bottom oven rack until the crust is golden brown, 30 to 35 minutes. Let cool slightly, cut into squares, and serve warm or at room temperature.

SERVES 4

Focaccia with Black Olives and Rosemary

Focaccia, a chewy Italian flatbread, is similar to pizza. But whereas pizza is usually oozing with toppings and eaten as a meal, focaccia is usually eaten with a meal or as a snack. Focaccia toppings tend to be spare, often just a sprinkling of herbs or chopped onion. In this version, I like the way the vibrant and contrasting flavors of the sweet onion, piquant olives, and fragrant rosemary complement one another.

3 tablespoons olive oil
1 small Vidalia or other sweet yellow onion, chopped
2 garlic cloves, minced
2 teaspoons chopped fresh rosemary leaves

1/2 cup pitted black olives, chopped or sliced
Salt and freshly ground black pepper
1 recipe Traditional Pizza Dough (page 423)

1. Preheat the oven to 400 degrees F.
2. Heat 2 tablespoons of the olive oil in a large skillet over medium heat. Add the onion and garlic, cover, and cook until softened, about 5 minutes. Stir in the rosemary. Remove from the heat, add the olives, and season with salt and pepper to taste. Set aside.
3. Punch the dough down. On a lightly floured work surface, roll out into a 12-inch circle or press into a 9 x 13-inch rectangle. Drizzle with the remaining 1 tablespoon olive oil, transfer to a lightly oiled pizza pan or baking sheet, and press the olive mixture into the top. Bake on the bottom oven rack until the crust is golden brown, 25 to 30 minutes. Serve warm or at room temperature.

SERVES 4

Portobello and Shallot Focaccia

Thin slices of portobello mushrooms and shallots are baked right into the top of this crusty flatbread.

2 large portobello mushrooms, stems
    removed and caps thinly sliced
2 shallots, halved lengthwise and
    thinly sliced
3 tablespoons olive oil

1/2 teaspoon dried marjoram
Salt and freshly ground black pepper
1 recipe Traditional Pizza Dough
    (page 423)

1. Preheat the oven to 400 degrees F.
2. Place the mushrooms and shallots in a medium-size bowl. Add the olive oil, marjoram, and salt and pepper to taste. Toss to coat well and set aside.
3. Punch the dough down. On a lightly floured work surface, roll out into a 12-inch circle or press into a 9 x 13-inch rectangle. Transfer to a lightly oiled pizza pan or baking sheet and press the mushroom mixture into the top, keeping the mushroom slices in a single layer. Bake on the bottom oven rack until the crust is golden brown, 25 to 30 minutes. Serve warm or at room temperature.

SERVES 4

Thai Pesto Focaccia

Sometimes when I'm eating hot Thai food, I wish for some crusty bread to help put out the fire. With this focaccia, I can enjoy the best of both worlds. Thai basil has a distinctive aromatic taste and fragrance that adds a special flavor to Thai cuisine. If it is unavailable, you can use regular basil, mint, or cilantro. Although the focaccia won't taste the same, it will still be tasty.

2 cups loosely packed fresh Thai basil
    leaves
2 garlic cloves, peeled
1/3 cup unsalted dry-roasted peanuts
1 or 2 small, fresh hot red chiles,
    to your taste, seeded

1/2 teaspoon salt
1/3 cup peanut oil
1 recipe Enriched Pizza Dough
    (page 424)

1. Preheat the oven to 400 degrees F.
2. In a food processor, combine the basil, garlic, peanuts, chile, and salt. Process until the mixture forms a paste. With the machine running, add the peanut oil through the feed tube and process until well blended. Set aside.
3. Punch the dough down. On a lightly floured work surface, roll out into a 12-inch circle or press into a 9 x 13-inch rectangle. Transfer to a lightly oiled pizza pan or baking sheet. Top with the pesto, pressing it lightly into the dough. Bake on the bottom oven rack until the crust is golden brown, 25 to 30 minutes. Serve warm or at room temperature.

SERVES 4

Spinach and Tofu Calzones

Calzones are made by folding pizza dough over a savory filling to create large turnovers, which are then sealed and baked. What you stuff inside a calzone is limited only by your imagination. Basically, whatever you would put on top of a pizza, you can put inside a calzone.

1 cup cooked chopped spinach,
   squeezed dry
4 ounces soft silken tofu, drained
Salt and freshly ground black pepper
1 tablespoon olive oil
2 garlic cloves, minced
One 16-ounce package extra-firm tofu,
   drained and crumbled

1 tablespoon minced fresh basil leaves
   or $1^{1}/_{2}$ teaspoons dried
1 teaspoon minced fresh oregano
   leaves or $^{1}/_{2}$ teaspoon dried
1 recipe Traditional Pizza Dough
   (page 423)

1. Preheat the oven to 375 degrees F.

2. In a blender or food processor, combine the spinach, silken tofu, and salt and pepper to taste. Blend until smooth and set aside.

3. Heat the olive oil in a medium-size skillet over medium heat. Add the garlic and cook until fragrant, about 30 seconds. Add the firm tofu, basil, oregano, and salt and pepper to taste. Cook, stirring, until any liquid evaporates, about 5 minutes. Remove from the heat and stir in the spinach mixture. Taste and adjust the seasonings, then set aside to cool.

4. Punch the dough down and divide it in half. On a lightly floured work surface, roll out each piece into a $^{1}/_{4}$-inch-thick circle. Divide the filling equally between the dough circles, leaving a 1-inch border around the edge. Fold the empty half of the dough over the filling and press down along the edge with your fingers, then seal with a fork.

5. Place on a lightly oiled pizza pan or baking sheet. Bake until the crust is golden brown, about 30 minutes. Let stand at room temperature for 10 minutes before serving.

SERVES 4

Spicy Soy Stromboli

If a calzone is a pizza turnover, a stromboli is a pizza roll. It's hard to imagine anyone wanting to improve on pizza, but this is one alternative to the familiar flat wedges.

2 tablespoons olive oil, plus more
    for brushing
1 large yellow onion, sliced
1 small red bell pepper, seeded
    and sliced
2 garlic cloves, minced
8 ounces white mushrooms, sliced
One 16-ounce package extra-firm tofu,
    drained and crumbled
One 14.5-ounce can diced tomatoes,
    drained

1 tablespoon minced fresh basil leaves
    or 1 1/2 teaspoons dried
1 teaspoon minced fresh oregano
    leaves or 1/2 teaspoon dried
1/2 teaspoon red pepper flakes
Salt and freshly ground black pepper
1 recipe Traditional Pizza Dough
    (page 423)

1. Place a baking sheet in the oven and preheat the oven to 400 degrees F.

2. Heat the olive oil in a large skillet over medium heat. Add the onion, cover, and cook until softened, about 5 minutes. Add the bell pepper and garlic, cover, and cook until softened, about 5 minutes. Stir in the mushrooms and cook, stirring a few times, until they release their liquid, about 3 minutes. Stir in the tofu, tomatoes, basil, oregano, red pepper flakes, and salt and pepper to taste. Cook until the liquid is evaporated, about 10 minutes. Remove from the heat and set aside to cool.

3. Punch the dough down. On a lightly floured work surface, roll out into a 9 x 13-inch rectangle. Top with the filling, spreading it to within 1 inch of the edges. Beginning on a long side, roll the stromboli into a log. Seal the dough by pinching it together along the ends and seam. Brush with olive oil.

4. Carefully place seam side down on the preheated baking sheet. Bake until the crust is golden brown, 30 to 40 minutes. Let stand at room temperature for 10 minutes before cutting crosswise into slices.

SERVES 4

16

Sandwiches, Wraps, & Burgers

Sandwiches have long been the mainstay of the American lunch, and with good reason. They are easy to make, portable, and tasty. But when they are made with animal products, they can also be loaded with fat and high in calories. Fortunately, many of our favorite sandwiches can be made with healthful vegan ingredients, so there's no need to deprive ourselves of that grilled Reuben, spicy po'boy, or juicy burger. We can enjoy these favorites and more when we start with ingredients such as tofu, tempeh, beans, and portobello mushrooms. In addition, natural food stores and many supermarkets now carry an assortment of meat-free burgers, hot dogs, and cold cuts. Just read the labels carefully to be sure they are vegan. In addition, some brands taste better than others, so experiment to find ones you like.

In my house, we have some favorites that are just as satisfying as the original. We especially like BLTs overflowing with tempeh bacon, crisp lettuce, and juicy tomatoes and slathered with soy mayonnaise.

Sandwiches are about more than the filling. The bread itself can be just as important as what is inside, and choices abound, from rustic artisan loaves to slender baguettes. Look to a variety of cultures for creative sandwich breads, including boules, tortillas, and pita breads. Add your favorite filling and garnish with the appropriate condiments—and lunch is served.

Pan Bagna

Pan bagna, or "bathed bread," is a layered vegetable sandwich that is popular picnic fare, since it must be prepared in advance and weighted down in order for the bread to soak up the flavors of the other ingredients. Crusty Italian bread is a must, and large round loaves are typically used. Slices of grilled portobello mushrooms, zucchini, or other vegetables can be added, if you like. The cannellini beans are added for substance, although a few thin slices of firm tofu work just as well—layered with the vegetables, the tofu will soak up all the surrounding flavors.

3/4 cup cooked or canned cannellini or other white beans, drained and rinsed

1/4 cup vegan pesto, homemade (page 157) or store-bought

1 loaf crusty Italian bread (round, if possible, about 9 inches in diameter)

2 large roasted red bell peppers (page 143), cut into strips

6 marinated artichoke hearts, sliced

1 large, ripe tomato, sliced

1/3 cup pitted and chopped black or green olives

1/4 cup balsamic vinaigrette, homemade (page 163) or store-bought

Salt and freshly ground black pepper

1. In a food processor, process the beans and vegan pesto together until smooth.
2. Using a serrated knife, cut the bread in half horizontally. Remove some of the inside of the loaf to make room for the filling.
3. Spread the pesto-bean mixture inside the bottom half of the loaf and top with layers of the roasted peppers, artichoke hearts, tomato, and olives. Drizzle with the vinaigrette and season with salt and pepper to taste.
4. Replace the top half of the loaf and wrap tightly in plastic. Place on a platter and top with a plate weighted down with some large canned goods or another weight. Refrigerate for at least 4 hours or up to 12 hours.
5. When ready to serve, unwrap the sandwich and cut into 4 wedges or slices.

SERVES 4

Chickpea and Avocado Muffaletta

Like Pan Bagna (page 445), the classic New Orleans muffaletta is usually made with a loaf of crusty bread. Although it traditionally contains several layers of meat and cheese, I maintain that its popularity is due primarily to the luscious olive salad that is an integral component of the filling. You can, of course, simply replace the meat and cheese with vegan cold cuts, but this version uses slices of creamy avocado and a tasty chickpea spread to complement the piquant olive mixture. A round loaf is traditional, but a long loaf or even individual sub rolls may be used instead.

1 1/2 cups cooked or one 15-ounce can chickpeas, drained and rinsed

1/2 cup chopped roasted red bell peppers (page 143)

1 cup chopped pimiento-stuffed green olives

1 cup pitted and chopped imported black olives

1/2 cup seeded and chopped banana peppers, peperoncini, or other mild pickled peppers

2 large garlic cloves, minced

2 tablespoons capers, drained

2 tablespoons chopped fresh parsley leaves

1 teaspoon dried oregano

1/4 cup olive oil

2 tablespoons white wine vinegar

Salt and freshly ground black pepper

1 loaf crusty Italian bread (round, if possible, about 9 inches in diameter)

2 small, ripe avocados, peeled, pitted, and sliced

1 large, ripe tomato, thinly sliced

1. In a food processor, process the chickpeas and roasted pepper until smooth. Set aside.

2. In a medium-size bowl, combine the olives, banana peppers, garlic, capers, parsley, oregano, olive oil, vinegar, and salt and pepper to taste. Set aside.

3. Using a serrated knife, cut the bread in half horizontally. Remove some of the inside of the loaf to make room for the filling. Spoon some of the liquid from the olive salad onto the cut sides of the bread. Spread the chickpea mixture over the bottom half. Layer the avocado and tomato on top, then spread the olive salad evenly over all. Replace the top half of the loaf. Using a serrated knife, cut the sandwich into 4 wedges and serve.

SERVES 4

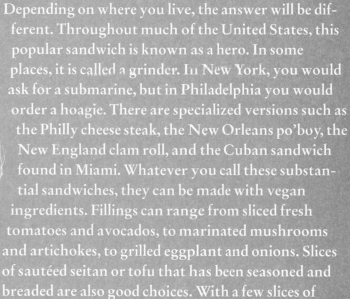

YOU SAY HERO, I SAY HOAGIE

What do you call a large sandwich made with an elongated loaf of bread sliced horizontally and stuffed with a variety of fillings? Depending on where you live, the answer will be different. Throughout much of the United States, this popular sandwich is known as a hero. In some places, it is called a grinder. In New York, you would ask for a submarine, but in Philadelphia you would order a hoagie. There are specialized versions such as the Philly cheese steak, the New Orleans po'boy, the New England clam roll, and the Cuban sandwich found in Miami. Whatever you call these substantial sandwiches, they can be made with vegan ingredients. Fillings can range from sliced fresh tomatoes and avocados, to marinated mushrooms and artichokes, to grilled eggplant and onions. Slices of sautéed seitan or tofu that has been seasoned and breaded are also good choices. With a few slices of vegan cold cuts, you can even make a classic cold cut sub complete with olive oil, oregano, and hot pepper spread.

Fried Green Tomato Po'boys

Two southern favorites—the po'boy and fried green tomatoes—team up for a tempting sandwich that may just start a new tradition in your home. Po'boys are often made with fried oysters, but succulent slices of fried green tomatoes make an engaging alternative. For added substance and flavor reminiscent of a BLT, I add a couple of strips of tempeh bacon.

3 small green tomatoes, halved lengthwise and cut into 1/2-inch-thick slices
Salt and freshly ground black pepper
3/4 cup dry bread crumbs
1/2 teaspoon Old Bay seasoning
3 tablespoons olive oil

4 strips tempeh bacon
Two 6-inch sub rolls
2 tablespoons soy mayonnaise, homemade (page 140) or store-bought
2 romaine lettuce leaves
Tabasco sauce, to your taste

1. Season the tomatoes with salt and pepper to taste. Combine the bread crumbs and Old Bay seasoning in a shallow bowl. Add the tomato slices and toss gently to coat evenly. Set aside.

2. Heat 1 tablespoon of the olive oil in a large skillet over medium heat. Add the tempeh bacon and cook until browned on both sides, about 4 minutes total. Transfer to paper towels to drain.

3. Add the remaining 2 tablespoons olive oil to the skillet and increase the heat to medium-high. Cook the tomato slices until golden brown on both sides, 5 to 6 minutes. Remove from the heat and transfer to paper towels to drain.

4. Cut the rolls horizontally and spread the cut sides with the soy mayonnaise. Line the bottom half of each roll with a lettuce leaf. Top each with 2 strips bacon. Arrange the tomatoes on top, sprinkle with Tabasco, and replace the top half of the roll. Serve with the bottle of Tabasco on the table.

SERVES 2

No-Egg Salad Sandwiches

This protein-rich sandwich filling tastes great and is quite similar to egg salad in texture and appearance—with no cholesterol. Here it is served on toasted whole-grain bread, but it's also good served on rolls or stuffed in a pita.

One 16-ounce package firm tofu, drained and crumbled
1 celery rib, minced
2 shallots, minced
1 tablespoon Dijon mustard
1 large dill pickle, minced
Pinch of turmeric

1/2 cup soy mayonnaise, homemade (page 140) or store-bought
Salt and freshly ground black pepper
8 slices whole-grain or other bread
4 lettuce leaves
1 large, ripe tomato, thinly sliced

1. Place the tofu in a large bowl. Add the celery, shallots, mustard, pickle, turmeric, 6 tablespoons of the soy mayonnaise, and salt and pepper to taste. Mix well. Cover and refrigerate for at least 1 hour to blend the flavors.

2. To assemble the sandwiches, toast the bread and place on a work surface. Spread a small amount of the remaining 2 tablespoons soy mayonnaise on one side of the toast. Top each of 4 slices of toast with a lettuce leaf and one or two tomato slices. Spoon a portion of the salad mixture onto each sandwich. Top the sandwiches with the remaining slices of toast, cut in half, and serve.

SERVES 4

Curried ChickenLess Salad Sandwiches

If you like the flavor of curry in a salad sandwich, look no further. This tasty blend of tempeh seasoned with a curry mayonnaise dressing features the sweetness of golden raisins and the crunch of slivered almonds. I usually serve this salad stuffed in pita pockets, but you can use the bread or roll of your choice.

One 12-ounce package tempeh, poached (page 14) and cooled
1 celery rib, minced
2 scallions, minced
2 tablespoons seeded and minced red bell pepper
1/4 cup golden raisins
2 tablespoons slivered almonds
1 tablespoon minced fresh parsley leaves

3/4 cup soy mayonnaise, homemade (page 140) or store-bought
1 tablespoon sweet pickle relish
2 teaspoons curry powder
1 teaspoon fresh lemon juice
1/2 teaspoon sugar or natural sweetener
Salt and freshly ground black pepper
Shredded romaine lettuce
2 large or 4 small white or whole wheat pita breads, cut in half

1. Grate or finely chop the tempeh and place in a large bowl. Add the celery, scallions, bell pepper, raisins, almonds, and parsley. Stir in the soy mayonnaise, relish, curry powder, lemon juice, sugar, and salt and pepper to taste. Mix until thoroughly combined. Cover and refrigerate for at least 30 minutes to allow the flavors to blend.

2. To assemble, stuff a small amount of shredded lettuce into each pita half. Spoon the tempeh mixture into each half, dividing it evenly among the halves. Tuck a little more lettuce into each sandwich, if desired, and serve.

SERVES 4

Tuna-Free Sandwich Filling

I'm always tinkering with ways to make a delicious tuna-free sandwich. This is my current favorite, which features a hearty blend of chickpeas with just a bit of kelp powder for a taste of the sea. Serve on your choice of bread, including rolls or pita pockets. Kelp powder is available at natural food stores.

1¹/₂ cups cooked or one 15-ounce can chickpeas, drained and rinsed
¹/₂ cup blanched almonds
1 tablespoon fresh lemon juice
1 teaspoon kelp powder
¹/₃ cup minced celery

1 scallion, minced
¹/₄ cup soy mayonnaise, homemade (page 140) or store-bought, or more as needed
1¹/₂ teaspoons Dijon mustard
Salt and freshly ground black pepper

1. In a food processor, pulse the chickpeas and almonds until coarsely chopped. Add the lemon juice and kelp powder. Blend until well combined. Transfer to a large bowl and add the celery, scallion, soy mayonnaise, mustard, and salt and pepper to taste. Mix well, adding a little more mayonnaise if the mixture seems dry.
2. Cover and refrigerate for at least 30 minutes before serving.

MAKES ABOUT 2 CUPS

Seitan Reuben

Thinly sliced seitan replaces the corned beef in this vegan version of the Reuben sandwich. Serve with vegan cole slaw, potato chips, and a dill pickle for a great deli-style lunch.

2 tablespoons soy mayonnaise, homemade (page 140) or store-bought
1 tablespoon ketchup
1 tablespoon sweet pickle relish
Salt and freshly ground black pepper

2 tablespoons olive oil
4 slices rye bread
6 ounces seitan, thinly sliced
1/4 cup sauerkraut, drained
4 ounces vegan cheese, thinly sliced

1. In a small bowl, combine the soy mayonnaise, ketchup, and relish. Season with salt and pepper to taste, blend well, and set aside.

2. Brush a small amount of the olive oil on one side of each slice of bread. Place the bread oiled side down on a flat surface and spread the mayonnaise mixture on the other side of each slice.

3. Layer the seitan, sauerkraut, and vegan cheese on 2 of the bread slices and top with the remaining 2 bread slices, oiled side up.

4. Heat the remaining olive oil in a large skillet over medium heat. Place the sandwiches in the skillet and cook, turning once, until golden brown on both sides, about 2 minutes per side. Remove from the skillet, cut in half, and serve hot.

SERVES 2

Tacos in No Time

There are many ways to make great vegan tacos, and one of the quickest is with vegetarian burger crumbles. If they are unavailable, substitute a package of veggie burgers (just thaw and chop or crumble). Grated tempeh or frozen, thawed, and crumbled firm tofu are good choices as well. Use crisp taco shells or soft tortillas, according to personal preference, and remember to read the labels carefully to be sure the products do not contain lard.

1 tablespoon olive oil
1/4 cup minced onion
1 garlic clove, minced
1 tablespoon chili powder
1/2 teaspoon ground cumin
1/2 cup Fresh Tomato Salsa (page 174) or your favorite salsa
3 cups vegetarian burger crumbles
Salt and freshly ground black pepper
8 taco shells or large flour tortillas

Toppings:
Shredded romaine lettuce
Chopped ripe tomatoes
Fresh Tomato Salsa (page 174) or your favorite salsa
Shredded vegan cheddar cheese
Vegan sour cream, homemade (page 139) or store-bought
Chopped red onion or scallions
Seeded and chopped fresh or canned jalapeños
Pitted and sliced black olives
Chopped avocado

1. Heat the olive oil in a large skillet over medium heat. Add the onion and garlic, cover, and cook until softened, about 5 minutes. Stir in the chili powder, cumin, salsa, burger crumbles, salt and pepper to taste. Simmer, stirring occasionally, until hot, 5 to 7 minutes. Reduce the heat to low and keep warm.
2. Preheat the oven to 375 degrees F. Wrap the taco shells or tortillas in aluminum foil and place in the oven to warm, 2 to 4 minutes.
3. To assemble the tacos, spoon about 1/4 cup of the taco filling into each taco shell or tortilla. Top as desired with any combination of lettuce, tomatoes, salsa, vegan cheese, vegan sour cream, onion, jalapeños, olives, and avocado and serve.

SERVES 4

Three-Bean Burritos

Using three kinds of beans gives these burritos a more complex flavor and texture than if you used only one type. The filling is also quite good for tacos or similar dishes. The recipe can be easily stretched by adding more beans. You can also add a cup of cooked corn kernels to give it a deliciously sweet accent.

One 15-ounce can refried pinto beans
1 cup cooked or canned black beans,
    drained and rinsed
1 cup cooked or canned dark red kidney
    beans, drained and rinsed
1/2 cup Fresh Tomato Salsa (page 174)
    or your favorite salsa

1 teaspoon chili powder
Salt and freshly ground black pepper
4 large flour tortillas, warmed
1/2 cup shredded vegan cheese
Minced red onion (optional)

1. In a large saucepan over medium heat, combine the refried beans, black beans, and kidney beans. Stir in the salsa, chili powder, and salt and pepper to taste. Cook, stirring, until the beans are hot, 7 to 10 minutes. Reduce the heat to low and keep warm.
2. Place the warmed tortillas on a flat work surface and spread a large spoonful of the bean mixture across the lower third of each tortilla. Sprinkle with the vegan

---

"Wrap" Stars

The popularity of Mexican food has brought tacos, burritos, fajitas, and many other "wrap" stars into our home kitchens. Virtually every cuisine has its own wrap foods, some of which are served sauced and eaten with a knife and fork, such as the French crepe, while others are eaten out of hand and served with a dipping sauce, like Asian spring rolls. There is also the popular Japanese sushi wrap, a rice and seaweed roll known as a *maki*. Wrap sandwiches can be made with tortillas, lavash, pita pockets, or other flatbreads and a wide variety of fillings, including grilled or marinated vegetables. Many different versions of a veggie wrap can be found on the menus of cafés and restaurants and even in bakeries and fast-food shops.

cheese and onion (if using). Fold up the burrito, first by bringing the bottom end over the filling, folding in the sides and then rolling it up. Serve at once, seam side down.

SERVES 4

Portobello Fajitas

F lavorful and juicy strips of portobello mushrooms are used to make these delicious fajitas.

2 tablespoons olive oil	1 teaspoon chili powder
1 large red onion, thinly sliced	1/2 teaspoon salt
1 large red bell pepper, seeded and	1/4 teaspoon cayenne (optional)
thinly sliced	4 large flour tortillas, warmed
4 large portobello mushrooms, stems	Fresh Tomato Salsa (page 174) or your
removed and caps cut into strips	favorite salsa, to your taste

1. Heat the olive oil in a large skillet over medium-high heat. Add the onion and bell pepper, cover, and cook until softened, about 5 minutes. Add the mushrooms and cook, stirring a few times, until tender, 1 to 3 minutes. Add the chili powder, salt, and cayenne (if using) and cook, stirring to coat the vegetables with the spices, for 3 to 5 minutes. Reduce the heat to low and keep warm.

2. Place the tortillas on a flat work surface and spread a large spoonful of the mushroom mixture across the lower third of each tortilla. Top each portion of filling with salsa. Roll up the fajitas to enclose the filling and serve at once.

SERVES 4

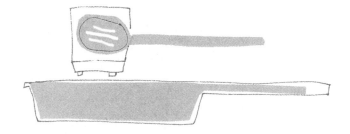

Soy Meets Grill Tortilla Wraps with Green Apple Salsa

Fruity, spicy, and oh soy good! Spice-rubbed slabs of grilled tempeh and bell pepper are cut into strips and wrapped inside a soft flour tortilla along with a generous helping of Green Apple Salsa.

1 teaspoon ground allspice

1 teaspoon sweet paprika

1 teaspoon light brown sugar or natural sweetener

3/4 teaspoon salt

1/4 teaspoon freshly grated nutmeg

1/4 teaspoon cayenne

One 12-ounce package tempeh, poached (page 14) and cut into 4 slabs

Olive oil

1 large red bell pepper, halved and seeded

4 large flour tortillas, warmed

1 cup Green Apple Salsa (page 173)

1. Preheat the grill. In a small bowl, combine the allspice, paprika, brown sugar, salt, nutmeg, and cayenne.

2. Coat the tempeh with olive oil and rub with the spice mixture. Place on the hot grill. Lightly oil the bell pepper halves and place cut side up on the grill. Grill until the tempeh is well browned on both sides and the bell peppers are blackened and tender, turning once, about 10 minutes total. When the peppers are cool enough to handle, scrape the black bits from the skin. Then cut the peppers and tempeh into thin strips.

3. Place the tortillas on a flat work surface and divide the tempeh and pepper strips among them, placing the strips across the lower third of each tortilla. Spoon some of the salsa alongside the strips, roll up, and serve at once.

SERVES 4

Grilled Vegetable Wraps

Grilled vegetables are great just about any way they are served, and wrap sandwiches are no exception. Lavash, a thin Middle Eastern flatbread, is best for these sandwiches, but large tortillas may be used as well. Lavash can be found in ethnic markets or bakeries, while tortillas are widely available in supermarkets. The flatbread should be at room temperature for easier rolling. Instead of the soy mayonnaise, you can use hummus or another bean spread for added flavor and nutrition, if you like.

A grill basket or perforated metal grill pan will help keep the zucchini and other smaller pieces of vegetables from falling through the rack. If unavailable, you can skewer the vegetables before grilling.

1 medium-size red onion, cut into
 $1/4$-inch-thick slices
1 large red bell pepper, halved and
 seeded
1 large portobello mushroom, stem
 removed
1 medium-size zucchini, cut into
 diagonal $1/4$-inch-thick slices

2 tablespoons olive oil
Salt and freshly ground black pepper
2 large lavash or flour tortillas
2 tablespoons soy mayonnaise,
 homemade (page 140) or
 store-bought

1. Preheat the grill. Brush the onion, pepper, mushroom, and zucchini with the olive oil and season with salt and pepper to taste. Grill the vegetables until tender on the inside and slightly charred on the outside, turning once. Cut the grilled vegetables into $1/2$-inch-wide strips.
2. Place the lavash on a flat surface. Spread a thin layer of soy mayonnaise over the surface and place the vegetable strips along the lower third of each flatbread. Beginning at the end with the filling, roll up into a cylinder. Cut each sandwich in half and serve seam side down.

SERVES 2 TO 4

Indian-Spiced Lentil Patties with Three-Fruit Chutney

Inspired by the flavors of India, these sandwiches are best made with roti or other Indian flatbread as the wrapper. If unavailable, use pita bread. A leftover baked potato is ideal for this recipe. Otherwise, peel, chop, and sauté or bake a medium-size potato until tender. (Cooking in water will add too much moisture to the recipe.)

3 tablespoons olive oil

1/2 cup minced onion

1 cup cooked brown lentils, well drained

1 cup chopped cooked potato (see headnote)

1/2 cup finely chopped unsalted dry-roasted cashews

2/3 cup dry bread crumbs

1 tablespoon minced fresh parsley leaves

1 teaspoon curry powder, or more to taste

1/2 teaspoon salt

1/8 teaspoon cayenne (optional)

4 roti or other Indian flatbread, warmed

Three-Fruit Chutney (page 168) or other chutney, to your taste

1. Heat 1 tablespoon of the olive oil in a large skillet over medium heat. Add the onion, cover, and cook until softened, about 5 minutes. Transfer to a food processor and add the lentils, potato, cashews, bread crumbs, parsley, curry powder, salt, and cayenne (if using). Process until well blended.

2. Shape the mixture into 8 small patties. Heat the remaining 2 tablespoons olive oil in a large skillet over medium heat. Add the patties and cook until browned on both sides, about 5 minutes per side.

3. Place 2 patties end to end on the lower third of each flatbread, spread with chutney, roll up, and serve hot.

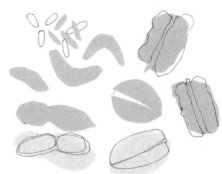

SERVES 4

Thai Peanut-Burger Wraps

This is a great way to enjoy fusion food: combine fragrant Thai ingredients to make an all-American burger, then surround it with a Middle Eastern or Mexican flatbread. The addition of Spicy Peanut Dipping Sauce may seem a bit over the top for these already peanutty burgers, but the result is delicious. If you're using large flatbreads, allow one-half sandwich per person. Otherwise, allow one sandwich per person.

1/2 cup chopped red onion
1/2 cup seeded and chopped green
    bell pepper
2 garlic cloves, minced
2 teaspoons peeled and minced
    fresh ginger
1/2 cup ground unsalted dry-roasted
    peanuts
8 ounces extra-firm tofu, drained
    and mashed
3 tablespoons smooth natural
    peanut butter

2 tablespoons chopped fresh Thai basil
    or cilantro leaves
2 tablespoons tamari or dark soy sauce
1/2 teaspoon Asian chili paste
Salt
1/2 cup dry bread crumbs
2 large or 4 small lavash, soft flour
    tortillas, or pita breads
Shredded romaine lettuce
1/2 cup Spicy Peanut Dipping Sauce
    (page 160)

1. Preheat the oven to 350 degrees F.

2. In a food processor, combine the onion, bell pepper, garlic, ginger, and peanuts. Pulse to blend, leaving some texture. Add the tofu, peanut butter, Thai basil, tamari, chili paste, and salt to taste and pulse until the mixture is well combined.

3. Shape the mixture into 4 large or 8 small patties and coat evenly with the bread crumbs. Arrange the burgers on a lightly oiled baking sheet and bake, turning once, until browned on both sides, 25 to 30 minutes total.

4. To assemble, cut the burgers into halves or thirds, if necessary, so that they roll up easily. Place them end to end on the lower third of the flatbreads. Top with the lettuce, drizzle with the peanut sauce, and roll up. Cut in half crosswise if using large breads and place seam side down on 4 individual plates. Serve immediately.

SERVES 4

Great Grain and Vegetable Burgers

Two grains and five vegetables add up to healthful veggie burgers that are loaded with flavor. Wheat gluten flour, also called vital wheat gluten or powdered wheat gluten, helps hold the burgers together. It is available in natural food stores. Serve these burgers on rolls, tucked into pitas, or on a plate topped with your favorite sauce.

1 cup cooked brown rice

1/2 cup cooked bulgur (220)

1 cup grated zucchini

1/4 cup grated onion

1/4 cup finely grated carrot

1 garlic clove, minced

1/2 cup wheat gluten flour (vital wheat gluten)

1/4 cup chopped roasted red bell pepper (page 143)

2 tablespoons minced fresh parsley leaves

Salt and freshly ground black pepper

2 tablespoons olive oil

1. Place the rice, bulgur, zucchini, onion, carrot, and garlic in a food processor and pulse to combine. Add the wheat gluten flour, roasted pepper, parsley, and salt and pepper to taste and process until well combined. Shape the mixture into four patties.
2. Heat the olive oil in a large skillet over medium-high heat. Cook the patties until golden brown on both sides, 5 to 8 minutes total. Or place the patties on an oiled baking sheet and bake at 350 degrees F until browned on both sides, turning once, 20 to 30 minutes total. Serve hot.

SERVES 4

Three-Nut Burgers

The rich flavors of lentils, walnuts, and cashews combine to make these hearty veggie burgers, which are bound with creamy almond butter. In addition to serving them on burger rolls, you can serve them as an entrée topped with Basic Brown Sauce (page 148). Instead of cooking the burgers on top of the stove, you may bake them in a preheated 350 degree F oven for 20 to 30 minutes.

3 tablespoons olive oil

1/2 cup minced onion

1 cup cooked brown lentils, well drained

1 cup chopped walnuts

1/2 cup chopped unsalted dry-roasted cashews

2 tablespoons almond butter

2/3 cup dry bread crumbs

1 tablespoon minced fresh parsley leaves

1/2 teaspoon salt

1/8 teaspoon freshly ground black pepper

1. Heat 1 tablespoon of the olive oil in a large skillet over medium heat. Add the onion, cover, and cook until softened, about 5 minutes. Transfer to a food processor and add the remaining ingredients except the remaining olive oil. Process until well blended.
2. Shape the mixture into 6 patties. Heat the remaining 2 tablespoons olive oil in a large skillet over medium heat and cook the burgers until well browned on both sides, about 5 minutes per side. Serve hot.

SERVES 6

Go Nuts!

Nuts add protein and "good" fat to your diet. Here are some great ways to "go nuts."

- Sprinkle chopped nuts on your cereal at breakfast.
- Spread nut butter on toast or use in sandwiches.
- Enjoy nuts and raisins as a snack at work, at school, or on the road.
- Add nuts to salads, stir-fries, and grain and vegetable dishes.
- Include nuts in muffins, tea breads, and desserts.
- Slather nut butter on celery sticks, apple slices, or bananas.

The Ultimate Veggie Burgers

Most homemade veggie burgers lack the firm texture found in some of the store-bought varieties. Flaxseeds and wheat gluten are used here to remedy that situation, resulting in protein-packed burgers. Wheat gluten flour is available at natural food stores, often sold as vital wheat gluten. I like to serve these on toasted burger rolls with lettuce, sliced tomato, and lots of ketchup.

1 tablespoon ground flaxseeds

2 tablespoons tamari or other soy sauce

1/2 cup walnut pieces

3/4 cup cooked brown lentils, well drained

1/4 cup grated onion

1 tablespoon minced fresh parsley leaves

1/3 cup wheat gluten flour (vital wheat gluten)

1/2 teaspoon browning sauce (see note)

Salt and freshly ground black pepper

2 tablespoons olive oil

1. In a blender, combine the flaxseeds and tamari, blending until viscous. Set aside.

2. In a food processor, pulse the walnuts to coarsely chop. Add the lentils, onion, parsley, wheat gluten flour, browning sauce, flax mixture, and salt and pepper to taste. Process until well combined but with some texture remaining. Shape the mixture into 4 patties and place on a platter. Refrigerate for 30 minutes.

3. Heat the olive oil in a large skillet over medium heat, add the patties, and cook until browned on both sides, about 4 minutes per side. Serve hot.

SERVES 4

Note: Carefully read the label before buying a browning sauce (located with the gravies and sauces in the supermarket) to be sure it does not contain meat extract. One popular brand, Gravy Master, states "contains no meat" on its label, and the ingredients are clearly identifiable.

Stuffed Mushroom Burgers

For anyone who ever enjoyed sautéed mushrooms on a burger, this is the ultimate combination—a sautéed portobello mushroom cap "stuffed" with a veggie burger. Serve on toasted rolls with ketchup and onions, if you like. Purchase flavorful veggie burgers, such as Original Vegan Boca Burgers, or use one of the burger recipes in this chapter. The mushrooms and burgers also may be cooked on a grill.

4 large portobello mushrooms,
    stems removed
2 tablespoons olive oil
Salt and freshly ground black pepper

4 veggie burgers, homemade
    (pages 460–462) or store-bought
4 burger rolls, lightly toasted

1. Using a small spoon or knife, remove the dark gills from the underside of the mushroom caps.

2. Heat 1 tablespoon of the olive oil in a large skillet over medium heat. Add the mushrooms and cook until they begin to soften, about 5 minutes. Turn over, season with salt and pepper to taste, and cook until browned and tender, about 5 minutes more. Keep warm over very low heat.

3. While the mushrooms are cooking, heat the remaining 1 tablespoon olive oil in another large skillet over medium heat. Add the burgers and cook, turning once, until browned on both sides and hot inside, 8 to 10 minutes total.

4. To serve, place a burger inside each mushroom cap and place on the rolls. Serve hot.

SERVES 4

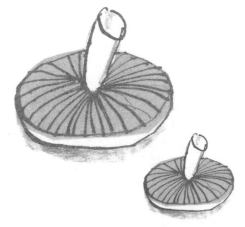

17

A Baker's Dozen of Breads

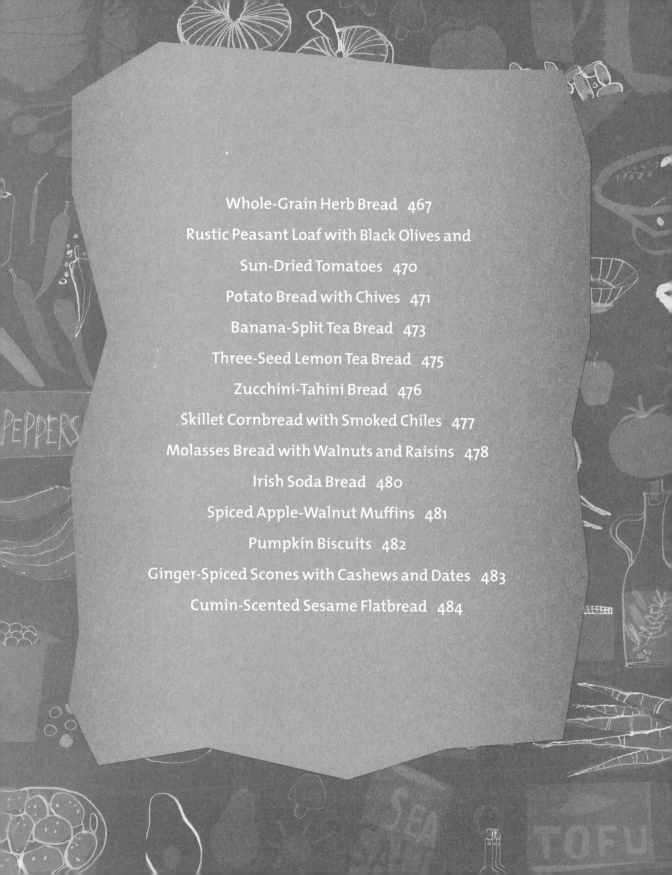

Over the centuries to the present time, people throughout the world have relied on traditional breads for basic sustenance, baking them with their same time-tested methods, be it on an open fire or in a clay oven. These days in American supermarkets, you can find rustic, freshly baked artisan breads as a pricey luxury item.

Although a loaf of bakery bread can taste great, nothing beats the aroma, flavor, and satisfaction of home-baked bread. In addition, there are no additives in home-made bread—just natural ingredients and lots of love. Being in control of the ingredients is especially important to vegans, since many commercial breads may contain eggs, dairy products, or honey.

Although hand-kneading can be relaxing, machines are often used to speed up the process, whether it be an electric mixer equipped with a dough hook or an electric bread machine that does all the work from kneading to baking. As for me, I prefer to work the dough with my hands the old-fashioned way.

At its most basic, this "staff of life" is little more than a blending of flour and water that has been put to heat. But variety abounds within the two main divisions—yeast breads and quick breads. Loaves can be sweet or savory and include flatbreads, skillet breads, muffins, and biscuits. Among the most nutritious breads are hearty multigrain loaves, some of which include whole or cracked grains, nuts, and seeds. This chapter consists of a baker's dozen of samplings from the wide range of the world's breads.

Whole-Grain Herb Bread

This wholesome bread is delicious served with meals or used in sandwiches. The herbs may be varied according to personal preference. I like the look of freeform round or long loaves, but you can use traditional loaf pans, if you prefer.

2¼ teaspoons (1 packet) active dry yeast

2¼ cups warm water

1 tablespoon pure maple syrup

2 tablespoons olive oil

1 tablespoon salt

4½ cups unbleached all-purpose flour

2 cups whole wheat flour, plus more for kneading

2 tablespoons minced fresh parsley leaves

1 teaspoon minced fresh chives

1 teaspoon dried marjoram

½ teaspoon dried thyme

1. In a large bowl, combine the yeast and ¼ cup of the water. Add the maple syrup and stir to dissolve. Let the mixture stand for 10 minutes, then stir in the remaining 2 cups water, the olive oil, and salt.
2. In a separate large bowl, combine the flours and stir until well mixed. Add about half of the flour mixture to the liquid mixture, stirring to blend, then work in the remaining flour mixture to form a stiff dough. Transfer to a lightly floured board.
3. Add the herbs and, with lightly floured hands, knead briefly to incorporate them. Dust your work surface with whole wheat flour as needed to prevent the dough from sticking and continue to knead well until smooth and elastic, 8 to 10 minutes.
4. Place in a lightly oiled large bowl and turn over once to coat with oil. Cover with a clean kitchen towel or a piece of lightly oiled plastic wrap. Let rise in a warm place until doubled in bulk, 1 to 2 hours.

5. Meanwhile, lightly oil 2 small baking sheets and set aside. Punch the dough down and turn out onto a lightly floured work surface. Divide the dough in half, shape into 2 round or long loaves, and place on the prepared baking sheets. Flatten the loaves slightly and cover with clean damp towels or lightly oiled plastic wrap. Set aside in a warm place and let rise again until doubled in bulk, about 1 hour.

6. Meanwhile, preheat the oven to 425 degrees F. Use a sharp knife to cut one to three $1/4$-inch-deep diagonal slashes in each loaf. Bake on the center oven rack for 10 minutes, then reduce the oven temperature to 350 degrees F and continue to bake until golden brown, about 30 minutes more. Tap the bottom of the loaves—if they sound hollow, the bread is done. Remove from the sheets and let cool on a wire rack before slicing.

MAKES 2 LOAVES

YEAST BREAD TYPES, TIPS, AND TECHNIQUES

Yeast breads can be made with unbleached all-purpose flour as well as whole-grain flours, such as whole wheat, to which other ingredients may be added, including other flours, vegetables, herbs, fruits, nuts, and seeds. Sourdough is a yeast bread that gets its name and distinctive flavor from a special yeast starter. Yeasted flatbreads include pita, focaccia, and pizza. Breakfast breads made with yeast include croissants, brioche, and cinnamon rolls, as well as skillet breads such as crumpets and English muffins.

- *Kneading and rising:* Yeast breads must be kneaded to activate the gluten-producing proteins in the flour. In addition, the dough needs

time to rise. To knead dough, push the dough down and away from you with the palms of your hands, then turn it, fold it over, and push it down again. Kneading should be done for several minutes to activate the proteins. Well-kneaded dough should be smooth and elastic. After kneading, cover the dough and set aside to rise in a warm place until doubled in bulk.

- *Baking:* For even baking, place the loaf in the center of the oven. The bread is done when the top is browned and the sides pull away from the pan and when a light tapping on the bottom produces a hollow sound.
- *Cooling and storing:* Bread should be removed from the pan as soon as it comes out of the oven and cooled on a wire rack. Cool the bread before slicing with a serrated knife, using a sawing motion. Cool the bread completely before storing to prevent condensation. Tightly wrapped bread will keep for several days at room temperature or for up to 3 months in the freezer (tightly wrap in plastic and aluminum foil).

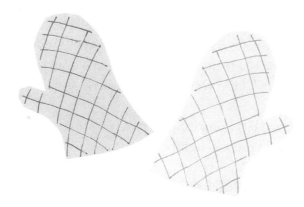

Rustic Peasant Loaf with Black Olives and Sun-Dried Tomatoes

Typical of the artisan breads popular in bakeries and gourmet markets, this rustic loaf is studded with bits of piquant olives and sun-dried tomatoes.

2¼ teaspoons (1 packet) active dry yeast

2 cups warm water

1 tablespoon sugar or natural sweetener

3 tablespoons olive oil

1 tablespoon salt

5 cups unbleached all-purpose flour, plus more for kneading

1 cup whole wheat flour

½ cup oil-packed or rehydrated sun-dried tomatoes, chopped

½ cup black olives, pitted and chopped

1. In a large bowl, combine the yeast and ¼ cup of the water. Add the sugar and stir to dissolve. Let the mixture stand for 10 minutes, then stir in the remaining 2 cups water, the olive oil, and salt.

2. In a separate large bowl, combine the flours and stir until well mixed. Add about half the flour to the liquid mixture, stirring to combine, then work in the remaining flour to form a stiff dough. Transfer to a lightly floured board.

3. Place the sun-dried tomatoes and olives on the dough and, using your hands, knead briefly to incorporate them. Continue to knead until smooth and elastic, 8 to 10 minutes. As you knead, keep your hands and work surface lightly floured so that the dough does not stick.

4. Place in a lightly oiled large bowl and turn over once to coat with oil. Cover with a clean kitchen towel or a piece of lightly oiled plastic wrap. Let rise in a warm place until doubled in bulk, 1 to 2 hours.

5. Meanwhile, lightly oil 2 small baking sheets and set aside. Punch the dough down and turn out onto a lightly floured work surface. Divide the dough in half, shape into 2 round or long loaves, and place on the prepared baking sheets. Flatten the loaves slightly and cover with clean damp towels or lightly oiled plastic wrap. Set aside in a warm place and let rise again until doubled in bulk, about 1 hour.

6. Meanwhile, preheat the oven to 375 degrees F. Use a sharp knife to cut one to three ¼-inch-deep diagonal slashes in each loaf. Bake on the center oven rack until golden brown, 40 to 45 minutes. Tap the bottom of the loaves—if they sound hollow, the bread is done. Remove from the sheets and let cool on a wire rack before slicing.

MAKES 2 LOAVES

Potato Bread with Chives

The addition of mashed potatoes gives this bread a moist, dense texture and delicate flavor that is accented by that of the chives. This bread is best eaten slightly warm from the oven on the day it is made. It is also good toasted.

2¼ teaspoons (1 packet) active dry yeast

1 cup warm water

1 teaspoon sugar or pure maple syrup

2 tablespoons corn oil

2 teaspoons salt

1 cup cold mashed potatoes

1 cup soy milk or other dairy-free milk

5 cups unbleached all-purpose flour, plus more for kneading

2 tablespoons minced fresh chives

1. In a large bowl, combine the yeast and ¼ cup of the water. Add the sugar and stir to dissolve. Let the mixture stand for 10 minutes, then stir in the remaining ¾ cup water, the corn oil, and salt. Mix in the potatoes, then stir in the soy milk. Add about half the flour, stirring to combine, then work in the remaining flour to form a stiff dough. Transfer to a lightly floured board.

2. Lightly flour your hands and work surface. Knead the dough well until it is smooth and elastic, 8 to 10 minutes, using more flour as necessary so the dough does not stick. Place in a lightly oiled large bowl and turn over once to coat with oil. Cover with a clean kitchen towel or a piece of lightly oiled plastic wrap. Let rise in a warm place until doubled in bulk, 1 to 2 hours.

3. Meanwhile, lightly oil a baking sheet and set aside. Punch the dough down and knead lightly. Turn out onto a lightly floured work surface, sprinkle with the chives, and knead until the dough is elastic and the chives are well distributed, 3 to 5 minutes. Shape the dough into 1 large or 2 small round loaves and place on the prepared baking sheet. Flatten the loaf or loaves slightly and cover with a clean damp towel or lightly oiled plastic wrap. Set aside in a warm place and let rise again until doubled in bulk, about 45 minutes.

4. Meanwhile, preheat the oven to 400 degrees F. Use a sharp knife to cut an X into the top of the loaf or loaves. Bake on the center oven rack until golden brown, 35 to 45 minutes, depending on size. Tap on the bottom of the loaf or loaves—if they sound hollow, the bread is done. Remove from the sheet and let cool somewhat on a wire rack before slicing.

MAKES 1 LARGE LOAF OR 2 SMALL LOAVES

Quick Breads

Since quick breads rise with the help of baking powder or baking soda, they require no rising or kneading time. Some varieties, called tea breads, are moist, slightly sweet loaves that are often made with pureed or grated fruits or vegetables and sometimes include nuts, seeds, and fragrant spices. Muffins resemble tea breads in flavor and texture—in fact, their recipes can be used interchangeably. The difference lies in the type of pan used and the baking time. Other quick breads include flaky and dropped biscuits, as well as many flatbreads, such as tortillas, chapatis, and parathas.

Banana-Split Tea Bread

This flavorful banana bread incorporates several banana-split ingredients for a surprising treat that sets it apart from ordinary tea breads. Vegan chocolate chips are available at natural food stores.

2½ cups unbleached all-purpose flour

2 teaspoons baking powder

½ teaspoon salt

3 medium-size, very ripe bananas,
    peeled and cut into chunks

½ cup soy milk or other dairy-free milk

¼ cup corn oil

¾ cup sugar or natural sweetener

1 teaspoon pure vanilla extract

¼ cup chopped unsalted dry-roasted
    peanuts or other nuts

¼ cup semisweet vegan chocolate chips

¼ cup drained crushed pineapple

¼ cup dried cherries

1. Preheat the oven to 375 degrees F. Lightly oil a 9 x 5-inch loaf pan and set aside.

2. In a large bowl, sift together the flour, baking powder, and salt and set aside.

3. In a food processor, combine the bananas, soy milk, corn oil, sugar, and vanilla and process until smooth. Add to the flour mixture and mix well. Fold in the peanuts, chocolate chips, pineapple, and cherries, then transfer to the prepared pan.

4. Bake on the center oven rack until a toothpick inserted in the center comes out clean, 50 to 60 minutes. Allow to cool in the pan on a wire rack before removing from the pan and slicing.

MAKES 1 LOAF

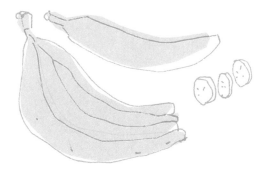

QUICK TIPS FOR QUICK BREADS

Mixing and baking: Because the leavening agents in quick breads react quickly with liquids, it is essential to mix the dry ingredients separately from the wet ingredients, combining them only at the last second. As you combine, avoid overmixing, which can toughen the bread. Quick breads should be baked in a preheated oven on the center oven rack. Test for doneness by inserting a toothpick in the center to see if it comes out clean.

Cooling and cutting: Cool quick breads in the pan before cutting. Use a serrated knife and a sawing motion to slice.

Storing: To store quick breads, cool in the pan for several minutes, then turn out onto a wire rack to cool completely before storing. (This prevents condensation.) Cooled bread that has been tightly wrapped in plastic will keep at room temperature for a day or two or in the refrigerator for several days. If stored tightly in the freezer in plastic wrap and aluminum foil, it will keep for up to 3 months.

Three-Seed Lemon Tea Bread

A fresh lemon taste is the backdrop for this protein-packed tea bread loaded with three kinds of nutritious seeds. The light, not-too-sweet flavor makes it a terrific breakfast bread.

2 tablespoons flaxseeds

1/3 cup water

1/2 cup sugar or natural sweetener

1 cup soy milk or other dairy-free milk

2 tablespoons corn oil

Juice and grated zest of 1 lemon

2 cups unbleached all-purpose flour

2 teaspoons baking powder

1 teaspoon salt

1/2 cup chopped hulled raw sunflower seeds

1/4 cup sesame seeds

1. Preheat the oven to 350 degrees F. Lightly oil a 9 x 5-inch loaf pan and set aside.

2. Grind the flaxseeds to a powder in a dry blender. Add the water and blend until thick, about 30 seconds. Set aside.

3. In a large bowl, combine the sugar, soy milk, corn oil, and lemon juice and zest. Blend in the flaxseed mixture and set aside.

4. In a medium-size bowl, sift together the flour, baking powder, and salt. Using a few swift strokes, add the dry ingredients to the wet ingredients until just combined. Fold in the sunflower seeds and sesame seeds, then transfer to the prepared pan.

5. Bake on the center oven rack until golden brown and a toothpick inserted in the center comes out clean, about 1 hour. Let cool in the pan on a wire rack before removing from the pan and slicing.

MAKES 1 LOAF

"The time will come when men such as I will look upon the murder of animals as they now look upon the murder of men."
—LEONARDO DA VINCI

Zucchini-Tahini Bread

Creamy sesame paste lends a delicious flavor to this zucchini bread, while also adding protein and calcium.

3 cups unbleached all-purpose flour
1 tablespoon baking powder
1 teaspoon ground ginger
1/2 teaspoon salt
Egg replacer for 1 egg (page 509)
3/4 cup firmly packed light brown sugar
    or natural sweetener

1/4 cup tahini (sesame paste)
1 cup soy milk or other dairy-free milk
1 1/2 cups grated zucchini, well drained
2 tablespoons sesame seeds

1. Preheat the oven to 350 degrees F. Lightly oil a 9 x 5-inch loaf pan and set aside.
2. In a large bowl, combine the flour, baking powder, ginger, and salt. Set aside.
3. In another large bowl, combine the egg replacer, brown sugar, tahini, and soy milk until well mixed. Stir in the zucchini. Combine the wet ingredients with the dry ingredients, stirring until just blended. Transfer to the prepared pan and sprinkle evenly with the sesame seeds.
4. Bake on the center oven rack until golden brown and a toothpick inserted in the center comes out clean, about 1 hour. Let cool in the pan on a wire rack before removing from the pan and slicing.

MAKES 1 LOAF

Skillet Cornbread with Smoked Chiles

This recipe can be baked in a glass or metal baking pan, but if you have a cast-iron skillet, this is a great way to use it. If canned chipotles are unavailable, use dried ones that have been soaked in very hot water to cover for 30 minutes. Alternatively, canned hot green chiles may be used to add heat, but they won't impart the same smoky flavor as the chipotles do.

1¼ cups yellow cornmeal

1 cup unbleached all-purpose flour

2½ teaspoons baking powder

1 teaspoon salt

1 cup soy milk or other dairy-free milk

3 tablespoons pure maple syrup

1 cup fresh, canned, or frozen corn kernels, cooked and drained

¼ cup corn oil

2 tablespoons finely chopped canned chipotle chiles in adobo sauce

1. Preheat the oven to 400 degrees F.

2. In a large bowl, combine the cornmeal, flour, baking powder, and salt and set aside.

3. In a medium-size bowl, combine the soy milk, maple syrup, corn kernels, corn oil, and chiles and set aside.

4. Heat a well-oiled cast-iron skillet over medium heat until hot. While the skillet is heating, add the wet ingredients to the dry ingredients and mix well with a few quick strokes. Transfer the batter to the hot skillet and bake on the center oven rack until golden brown and a toothpick inserted in the center comes out clean, 25 to 30 minutes. Serve hot or warm.

MAKES 1 LOAF

Flour Storage

Keep whole-grain flours tightly covered and stored in the refrigerator or freezer to prevent them from getting rancid.

Molasses Bread with Walnuts and Raisins

This soft, luscious bread made with nutrient-rich walnuts, molasses, and raisins tastes great on its own or served with baked beans or a hearty stew.

1¼ cups soy milk or other dairy-free milk

1½ tablespoons white vinegar

2 cups unbleached all-purpose flour

1 cup yellow cornmeal

1 teaspoon salt

1 teaspoon baking soda

¾ cup molasses

½ cup coarsely chopped walnuts

½ cup raisins

1. Preheat the oven to 350 degrees F. Lightly oil a 9 x 5-inch loaf pan and set aside.
2. In a small bowl combine the soy milk and vinegar and set aside.
3. In a large bowl, combine the flour, cornmeal, salt, and baking soda, mixing well. Add the molasses and soy milk mixture and stir until the batter is just mixed. Stir in the walnuts and raisins with a few quick strokes, then transfer to the prepared pan.
4. Bake on the center oven rack until firm and a toothpick inserted in the center comes out clean, about 1 hour. Let cool in the pan for 10 minutes before removing from the pan and slicing. Serve warm, soon after it is made.

MAKES 1 LOAF

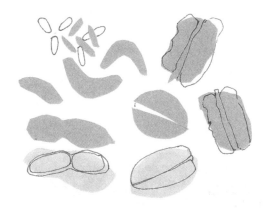

Marvelous Molasses

A byproduct of the sugar-refining process, molasses is a syrupy liquid that can vary in sweetness and color depending on what phase, or "boiling," it is extracted from. The finest-quality molasses is unsulphured molasses from the first boiling, which is quite sweet and light in color, especially compared to blackstrap molasses, which is dark, aromatic, and only slightly sweet. Nutritionally, however, blackstrap shines. It is extremely high in iron and calcium and for that reason is more of a nutritional supplement than a sweetener, although its distinctive, slightly sweet flavor works well in dark breads, baked beans, and spice cookies. Whether you choose light or dark molasses, be sure it is labeled "unsulfured." Sulfured molasses is made from immature green sugar cane that has been treated with sulfur fumes during the sugar-extracting process. The residue of this sulfur can remain in the molasses.

Irish Soda Bread

I've been making soda bread on St. Patrick's Day for as long as I can remember. It's ideal served with a hearty stew or eaten on its own, still warm from the oven.

1½ cups soy milk or other dairy-free milk

1½ tablespoons white vinegar

4 cups unbleached all-purpose flour

1½ teaspoons salt

1 teaspoon baking soda

½ teaspoon baking powder

1. Preheat the oven to 375 degrees F. Lightly oil a baking sheet and set aside.

2. Combine the milk and vinegar in a measuring cup and set aside.

3. In a large bowl, combine the flour, salt, baking soda, and baking powder and mix until blended. Add enough of the milk mixture to make a soft dough that is not too sticky. Knead just until the dough is smooth, about 3 minutes. Shape the dough into a round loaf and use a sharp knife to cut an X in the top. Place on the prepared baking sheet.

4. Bake on the center oven rack until golden brown, about 45 minutes. The bread is done when it sounds hollow when tapped on the bottom. Remove from the sheet and let cool on a wire rack before slicing. This bread is best eaten the same day it is made.

MAKES 1 LOAF

Spiced Apple-Walnut Muffins

To save time, you may use a cup of applesauce instead of the grated fresh apple, if desired. For extra apple flavor, serve slices of this bread spread with apple butter.

1 large Granny Smith apple, peeled and cored

3/4 cup soy milk or other dairy-free milk

Egg replacer for 1 egg (page 509)

1/2 cup firmly packed light brown sugar or natural sweetener

3 tablespoons corn oil

2 cups unbleached all-purpose flour

2 1/2 teaspoons baking powder

3/4 teaspoon salt

3/4 teaspoon ground cinnamon

1/4 teaspoon ground allspice

1/2 cup chopped walnuts

1. Preheat the oven to 400 degrees F. Lightly oil a muffin pan and set aside.
2. Grate the apple into a large bowl. Add the soy milk, egg replacer, brown sugar, and corn oil and blend until smooth. Set aside.
3. In a medium-size bowl, sift together the flour, baking powder, salt, cinnamon, and allspice. Using a few swift strokes, mix the dry ingredients into the wet ingredients until just blended. Fold in the walnuts, then transfer the batter to the prepared pan, filling the cups about two-thirds full.
4. Bake on the center oven rack until golden brown and a toothpick inserted in a muffin comes out clean, about 30 minutes. Let cool in the pan for 5 to 10 minutes. Serve warm.

MAKES 12 MUFFINS

Pumpkin Biscuits

Biscuits are convenient by nature because they are easy to put together and bake quickly. This variation on the classic sweet potato biscuit uses canned pumpkin, which I find even more convenient. These biscuits are ideal served with any autumn meal, from a bowl of chili to Thanksgiving dinner. For tender biscuits, be sure to mix lightly, since overmixing can result in tough biscuits.

2 cups unbleached all-purpose flour

1 tablespoon baking powder

3/4 teaspoon salt

1/2 teaspoon ground allspice

3/4 cup canned pumpkin

1/2 cup soy milk or other dairy-free milk

3 tablespoons corn oil

1 tablespoon pure maple syrup

1. Preheat the oven to 450 degrees F. Lightly oil a baking sheet and set aside.
2. In a large bowl, sift together the flour, baking powder, salt, and allspice and set aside.
3. In a medium-size bowl, combine the pumpkin, soy milk, corn oil, and maple syrup and blend until smooth. Combine the pumpkin mixture with the flour mixture, stirring until the dough is just mixed and holds together.
4. Transfer to a lightly floured work surface and roll out to about 1/2 inch thick. Using a biscuit cutter or small drinking glass, cut the dough into 2-inch rounds and place on the prepared baking sheet. Reroll the dough scraps and cut out more biscuits.
5. Bake on the center oven rack until golden brown on top, 12 to 14 minutes. Serve hot.

MAKES ABOUT 20 BISCUITS

Ginger-Spiced Scones with Cashews and Dates

I think of scones as elegant biscuits. Unlike biscuits, which are usually served with a meal, scones are often served as a snack, much like muffins and tea breads. One of the great pleasures in life is a freshly baked scone served with a cup of hot coffee or tea.

2 cups unbleached all-purpose flour

3/4 cup sugar or natural sweetener

2 teaspoons baking powder

1 teaspoon baking soda

1/2 teaspoon ground ginger

1/2 teaspoon salt

1/2 cup soy margarine, softened

1/3 cup dates, pitted and chopped

1/4 cup chopped unsalted dry-roasted cashews

1/4 cup soy milk or other dairy-free milk

Egg replacer for 2 eggs (page 509)

1. Preheat the oven to 425 degrees F. Lightly oil a baking sheet and set aside.

2. In a large bowl, sift together the flour, sugar, baking powder, baking soda, ginger, and salt. Cut the soy margarine into the flour mixture until crumbly. Mix in the dates, cashews, soy milk, and egg replacer, stirring until just blended. Do not over-work the dough.

3. Transfer the dough to a lightly floured work surface. Using a lightly floured rolling pin, roll out into a circle about 3/4 inch thick. Cut into 12 wedges and place on the prepared baking sheet.

4. Bake on the center oven rack until golden brown, 12 to 15 minutes. Serve warm.

MAKES 12 SCONES

Cumin-Scented Sesame Flatbread

Simple flatbreads are made throughout the world—some with yeast, others without. This version uses no yeast and can, therefore, be prepared quickly. The cumin in this bread makes it especially complementary to Mexican or Indian foods.

2 cups unbleached all-purpose flour
1/2 teaspoon salt
3/4 cup water, or as needed

Olive oil for brushing
2 tablespoons sesame seeds
3/4 teaspoon ground cumin

1. In a medium-size bowl, combine the flour and salt. Add enough water for the dough to hold together. Knead until smooth, about 5 minutes. Wrap in plastic and set aside at room temperature for 15 minutes.
2. Divide the dough into 6 pieces. Lightly flour your hands and work surface, then shape the dough into balls and flatten them. Roll out into circles about 6 inches in diameter. Brush lightly with olive oil, then sprinkle with the sesame seeds and cumin, pressing lightly so the seeds adhere to the dough.
3. Lightly oil a large skillet and heat over medium-high heat. Place a dough circle in the skillet and cook, turning once, until brown spots begin to appear, about 3 minutes per side. Transfer to a platter and cover with aluminum foil or a clean towel to keep warm while you cook the rest. Serve at once.

MAKES 6 FLATBREADS

GETTING A RISE

From baking powder to yeast, leavening agents are what make baked goods rise. Here are the most commonly used leaveners.

Active dry yeast: This leavening agent is a living organism that makes bread rise by feeding off the sugars found in flour and giving off carbon dioxide bubbles, which makes the dough expand. Sold in granular form, it keeps well under refrigeration through the expiration date. Breads made with yeast require kneading and rising before they can be baked. Yeast should be dissolved in water that is around 110 degrees F. If the water is too hot, it will kill the yeast; if it is too cool, the yeast will stay dormant.

Quick-rising yeast: Made up of smaller particles than active dry yeast, this leavener works faster than the active variety but may be used in equal measure.

Fresh yeast: Available in moist, crumbly cakes, it is highly perishable and less convenient than dry yeast. It can be stored in the refrigerator for about 2 weeks or until the expiration date.

Baking soda: Breads made with this leavening agent require no kneading or rising time, but an acidic ingredient, such as vinegar, must be added for the bread to rise. Stored in an airtight container in a cool, dry place, baking soda will keep for up to 1 year.

Baking powder: Like baking soda, this leavening agent requires no kneading or rising time to work. Baking powder is a combination of baking soda and cream of tartar or another acidic agent, so no additional acidic ingredient is needed. When stored in a cool, dry place, baking powder will keep for up to 6 months.

Dessert Heaven

Although meat eaters and vegetarians may disagree on their entrées, most can find common ground at the dessert table. This is often not the case for vegans, since many popular desserts contain eggs or some form of dairy. Anyone who bakes knows that cakes, cookies, and other baked goods often rely on eggs and dairy products for their flavor and texture.

Fortunately, many traditional desserts can be made with vegan ingredients that produce similar results. For example, soy milk can be used instead of dairy milk, corn oil or soy margarine may replace butter, and egg replacer can be blended with water to use instead of eggs in most recipes.

Even such normally dairy-rich desserts as cheesecake, pudding, and ice cream can be made egg- and dairy-free. This comes as good news not only to vegans but also to people with dairy allergies or those looking for ways to reduce their cholesterol intake. In addition, many vegan desserts offer delicious opportunities to eat more soy foods.

Although I wouldn't recommend trying to replicate a particularly egg-centered dessert such as a vanilla soufflé, most recipes with only one or two eggs can be reproduced quite successfully. Some people may find that certain cakes made with vegan ingredients are denser than those prepared with eggs and butter, but the fact remains that vegan desserts are better for your health and can be delicious. Most vegans I know have quite a sweet tooth, and they readily devour every vegan dessert set before them with gusto. Still, I would be remiss if I did not point out that it may take some trial and error to get used to baking with egg and dairy alternatives—especially when trying to convert your favorite recipes. I have tried to include a variety of dessert recipes that everyone will enjoy and that are easy to make, even for the beginner.

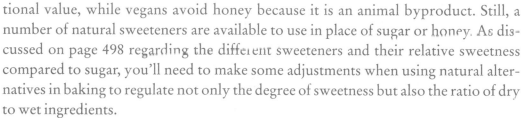

Regarding sweeteners, many health-conscious people choose to avoid sugar because of its lack of nutritional value, while vegans avoid honey because it is an animal byproduct. Still, a number of natural sweeteners are available to use in place of sugar or honey. As discussed on page 498 regarding the different sweeteners and their relative sweetness compared to sugar, you'll need to make some adjustments when using natural alternatives in baking to regulate not only the degree of sweetness but also the ratio of dry to wet ingredients.

Once you become familiar with using egg and dairy alternatives in your dessert recipes, you will soon be able to whip up many of your favorite desserts without blinking an eye—and feel better for it.

Substituting Sweet for Sweet

When substituting a natural liquid sweetener for granulated sugar in recipes, you will need to reduce the amount of the other liquids in the recipe so that the finished product retains the intended texture. For each cup of liquid sweetener added, figure on reducing the total liquid by $1/4$ cup.

Coconut-Macadamia "Cheesecake"

This taste of the tropics cheesecake is decadent and delicious. For an added taste treat and lovely color contrast, serve it with sliced fresh mango or mango puree.

1/2 cup plus 2 tablespoons ground
    macadamia nuts
11/2 cups vegan graham cracker or
    vanilla cookie crumbs
2 tablespoons pure maple syrup
1/4 cup soy margarine, melted
One 16-ounce package firm silken tofu,
    drained

One 8-ounce package vegan cream
    cheese
1 cup sugar or natural sweetener
1/4 cup unsweetened coconut milk
1 teaspoon pure coconut extract
1/3 cup unsweetened shredded coconut,
    toasted (page 491)

1. Bring the ingredients to room temperature. Preheat the oven to 350 degrees F. Lightly oil a 9-inch springform pan.

2. In a large bowl or food processor, combine the 2 tablespoons macadamia nuts, the crumbs, maple syrup, and soy margarine until well blended. Transfer to the prepared pan and press the mixture against the bottom and side of the pan. Bake for 5 minutes, then set aside to cool.

3. Place the tofu and vegan cream cheese in a food processor and process until smooth. Add the sugar, coconut milk, and coconut extract and process again until smooth. Pour into the prepared crust and bake on the center oven rack until firm, about 40 minutes. Turn the oven off and leave the cheesecake inside for 30 minutes.

4. Remove from the oven and let cool to room temperature, then refrigerate for several hours before serving.

5. To serve, remove the pan sides, sprinkle the top evenly with the 1/2 cup macadamia nuts and the coconut, and cut into pieces.

SERVES 8

Toasting Coconut

Spread unsweetened shredded coconut in a dry skillet over low heat and cook, stirring frequently, until it begins to turn light brown. Or spread it on a baking sheet and toast in a preheated 325 degree F oven, stirring occasionally, for about 10 minutes. Coconut browns quickly and should be removed from the skillet or baking sheet right away to prevent overbrowning. Cool the coconut completely and store in an airtight container until ready to use. Properly stored, it will keep in the refrigerator for 1 to 2 weeks or in the freezer for up to 3 months.

Key Lime "Cheesecake"

The light and refreshing taste of this cheesecake makes it ideal to serve after a hot, spicy meal. This recipe uses regular limes, since Key limes are not widely available and are quite expensive. I use vegan gingersnaps for the crust because I like the combination of ginger and lime, but you may use vegan graham crackers instead.

1½ cups vegan gingersnap crumbs
1 cup plus 1 tablespoon sugar or
    natural sweetener
6 tablespoons soy margarine, melted
Two 12-ounce packages firm silken
    tofu, drained

One 8-ounce package vegan cream
    cheese
⅓ cup fresh lime juice (2 to 3 limes)
1 tablespoon grated lime zest

1. Bring the ingredients to room temperature. Preheat the oven to 350 degrees F. Lightly oil a 9-inch springform pan.
2. In a medium-size bowl or food processor, combine the crumbs, the 1 tablespoon sugar, and the soy margarine and mix well. Transfer to the prepared pan and press the mixture against the bottom and side of the pan. Bake for 5 minutes, then set aside to cool.
3. In a food processor, process the tofu and vegan cream cheese together until smooth. Add the 1 cup sugar, the lime juice, and lime zest and process again until smooth. Pour into the prepared crust and bake on the center oven rack until firm, about 40 minutes. Turn the oven off and leave the cheesecake inside for 30 minutes.
4. Remove from the oven and let cool to room temperature, then refrigerate for several hours before serving. Remove the sides of the pan before cutting.

SERVES 8

Banana Swirl "Cheesecake"

Chocolate, bananas, and peanut butter are one of my favorite combinations, and for pure decadent indulgence, I can think of no better way to enjoy them than in this blissfully rich cheesecake. The three flavors are swirled together to create a marbleized cake that tastes as good as it looks.

1½ cups vegan chocolate cookie crumbs
¾ cup plus 1 tablespoon sugar or
    natural sweetener
6 tablespoons soy margarine, melted
One 16-ounce package firm silken tofu,
    drained

½ cup soy milk or other dairy-free milk
¼ cup smooth natural peanut butter
3 large, ripe bananas, peeled and
    mashed
½ cup semisweet vegan chocolate
    chips, melted

1. Bring the ingredients to room temperature. Preheat the oven to 350 degrees F. Lightly oil a 9-inch springform pan.
2. In a medium-size bowl or food processor, combine the crumbs, the 1 tablespoon sugar, and the soy margarine and mix well. Transfer to the prepared pan and press the mixture against the bottom and side of the pan. Bake for 5 minutes, then set aside to cool.
3. In a food processor, process half the tofu, half the soy milk, and the peanut butter until smooth. Pour into the prepared crust and set aside.
4. In the same food processor, process the bananas, remaining tofu, remaining soy milk, and the ¾ cup sugar until smooth. Pour over the peanut butter mixture and set aside.
5. Melt the vegan chocolate chips in a small saucepan over low heat or in the microwave. Stir until smooth. Using a circular motion, pour the melted chocolate over the banana mixture and use a thin spatula or knife to swirl all the fillings around to create a marbleized pattern. Bake on the center oven rack until firm, 40 to 45 minutes. Turn the oven off and leave the cheesecake inside for 30 minutes.
6. Remove from the oven and let cool to room temperature, then refrigerate for several hours before serving. Remove the pan sides before cutting.

SERVES 8

Strawberry-Topped "Cheesecake"

You can serve this vegan version of the classic cheesecake plain or with a different fruit topping, if you prefer. The strawberries may be arranged on top of the cheesecake whole or sliced, depending on their size.

1½ cups vegan graham cracker crumbs

⅓ cup soy margarine, melted

1 cup plus 1 tablespoon sugar or
    natural sweetener

Two 12-ounce packages firm silken
    tofu, drained

One 8-ounce package vegan cream
    cheese

1 teaspoon pure vanilla extract

½ cup fruit-sweetened strawberry
    spread

1 tablespoon water, fruit juice, or
    liqueur

2 to 3 cups fresh strawberries, hulled

1. Bring the ingredients to room temperature. Preheat the oven to 350 degrees F. Lightly oil a 9-inch springform pan.

2. In a medium-size bowl or food processor, combine the crumbs, soy margarine, and the 1 tablespoon sugar until well blended. Transfer to the prepared pan and press the mixture into the bottom and side of the pan. Bake for 5 minutes, then set aside to cool.

3. In a food processor, process the tofu and vegan cream cheese until smooth. Add the 1 cup sugar and the vanilla and process again until smooth. Pour into the prepared crust and bake on the center oven rack until firm, about 40 minutes. Turn the oven off and leave the cheesecake inside for 30 minutes.

4. Remove from the oven and let cool to room temperature, then refrigerate for several hours.

5. While the cake is chilling, combine the strawberry spread and water in a small saucepan over medium heat, stirring until smooth. Set aside to cool.

6. Once the cake is chilled, slice the strawberries if they are large or vary greatly in size, or leave whole if they are small and uniform in size. Remove the sides of the pan. Arrange the strawberries on top of the cheesecake and brush with the strawberry glaze.

SERVES 8

There's Nothing Better Than a Strawberry

Anyone who bites into a freshly picked strawberry still warm from the sun has to agree with William Butler, who wrote, "Doubtless God could have made a better berry, but doubtless God never did."

Strawberries are said to have gotten their name from the English practice of placing straw around the plants for protection, although some sources maintain that the name is derived from the Anglo-Saxon verb "to strew" (spread), because of the runners that spread outward from the plant.

Naturally sweet, this most popular berry is high in vitamins A and C and folic acid, among other vitamins and minerals. Eight medium-size strawberries contain only 45 calories and no fat, while providing an amazing 160 percent of our daily requirement of vitamin C.

Besides eating them out of hand, you can serve strawberries in a number of delicious ways. At breakfast, slice them onto cereals, pancakes, or waffles. Whir them in a blender with a splash of orange juice for a great smoothie—add some tofu to boost the protein and calcium for a well-balanced meal. Enjoy them at lunch or dinner as a chilled soup or a colorful ingredient in a salad. Or use this versatile berry to make sweet jams, fiery salsas, chutneys, and other condiments.

But it is in desserts that the strawberry really takes the cake—strawberry shortcake, that is. You can also combine them with rhubarb and bake them into a pie, or let them star in their own pie, pudding, or other confection. Try dipping long-stemmed berries into melted vegan chocolate. If less decadence is in order, puree fresh strawberries into a sauce for a fruit sorbet or a dipping sauce for other cut fruit. For a sophisticated surprise, toss berries with a splash of balsamic vinegar and a little freshly ground black pepper. No matter how you prepare them, nothing can compare to the locally grown berries you pick yourself at the peak of the season. This is when I can think of no better preparation for these sweet crimson jewels than this: pick berry, place in mouth, repeat.

Five-Spice Chocolate Layer Cake

Fragrant spices transform a basic vegan chocolate cake into gourmet fare. It is especially yummy served with a scoop of dairy-free vanilla ice cream dusted with ground ginger.

Cake:

2 1/2 cups unbleached all-purpose flour
2/3 cup unsweetened cocoa powder
1/3 cup sugar or natural sweetener
2 teaspoons baking powder
1 teaspoon baking soda
3/4 teaspoon ground cinnamon
1/2 teaspoon ground allspice
1/2 teaspoon ground ginger
1/4 teaspoon freshly grated nutmeg
1/4 teaspoon ground cloves
1/2 teaspoon salt
1 cup pitted prunes, soaked in 1 cup
    hot water
6 ounces soft silken tofu, drained

1 cup molasses
1/4 cup corn oil
2 teaspoons pure vanilla extract
1 1/2 teaspoons rice or cider vinegar
1 1/2 cups water

Maple-chocolate frosting:

One 16-ounce package soft silken tofu,
    drained
1/2 cup unsweetened cocoa powder
1/2 cup pure maple syrup or other
    natural liquid sweetener
1/4 cup soy milk or other dairy-free milk
2 teaspoons pure vanilla extract

1. Preheat the oven to 350 degrees F. Oil and lightly flour two 9-inch cake pans.

2. To make the cake, in a large bowl sift together the flour, cocoa powder, sugar, baking powder, baking soda, spices, and salt. Set aside.

3. In a blender or food processor, combine the prunes and their soaking liquid, the tofu, molasses, corn oil, vanilla, and vinegar. Add the water and blend until smooth, then transfer to a large bowl.

4. Whisk the dry ingredients into the wet ingredients, blending until smooth. Divide the batter evenly between the prepared pans and bake on the center oven rack until the cakes spring back when lightly touched, about 30 minutes. Let cool in the pans for 15 minutes, then transfer to wire racks to cool completely before removing from the pans and frosting.

5. To make the frosting, in a blender or food processor, combine all the ingredients and process until smooth. Transfer to a bowl, cover, and refrigerate until well chilled.

6. To frost the cake, place one layer on a cake plate and spread with about $3/4$ cup of the frosting. Top with the second layer and spread the top and sides of the cake with the remaining frosting.

SERVES 8 TO 10

Pumpkin-Rum Couscous Cake

This unusual no-bake cake has a moist texture similar to that of bread pudding, but it is made in a springform pan and is cut into wedges like a cheesecake.

1 cup drained soft silken tofu

$3/4$ cup canned pumpkin

$1/2$ cup firmly packed light brown sugar or natural sweetener

2 tablespoons rum

1 teaspoon pure vanilla extract

$1/2$ teaspoon ground cinnamon

$1/4$ teaspoon ground allspice

$1/4$ teaspoon freshly grated nutmeg

$1^{1}/2$ cups apple juice

Pinch of salt

1 cup instant couscous

1. In a food processor or blender, process the tofu, pumpkin, $1/4$ cup of the brown sugar, the rum, and vanilla until smooth. Add the spices and blend thoroughly until well combined. Set aside.

2. In a medium-size saucepan, combine the apple juice, remaining $1/4$ cup brown sugar, and salt and bring to a boil. Reduce the heat to low and stir in the couscous. Cover and simmer for 2 minutes, then turn off the heat and let stand for 5 minutes.

3. In a large bowl, combine the couscous and the pumpkin mixture until well blended. Spread in a lightly oiled 9-inch springform pan, pressing the mixture firmly and evenly in the pan. Chill for several hours or overnight for easier slicing. Remove the sides of the pan before cutting.

SERVES 8

Sweet Choices

Following are explanations of the different sweeteners, from sugar to stevia. See page 30 for substitution guidelines.

- *Table sugar, or sucrose:* A highly refined sweetener that contains empty calories and provides no nutritional benefit.
- *Brown sugar:* White sugar that contains a small amount of molasses.
- *Turbinado sugar:* A refined, light brown sugar that has not been bleached. No nutritional benefit.
- *Raw sugar:* Made from sugar cane juice that is dehydrated and then milled into granulated powder. Retains its natural, though minimal, vitamins and minerals (brand names include Rapadura, Sucanat, and Florida Crystals).
- *Date or palm sugar:* Made from the fruit of the date palm tree, it has a rich, distinctive flavor and doesn't dissolve well in recipes. It is usually sold in Asian markets.
- *Stevia:* A heat-stable, highly concentrated natural sugar alternative with zero calories available at natural food stores in liquid or powder form. Just a minuscule amount is needed for sweetening, but too much can produce a strong aftertaste.
- *Barley malt syrup:* A dark, thick sweetener made from roasted sprouted barley. Can replace honey or molasses in most baked goods.
- *Brown rice syrup:* A mild-tasting natural liquid sweetener made by adding sprouted barley or rice enzymes to cooked rice. It is about half as sweet as sugar.
- *Maple syrup:* Made by boiling the sap from maple trees, it has minimal nutrition. Buy only "pure maple syrup." Avoid pancake syrup, which can be little more than colored corn syrup.
- *Molasses:* This is the dark, thick liquid that remains after the sugar-making process. Blackstrap molasses is rich in iron and calcium. Generally, the darker the molasses, the greater its nutritional value.

Brandy-Apple Pie

A touch of brandy adds a bit of sophistication to "Mom's apple pie." You can, of course, omit it, if you prefer. Serve warm with a scoop of dairy-free vanilla ice cream for nostalgic decadence at its best.

2 cups unbleached all-purpose flour
1 teaspoon salt
2/3 cup plus 1 tablespoon soy margarine, cut into small pieces
1/4 cup ice water, or as needed
5 large Granny Smith or other tart apples

1/2 cup firmly packed light brown sugar or natural sweetener
1 teaspoon ground cinnamon
1/4 teaspoon ground allspice
1 tablespoon fresh lemon juice
1 tablespoon cornstarch
2 tablespoons brandy

1. Combine the flour and salt in a food processor. Blend in the 2/3 cup soy margarine with short pulses until the mixture becomes crumbly. With the machine running, add just enough of the water through the feed tube until the dough just starts to hold together. Transfer to a work surface, divide in half, and flatten to form 2 disks. Wrap in plastic and refrigerate for 30 minutes.

2. Preheat the oven to 450 degrees F. On a lightly floured work surface, roll out 1 piece of dough to fit a 9-inch pie plate. Fit the dough into the pie plate and trim and flute the edges. Roll out the remaining dough for the top crust and set aside or refrigerate if you will not be using right away. Refrigerate the pie plate.

3. Peel, core, and slice the apples and place in a large bowl. Add the brown sugar, cinnamon, allspice, lemon juice, cornstarch, and brandy and stir to mix well. Spoon the apple mixture into the prepared bottom crust and dot with the 1 tablespoon soy margarine.

4. Place the top crust on the fruit, seal with the bottom crust, and flute the edges. Use a fork or knife to create several steam holes in the top crust. Bake for 10 minutes, then reduce the oven temperature to 350 degrees F and bake until golden brown, 40 to 45 minutes more. Let cool to room temperature before serving.

SERVES 8

Asian Pear Tart with Toasted Almond Crust and Orange-Ginger Glaze

Asian pears, more widely available in recent years, taste and look like a cross between a pear and an apple. Primarily enjoyed raw and unadorned for their sweet flavor and crisp, juicy texture, Asian pears retain their shape and texture when cooked. Look for firm-fleshed, unbruised fruits that are heavy for their size. Color will range from pale yellow to golden brown. For a more traditional tart, use ripe regular pears, such as Anjou or Bartlett. Other fruits also may be used.

2 cups raw almonds, toasted (page 110)
1/2 cup dates, pitted
4 Asian pears, peeled, cored, and thinly sliced
1 tablespoon plus 2 teaspoons fresh lemon juice

1/4 cup firmly packed light brown sugar or natural sweetener
1/4 teaspoon ground ginger
1/3 cup orange marmalade
1/2 teaspoon peeled and minced fresh ginger

1. Preheat the oven to 375 degrees F. In a food processor, coarsely grind the almonds. Add the dates and process until thoroughly combined. Press the mixture into a lightly oiled 9-inch tart pan, pie plate, or springform pan.

2. Toss the pears with the 2 teaspoons lemon juice and arrange in the crust in a circular pattern. Sprinkle with the brown sugar and ground ginger and bake on the center oven rack until the pears soften, about 30 minutes. Let cool to room temperature.

3. In a small saucepan over low heat, combine the marmalade, the 1 tablespoon lemon juice, and the fresh ginger, stirring until blended. Brush on the pear slices and serve.

SERVES 6 TO 8

Fresh Peach Crisp with Almond Butter Cream

Besides eating them out of hand, this is my favorite way to enjoy fresh, ripe peaches. The crunchy topping, rather than a crust, allows the juicy fruit to take center stage. This dessert is best served warm out of the oven.

6 large, ripe peaches, peeled, pitted, and sliced

1/2 cup slivered almonds

1/2 cup plus 1 tablespoon unbleached all-purpose flour

3/4 cup firmly packed light brown sugar or natural sweetener

2 tablespoons fresh lemon juice

3/4 teaspoon ground allspice

1/2 cup old-fashioned rolled oats

3 tablespoons corn oil

1 recipe Almond Butter Cream (page 502)

1. Preheat the oven to 375 degrees F. Lightly oil a 10-inch baking dish and set aside.

2. In a large bowl, combine the peaches, almonds, the 1 tablespoon flour, 1/4 cup of the brown sugar, the lemon juice, and 1/4 teaspoon of the allspice. Mix gently and transfer to the prepared dish.

3. In small bowl, combine the 1/2 cup flour, remaining 1/2 cup brown sugar, the oats, corn oil, and remaining 1/2 teaspoon allspice. Use your hands or a pastry blender to mix well until crumbly. Sprinkle evenly over the peach mixture and bake on the center oven rack until the fruit bubbles in the middle and the topping is browned, 30 to 40 minutes.

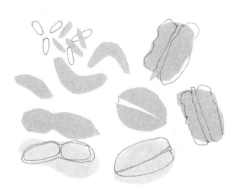

4. To serve, spoon into 8 individual dishes while still warm and top with a dollop of the almond cream.

SERVES 8

ALMOND BUTTER CREAM

Seductively rich and deceptively healthful, this versatile topping can be served on pies, bread pudding, fruit, and even pancakes—just use your imagination.

3 or 4 dates, pitted

1/2 cup hot water

1 cup blanched almonds

1. Soak the dates in the water until soft.

2. Place the dates and their soaking liquid in a blender, add the almonds, and blend until smooth and creamy. Store in the refrigerator, tightly covered, until ready to use, up to 1 week.

MAKES ABOUT 1¹/₂ CUPS

Red, White, and Blueberry Cobbler

This is an ideal Fourth of July dessert, since fresh strawberries and blueberries are usually available at that time. The patriotic colors can be provided by the red and blue berries and the white crust, or you can go a step further and add a scoop of dairy-free vanilla ice cream topped with Strawberry–Grand Marnier Sauce (recipe follows) and a few fresh blueberries for garnish. Either way, you have a delicious all-American dessert.

3 cups fresh blueberries, picked over

3 cups fresh strawberries, hulled

2/3 cup plus 2 tablespoons sugar or
    natural sweetener

1¹/₂ cups plus 1 tablespoon unbleached
    all-purpose flour

1/2 teaspoon ground cinnamon

2 teaspoons baking powder

1/2 teaspoon salt

6 tablespoons soy margarine, cut
    into small pieces

About 1/2 cup soy milk or other
    dairy-free milk

1. Preheat the oven to 375 degrees F.

2. In a medium-size saucepan over medium heat, combine the blueberries, straw-berries, the ²/₃ cup sugar, the 1 tablespoon flour, and the cinnamon. Stir to blend and bring to a boil, then reduce the heat to low and stir gently until slightly thickened. Remove from the heat and spoon into the bottom of a 9-inch baking dish.

3. In a food processor, combine the 1¹/₂ cups flour, the baking powder, salt, and the 2 tablespoons sugar. Blend in the soy margarine with short pulses, until the mix-ture becomes crumbly. With the machine running, add the soy milk through the feed tube and blend until the dough just starts to hold together.

4. Drop by large spoonfuls on top of the fruit. Bake until the fruit is bubbly and the crust is golden brown, 30 to 40 minutes. Serve warm.

SERVES 8

STRAWBERRY-GRAND MARNIER SAUCE

This multipurpose sauce can be used to top Red, White, and Blueberry Cobbler or to adorn a plain vegan cheesecake or a scoop of dairy-free ice cream.

2 cups ripe strawberries, hulled
2 tablespoons Grand Marnier or other
  orange-flavored liqueur

1 teaspoon orange juice or fresh lemon
  juice
Confectioners' sugar

1. Place the strawberries in a food processor and process until smooth, or run them through a food mill.

2. Pour the puree into a bowl and stir in the liqueur, juice, and confectioners' sugar to taste. Use at once, or cover and refrigerate for up to 2 days.

MAKES ABOUT 2 CUPS

Mango-Coconut Bread Pudding

Old-fashioned bread pudding takes a decidedly tropical turn with creamy coconut milk and luscious mangoes.

1 large, ripe mango, peeled, pitted, and pureed
1/2 cup drained soft silken tofu
2 1/2 cups unsweetened coconut milk
1/2 cup firmly packed light brown sugar or natural sweetener

1 teaspoon pure vanilla extract
8 to 10 slices white bread, crusts removed
1/4 cup unsweetened shredded coconut
1 large, ripe mango (optional), peeled, pitted, and diced, for garnish

1. Preheat the oven to 350 degrees F. Lightly oil a shallow 10-inch baking dish.
2. In a blender or food processor, process the mango puree, tofu, 1 cup of the coconut milk, the brown sugar, and vanilla until smooth. Set aside.
3. Cut the bread into small pieces and arrange in the bottom of the prepared dish. Pour the remaining 1 1/2 cups coconut milk over the bread, tossing to coat and soak up the liquid. Add the mango mixture and bake on the center oven rack for 35 minutes. Remove from the oven and sprinkle with the coconut. Return to the oven and back until firm, about 10 minutes more.
4. Serve warm or chilled, garnished with the diced mango, if desired.

SERVES 8

Coconut-Cardamom Rice Pudding

Since I usually have cooked rice in the house, I often make rice pudding for a quick and wholesome dessert. Rose water adds a heavenly accent and is available at gourmet markets and Indian grocery stores. If unavailable, vanilla extract may be used instead.

2½ cups cooked basmati rice
2½ cups unsweetened coconut milk
½ cup sugar or natural sweetener
½ teaspoon ground cardamom

Pinch of salt
½ cup coarsely chopped raw pistachios
1½ teaspoons rose water

1. Place the rice, coconut milk, and sugar in a medium-size saucepan over low heat and simmer for 20 minutes, stirring occasionally. Stir in the cardamom and salt and simmer until thick and creamy, 5 to 10 minutes.

2. Remove from the heat and stir in the pistachios and rose water. Let cool to room temperature before serving, or cover and refrigerate to serve chilled.

SERVES 4

Chocolate Pudding Parfaits

A creamy chocolate pudding made with silken tofu is a great way to enjoy soy. This can be delicious on its own, but I enjoy serving it in parfait glasses (wineglasses also will work), layered with creamy whipped topping and chopped nuts. Crown each parfait with a fresh berry, and you have an easy and elegant dessert that's good for you, too.

1 cup semisweet vegan chocolate chips

1/2 cup pure maple syrup

One 12-ounce package soft silken tofu, drained

1 teaspoon pure vanilla extract

1 cup Creamy Whipped Topping (recipe follows)

1/2 cup chopped almonds or other nuts, toasted (page 110)

4 fresh strawberries, hulled, or fresh raspberries (optional)

1. Place the vegan chocolate chips and maple syrup in the top half of a double boiler and simmer over medium heat until the chocolate is melted, stirring to blend. Set aside to cool.

2. Place the tofu and vanilla in a blender or food processor and process until smooth. Add the chocolate mixture and process until smooth and well combined.

3. Spoon a small amount of the pudding into individual parfait glasses. Top with a small amount of the whipped topping, and sprinkle lightly with nuts. Repeat the process until the glasses are full, ending with the chopped nuts. Cover tightly with plastic wrap and refrigerate for at least 2 hours before serving.

4. When ready to serve, top each serving with a fresh berry, if desired.

SERVES 4

CREAMY WHIPPED TOPPING

This is a healthful soy-based alternative to whipped cream that can be used with abandon on cakes, pies, and other desserts. Unlike most commercial nondairy whipped toppings, this does not contain hydrogenated fat or additives and is rich in soy protein. If you're using sugar or another granular sweetener, it is best to dissolve it before using it in the recipe for the best texture. To do this, combine 1/4 cup of sugar or other granular sweetener with 1/4 cup water in a small saucepan over medium heat and bring to a boil. Reduce the heat to low and cook, stirring, until the sugar is dissolved, about 1 minute. Remove from the heat and allow to cool before using. If you're not using sugar, use a light-tasting natural sweetener so it doesn't overpower the flavor of the topping.

1 cup drained and blotted soft silken tofu

2 tablespoons confectioners' sugar or 1/4 cup sugar syrup (see headnote) or natural liquid sweetener

1 tablespoon safflower or other neutral-tasting oil

1 teaspoon pure vanilla extract

1/4 teaspoon fresh lemon juice

1. Place the tofu, confectioners' sugar, oil, vanilla, and lemon juice in a blender or food processor and process until smooth and creamy.

2. Transfer to a small container, cover, and refrigerate for 30 minutes before serving. This topping should be used within a few hours after making it.

MAKES ABOUT 1 CUP

Chocolatey Peanut Butter Brownies

Chocolate and peanut butter join forces in these rich and chewy brownies. For regular brownies, simply omit the peanut butter and extra 2 tablespoons corn oil and proceed with the recipe.

1/3 cup smooth natural peanut butter
1/4 cup plus 2 tablespoons corn oil
4 ounces semisweet vegan chocolate
    chips
Egg replacer for 2 eggs (page 509)

3/4 cup sugar or natural sweetener
1 teaspoon pure vanilla extract
1 cup unbleached all-purpose flour
1 teaspoon baking powder

1. Bring the peanut butter to room temperature, then combine it with the 2 tablespoons corn oil until smooth. Set aside.

2. Preheat the oven to 350 degrees F. Lightly oil an 8-inch square baking pan and set aside.

3. In a small saucepan over low heat, combine the 1/4 cup corn oil and the vegan chocolate chips, stirring occasionally, until melted. Remove from the heat and set aside.

4. Place the egg replacer in a large bowl. Add the sugar and vanilla and blend well. Stir in the chocolate mixture and blend well. Stir in the flour and baking powder, mixing well. Spoon the batter into the prepared pan and swirl in the peanut butter mixture.

5. Bake until the top springs back when touched, 20 to 25 minutes. Let cool before cutting into squares.

MAKES 16 BROWNIES

Orange-Scented Almond Biscotti

These crisp, delicious biscotti with a hint of orange are ideal companions for a cup of tea or coffee, whether served alone or alongside a scoop of your favorite frozen dessert.

⅓ cup soy margarine, softened
⅔ cup sugar or natural sweetener
Egg replacer for 2 eggs (see box above)
1 teaspoon pure vanilla extract

2 cups unbleached all-purpose flour
1½ teaspoons baking powder
1½ teaspoons grated orange zest
½ cup slivered almonds

1. Preheat the oven to 350 degrees F.

2. In a large bowl, cream the soy margarine and sugar until light and fluffy. Blend in the egg replacer and vanilla. Mix in the flour and baking powder. Stir in the orange zest and almonds. Chill for 10 minutes.

3. Divide the chilled dough in half and roll each half out into a slab about 2 inches thick. Place the slabs on lightly oiled baking sheets and flatten slightly. Bake until golden brown and a toothpick inserted in the center comes out clean, 25 to 30 minutes. Remove from the oven and reduce the oven temperature to 275 degrees F.

4. Let the slabs cool for 10 minutes, then cut each slab into $1/2$-inch-wide slices. Place the sliced biscotti on their sides on an ungreased baking sheet and bake until crisp and dry, 8 to 10 minutes. Let cool completely before storing in an airtight container, where they will keep for several days.

MAKES 36 BISCOTTI

Mom's Best Chocolate Chip Cookies—Only Better

I gave my mom's time-tested recipe a vegan makeover using egg replacer, vegan chocolate chips, and corn oil instead of butter. Family and friends devour them with as much fervor as the originals.

2 cups unbleached all-purpose flour
$1/2$ teaspoon baking soda
$1/2$ teaspoon salt
1 cup firmly packed light brown sugar
   or natural sweetener
$1/4$ cup pure maple syrup
$1/2$ cup corn oil

Egg replacer for 2 eggs (page 509)
1 teaspoon pure vanilla extract
$1^{1}/2$ cups semisweet vegan chocolate
   chips
$1/2$ cup chopped nuts of your choice
   (optional)

1. Preheat the oven to 350 degrees F. Lightly oil two baking sheets.
2. In a medium-size bowl, combine the flour, baking soda, and salt. Set aside.
3. In a large bowl, combine the brown sugar, maple syrup, corn oil, egg replacer, and vanilla, mixing until blended. Add half of the dry ingredients and mix until just combined. Add the remaining dry ingredients and mix until just combined. Fold in the vegan chocolate chips and nuts (if using). Drop the dough by the spoonful onto the prepared baking sheets, about 2 inches apart.
4. Bake until golden brown, 15 to 18 minutes. Let cool completely before storing in an airtight container.

MAKES ABOUT 36 COOKIES

Cranberry-Walnut Oatmeal Cookies

Bejeweled with bits of cranberry and studded with walnuts, these tempting oatmeal cookies will disappear before you know it. You may substitute other dried fruits and nuts, if you prefer.

1¼ cups unbleached all-purpose flour
1 teaspoon baking powder
¾ teaspoon ground cinnamon
Pinch of salt
½ cup corn oil
¾ cup firmly packed light brown sugar
    or natural sweetener

Egg replacer for 2 eggs (page 509)
¼ cup soy milk or other dairy-free milk
1 teaspoon pure vanilla extract
1¾ cups old-fashioned rolled oats
½ cup chopped sweetened dried
    cranberries
½ cup chopped walnuts

1. Preheat the oven to 350 degrees F. Lightly oil two baking sheets.

2. In a medium-size bowl, combine the flour, baking powder, cinnamon, and salt. Set aside.

3. In a large bowl, combine the corn oil, brown sugar, egg replacer, soy milk, and vanilla, mixing until blended. Add the dry ingredients along with the oats, cranberries, and walnuts, stirring to mix well. Drop by the spoonful onto the prepared baking sheets about 2 inches apart.

4. Bake until golden, 12 to 15 minutes. Let cool completely before storing in an airtight container.

MAKES ABOUT 30 COOKIES

Chocolate Macadamia Clusters

These tasty treats are sweetened only with dates, so they're better for you than a sugary candy bar, while still being immensely satisfying. You may substitute a less pricey nut for the macadamias, if you prefer.

1½ cups dates, pitted and soaked in
hot water to cover until soft
1½ cups macadamia nuts
¼ cup unsweetened cocoa powder

1 teaspoon pure vanilla extract
1 cup unsweetened finely shredded
coconut

1. Drain the dates and set aside.
2. Chop 1 cup of the macadamia nuts and set aside.
3. Place the remaining ½ cup macadamia nuts in a food processor and grind to a powder. Slowly add the dates until thoroughly mixed. Add the cocoa powder and vanilla and process until well blended. Stir in the chopped macadamia nuts.
4. Roll the mixture between your palms into 1-inch balls. Roll the balls in the coconut and flatten them somewhat. Arrange them on a platter and serve at once, or cover and refrigerate until ready to use. Tightly covered and refrigerated, they will keep for up to 2 weeks.

MAKES ABOUT 36 CLUSTERS

Date and Cashew Nut Truffles

Easy to make and infinitely versatile, these delicious morsels can be made with a different nut or the addition of grated orange zest. Instead of rolling them in ground nuts, you can coat them with unsweetened cocoa powder or finely shredded coconut.

1¹/₂ cups dates, pitted and soaked in hot water to cover until soft
2 cups raw cashews

¹/₄ cup soy milk or other dairy-free milk, or as needed

1. Drain the dates and set aside.

2. Process the cashews in a blender or food processor until finely ground. Reserve ¹/₂ cup and set aside. Add the dates to the remaining cashews and process until well blended. Add just enough soy milk for the mixture to hold together.

3. Roll the mixture between your palms into 1-inch balls. Roll in the reserved cashews and place on a platter or baking sheet. Cover and refrigerate until ready to serve. Tightly covered and refrigerated, they will keep for up to 2 weeks.

MAKES ABOUT 36 TRUFFLES

Dairy-Free "Plain Vanilla" Ice Cream

With so many fruits and other flavorings available, I never make this as "plain vanilla" but rather use it as the base for flavored "ice creams." To do so, substitute 1/2 cup of pureed fruit for 1/2 cup of the soy milk. You may add other ingredients, such as chopped nuts or extracts, if you wish, but keep the volume about the same.

2 tablespoons arrowroot

4 cups cold soy milk or other dairy-free milk

1/2 cup sugar or natural sweetener

1 teaspoon pure vanilla extract

1. In a small bowl, combine the arrowroot and 1/4 cup of the soy milk. Blend until smooth and set aside.

2. In a medium-size saucepan over medium heat, heat the remaining 3 3/4 cups soy milk to a simmer, stirring constantly, then add the arrowroot mixture, stirring to thicken. Do not let boil.

3. Once the mixture thickens slightly, remove from the heat and add the sugar, stirring until it dissolves. Stir in the vanilla and let cool to room temperature.

4. Refrigerate until chilled, then freeze in an ice-cream maker according to the manufacturer's directions.

MAKES ABOUT 1 QUART

Dairy-Free Double-Chocolate Ice Cream

Real chocoholics may want to add more vegan chocolate chips or other bits of vegan chocolate near the end of the freezing process. Chopped nuts make a good addition as well.

4 cups cold soy milk or other dairy-free milk

2 tablespoons arrowroot

1/4 cup unsweetened cocoa powder

3/4 cup sugar or natural sweetener

1/2 cup semisweet vegan chocolate chips

1 tablespoon pure vanilla extract

1. In a small bowl, combine 1/4 cup of the soy milk and the arrowroot. Blend well and set aside.

2. Place the remaining 3 3/4 cups soy milk in a medium-size saucepan over medium heat. Add the cocoa powder and sugar and bring to a simmer, stirring to dissolve the sugar. Stir in the arrowroot mixture, stirring constantly until the mixture thickens and starts to bubble, about 5 minutes. Do not let boil. Remove from the heat and add the vegan chocolate chips. Let the chips sit in the hot liquid for a few minutes before whisking to combine thoroughly. Stir in the vanilla and let cool to room temperature.

3. Refrigerate until chilled, then freeze in an ice-cream maker according to the manufacturer's directions.

MAKES ABOUT 1 QUART

Frozen Coconut "Thaiphoon" with Mango, Lime, and Peanuts

When I first received my ice-cream maker as a gift, I was anxious to create a vegan ice cream that would complement a spicy Thai meal. The result was this creamy and delicious "Thaiphoon," redolent of the flavors of Thailand.

2 tablespoons arrowroot

1/4 cup cold soy milk or other dairy-free
   milk

3 cups unsweetened coconut milk

1/2 cup sugar or natural sweetener

1 large, ripe mango, peeled and pitted

1 tablespoon fresh lime juice

1 teaspoon grated lime zest

1 teaspoon pure vanilla extract

1/4 cup unsweetened shredded coconut,
   toasted (page 491), for garnish

1/4 cup chopped unsalted dry-roasted
   peanuts for garnish

1. In a small bowl, combine the arrowroot and soy milk. Blend until smooth and set aside.

2. In a medium-size saucepan over medium heat, heat the coconut milk to a simmer, stirring constantly. Add the arrowroot mixture and heat, stirring, to thicken slightly, about 5 minutes. Do not let boil. Remove from the heat and add the sugar, stirring until it dissolves. Puree half of the mango and stir it into the mixture along with the lime juice, lime zest, and vanilla. Let cool to room temperature.

3. Refrigerate until chilled, then freeze in an ice-cream maker according to the manufacturer's directions.

4. Cut the remaining half of the mango into dice. Garnish each serving with the mango, coconut, and peanuts and serve.

MAKES ABOUT 1 QUART

Double Espresso Affogato

This variation on the classic Italian dessert usually made with vanilla gelato is a coffee and chocolate lover's dream. For a dramatic presentation, bring the brewed espresso to the table and pour it over the ice cream at the last minute. Note: If using warm espresso rather than cold, be sure it isn't too hot, or it may crack the serving glasses.

4 cups soy milk or other dairy-free milk
2 tablespoons arrowroot
1/4 cup unsweetened cocoa powder
3/4 cup sugar or natural sweetener

1 tablespoon instant espresso powder
1/2 cup semisweet vegan chocolate chips
1 tablespoon pure vanilla extract
1 cup warm or cold brewed espresso

1. In a small bowl, combine 1/4 cup of the soy milk and the arrowroot. Blend well and set aside.

2. Place the remaining 3 3/4 cups soy milk in a large saucepan over medium heat. Add the cocoa powder, sugar, and instant espresso and bring to a simmer, stirring to dissolve. Stir in the arrowroot mixture, stirring constantly until the mixture thickens and starts to bubble, about 5 minutes. Do not let boil. Turn off the heat and add the vegan chocolate chips. Let the chips sit in the hot liquid for a few minutes before whisking to combine thoroughly. Stir in the vanilla and let cool to room temperature.

3. Refrigerate until chilled, then freeze in an ice-cream maker according to the manufacturer's directions.

4. To serve, spoon the frozen dessert into stemmed glasses (martini glasses are best) and top with a few tablespoons of the brewed espresso.

MAKES ABOUT 1 QUART

Fresh Peach Sorbet

Use this recipe as a guide for making sorbet from your favorite fresh fruit. Peel, pit, or seed the fruit as necessary. Keep the amount of pureed fruit between 3 and 4 cups, using additional sugar if needed, depending on the sweetness of the fruit. Lemon juice is added here to help retain the color and to brighten the flavor of the peaches. Depending on the fruit you use, a splash of citrus juice or other flavoring is optional.

4 or 5 large, ripe peaches, peeled, pitted, and cut into chunks

¾ cup sugar or natural sweetener
1 teaspoon fresh lemon juice

1. Process the peaches in a food processor until smooth. You should have a little over 3 cups of puree. Transfer to a medium-size bowl.
2. Place the sugar in a small saucepan over low heat. Add enough of the puree to moisten the sugar and heat, stirring, to dissolve. Stir into the remaining puree along with the lemon juice.
3. Refrigerate until chilled, then freeze in an ice-cream maker according to manufacturer's directions.

MAKES ABOUT 3½ CUPS

Cranberry-Walnut Sorbet with a Hint of Orange

The walnuts offer a surprising crunch in this light and refreshing sorbet, although you can make it without them if you prefer a smooth texture. Especially festive when served in champagne flutes, this sorbet can be presented as an elegant dessert or an *intermezzo*. Or it can be used as an intriguing stand-in for cranberry sauce at holiday meals.

2¼ cups cranberry juice cocktail
2 cups fresh cranberries, picked over
1 cup sugar or natural sweetener
Juice and grated zest of 1 orange

½ cup chopped walnuts (optional)
Candied orange peel for garnish
   (optional)

1. In a medium-size saucepan over medium heat, combine the cranberry juice, cranberries, and sugar and bring to a boil. Reduce the heat to low and simmer until the cranberries pop, about 5 minutes. Remove from the heat, then strain or run through a food mill to remove the skins. Set aside to cool.
2. Stir in the orange juice and zest and refrigerate until chilled. Freeze in an ice-cream maker according to the manufacturer's directions, adding the chopped walnuts, if using, about halfway through the freezing process.
3. Serve garnished with candied orange peel, if desired.

MAKES ABOUT 1 QUART

19

Smoothies, Shakes, & Other Quenchers

Smoothies are luscious, velvety blender beverages usually made with fresh or frozen fruits and naturally sweet fruit juices. They have been served at health food restaurants and juice bars for years and are now made in homes nationwide. Their growing popularity is proof positive that you don't need dairy products to enjoy a creamy, delicious drink. In addition to using fruits and juices, you can boost the nutritional content by adding a scoop of soy protein powder, soy milk, or tofu. Ground flaxseeds, rich in essential omega-3 fatty acids, also can be added to increase the nutritional value. People who normally skip breakfast may welcome a refreshing smoothie to provide the energy they need to get them through the morning. But don't let the virtuous health benefits fool you. Some of these concoctions can be as rich as the most decadent dessert.

Whether you're already a card-carrying smoothie addict or closet milk shake quaffer or you're simply looking for a healthful yet flavorful treat, you're sure to enjoy the drinks in this chapter, from cooling tropical smoothies to nutritious breakfast shakes.

Almond Milk

Versatile almonds can be used to make a nutritious milk alternative with a delicate nutty flavor. Although you can purchase almond milk in natural food stores, you can make it easily from scratch at home. Soaking the almonds overnight softens them and activates their enzymes, making them more digestible.

1 cup raw almonds   4 cups water

1. Soak the almonds in the water overnight.
2. Drain the almonds, reserving the soaking liquid. Place the almonds in a blender with about half the soaking liquid and blend until smooth. Add the remaining liquid and continue blending until very smooth.
3. Place a fine-mesh strainer over a bowl and strain the almond milk, stirring to push the liquid through. Refrigerate in a covered jar or airtight container and shake before using. Properly stored, almond milk will keep for 4 to 5 days.

MAKES ABOUT 1 QUART

GOT MILK ALTERNATIVES?

There are lots of ways to have your milk without the moo. Choose among the following:

- *Soy milk:* Can be used to replace milk in recipes or used on cereal or to make smoothies. Be aware that the flavors and textures vary by manufacturer, and you should experiment to find one you like.
- *Rice milk:* This milk alternative is thinner than soy milk but can be used in the same ways if you don't like soy.
- *Oat milk:* Has a mild flavor and thick, creamy texture. A good choice for "cream" soups and sauces.
- *Nut milks:* Can be expensive to buy but easy to make at home, with all the nutrients of the nut it is made from. Use wherever a nutty flavor is desired.
- *Coconut milk:* Use to make Indian, Thai, or Indonesian dishes or in desserts or other dishes where a coconut flavor is desired. Make sure you buy unsweetened coconut milk, not coconut cream.

Smoothie Savvy

The main rule about smoothies is that there are no rules. Use these recipes as guidelines to create your own concoctions. Here are some tips.

- *Frozen fruit:* Buy extra bananas to peel, cut into chunks, and keep on hand in the freezer to add creaminess, sweetness, and nutrients to almost any smoothie. It's also a good way to use up bananas that are very ripe. Frozen berries work well this way, too, because they thicken and chill the drink without diluting it the way ice can. You can freeze fruit juice in an ice cube tray for this purpose. If no frozen fruit or juice is on hand, a few ice cubes can be blended into your smoothie.
- *Soy:* With all the benefits of soy, people are looking for ways to add it to their diets. Smoothies are the answer. Whether you add soy milk, tofu, or a scoop of soy protein powder, you can get an extra serving of soy whenever you enjoy a smoothie. And smoothies are a great way to introduce soy to your family.
- *Flax:* Flaxseeds are rich in essential omega-3 fatty acids, so when you add a tablespoon of ground flaxseeds to your smoothie, you increase its nutritional value.
- *Snack appeal:* A nutritious smoothie can help fill you up and not out, and it's a great way to curb your appetite between meals. Reach for the blender next time you crave something delicious.
- *Sweet stuff:* Add softened dates, pure maple syrup, or another sweetener, if needed. All tastes are different, and some fruit is sweeter than others, so feel free to add a little sweetener.
- *Extra flavor:* Add vanilla or another extract to boost and brighten the flavor of a smoothie.
- *Extra liquid:* Despite the juiciness of many fruits, a certain amount of liquid is needed to make a smoothie. The liquid can be in the form of fruit juice, soy milk or other dairy-free milk (including coconut milk), or water.
- *Chill out:* Start with chilled ingredients for best results.

Mango Tango Smoothie

It takes two to tango—in this case, a luscious ripe mango and a creamy banana. A splash of orange juice brings the two together. Frozen bananas make the smoothie thicker and creamier than unfrozen and do not dilute the smoothie the way ice can. Keep frozen chunks of peeled ripe bananas on hand for spontaneous smoothie making.

1 large, ripe mango, peeled, pitted, and cut into chunks
1 cup cold orange juice

1 large, ripe banana, peeled, cut into chunks, and frozen

1. In a blender, combine the mango chunks and orange juice and process until smooth. Add the banana chunks and blend until thick and frothy.
2. Pour into 2 glasses and serve at once.

SERVES 2

Ambrosia Breakfast Smoothie

Inspired by the classic dessert, this refreshing drink combines the flavors of banana, orange, and coconut with the nutritional value of silken tofu and ground flaxseeds. It's loaded with potassium, vitamin C, and essential omega-3 fatty acids.

1/4 cup drained soft silken tofu
2 tablespoons finely ground flaxseeds
1 cup cold unsweetened coconut milk

1 cup cold orange juice
2 medium-size, ripe bananas, peeled, cut into chunks, and frozen

1. In a blender, combine the tofu, flaxseeds, and coconut milk and process until well blended. Add the orange juice and banana chunks and blend until thick and smooth.
2. Pour into 2 glasses and serve at once.

SERVES 2

Berry Delicious Smoothie

This is a great way to enjoy fresh berries in season or frozen berries the rest of the year. The banana adds creaminess, but silken tofu and a little pure maple syrup may be used instead.

1 cup fresh strawberries, hulled, or
    frozen strawberries
1/2 cup fresh blueberries, picked over,
    or frozen blueberries

1 cup cranberry juice cocktail
1 medium-size, ripe banana, peeled,
    cut into chunks, and frozen

1. In a blender, combine the strawberries, blueberries, and cranberry juice and process until smooth. Add the banana and blend until thick and smooth, about 30 seconds.
2. Pour into 2 glasses and serve at once.

SERVES 2

Peaches and "Cream" Smoothie

Make this smoothie when fresh peaches are in season; canned peaches just don't do the trick. The "cream" is nutritious and delicious almond milk. As with any smoothie, you can add some pure maple syrup, softened dates, or other natural sweetener, if desired. The ice cubes help to thicken it.

3 medium-size, ripe peaches, peeled,
    pitted, and quartered
1 cup cold almond milk, homemade
    (page 523) or store-bought

2 or 3 ice cubes

1. Place all the ingredients in a blender and process until smooth.
2. Pour into 2 glasses and serve at once.

SERVES 2

Tutti-Frutti Smoothie

Anything goes in this "fruit-full" smoothie. Use whatever fruit is on hand to create a creamy, fruity concoction whenever the mood strikes.

2 dates, pitted, soaked in hot water to
  cover until soft and drained
1/2 cup fresh or canned pineapple chunks
1/2 cup fresh strawberries, hulled, or
  frozen strawberries

4 ounces soft silken tofu, drained
1 medium-size, ripe banana, peeled,
  cut into chunks, and frozen
1 cup apple juice

1. In a blender, combine the dates, pineapple, strawberries, and tofu and process until smooth. Add the banana and apple juice and blend until thick and smooth.
2. Pour into 2 glasses and serve at once.

SERVES 2

Cantaloupe Tonight Melon Smoothie

Although this is best made with sweet, ripe melons, I've found that it can be a great way to use up a cantaloupe that is less than wonderful—the banana and citrus juice work wonders at transforming the flavor into a luscious smoothie.

1/2 medium-size, ripe cantaloupe,
  seeded and cut from the rind
1/2 cup orange juice
Juice of 2 limes

1 medium-size, ripe banana, peeled,
  cut into chunks, and frozen
Fresh mint leaves for garnish (optional)

1. Cut the cantaloupe into chunks and place in a blender. Add the orange juice, lime juice, and banana and process until thick and creamy.
2. Pour into 2 glasses, garnish with mint leaves, if desired, and serve at once.

SERVES 2

Going Bananas

Bananas are a natural, ready-to-eat snack that comes in their own package. Sweet and delicious, they are also rich in potassium, magnesium, and vitamins A and B complex and have twice the vitamin C as apples. With 60 percent of bananas produced in the world consumed in the United States, there's no denying that Americans love bananas. So why do we take them for granted?

We romanticize other fruits because we think of them seasonally. We associate apples and pears with the crispness of autumn. Oranges and other citrus fruits nurse us through the winter cold season. Spring holds the promise of freshly picked strawberries, while the heat of July and August brings an abundance of sweet melons, juicy peaches, and other favorites that can mean only summer.

Bananas are technically tropical, but we usually don't think of them as exotic, the way we do papayas, mangoes, and guavas. The banana is all but forgotten during holiday meals and seasonal celebrations, where other fruits take center stage. Thanksgiving provides the backdrop for pumpkin pie. Independence Day is made more festive with strawberry shortcake. Yet the dependable banana is available year round, when other fruits are out of season or prohibitively expensive.

You can buy green-tipped bananas and know they'll ripen in a few days. Even overripe bananas are ready to go to work in banana bread, cookies, and muffins. They can be peeled, cut, and frozen to make smoothies, or mashed to make an instant treat for babies. Banana chunks can be rolled in coconut or chopped nuts as a special snack for children and adults. They can be dried as crunchy chips or baked or grilled for an unusual dessert.

Who didn't grow up enjoying sliced bananas on their breakfast cereal or the sumptuous delight of a banana split? Who can forget Elvis Presley's infamous fried banana and peanut butter sandwiches? Yet we never hear the phrase "as American as banana pie" or see banana shortcake served on the Fourth of July. And although no one ever says, "Life is just a bowl of bananas," the reliable banana remains a perennial comfort food. As I often say, "When life gives you bananas, make smoothies."

Spiced Pumpkin Smoothie

This is a favorite autumn drink at my house and a festive addition to holiday gatherings from Halloween right through the Christmas season, when it makes a colorful and delicious alternative to eggnog.

1/2 cup canned pumpkin
3 tablespoons pure maple syrup
1 teaspoon pure vanilla extract
1/2 teaspoon ground cinnamon

1/4 teaspoon freshly grated nutmeg
1/4 teaspoon ground allspice
2 cups soy milk or other dairy-free milk

1. Combine the pumpkin, maple syrup, vanilla, cinnamon, nutmeg, and allspice in a blender and process until smooth. Add the soy milk and blend again until smooth.
2. Pour into 2 glasses and serve at once.

SERVES 2

Make Mine Mocha

The popular combination of coffee and chocolate turns up in this delicious blender drink. It tastes like coffee and dessert all rolled into one.

2 cups soy or other dairy-free milk
2 tablespoons unsweetened cocoa
   powder
2 tablespoons sugar or natural
   sweetener

1/2 cup strong brewed coffee, chilled or
   frozen into ice cubes
1 teaspoon pure vanilla extract

1. Place all the ingredients in a blender and process until thick and smooth.
2. Pour into 2 glasses and serve at once.

SERVES 2

Sorbet Frappe

Blend your favorite fruit sorbet with soy milk and a splash of vanilla extract for a cool and creamy blender drink. For a lighter version, substitute seltzer water for the soy milk and omit the vanilla.

3/4 cup fruit sorbet of your choice
1 cup soy or other dairy-free milk

1 teaspoon pure vanilla extract

1. Combine all the ingredients in a blender and process until smooth and creamy.
2. Pour into 2 glasses and serve at once.

SERVES 2

Chocolate-Banana Shake

Bananas and chocolate are one of my favorite combinations, and they live up to my expectations in this decadent shake.

2 medium-size, ripe bananas, peeled, cut into chunks, and frozen
1/2 cup dairy-free chocolate ice cream
1 cup soy or other dairy-free milk

1 tablespoon chocolate syrup (optional)
2 fresh strawberries for garnish (optional)

1. In a blender, combine the bananas, nondairy ice cream, soy milk, and chocolate syrup (if using), and process until thick and smooth.
2. Pour into 2 glasses, garnish each with a strawberry, if desired, and serve at once.

SERVES 2

Banana Tips

- Unless you need to use them the same day, buy bananas with green tips. Then they can ripen at room temperature.
- Bananas will ripen faster if placed in a paper bag.
- Bananas are ripe when they turn yellow and brown speckles begin to appear.
- Once ripe, bananas may be stored in the refrigerator if you won't be using them right away. Refrigeration will turn the skin brown, but the inside will be fine.
- Ripe, peeled bananas may be cut or mashed and frozen for later use in baking or making smoothies.

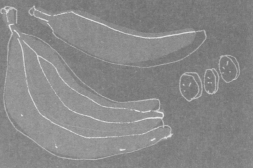

Creamy Cashew-Cardamom Shake

Naturally sweet and creamy, cashews are easily incorporated into a thick and delicious blender drink that is further enhanced by fragrant cardamom.

1/2 cup raw cashews

1 cup soy milk or other dairy-free milk

2 tablespoons pure maple syrup

1 teaspoon pure vanilla extract

1/2 teaspoon ground cardamom

1 medium-size, ripe banana, peeled, cut into chunks, and frozen

1. In a blender, grind the cashews to a powder. Add the soy milk, maple syrup, vanilla, and cardamom and blend until smooth. Add the banana chunks and blend until thick and creamy.

2. Pour into 2 glasses and serve at once.

SERVES 2

Creamsicle Redux

This smoothie is like a Creamsicle-in-a-glass for grown-up tastes, especially if you add the optional Grand Marnier.

1/2 cup dairy-free vanilla ice cream

1 1/2 cups orange juice

1/2 teaspoon pure vanilla extract

2 tablespoons Grand Marnier or other orange-flavored liqueur (optional)

1. In a blender, combine all the ingredients and process until smooth.
2. Pour into 2 glasses and serve at once.

SERVES 2

Rum Soy Nog

This vegan eggnog is always a hit at holiday parties. People are amazed at how rich and delicious it is, even though it contains no eggs or dairy products. I usually make it with rum, but you can substitute a teaspoon of rum extract, if you like, or omit it altogether.

1 1/2 cups dairy-free vanilla ice cream

1 1/2 cups soy milk or other dairy-free milk

1/4 teaspoon freshly grated nutmeg, plus more for dusting, if desired

3 tablespoons dark rum, or to taste (optional)

1. In a blender, combine all the ingredients and process until smooth.
2. Pour into 6 eggnog cups, dust with an extra bit of nutmeg, if desired, and serve at once.

SERVES 6

Luscious Lemon-Cranberry Cooler

This refreshing drink hits the spot on a hot, steamy day or warm, balmy evening. Use limeade concentrate instead of lemonade, if you like.

1/4 cup frozen lemonade concentrate

2 cups cold cranberry juice cocktail

4 ice cubes

1. Combine all the ingredients in a blender and process until smooth.
2. Pour into 2 glasses and serve at once.

SERVES 2

Tropical Paradise Quencher

A variety of sweet, ripe tropical fruits go into this refreshing smoothie. Feel free to vary the combination according to personal preference and availability.

1 medium-size, ripe banana, peeled, cut into chunks, and frozen

1 small, ripe papaya, peeled, seeded, and diced

1 small, ripe mango, peeled, pitted, and diced

1/2 cup cold pineapple juice

2 fresh strawberries or fresh or canned pineapple chunks for garnish

1. In a blender, combine the banana, papaya, mango, and pineapple juice and process until smooth.
2. Pour into 2 glasses, garnish each with a strawberry, and serve at once.

SERVES 2

20

Don't Skip Breakfast

Just because eggs and bacon are not on your menu doesn't mean you can't enjoy a hearty breakfast. Healthy vegan choices that are both satisfying and delicious abound. And they don't have to take extra time either.

If you enjoy cereal in the morning, simply substitute soy or other nondairy milk for cow's milk, and you're on your way. Instead of butter, consider spreading your whole-grain toast with nut butter for a nutritious option, or try the yummy bagel spreads on page 555. If you don't care for a sit-down breakfast but realize you need a boost to get yourself through to lunch, whip up a smoothie such as the ones in Chapter 19. For extra protein to start the day, add a scoop or two of soy protein powder and some ground flaxseeds.

Tofu and other soy foods make ideal alternatives to many high-cholesterol egg dishes: consider *Tomato-Zucchini Frittata* or *Spanish Tofu Omelet*. There are also several recipes for breakfast casseroles, wraps, and hash, as well as the more traditional pancakes and even French toast that can help make breakfast not just the most important meal of the day but perhaps the best-tasting one, too. And there's no need to stop at breakfast. Many of these recipes make great choices for lunch or dinner as well.

To accompany these dishes, check out the freezer case of your supermarket and natural food store for convenient vegan bacon, sausage, and even cream cheese that can be enjoyed as part of a satisfying and healthy meal.

Spicy Soy and Vegetable Scramble

Protein-rich tofu is a great way to start the day, especially when combined with soy sausage, spicy seasonings, and flavorful vegetables in this tasty breakfast scramble.

1½ tablespoons olive oil

¼ cup minced onion

½ small red bell pepper, seeded and chopped

1 cup sliced white mushrooms

1 cup chopped or crumbled soy sausage

½ teaspoon red pepper flakes

Pinch of cayenne (optional)

One 16-ounce package firm tofu, drained and crumbled

¼ teaspoon turmeric

Salt and freshly ground black pepper

1. Heat 1 tablespoon of the olive oil in a large skillet over medium heat. Add the onion and bell pepper, cover, and cook until softened, about 5 minutes. Add the mushrooms and cook until they begin to release their liquid, about 3 minutes. Using a slotted spoon, transfer the vegetables to a medium-size bowl and set aside.

2. Heat the remaining ½ tablespoon olive oil in the same skillet over medium heat. Add the soy sausage, red pepper flakes, and cayenne (if using) and cook, stirring, until the sausage is browned, about 5 minutes. Stir in the crumbled tofu, turmeric, and salt and pepper to taste. Add the sautéed vegetables and cook, stirring, until any remaining liquid is evaporated and the ingredients are hot, 5 to 7 minutes. Serve hot.

SERVES 4

Tomato-Zucchini "Frittata"

Tofu replaces eggs in this interpretation of a frittata, the classic Italian flat omelet. In a frittata, the filling sets right in the eggs (or tofu, in this case) rather than being folded or rolled up inside, as with an omelet. Vary the filling ingredients according to personal preference: cooked asparagus or mushrooms are good choices.

1 tablespoon olive oil
1 small Vidalia or other sweet yellow
    onion, minced
1 small zucchini, shredded
1 large, firm, ripe tomato, peeled,
    seeded, and chopped
1/2 teaspoon dried basil

Salt and freshly ground black pepper
One 16-ounce package firm tofu,
    drained
1 tablespoon arrowroot dissolved in
    2 tablespoons water
1/8 teaspoon turmeric

1. Heat the olive oil in a large skillet over medium heat. Add the onion, cover, and cook until softened, about 5 minutes. Add the zucchini, cover, and cook, stirring occasionally, until softened, about 3 minutes. Stir in the tomato, basil, and salt and pepper to taste. Transfer to a lightly oiled, shallow round baking dish and set aside.
2. Preheat the oven to 375 degrees F. In a blender, combine the tofu, arrowroot mixture, turmeric, and salt and pepper to taste and process until smooth. Pour over the vegetables in the baking dish and bake until the tofu is set and the top is golden brown, about 30 minutes.
3. To serve, cut into wedges and serve hot.

SERVES 4

The Downside of "Sunny-Side Up"

Many vegetarians look to eggs as a source of protein, since no animal has to die to supply the product. But perhaps there is a fate worse than death, such as the short, miserable existence of "battery" hens. These naturally active birds are crammed into small cages for life, cruelly debeaked, and starved for periods of time to manipulate egg production. They become completely stressed-out and often develop diseases such as cancer. In addition, after being imprisoned for a year or two in this way, they are slaughtered as soon as their egg production stops. Contrary to popular belief, free-range hens don't have it much better.

To vegans, therefore, the most compelling reason to give up eggs is often an ethical one, but there are a number of health reasons as well. Bacteria such as salmonella, poisonous ammonia fumes, and high doses of antibiotics can be passed into the eggs. In addition, an average egg contains more than 200 milligrams of cholesterol and is about 70 percent fat. In fact, the yolk of a chicken egg is one of the densest concentrations of animal fat there is. When eaten, it can raise cholesterol and help clog arteries. At the same time, albumin, which is concentrated animal protein, can leach the calcium out of your bones. A healthier alternative is to use tofu and other soy products to replace eggs in your diet.

Spanish Tofu "Omelet"

In this vegan version of a Spanish omelet, tofu stands in for the eggs, while the tangy tomato salsa adds flavor and saves chopping time. I prefer to spoon the salsa on top of the "omelet" rather than use it as a filling.

1 tablespoon olive oil
1 small yellow onion, minced
One 16-ounce package firm tofu,
   drained and crumbled

¼ teaspoon turmeric
Salt and freshly ground black pepper
¾ cup Fresh Tomato Salsa (page 174)
   or your favorite salsa

1. Heat the olive oil in a medium-size skillet over medium heat. Add the onion, cover, and cook until softened, about 5 minutes. Add the tofu, turmeric, and salt and pepper to taste, stirring to blend the seasonings into the tofu. Cook until heated through and all the liquid is absorbed, about 5 minutes.

2. Divide the tofu mixture among 4 individual plates, top each with a spoonful of the salsa, and serve hot.

SERVES 4

Soy Sausage Breakfast Casserole

This satisfying casserole can be enjoyed for breakfast, brunch, or supper. It can be assembled ahead of time and baked shortly before serving.

2 tablespoons olive oil

1 medium-size yellow onion, chopped

3 cups chopped or crumbled soy
    sausage

One 16-ounce package soft tofu,
    drained and crumbled

2 cups soy milk or other dairy-free milk

1/2 teaspoon dried thyme

1/4 teaspoon ground fennel seeds

Salt and freshly ground black pepper

8 to 10 slices bread

1. Heat the olive oil in a large skillet over medium heat. Add the onion, cover, and cook until softened, about 5 minutes. Add the soy sausage and cook, stirring occasionally, until browned, about 5 minutes. Remove from the heat and set aside.
2. In a large bowl, combine the tofu, soy milk, thyme, fennel seeds, and salt and pepper to taste. Mix well, then blend in the sausage mixture and set aside.
3. Tear the bread into bite-size pieces and place in a lightly oiled shallow 9 x 13-inch baking dish. Pour the sausage mixture evenly over the bread and set aside until the liquid is absorbed, about 20 minutes or overnight. (If refrigerating overnight, bring back to room temperature before baking.)
4. Preheat the oven to 350 degrees F. Bake until puffy and lightly browned, about 45 minutes. Let stand for 10 minutes before cutting into squares. Serve warm.

SERVES 8

Savory Spinach Bread Pudding

This is an ideal brunch dish because it can be assembled the night before and baked shortly before serving. For a heartier casserole, add some crumbled soy sausage to the mixture.

2 tablespoons olive oil
1 large Vidalia or other sweet yellow
    onion, chopped
One 10-ounce package frozen chopped
    spinach, cooked according to
    package directions and well
    drained

One 16-ounce package soft tofu,
    drained and crumbled
3 cups soy milk or other dairy-free milk
1 tablespoon Dijon mustard
1 teaspoon dillweed
Salt and freshly ground black pepper
1 loaf bread, sliced

1. Heat the olive oil in a large skillet over medium heat. Add the onion, cover, and cook until softened, about 5 minutes. Set aside.

2. In a large bowl, combine the spinach, tofu, 1 cup of the soy milk, the mustard, dillweed, and salt and pepper to taste. Mix well, then blend in the onion mixture and the remaining 2 cups soy milk. Set aside.

3. Tear the bread into bite-size pieces and place in a lightly oiled shallow 9 x 13-inch baking dish. Pour the spinach mixture over the bread, spreading it out evenly. Set aside until the liquid is absorbed, about 20 minutes or overnight. (If refrigerating overnight, bring back to room temperature before baking.)

4. Preheat the oven to 350 degrees F. Bake until lightly browned and puffed, about 45 minutes. Let stand for 10 minutes before cutting into squares. Serve warm.

SERVES 8

Flax-Berry Pancakes

Many people include flaxseeds as part of their daily diets because they are an important source of omega-3 fatty acids. Ground flaxseeds blended with water are used to replace eggs in this pancake recipe—a nutritious way to start your day. Blueberries are the classic fruit choice, but feel free to substitute another fruit, if you like. Serve with pure maple syrup.

1¹/₂ cups unbleached all-purpose flour

2 tablespoons sugar or natural
   sweetener

2 teaspoons baking powder

¹/₂ teaspoon salt

2 tablespoons ground flaxseeds

¹/₄ cup water

1¹/₄ cups soy milk or other dairy-free
   milk

1 teaspoon pure vanilla extract

³/₄ cup fresh blueberries, picked over,
   or frozen blueberries, thawed

1. In a large bowl, combine the flour, sugar, baking powder, and salt and set aside.
2. In a blender, combine the flaxseeds and water and blend until thick, about 30 seconds. Add the soy milk and vanilla and process until smooth.
3. Pour the wet ingredients into the dry ingredients, mixing with a few swift strokes until just moist. Fold in the berries.
4. Preheat the oven to 200 degrees F. Heat a lightly oiled griddle or large nonstick skillet over medium heat. Ladle about 3 tablespoons of the batter onto the hot griddle. Cook on one side until small bubbles appear on top, about 2 minutes. Flip the pancake with a metal spatula and cook until the other side is lightly browned, about 1 minute more. Keep the cooked pancakes warm in the oven while you prepare the remaining pancakes.

SERVES 4

Spiced Banana Pancakes

Banana pancakes are a special treat, and this recipe takes full advantage of that great banana flavor by using both sliced and pureed bananas in the batter. Top with pure maple syrup or blueberry syrup, as desired.

1 1/2 cups unbleached all-purpose flour

2 tablespoons sugar or natural sweetener

2 teaspoons baking powder

1/2 teaspoon salt

1/8 teaspoon ground cinnamon

1/8 teaspoon ground allspice

1 1/4 cups soy milk or other dairy-free milk

3 medium-size, ripe bananas, peeled and sliced

1. In a large bowl, combine the flour, sugar, baking powder, salt, cinnamon, and allspice and set aside.

2. In a food processor or blender, combine the soy milk and half of the bananas and process until smooth. Pour the wet ingredients into the dry ingredients, mixing with a few swift strokes until just combined. Fold in the remaining bananas.

3. Preheat the oven to 200 degrees F. Heat a lightly oiled griddle or large nonstick skillet over medium heat. Ladle about 3 tablespoons of the batter onto the hot griddle. Cook on one side until small bubbles appear on top, about 2 minutes. Flip the pancake with a metal spatula and cook until the other side is lightly browned, about 1 minute more. Keep the cooked pancakes warm in the oven while you prepare the remaining pancakes.

SERVES 4

Pumpkin Pie Pancakes

The great taste of pumpkin pie in these moist, flavorful pancakes can make any morning special. Top with pure maple syrup or, for a delicious treat, Almond Butter Cream (page 502).

1½ cups unbleached all-purpose flour

3 tablespoons sugar or natural
   sweetener

1 tablespoon baking powder

½ teaspoon salt

¼ teaspoon pumpkin pie spice

1¼ cups soy milk or other dairy-free
   milk

⅓ cup canned pumpkin

1 tablespoon corn oil

1. In a large bowl, combine the flour, sugar, baking powder, salt, and pumpkin pie spice and set aside.

2. In a food processor or blender, combine the soy milk, pumpkin puree, and corn oil and process until well blended. Pour the wet ingredients into the dry ingredients, mixing with a few swift strokes until just combined.

3. Preheat the oven to 200 degrees F. Heat a lightly oiled griddle or large nonstick skillet over medium heat. Ladle about 3 tablespoons of the batter onto the hot griddle. Cook on one side until small bubbles appear on top, about 2 minutes. Flip the pancakes with a metal spatula and cook until the other side is lightly browned, about 1 minute more. Keep the cooked pancakes warm in the oven while you prepare the remaining pancakes.

SERVES 4

Maple-Pecan French Toast

The scent of pecans and maple from the kitchen can help warm up even the coldest winter morning. I like to use a heartier whole-grain or sprouted bread in this recipe, although it can be made with just about any bread you like.

3/4 cup chopped pecans, toasted
   (page 110)
1 1/4 cups soy milk or other dairy-free
   milk

4 ounces soft silken tofu, drained
1 teaspoon pure vanilla extract
3/4 cup pure maple syrup
8 slices whole-grain or sprouted bread

1. Place 1/4 cup of the pecans in a blender and grind into a powder. Add the soy milk, tofu, vanilla, and 1/4 cup of the maple syrup and process until smooth.

2. Pour into a large, shallow bowl and dip in the bread, coating both sides evenly with the batter.

3. Preheat the oven to 200 degrees F. Heat a lightly oiled griddle or large skillet over medium-high heat. Add the prepared bread in batches and cook until browned on both sides, 4 to 5 minutes total. Keep the cooked French toast warm in the oven while you prepare the remaining slices.

4. In a small saucepan, combine the remaining 1/2 cup maple syrup and the remaining 1/2 cup pecans and heat until warm. Spoon over the French toast and serve at once.

SERVES 4

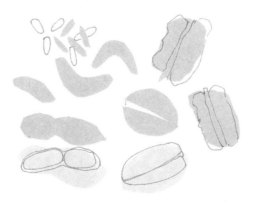

Apple-Cinnamon French Toast

Applesauce and cinnamon are blended into the batter in this egg- and dairy-free version of French toast. Instead of the usual maple syrup, the topping is warm sautéed apple slices. For an easy autumn supper, serve with soy sausage patties or links.

1 cup soy milk or other dairy-free milk

1/2 cup unsweetened applesauce

1/4 cup drained soft silken tofu

2 tablespoons light brown sugar or
    natural sweetener

1 teaspoon ground cinnamon

8 slices bread

2 tablespoons corn oil

1 large apple, peeled, cored, and thinly
    sliced

1 teaspoon fresh lemon juice

1. Combine the soy milk, applesauce, tofu, 1 tablespoon of the brown sugar, and the cinnamon in a food processor or blender and process until smooth.

2. Pour into a large, shallow bowl and dip in the bread, coating both sides evenly with the batter.

3. Preheat the oven to 275 degrees F. Heat 1 tablespoon of the corn oil in a large skillet over medium-high heat. Add the prepared bread in batches and cook until just browned on both sides, 4 to 5 minutes total. Keep the cooked French toast warm in the oven while you prepare the remaining slices.

4. Heat the remaining 1 tablespoon corn oil in a skillet over medium heat. Add the apple slices, lemon juice, and remaining 1 tablespoon brown sugar and cook, stirring, until the apples are tender, about 5 minutes. Spoon the topping over the French toast and serve hot.

SERVES 4

Spicy Sweet-Potato Hash

This colorful hash is a yummy addition to a hearty breakfast, but it also makes a great lunch or dinner entrée. It's especially good served with a sweet, mild chutney. Adjust the amount of cayenne according to your heat tolerance. The hash is delicious without it, too. This is a great way to use leftover baked sweet potatoes. Otherwise, the potatoes should be peeled and diced, placed on a lightly oiled baking sheet, and baked at 375 degrees F until tender, 15 to 20 minutes.

1 tablespoon olive oil

1 large yellow onion, chopped

1 small red bell pepper, seeded and chopped

1 1/2 pounds sweet potatoes, peeled, diced, and cooked (see headnote)

2 frozen veggie burgers, thawed and chopped or crumbled

1/4 teaspoon cayenne, or to taste

Salt and freshly ground black pepper

Heat the olive oil in a large skillet over medium heat. Add the onion and bell pepper, cover, and cook until softened, about 5 minutes. Add the potatoes, veggie burgers, cayenne, and salt and pepper to taste. Cook, stirring frequently, until lightly browned, about 10 minutes. Serve hot.

SERVES 4

Skillet Vegetable Hash

Feel free to substitute different ingredients, including any leftover cooked vegetables you may have on hand. This is especially good made with leftover roasted or grilled vegetables, because they add an extra dimension of flavor. Serve with ketchup.

2 tablespoons olive oil

1 large red onion, chopped

1 small red or yellow bell pepper, seeded and chopped

1 medium-size zucchini, grated and well drained

1 pound all-purpose potatoes, peeled, diced, and cooked until tender

1/2 cup frozen green peas, thawed

1 tablespoon tamari or other soy sauce

Salt and freshly ground black pepper

Heat the olive oil in a large skillet over medium heat. Add the onion, cover, and cook until softened, about 5 minutes. Add the bell pepper and zucchini, cover, and cook until softened, about 5 minutes. Add the potatoes and cook, stirring frequently, until lightly browned, about 5 minutes. Add the peas, tamari, and salt and pepper to taste and cook until heated through, about 5 minutes. Serve hot.

SERVES 4 TO 6

Soy Nut Butter

Soy nut butter is made by grinding roasted soybeans, called soy nuts, to a paste that is similar in appearance to peanut butter but milder in taste. Soy nut butter has 30 percent less fat and more protein than peanut butter, and it can be used as an alternative to peanut or other nut butters. Although it is also delicious on your morning toast, soy nut butter should not be confused with soy margarine, which is made to resemble butter or margarine and may contain hydrogenated oil.

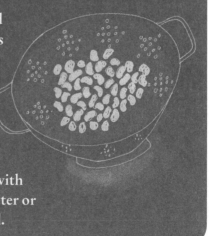

Pan-Seared Breakfast Mushrooms

I like to serve these mushrooms stuffed with Skillet Vegetable Hash (page 549) or Spicy Soy and Vegetable Scramble (page 537). Alternatively, the mushrooms may be cut into ¼-inch-thick slices and fanned out on the plate.

1 tablespoon peanut oil

4 large portobello mushrooms, stems removed

1 tablespoon tamari or other soy sauce

3 tablespoons pure maple syrup

1. Heat the peanut oil in a large skillet over medium-high heat. Add the mushrooms and sear until well browned on the outside and slightly softened on the inside, about 5 minutes, turning once. Add the tamari and maple syrup and cook, turning to coat, until the mushrooms are glazed, 3 to 5 minutes.

2. Serve the mushrooms whole or sliced, as described in the headnote.

SERVES 4

Soy-Salsa Breakfast Wraps

Wrap sandwiches are a popular lunchtime meal, and now they can be a breakfast favorite as well.

1 tablespoon olive oil
1 small red or yellow bell pepper, seeded and chopped
2 scallions, chopped
One 16-ounce package firm tofu, drained and chopped
2 teaspoons chili powder

Salt and freshly ground black pepper
3 tablespoons minced fresh cilantro leaves
4 large flour tortillas, warmed
1 cup Fresh Tomato Salsa (page 174) or your favorite salsa

1. Heat the olive oil in a large skillet over medium heat. Add the bell pepper, cover, and cook until softened, about 5 minutes. Add the scallions and cook for 2 minutes. Stir in the tofu, chili powder, and salt and pepper to taste, stirring to combine. Cook until the tofu is hot and any liquid is evaporated, about 5 minutes. Remove from the heat, stir in the cilantro, and set aside.

2. Place the tortillas on a work surface. Divide the tofu mixture among the tortillas, topping each with 1/4 cup of the salsa. Roll up each tortilla to enclose the filling. Use a serrated knife to cut each wrap in half. Transfer to plates, seam side down, and serve at once.

SERVES 4

Couscous Breakfast Cake with Pear and Dried Plum Compote

This unusual cake is an ideal addition to a brunch or breakfast for guests, as it can be prepared the day before. Made with couscous and fruit juice, the cake is dense and moist without being too sweet—a great way to start the day.

2½ cups apple or pear juice
Pinch of salt
2 cups instant couscous

Pear and Dried Plum Compote
(page 553)

1. Place the juice and salt in a medium-size saucepan over high heat and bring to a boil. Reduce the heat to low and stir in the couscous. Cover and simmer for 2 minutes, then turn off the heat and set aside, covered, for 10 minutes.
2. Lightly oil an 8-inch springform pan and spoon the couscous into it, spreading it evenly. Use the back of a spoon or a spatula to press the couscous firmly into the pan. Cover and refrigerate for several hours or overnight to make it easier to slice.
3. To serve, remove the sides of the pan, cut into wedges, and top with the compote.

SERVES 6

Pear and Dried Plum Compote

This compote is ideal with Couscous Breakfast Cake (page 552), but it is also wonderful on its own or served with Potato Pierogi with Savoy Cabbage (page 266).

3 medium-size, ripe pears, peeled,
   cored, and sliced
2 cups dried pitted plums (prunes)
1/2 cup mixed dried fruit, chopped
1/3 cup sugar or natural sweetener
Grated zest and juice of 1 lemon

Grated zest and juice of 1 orange
1 cinnamon stick
1/4 teaspoon ground allspice
1/8 teaspoon freshly grated nutmeg
2 cups water

1. In a medium-size saucepan over medium heat, combine all the ingredients and bring to a boil. Reduce the heat to low and simmer until the pears soften and the dried fruit plumps up, about 15 minutes. Set aside to cool, then transfer to a medium-size bowl, cover, and refrigerate for at least several hours.
2. When ready to serve, return to room temperature for the best flavor. This will keep for up to 1 week in the refrigerator.

SERVES 6 TO 8

Maple-Cinnamon Oatmeal with Slivered Almonds and Dried Cranberries

Few breakfasts are more satisfying on a cold winter morning than this fragrant oatmeal, studded with sweet-tart cranberries and crunchy toasted almonds. Serve with a little soy milk or an additional drizzle of maple syrup and a light dusting of cinnamon.

4 cups water

2 cups old-fashioned rolled oats

3/4 teaspoon ground cinnamon

Pinch of salt

1/4 cup sweetened dried cranberries

2 tablespoons pure maple syrup

1/4 cup slivered almonds, toasted (page 110), for garnish

1. Bring the water to a boil in a medium-size saucepan over high heat. Reduce the heat to low and stir in the oats, cinnamon, and salt. Cover and simmer for 5 minutes, stirring occasionally.

2. Remove from the heat and stir in the cranberries and maple syrup. Cover and let stand for 2 to 3 minutes.

3. To serve, spoon the oatmeal into bowls and garnish with the almonds.

SERVES 4

Bagels-for-Breakfast Spread (Sweet)

This nutritious spread, loaded with protein, calcium, and potassium, is a great way to start your day. You can make it the night before so that you can quickly spread it on toast or a bagel the next morning.

4 ounces soft silken tofu, drained
1 medium-size, ripe banana, peeled
   and sliced
2 tablespoons almond butter

2 tablespoons pure maple syrup
1 teaspoon pure vanilla extract
$1/2$ teaspoon ground cinnamon
$1/4$ teaspoon ground allspice

In a food processor or blender, combine all the ingredients and process until smooth. Transfer to a small bowl, cover, and refrigerate for several hours to allow the flavors to develop. This will keep for about 3 days in the refrigerator.

MAKES ABOUT 1$1/4$ CUPS

Bagels-for-Breakfast Spread (Savory)

This high-protein, calcium-rich spread is a wholesome, cholesterol-free way to enjoy your bagel or toast.

4 ounces soft silken tofu, drained
$1/3$ cup tahini (sesame paste)

$1/4$ cup miso paste
1 tablespoon fresh lemon juice

In a food processor or blender, combine all the ingredients until well blended. Transfer to a small bowl, cover, and refrigerate until ready to use, up to 3 to 5 days.

MAKES ABOUT 1$1/4$ CUPS

Resources

The following list of organizations, mail-order sources, and other resources is provided as a starting point for those interested in a vegan lifestyle. The list contains a representative sampling of what is available and is by no means exhaustive. Some of the sites listed may not be entirely vegan.

MAIL-ORDER PRODUCTS

These sources can be especially useful for hard-to-find ingredients or if you live in an area that does not have a natural food store.

Garden Spot Distributors
438 White Oak Road
New Holland, PA 17557
(800) 829-5100
www.gardenspotsfinest.com
Vegan foods such as cereals, grains, beans, dried fruits, soy products, convenience foods, and organic produce.

Gold Mine Natural Food Co.
7805 Arjons Drive
San Diego, CA 92126
(800) 475-3663
www.goldminenaturalfood.com
Vegan staples, including grains, beans, and Asian foods such as tamari, shoyu, miso, and dried shiitake mushrooms.

The Mail-Order Catalog for
   Healthy Eating
413 Farm Road
P.O. Box 180
Summertown, TN 38483
(800) 695-2241
www.healthy-eating.com
Vegan food products, including tofu,
textured vegetable protein (TVP), wheat
gluten flour, and nutritional yeast, as well as
cookbooks.

Mountain Ark Trading Company
799 Old Leicester Highway
Asheville, NC 28806
(800) 643-8909
www.cybermacro.com/public_html
Vegan and macrobiotic foods, including tofu,
beans, grains, flours, sea vegetables, Asian
noodles, nuts, and dried fruits.

Pangea
2381 Lewis Avenue
Rockville, MD 20851
(800) 340-1200
www.veganstore.com
Vegan shoes, clothing, and accessories,
as well as food items and personal care
products.

Vegan Essentials
7722 West Menomonee River Parkway
Wauwatosa, WI 53213
(888) 88-VEGAN
www.veganessentials.com
Vegan personal care products, clothing,
supplements, and food.

ORGANIZATIONS

For more information on various aspects of
veganism, contact or visit the Web sites of
these nonprofit organizations.

American Vegan Society (AVS)
56 Dinshah Lane
P.O. Box 369
Malaga, NJ 08328
(856) 694-2887
www.americanvegan.org
Offers books and tapes by mail to promote a
vegan lifestyle. Spearheads an annual vegan
conference and publishes a magazine called
American Vegan (formerly *Ahimsa*).

EarthSave International
1509 Seabright Avenue, Suite B1
Santa Cruz, CA 95062
(800) 362-3648
www.earthsave.org
Provides information regarding food choices
in relation to health and environmental concerns. Coordinates local groups nationwide.

Farm Animal Reform Movement (FARM)
P.O. Box 30654
Bethesda, MD 20824
(888) 275-3276
www.farmusa.org
Works to stop animal abuse in agricultural in-
dustries. Sponsors the annual Great American
Meatout (March 20), among other campaigns.

Farm Sanctuary East
P.O. Box 150
Watkins Glen, NY 14891
(607) 583-2225
www.farmsanctuary.org

Farm Sanctuary West
P.O. Box 1065
Orland, CA 95963
(530) 865-4617
www.farmsanctuary.org
Two sanctuaries for rescued injured and abused farm animals. Sponsors conferences and other events and publishes books and educational materials.

North American Vegetarian Society
    (NAVS)
P.O. Box 72
Dolgeville, NY 13329
(518) 568-7970
www.navs-online.org
Promotes vegan and vegetarian lifestyles. Sponsors the annual Vegetarian Summerfest and World Vegetarian Day (October 1). Publishes *Vegetarian Voice* magazine.

People for the Ethical Treatment of
    Animals (PETA)
501 Front Street
Norfolk, VA 23510
(757) 622-7382
www.vegnow.com; www.peta-online.org
Works to protect and defend animals subjected to all types of abuse and exploitation. Offers vegan dietary information, books, literature, and merchandise.

Physicians Committee for Responsible
    Medicine (PCRM)
5100 Wisconsin Avenue, Suite 400
Washington, DC 20016
(202) 686-2210
www.pcrm.org
Provides vegan nutritional information and works to promote ethical and compassionate research and medical practices and policies. Publishes *Good Medicine* magazine.

United Poultry Concerns (UPC)
P.O. Box 150
Machipongo, VA 23405
(757) 678-7875
www.upc-online.org
Dedicated to the compassionate and ethical treatment of chickens, turkeys, and other domestic fowl.

Vegetarian Resource Group (VRG)
P.O. Box 1463
Baltimore, MD 21203
(410) 366-8343
www.vrg.org
Provides vegetarian and vegan information about health, nutrition, and the environment. Publishes books and *Vegetarian Journal* magazine.

MORE WEB SITES
In addition to the sites listed above, check out these vegan and vegetarian sites:
www.notmilk.com
www.robinrobertson.com
www.vegan.com
www.vegan.org
www.veganoutreach.com
www.vegansociety.com
www.vegdining.com
www.vegsource.com

RECOMMENDED READING

Books
I consider these titles among the best resources on the various facets of veganism, from health and nutrition to environmentalism to animal rights.

Animal Factories, Jim Mason and
     Peter Singer
*Becoming Vegan: The Complete Guide to
     Adopting a Healthy Plant-Based Diet*,
     Brenda Davis, R.D., and Vesanto
     Melina, M.S., R.D.
Diet for a New America, John Robbins
Food for Life, Neal Barnard, M.D.
*The Food Revolution: How Your Diet Can
     Help Save Your Life and the World*,
     John Robbins
*Mad Cowboy: Plain Truth from the Cattle
     Rancher Who Won't Eat Meat*, Howard
     F. Lyman
*Prisoned Chickens, Poisoned Eggs:
     An Inside Look at the Modern Poultry
     Industry*, Karen Davis
*Slaughterhouse: The Shocking Story of
     Greed, Neglect, and Inhumane
     Treatment Inside the U.S. Meat
     Industry*, Gail A. Eisnitz
Vegan: The New Ethics of Eating, Erik
     Marcus
Vegan Nutrition: Pure and Simple, Michael
     Klaper, M.D.
The Vegan Sourcebook, Joanne Stepaniak
*When Elephants Weep: The Emotional Lives
     of Animals*, Jeffrey Moussaieff Masson
     and Susan McCarthy
*You Can Save the Animals: 251 Simple Ways
     to Stop Thoughtless Cruelty*, Ingrid
     Newkirk

Magazines
In addition to the membership magazines published by the organizations listed earlier, the following magazines, though not 100 percent vegan, are good sources for vegan recipes and other information.

Vegetarian Times
P.O. Box 420166
Palm Coast, FL 32142
(877) 717-8923
www.vegetariantimes.com

VegNews Magazine
P.O. Box 320130
San Francisco, CA 94132
(415) 665-NEWS
www.vegnews.com

Index

Gratin
    Artichoke and Root
        Vegetable, 355–356
    Basil-Scented Fennel and
        Tomato, 357
    Cheesy Potato-Chili, 359
    Spring Vegetable, 358
    Sweet Potato, with Pineapple
        and Coconut Milk, 360
Green Bean(s)
    and Chickpea Tagine, 282
    Moroccan-Spiced Fava Bean
        Stew, 305
    Pasta Salad Niçoise, 130
    and Portobello Ragout with
        Madeira, 299–300
    Sautéed, with Tomatoes and
        Garlic, 193
    and Shallots, Shredded Seitan
        with, 348
    Szechuan String Beans, 196
Greens. *See also specific greens*
    nutrients in, 123, 387
    preparing and storing, 387
Gremolata, 243
Gremolata, Orange, 195
grits, 217
Guacamole, Blushing, 50
Gumbo, Sassy Vegetable, 90–91
gumbo soups, 91

H
Harissa, 159
Hash, Skillet Vegetable, 549
Hash, Spicy Sweet-Potato, 548
hazelnuts, 24, 110
heart disease, xii
Herb(s). *See also specific herbs*
    Basil Pesto with Variations,
        157
    Bread, Whole Grain, 467–468
    Fresh, and Scallion Dressing,
        162
    fresh, cooking with, 115
    Gremolata, 243
    Marinade, Garlicky, 161
high blood pressure, xii
hijiki, 28
Hoisin-Braised Baby Bok Choy
    and Shiitake Mushrooms,
    197
Hoisin-Drenched Garlic Seitan
    with Baby Bok Choy, 349

Hollandaise, Eggless, 144
honey, 30, 31, 498
Hummus, Hot for, 48

I
Ice Cream
    Dairy-Free Double-
        Chocolate, 515
    Dairy-Free "Plain Vanilla,"
        514
    Double Espresso Affogato, 517
    Frozen Coconut
        "Thaiphoon" with Mango,
        Lime, and Peanuts, 516
Indian-Spiced Lentil Patties
    with Three-Fruit Chutney,
    458
Indian-Spiced Lentil Soup, 78
Indian-Spiced Quinoa with
    Raisins and Pine Nuts, 229
Indonesian-Inspired Tempeh
    Stew, 310
Indonesian-Style Rice with
    Tempeh, 235
Indonesian-Style Vegetable
    Salad, 107–108
Irish Soda Bread, 480
iron, 5, 11, 23, 307, 314, 332
Italian Wedding Soup, 93

J
Jambalaya, Tempeh and Red
    Bean, with Chipotle Chiles,
    311
Japanese-style tofu, 12. *See also*
    Tofu
jasmine rice, 219
Jasmine Rice, Spicy, with
    Carrots and Cashews, 234

K
Kale, 387
    Balsamic-Glazed Carrots and,
    200
    and Tofu Spanakopita,
    386–387
Kamut, 218, 220
    Ancient Grains on Wild
        Greens, 126
kasha. *See* Buckwheat
kelp, 28
Ketchup, Tangy Tomato, 187
Key Lime "Cheesecake," 492

Kidney Beans, 276
    African Sweet Potato and
        Peanut Stew, 302
    Autumn Vegetable Stew,
        298–299
    Backyard Barbecue Chili, 324
    Baked Polenta with Red
        Beans and Fresh Tomato
        Salsa, 227
    Caribbean Rice with Red
        Beans and Chiles, 233
    East Coast Chili, 322
    Farmhouse Vegetable Soup, 89
    Red Bean and Sweet Potato
        Curry, 286
    Red Bean Cakes with Creamy
        Coconut Sauce, 288
    Sweet and Spicy Chili, 321
    Tempeh and Red Bean
        Jambalaya with Chipotle
        Chiles, 311
    Three-Bean Burritos, 454–455
    Three-Bean Chili, 314
    Three-Bean Dal, 285
    West Coast Chili, 323
kitchen timesavers, 61
knives, kitchen, 52
kombu, 28

L
Lasagna
    Butternut Squash and Wild
        Mushroom, 381–382
    Eggplant and Spinach, 380
    Primavera, 378–379
    Spirals, Tomato-Basil,
        382–383
leaveners, 485
Lebanese Bread Salad
    (Fattoush), 119
legumes. *See* Beans, dried
Lemon(s)
    -Cranberry Cooler, Luscious,
        533
    Gremolata, 243
    Risotto with Peas and
        Scallions, 237
    and Roasted Garlic
        Marmalade, 184
    Tea Bread, Three-Seed, 475
Lentil(s), 276, 284
    Curried, with Carrots and
        Peas, 306